A short breather (heh).

- Takeshi Konomi

About Takeshi Konomi

Takeshi Konomi exploded onto the manga scene with the incredible **THE PRINCE OF TENNIS**. His refined art style and sleek character designs proved popular with **Weekly Shonen Jump** readers, and **THE PRINCE OF TENNIS** became the number one sports manga in Japan almost overnight. Its cast of fascinating male tennis players attracted legions of female readers even though it was originally intended to be a boys' comic. The manga continues to be a success in Japan and has inspired a hit anime series, as well as several video games and mountains of merchandise.

THE PRINCE OF TENNIS
VOL. 18
The SHONEN JUMP Manga Edition

**STORY AND ART BY
TAKESHI KONOMI**

English Adaptation/Michelle Pangilinan
Translation/Joe Yamazaki
Touch-up Art & Lettering/Andy Ristaino
Design/Sam Elzway
Editor/Joel Enos

Managing Editor/Frances E. Wall
Editorial Director/Elizabeth Kawasaki
VP & Editor in Chief/Yumi Hoashi
Sr. Director of Acquisitions/Rika Inouye
Sr. VP of Marketing/Liza Coppola
Exec. VP of Sales & Marketing/John Easum
Publisher/Hyoe Narita

Printed in the U.S.A.

Published by VIZ Media, LLC
P.O. Box 77010
San Francisco, CA 94107

SHONEN JUMP Manga Edition
10 9 8 7 6 5 4 3 2 1
First printing, March 2007

www.viz.com

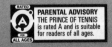

PARENTAL ADVISORY
THE PRINCE OF TENNIS
is rated A and is suitable
for readers of all ages.

THE WORLD'S
MOST POPULAR MANGA

SHONEN JUMP

www.shonenjump.com

テニスの王子様

THE PRINCE OF TENNIS™

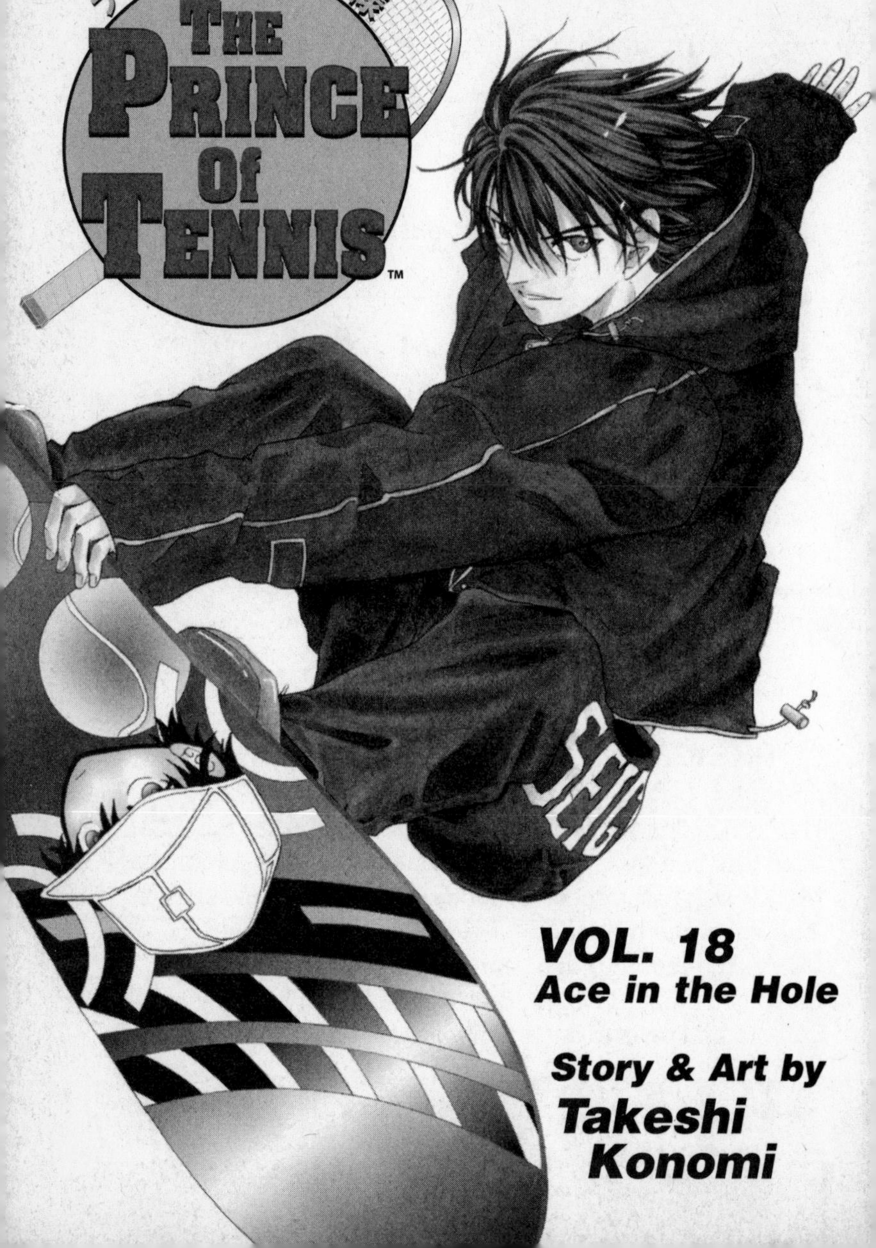

VOL. 18
Ace in the Hole

Story & Art by
Takeshi Konomi

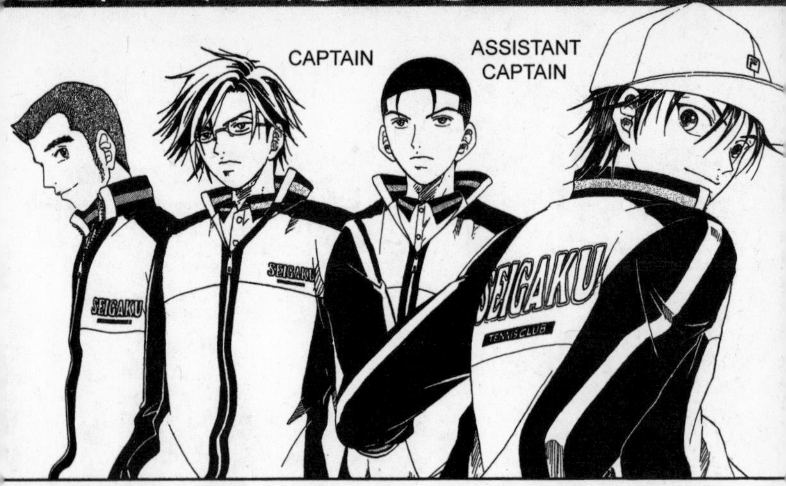
CAPTAIN
ASSISTANT CAPTAIN
SEIGAKU
SEIGAKU
SEIGAKU
SEIGAKU
TENNIS CLUB

●TAKASHI KAWAMURA●KUNIMITSU TEZUKA●SHUICHIRO OISHI● RYOMA ECHIZEN ●

Ryoma Echizen, a student at Seishun Academy, is a tennis prodigy who won four consecutive U.S. Junior tournaments. He became a starter as a 7th grader and led his team to the District Preliminaries! Despite a few mishaps, Seishun won the District Prelims and City Tournament, and earned a ticket to the Kanto Tournament.

The Kanto Tournament is underway. Seishun's first-round opponent is last year's Nationals runner-up — Hyotei Academy! After four matches, Seishun has the lead with two wins, one loss, and one forfeited match. Advancing to the second round rests on Kunimitsu's shoulders, but his opponent, Keigo, is a skilled player who's ranked No. 1 in a team of 200 Hyotei players. Early in the match, Keigo spots Kunimitsu's arm injury and plots to destroy his arm for good!

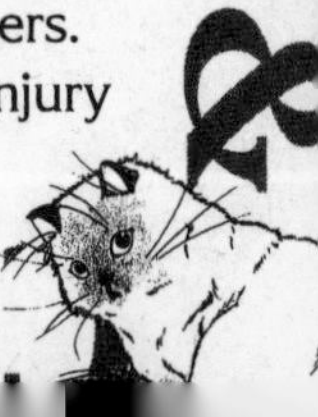

SEIGAKU T

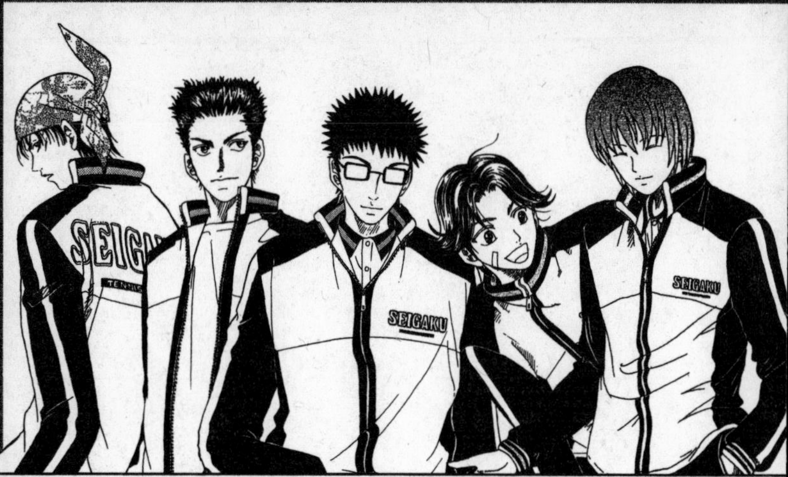
SEIGAKU
SEIGAKU
SEIGAKU

● KAORU KAIDO ● TAKESHI MOMOSHIRO ● SADAHARU INUI ● EIJI KIKUMARU ● SHUSUKE FUJI ●

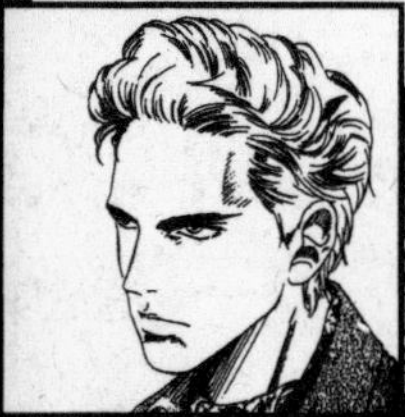
HYOTEI ACADEMY TENNIS COACH
TARO SAKAKI

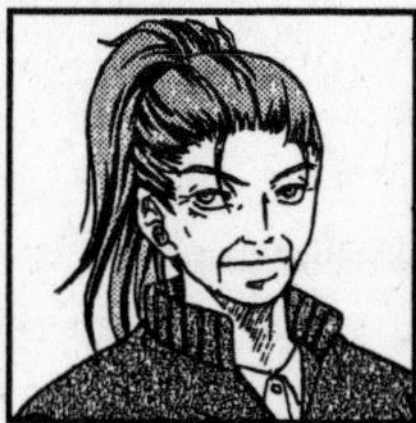
SEISHUN ACADEMY TENNIS TEAM COACH
SUMIRE RYUZAKI

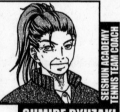

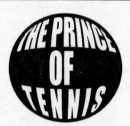

THE PRINCE OF TENNIS

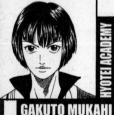

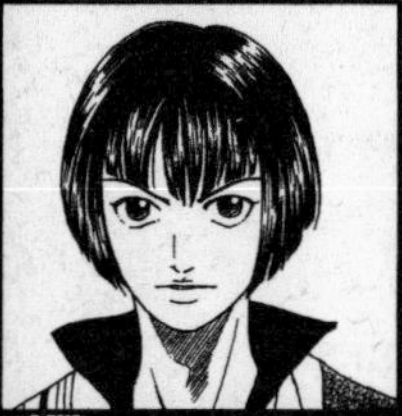
HYOTEI ACADEMY
GAKUTO MUKAHI

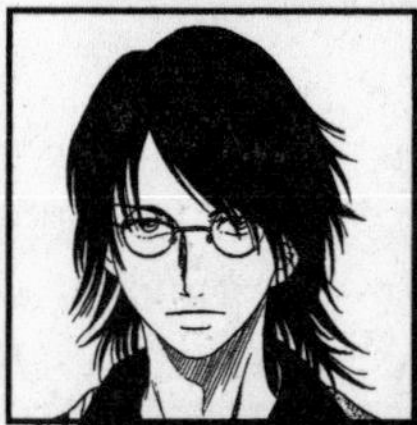
HYOTEI ACADEMY
YUSHI OSHITORI

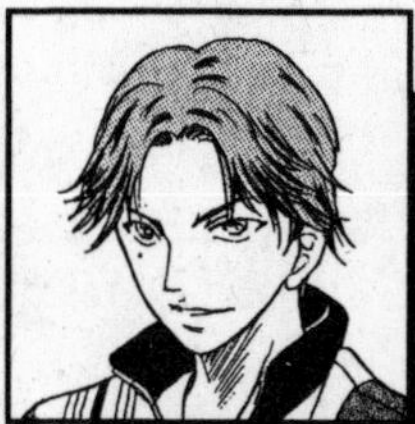
HYOTEI ACADEMY
KEIGO ATOBE

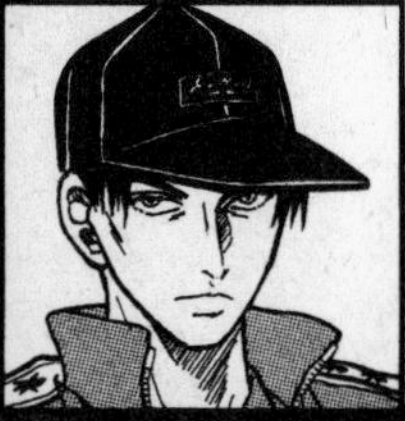
RIKKAI UNIVERSITY JUNIOR HIGH SCHOOL
GENICHIRO SANADA

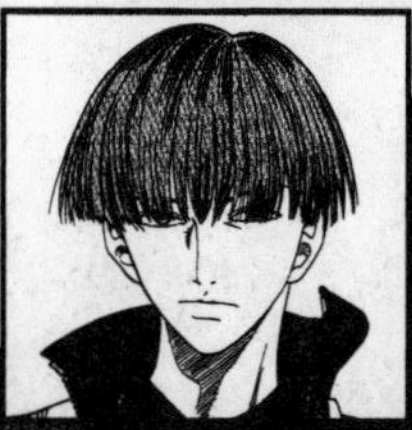
HYOTEI ACADEMY
WAKASHI HIYOSHI

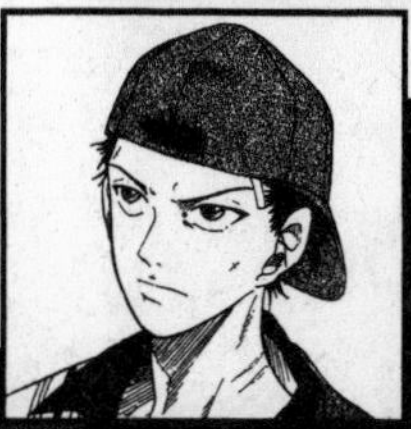
HYOTEI ACADEMY
RYO SHISHIDO

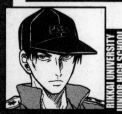

CONTENTS

Vol.18
Ace in the Hole

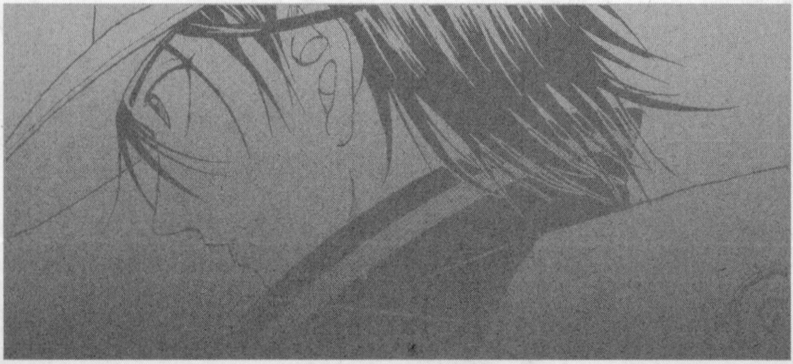

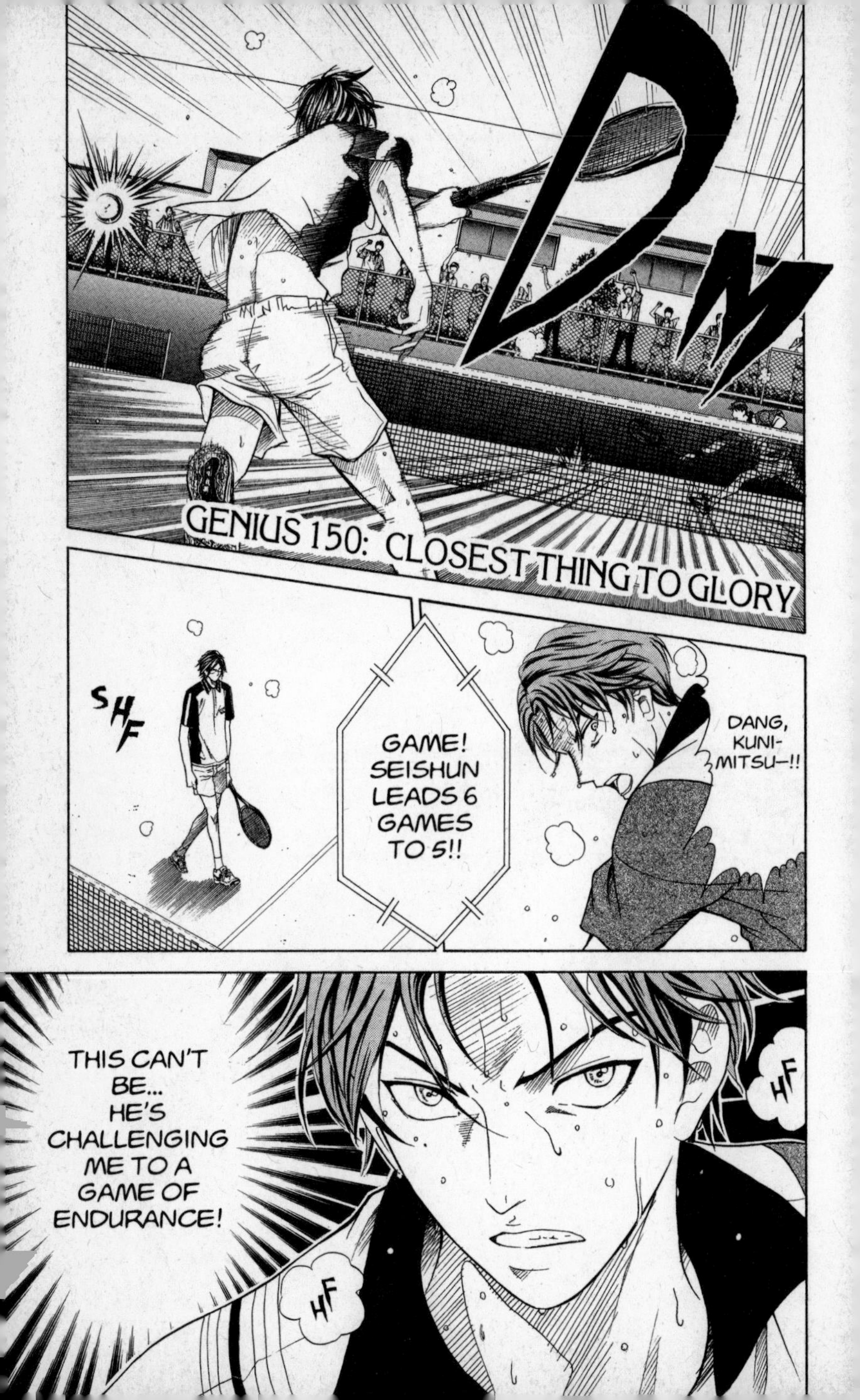
DM
GENIUS 150: CLOSEST THING TO GLORY
DANG, KUNI-MITSU—!!
GAME! SEISHUN LEADS 6 GAMES TO 5!!
SHF
HF
THIS CAN'T BE... HE'S CHALLENGING ME TO A GAME OF ENDURANCE!
HF

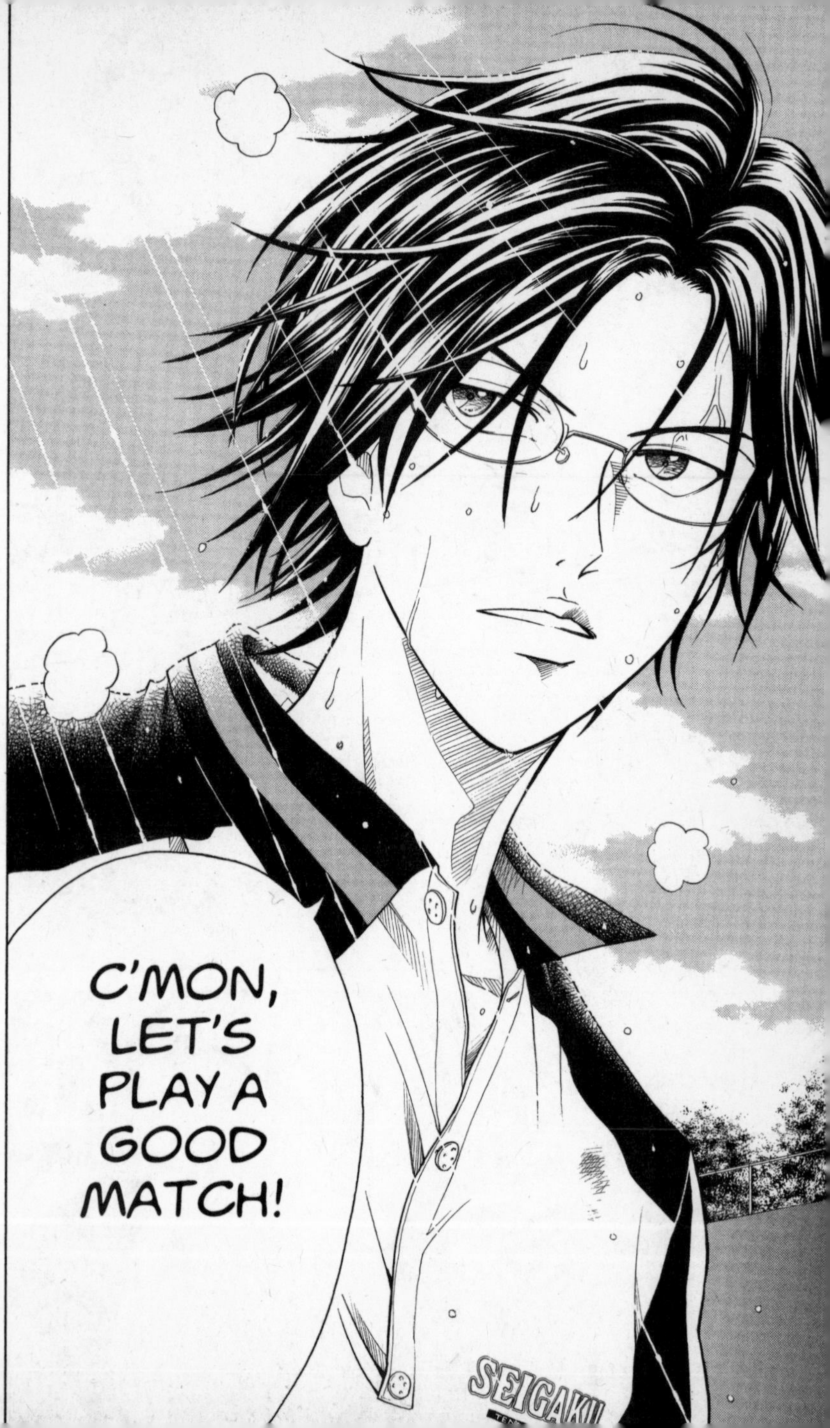
C'MON, LET'S PLAY A GOOD MATCH!
SEIGAKU

GENIUS 150: CLOSEST THING TO GLORY

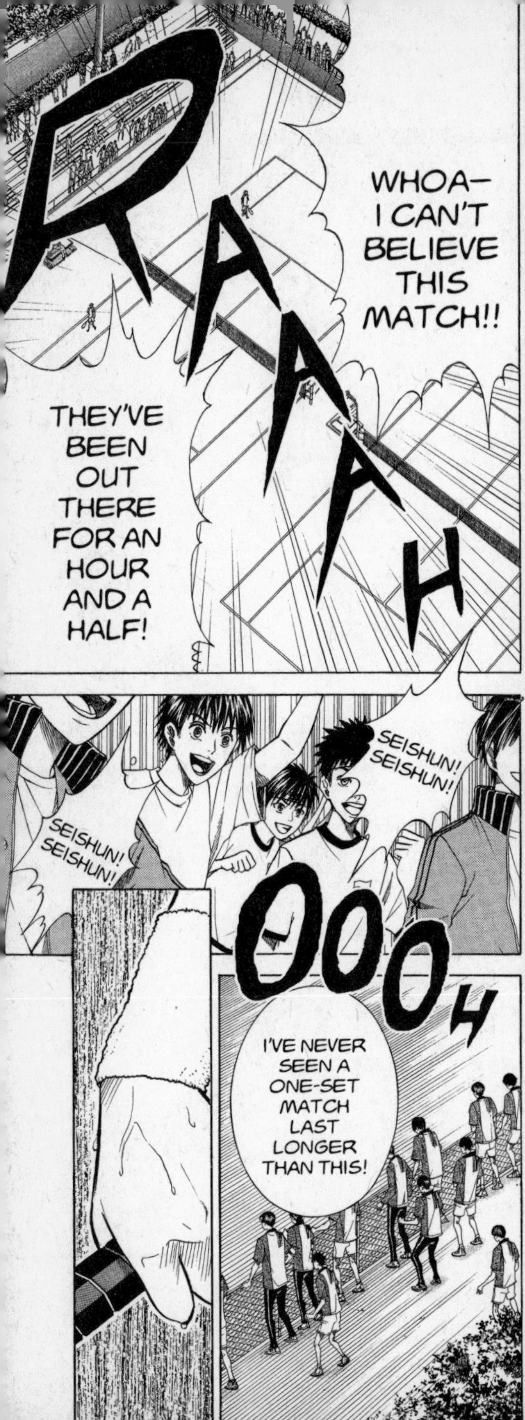
RAAAH
WHOA- I CAN'T BELIEVE THIS MATCH!!
THEY'VE BEEN OUT THERE FOR AN HOUR AND A HALF!
SEISHUN! SEISHUN!
SEISHUN! SEISHUN!
OOOH
I'VE NEVER SEEN A ONE-SET MATCH LAST LONGER THAN THIS!

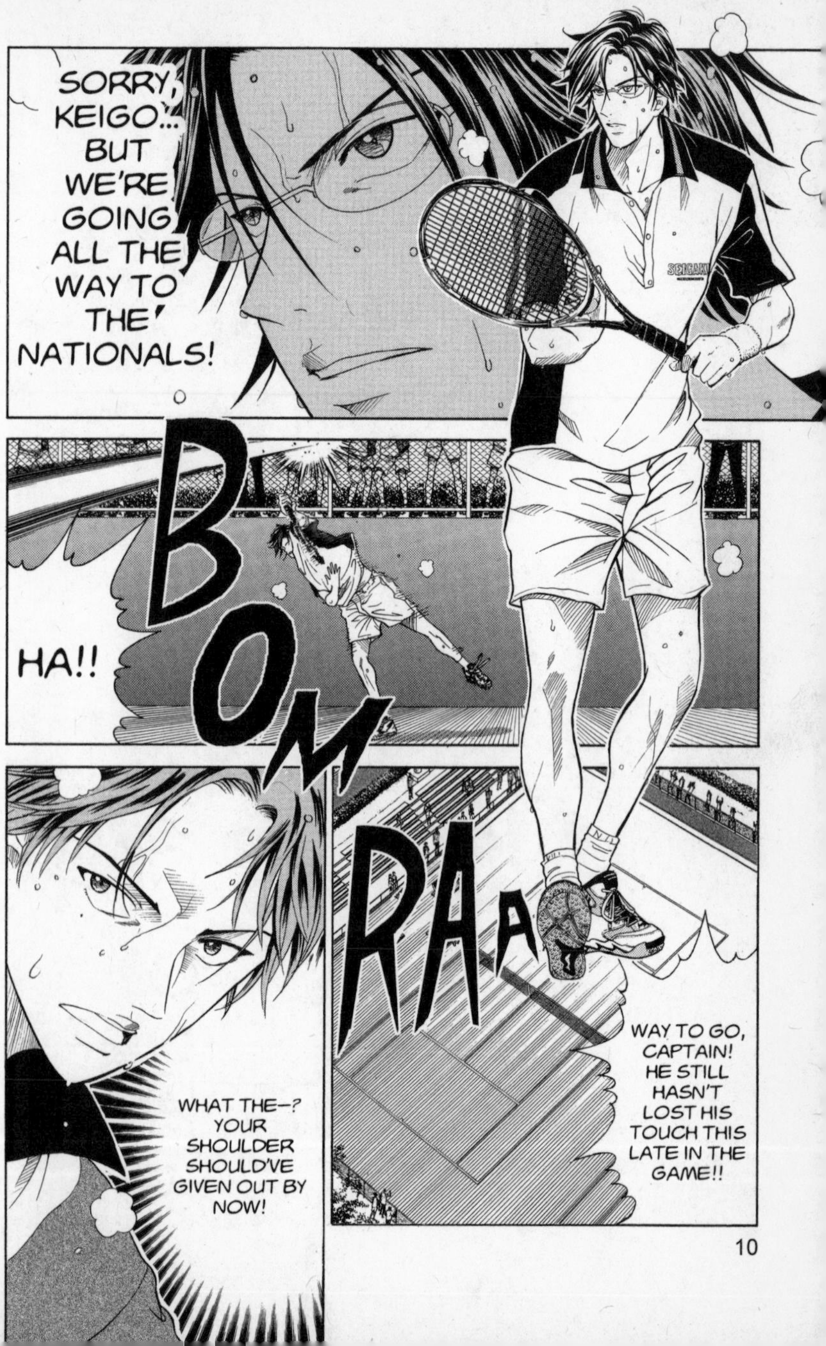
SORRY, KEIGO... BUT WE'RE GOING ALL THE WAY TO THE NATIONALS!
HA!!
BOMRAA
WAY TO GO, CAPTAIN! HE STILL HASN'T LOST HIS TOUCH THIS LATE IN THE GAME!!
WHAT THE--? YOUR SHOULDER SHOULD'VE GIVEN OUT BY NOW!

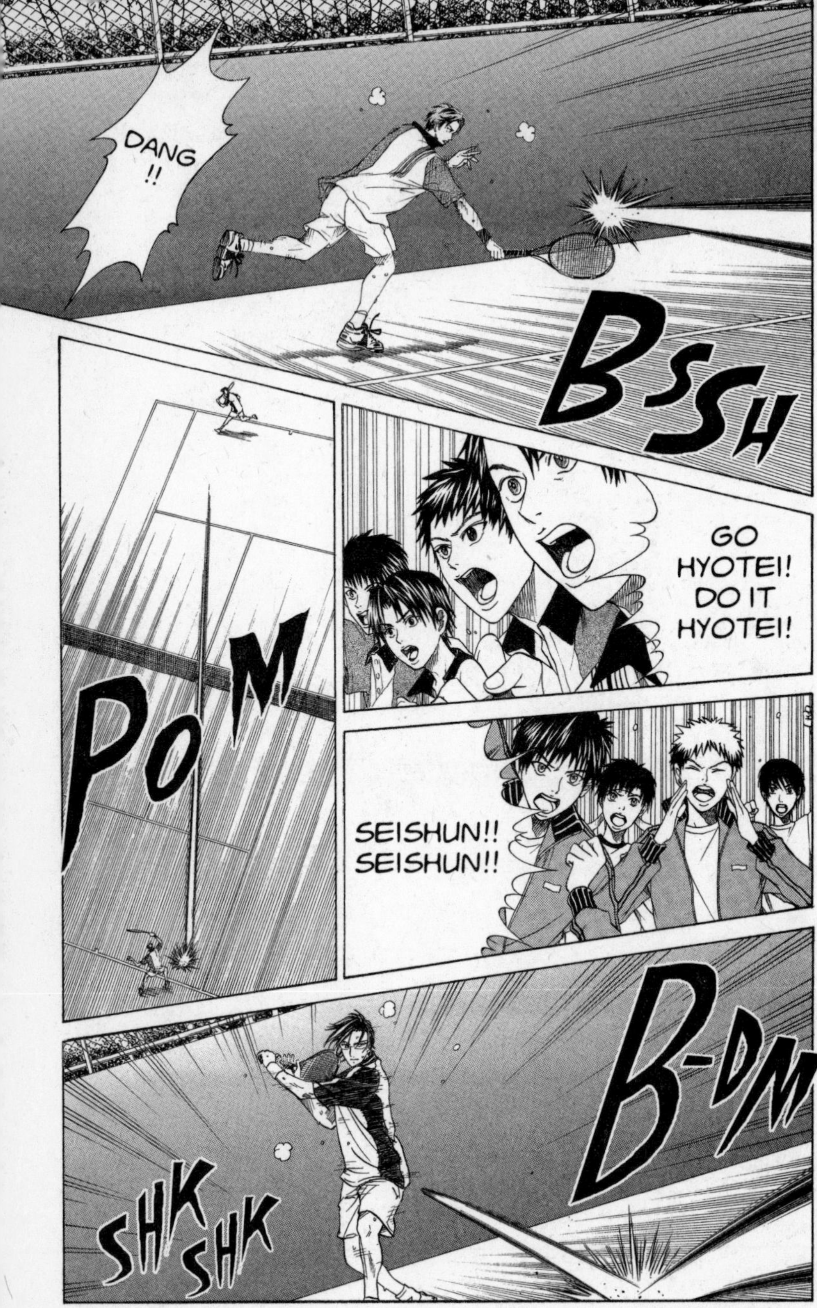
DANG!!
BSSH
GO HYOTEI! DO IT HYOTEI!
SEISHUN!! SEISHUN!!
POM
B-DM
SHK SHK

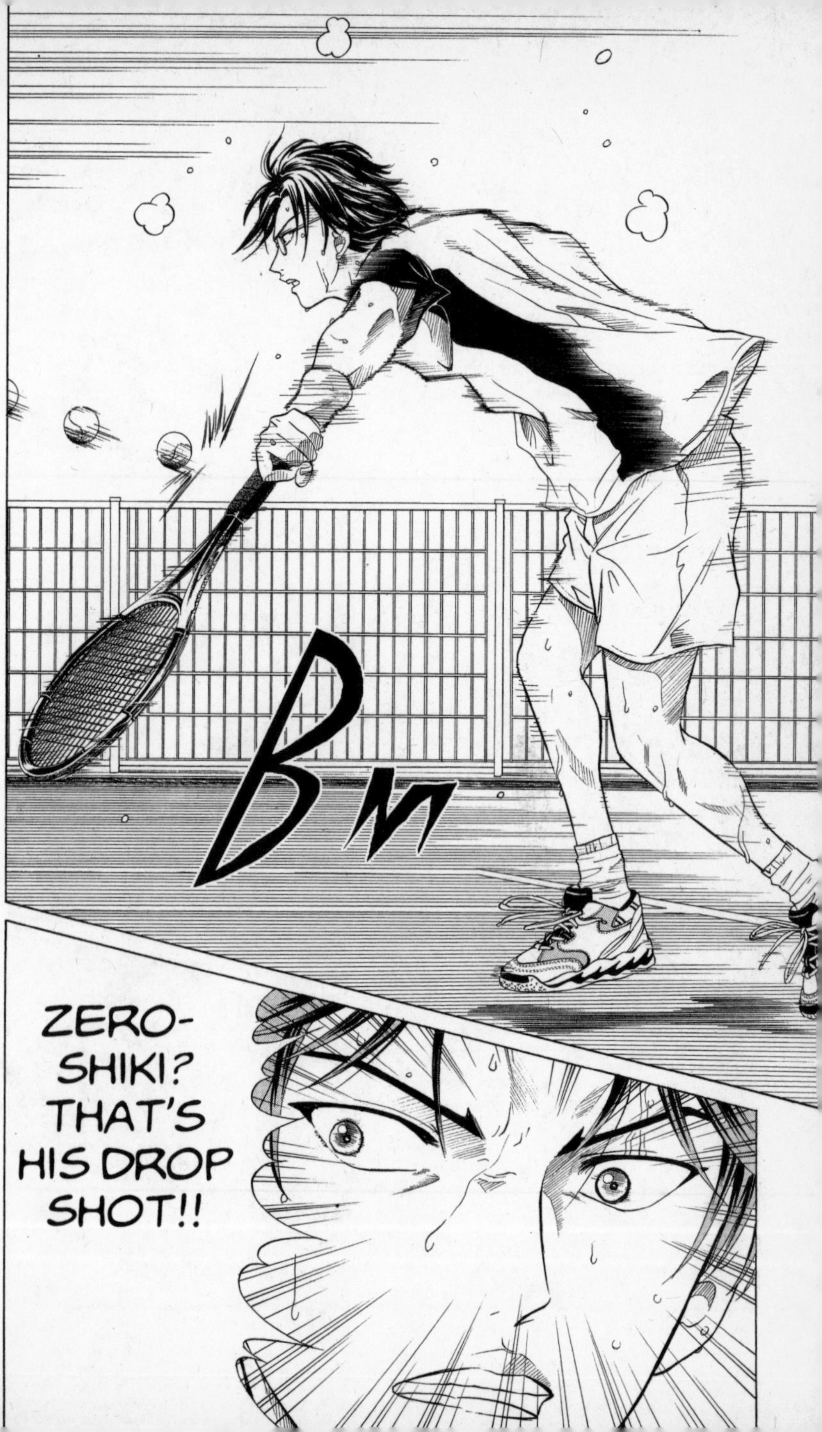
Bn
ZERO-SHIKI? THAT'S HIS DROP SHOT!!

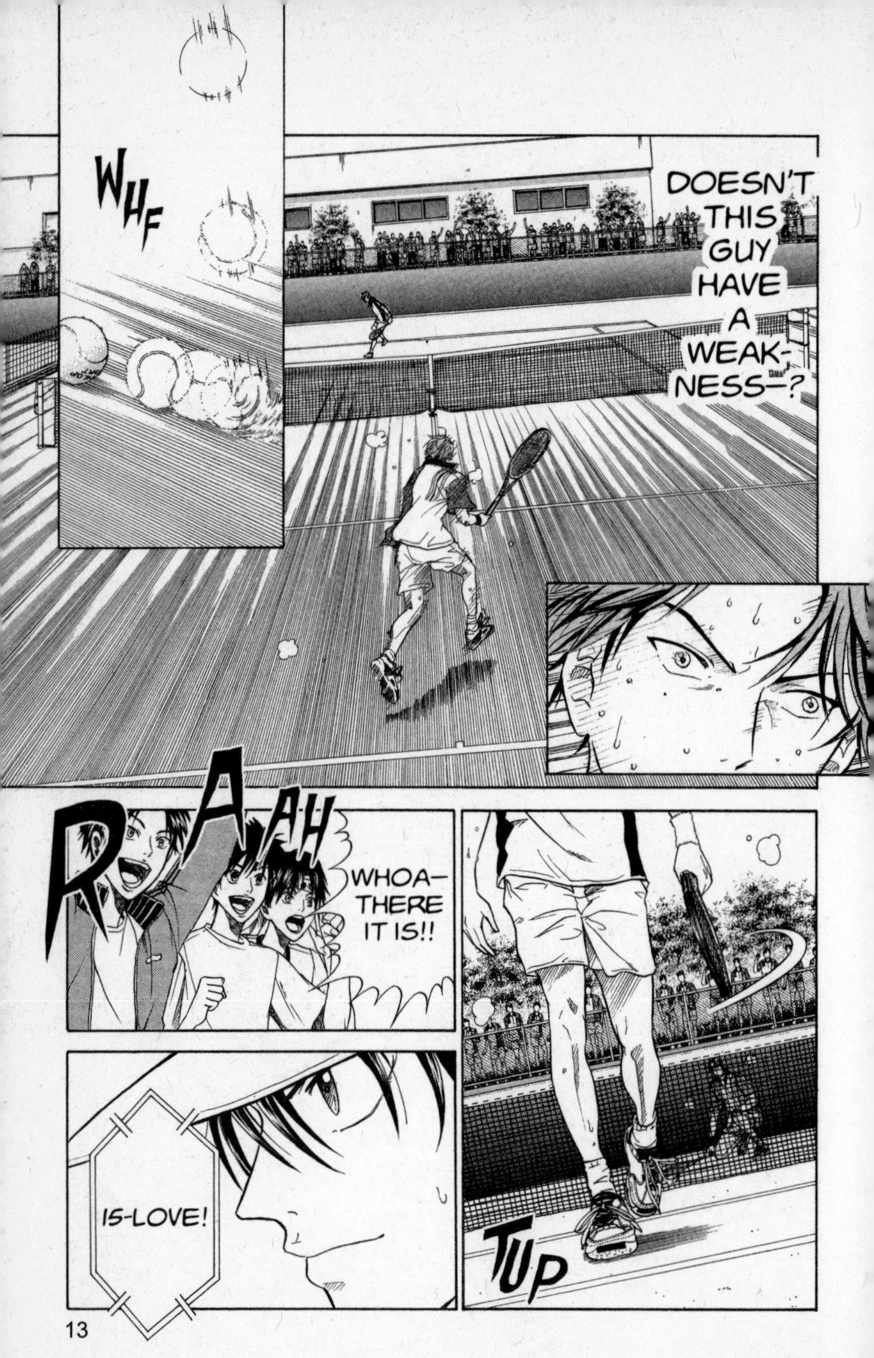

DOESN'T THIS GUY HAVE A WEAK-NESS--?
WHF
TUP
RAAH
WHOA-- THERE IT IS!!
IS-LOVE!

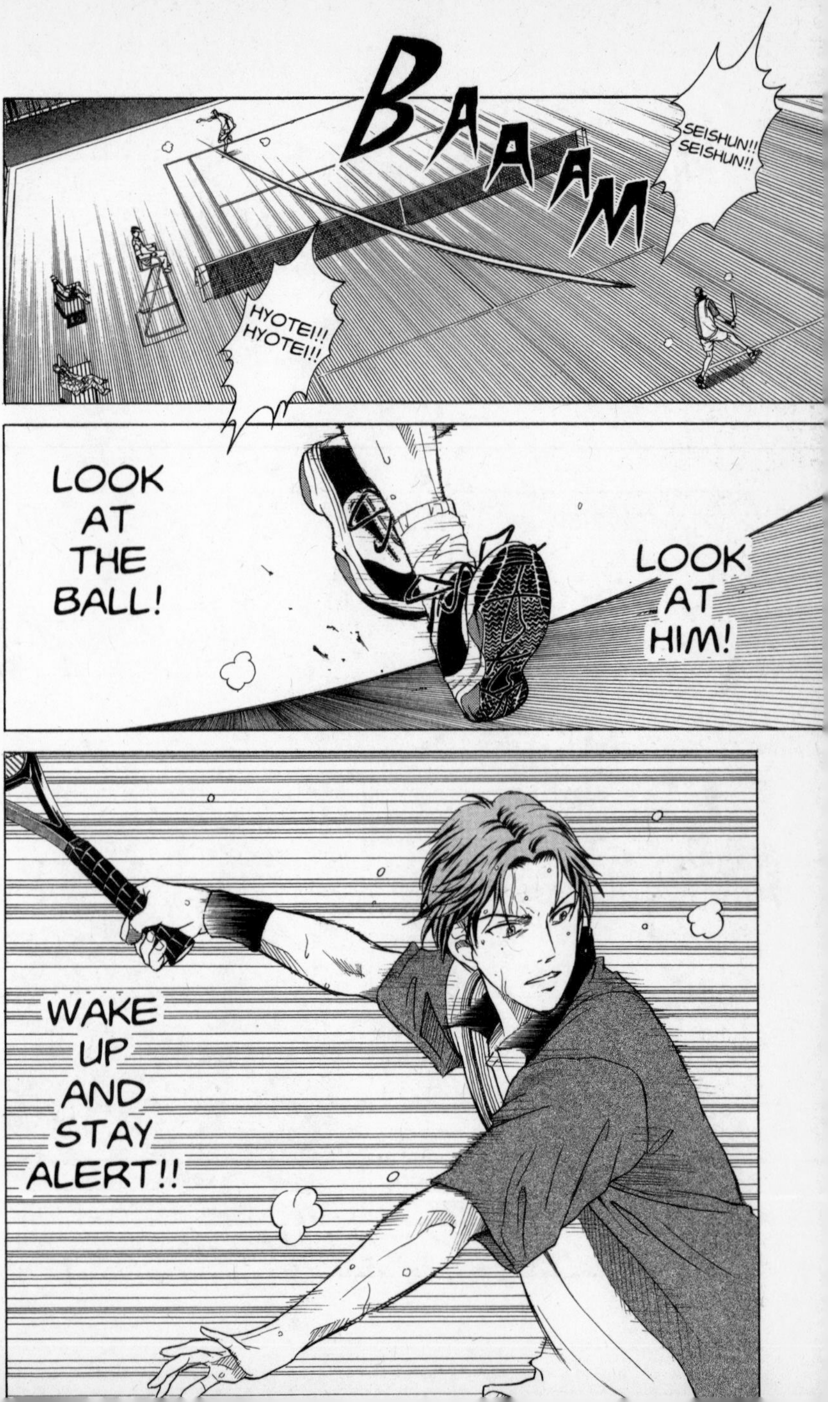
SEISHUN!! SEISHUN!!
BAAAM
HYOTEI!! HYOTEI!!
LOOK AT HIM!
LOOK AT THE BALL!
WAKE UP AND STAY ALERT!!

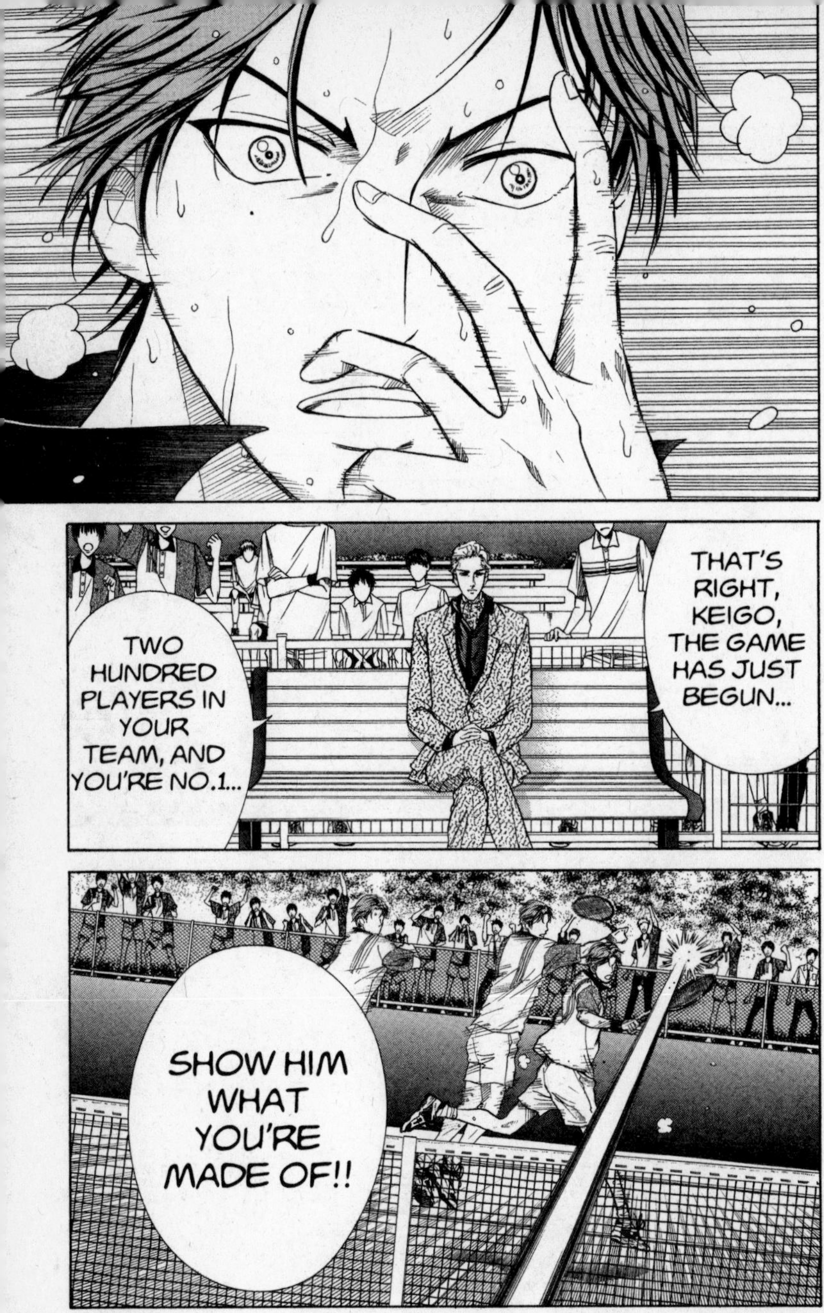
THAT'S RIGHT, KEIGO, THE GAME HAS JUST BEGUN...
TWO HUNDRED PLAYERS IN YOUR TEAM, AND YOU'RE NO.1...
SHOW HIM WHAT YOU'RE MADE OF!!

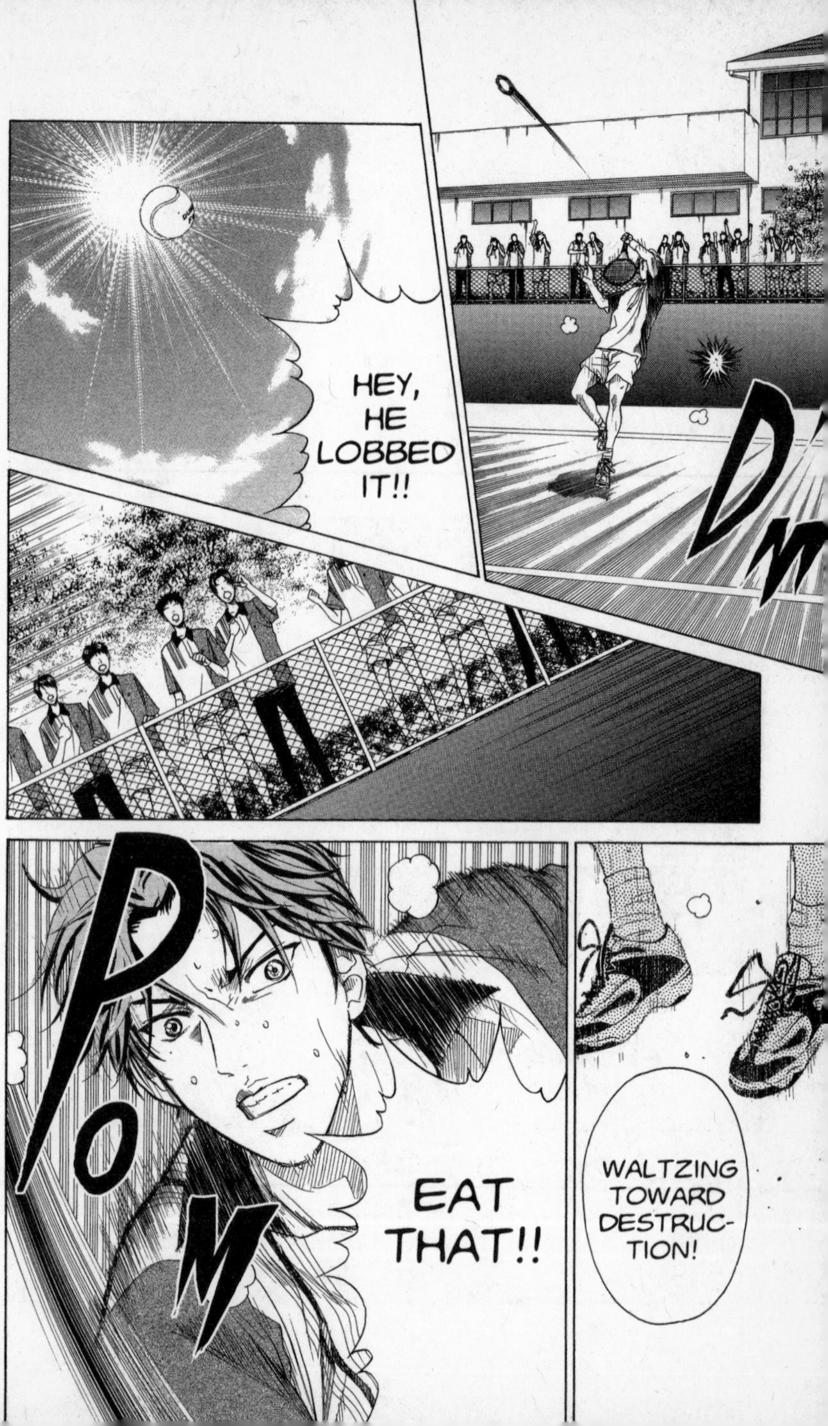
HEY, HE LOBBED IT!!
WALTZING TOWARD DESTRUC-TION!
POM
EAT THAT!!

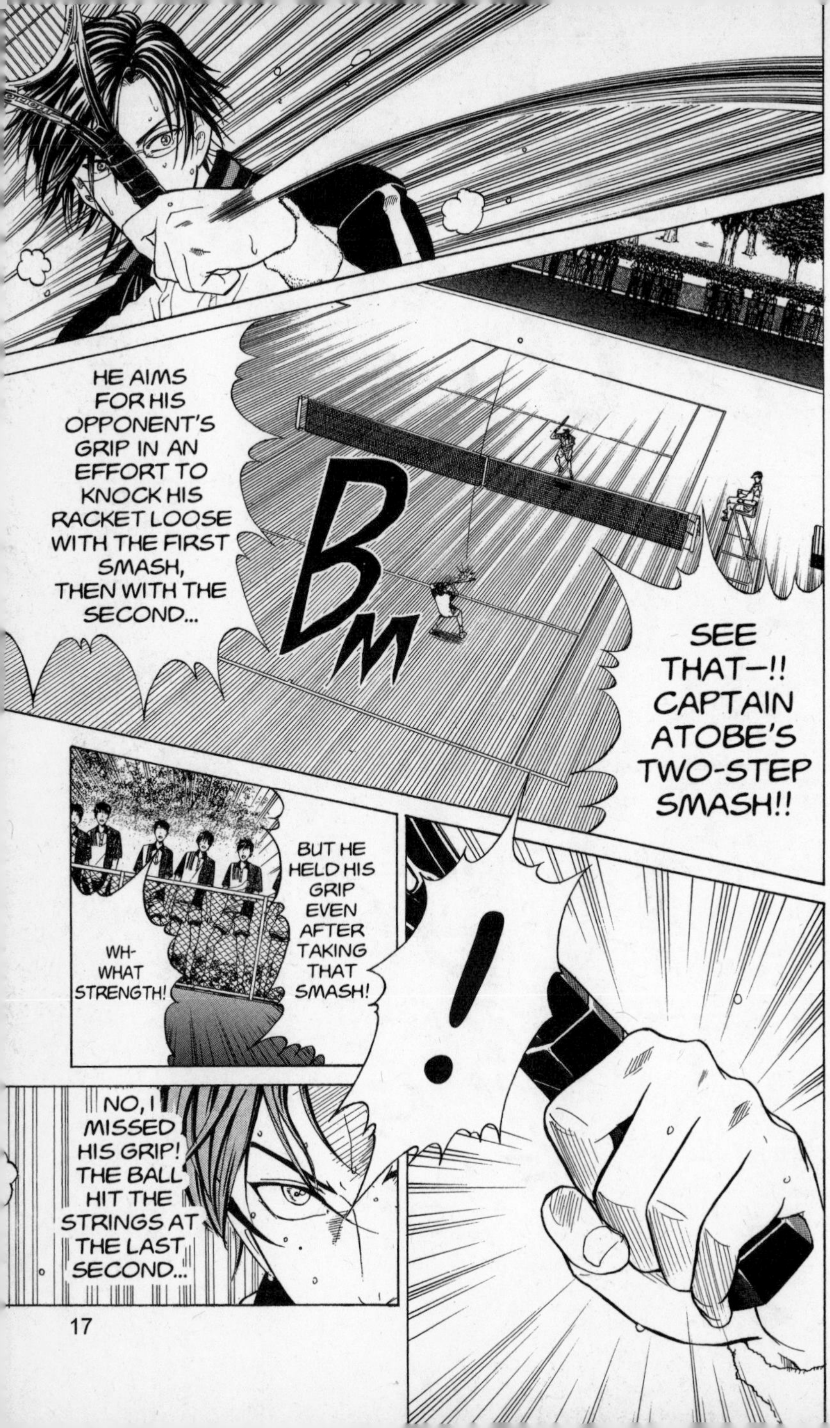
SEE THAT—!! CAPTAIN ATOBE'S TWO-STEP SMASH!!
BM
HE AIMS FOR HIS OPPONENT'S GRIP IN AN EFFORT TO KNOCK HIS RACKET LOOSE WITH THE FIRST SMASH, THEN WITH THE SECOND...
!
BUT HE HELD HIS GRIP EVEN AFTER TAKING THAT SMASH!
WH-WHAT STRENGTH!
NO, I MISSED HIS GRIP! THE BALL HIT THE STRINGS AT THE LAST SECOND...

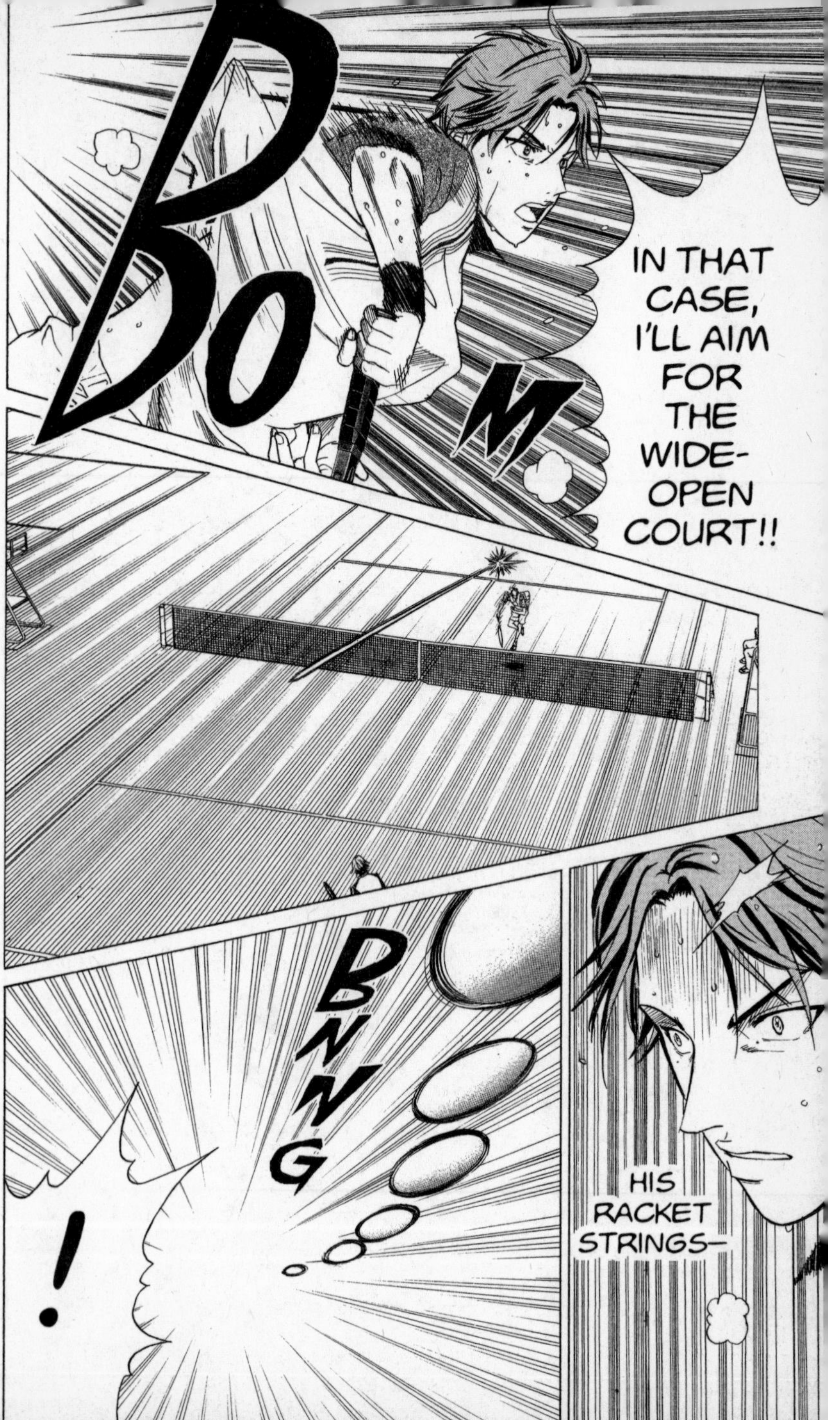
IN THAT CASE, I'LL AIM FOR THE WIDE-OPEN COURT!!
BOOM
HIS RACKET STRINGS—
BNNG
!

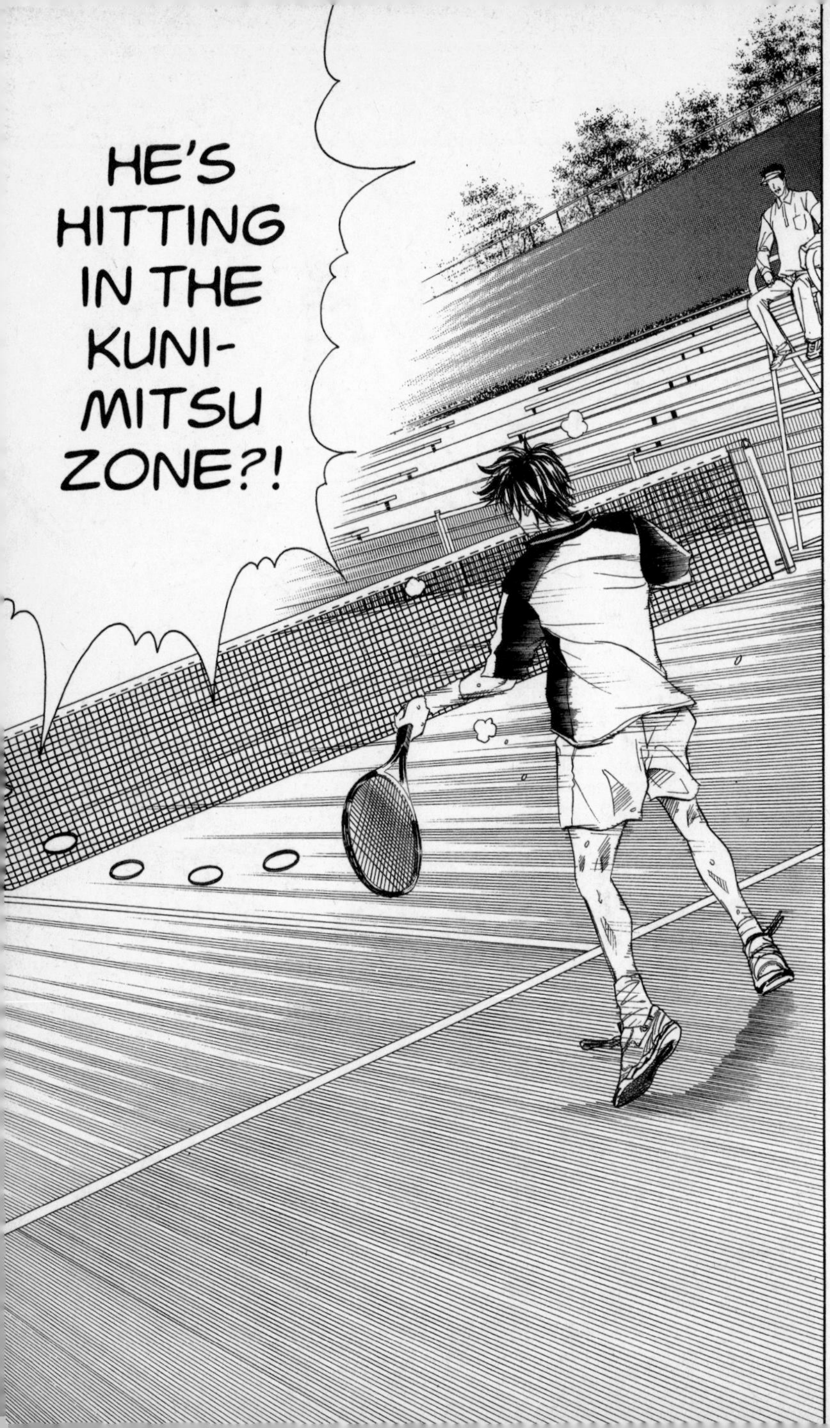
HE'S HITTING IN THE KUNI-MITSU ZONE?!

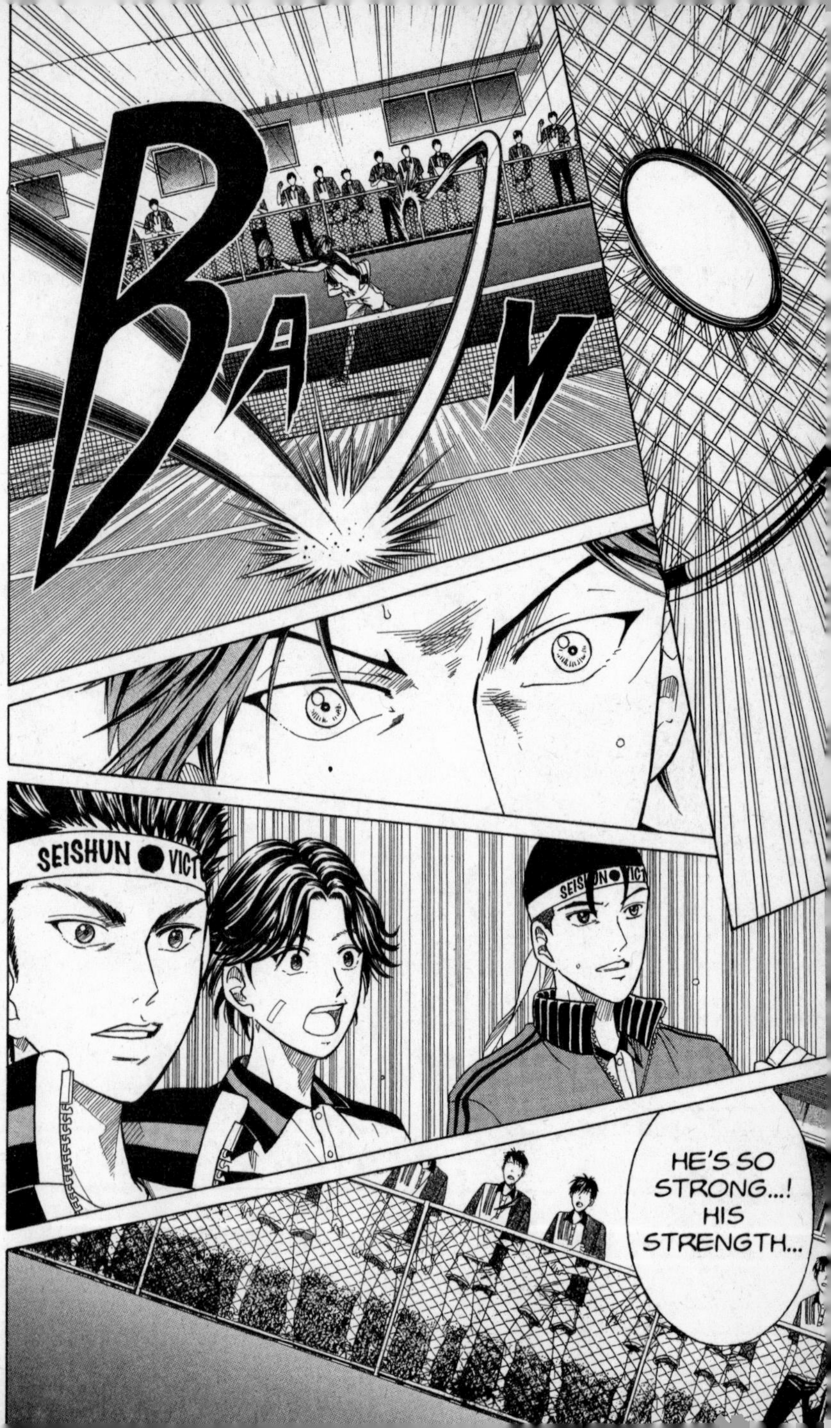
BAM
SEISHUN VICT
SEISHUN VICT
HE'S SO STRONG...! HIS STRENGTH...

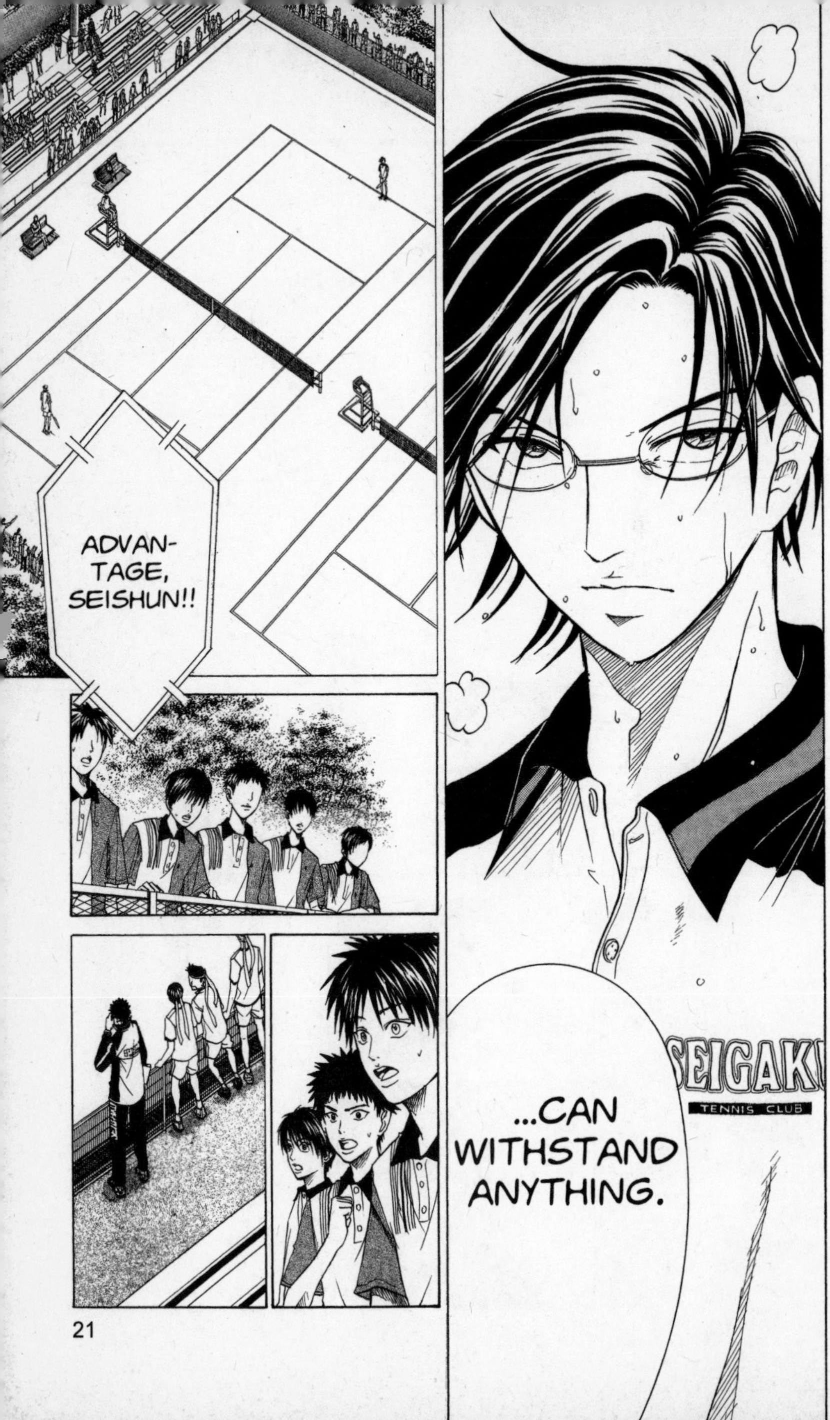
...CAN WITHSTAND ANYTHING.
SEIGAKU
TENNIS CLUB
ADVAN-TAGE, SEISHUN!!

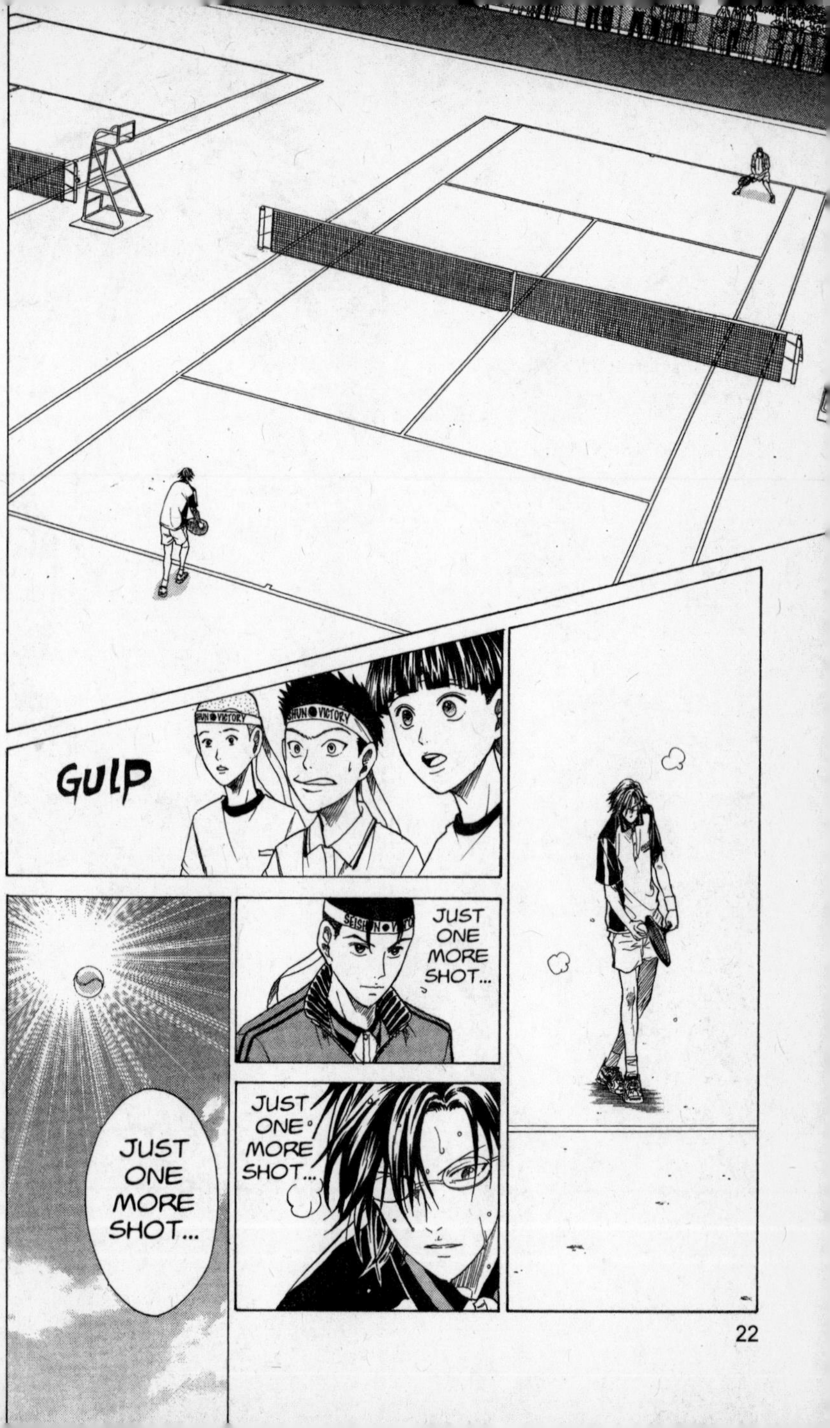
GULP
JUST ONE MORE SHOT...
JUST ONE MORE SHOT...
JUST ONE MORE SHOT...

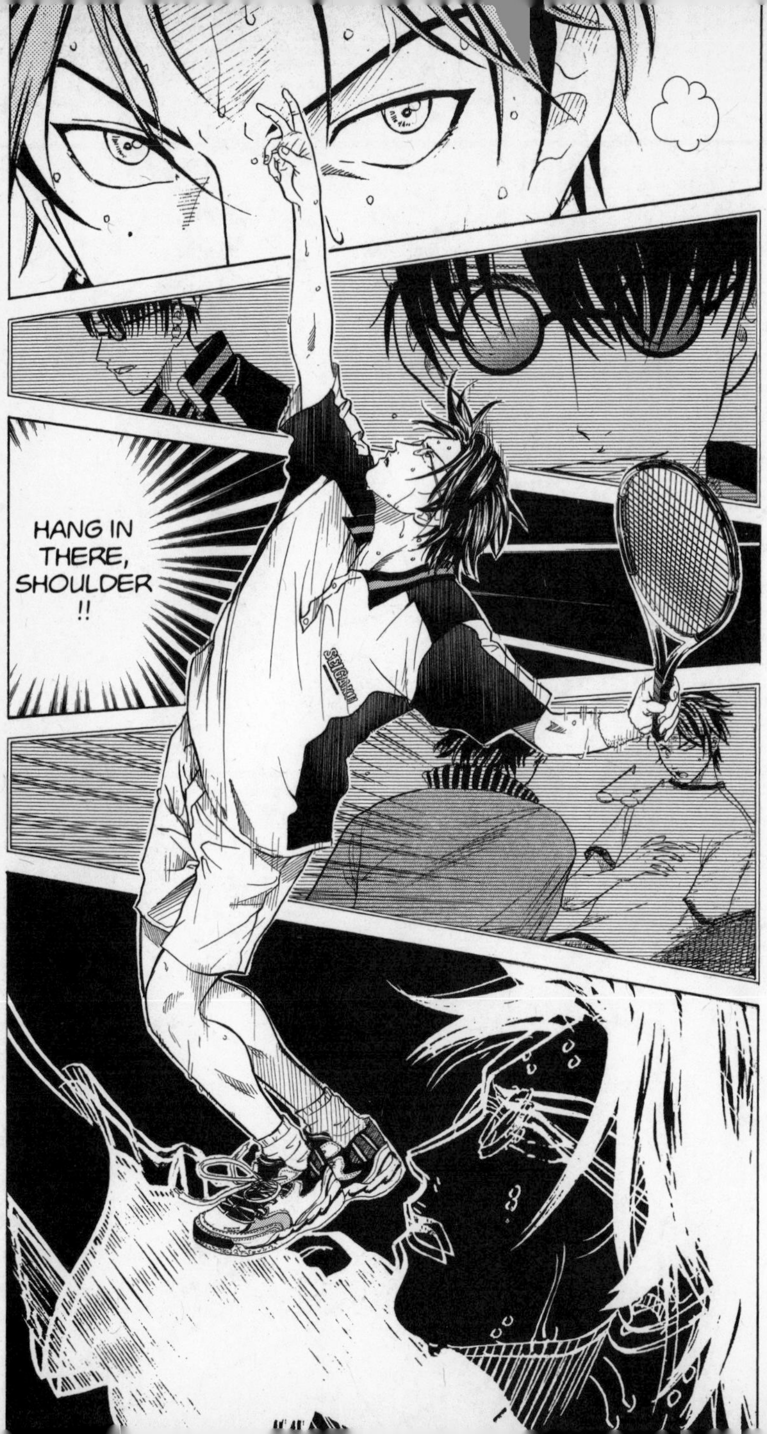
HANG IN THERE, SHOULDER !!

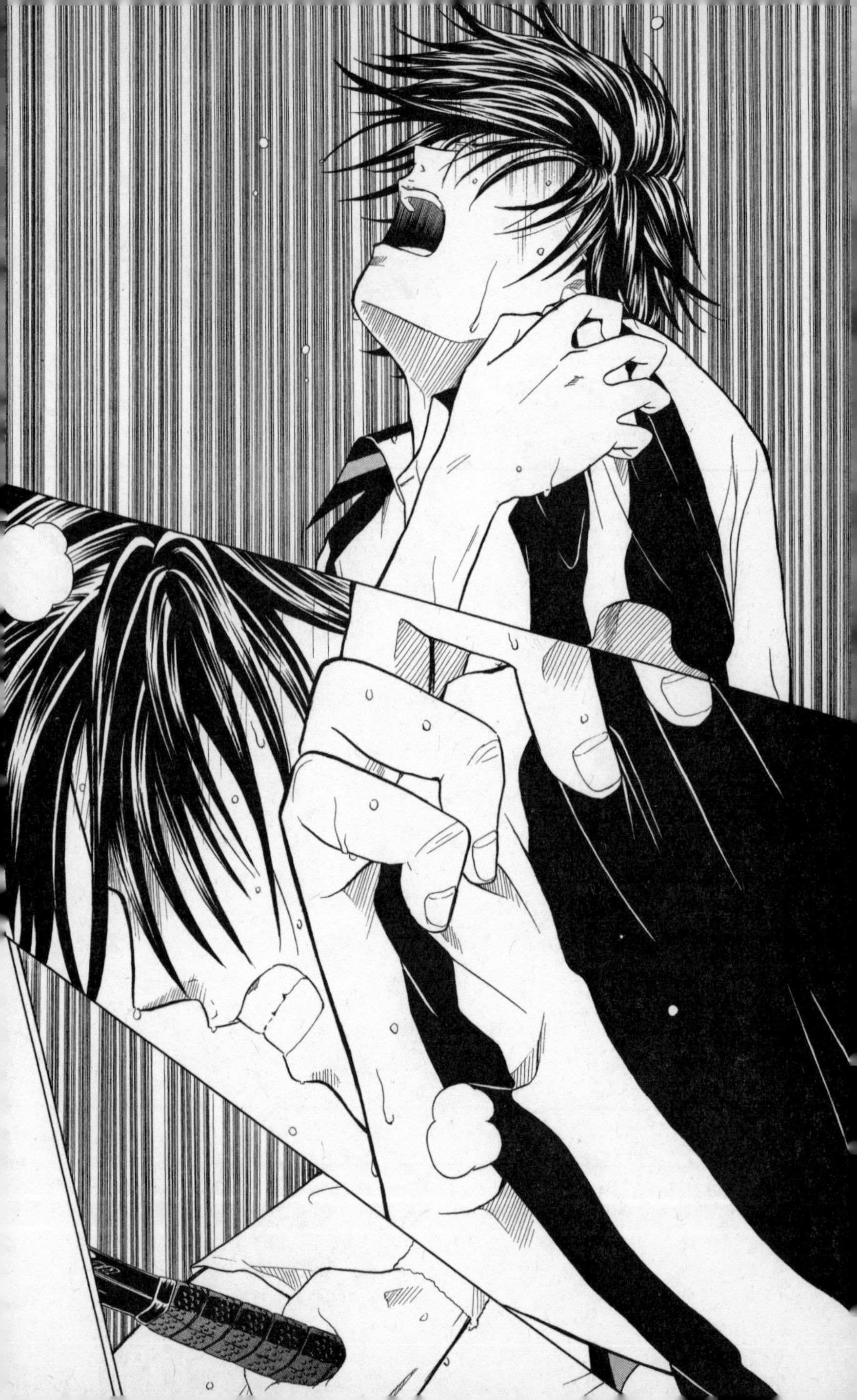

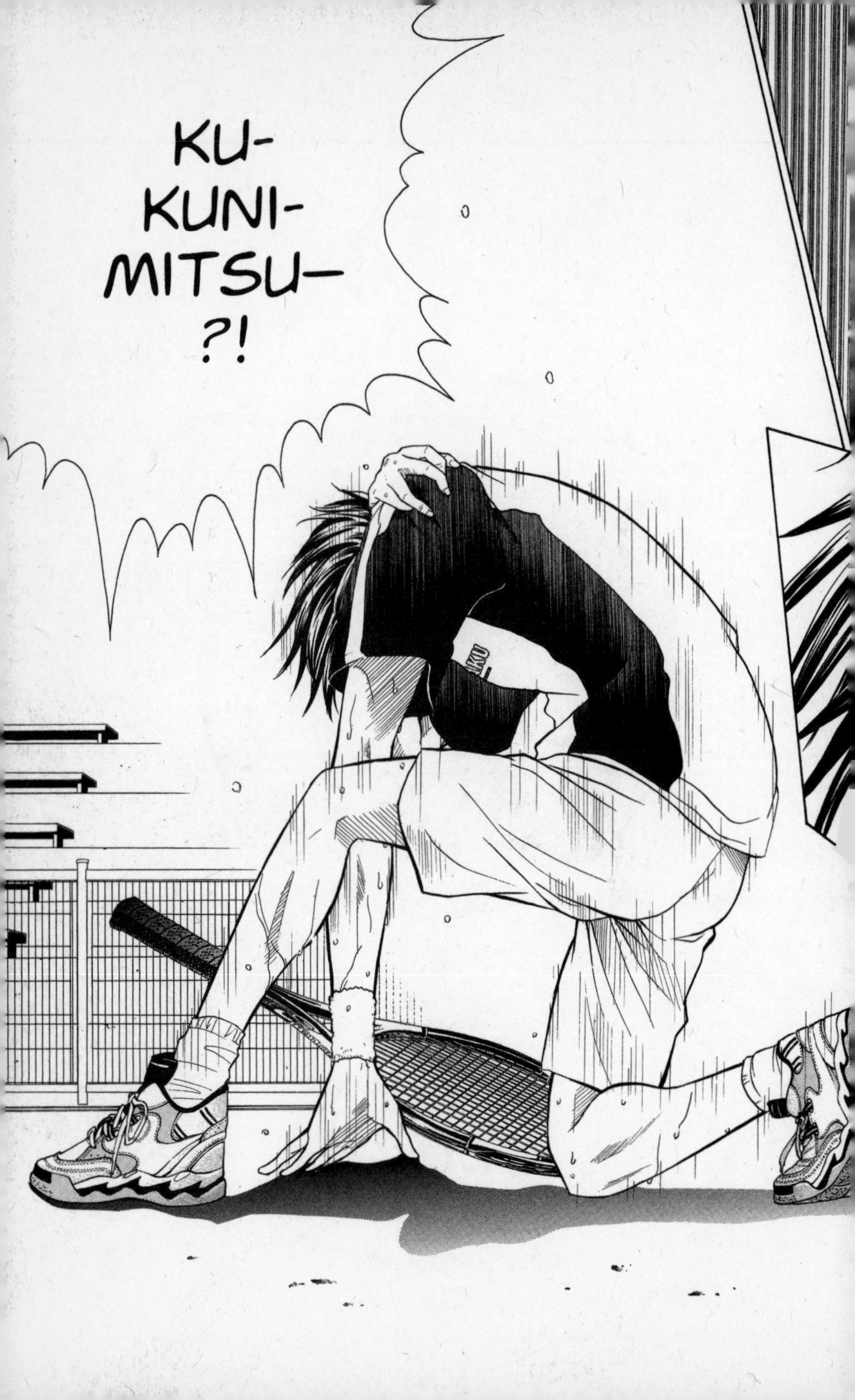
KU-
KUNI-
MITSU-
?!

テニスの王子様

THE PRINCE OF TENNIS™

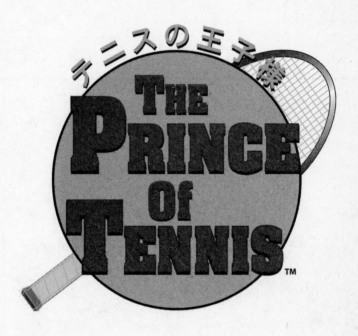

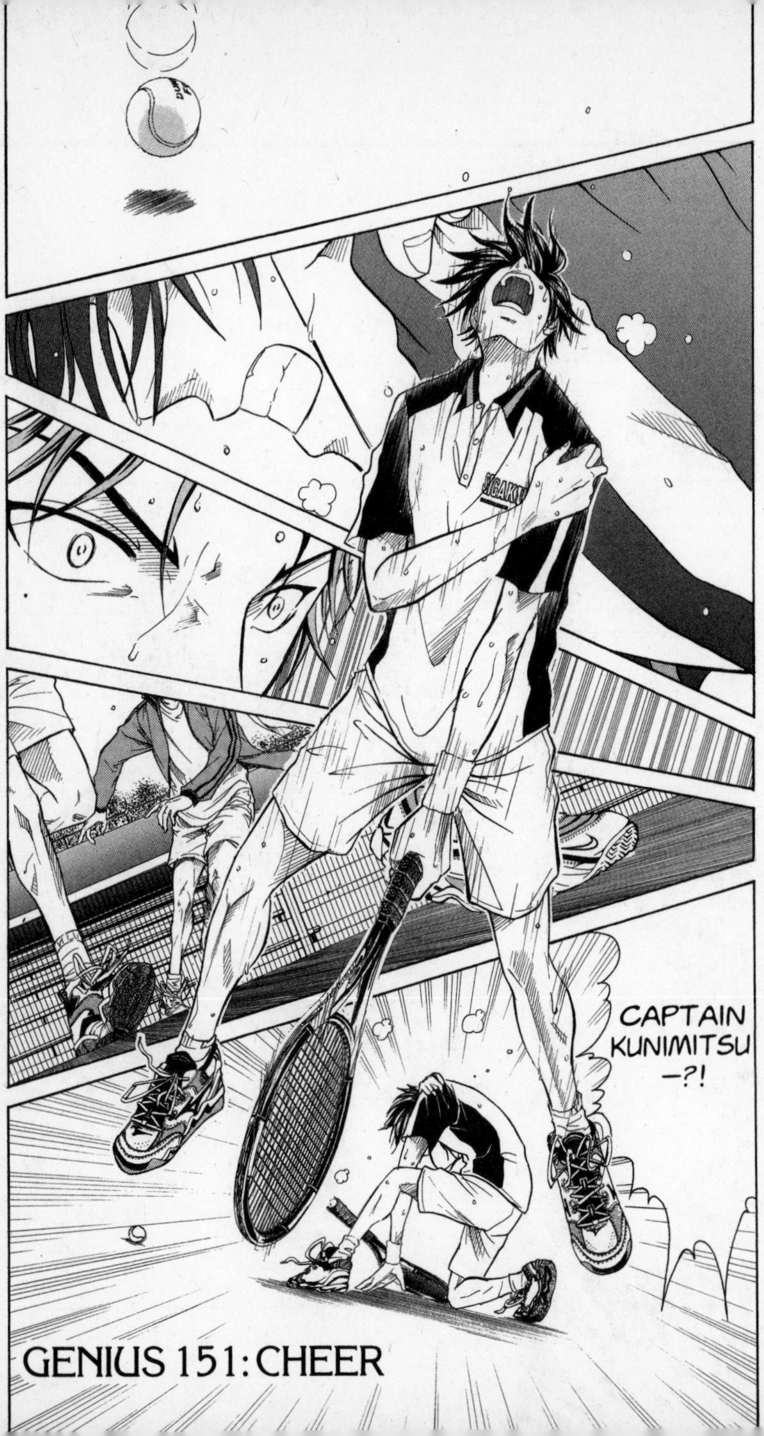
CAPTAIN KUNIMITSU—?!
GENIUS 151: CHEER

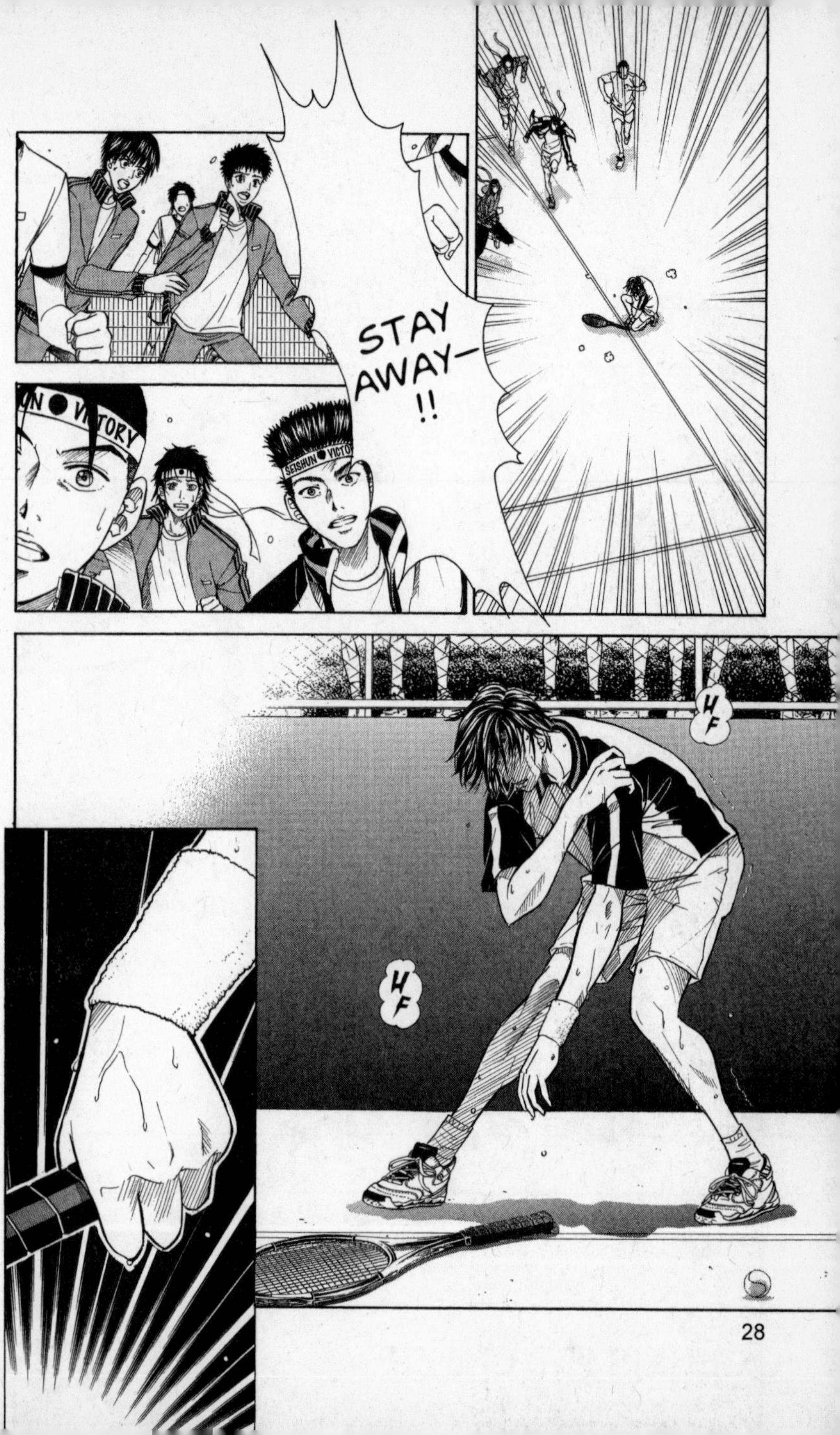
STAY AWAY—!!
SEISHUN VICTORY
HF
HF

GENIUS 151: CHEER

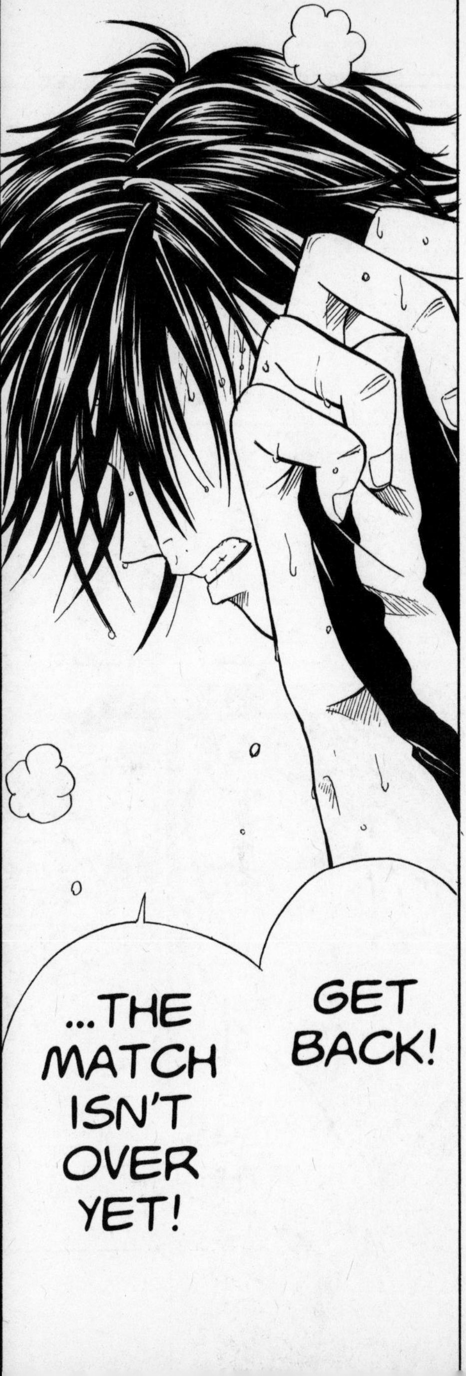
GET BACK!
...THE MATCH ISN'T OVER YET!

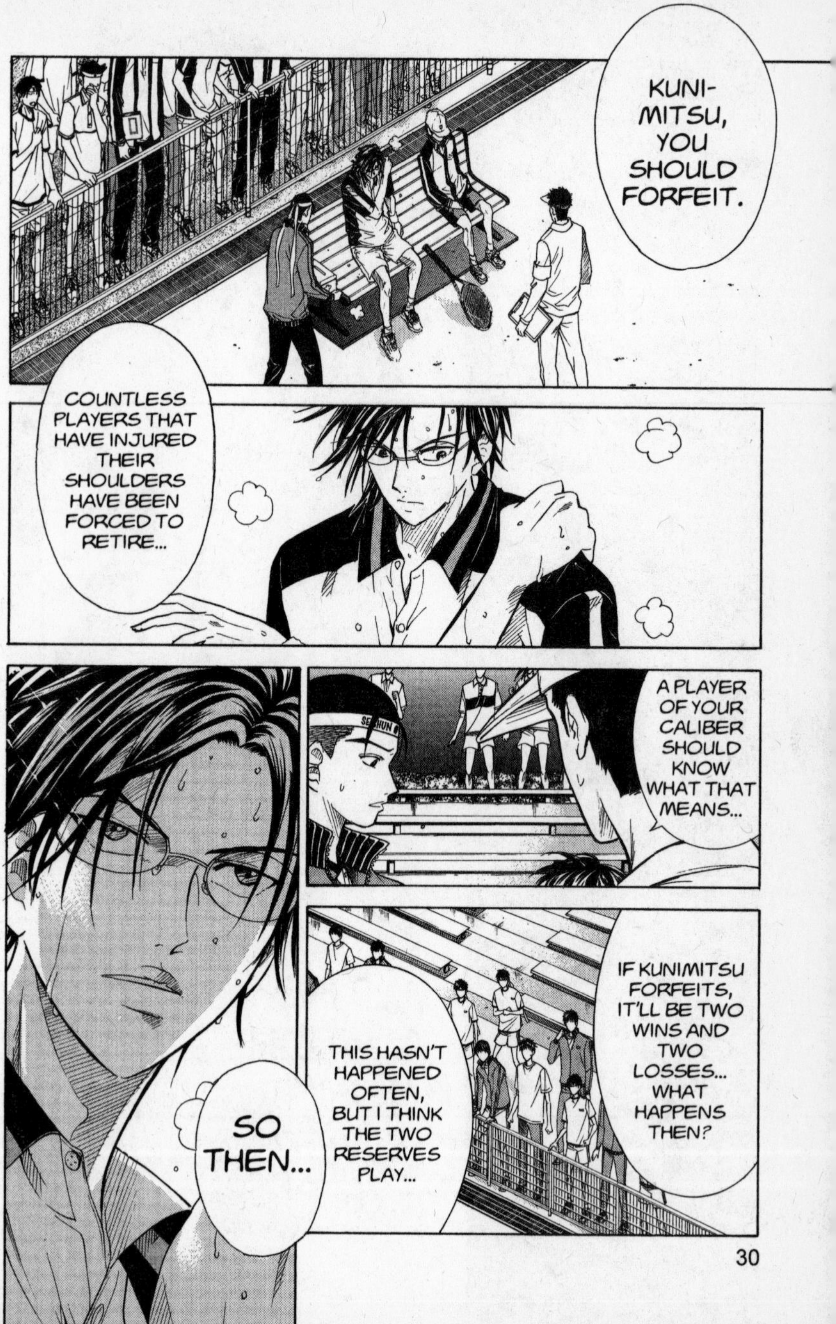
KUNI-MITSU, YOU SHOULD FORFEIT.
COUNTLESS PLAYERS THAT HAVE INJURED THEIR SHOULDERS HAVE BEEN FORCED TO RETIRE...
A PLAYER OF YOUR CALIBER SHOULD KNOW WHAT THAT MEANS...
IF KUNIMITSU FORFEITS, IT'LL BE TWO WINS AND TWO LOSSES... WHAT HAPPENS THEN?
THIS HASN'T HAPPENED OFTEN, BUT I THINK THE TWO RESERVES PLAY...
SO THEN...

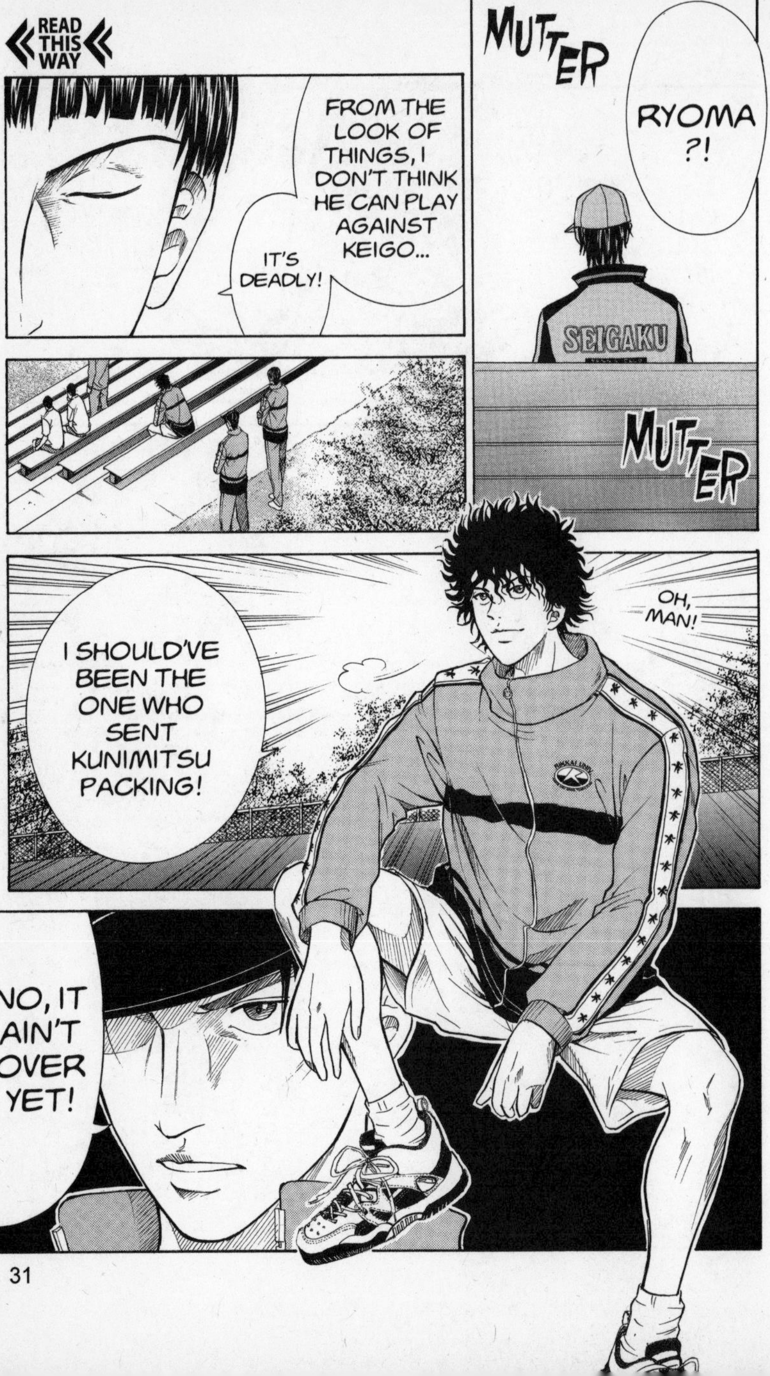
READ THIS WAY
MUTTER
RYOMA ?!
MUTTER
FROM THE LOOK OF THINGS, I DON'T THINK HE CAN PLAY AGAINST KEIGO...
IT'S DEADLY!
OH, MAN!
I SHOULD'VE BEEN THE ONE WHO SENT KUNIMITSU PACKING!
NO, IT AIN'T OVER YET!

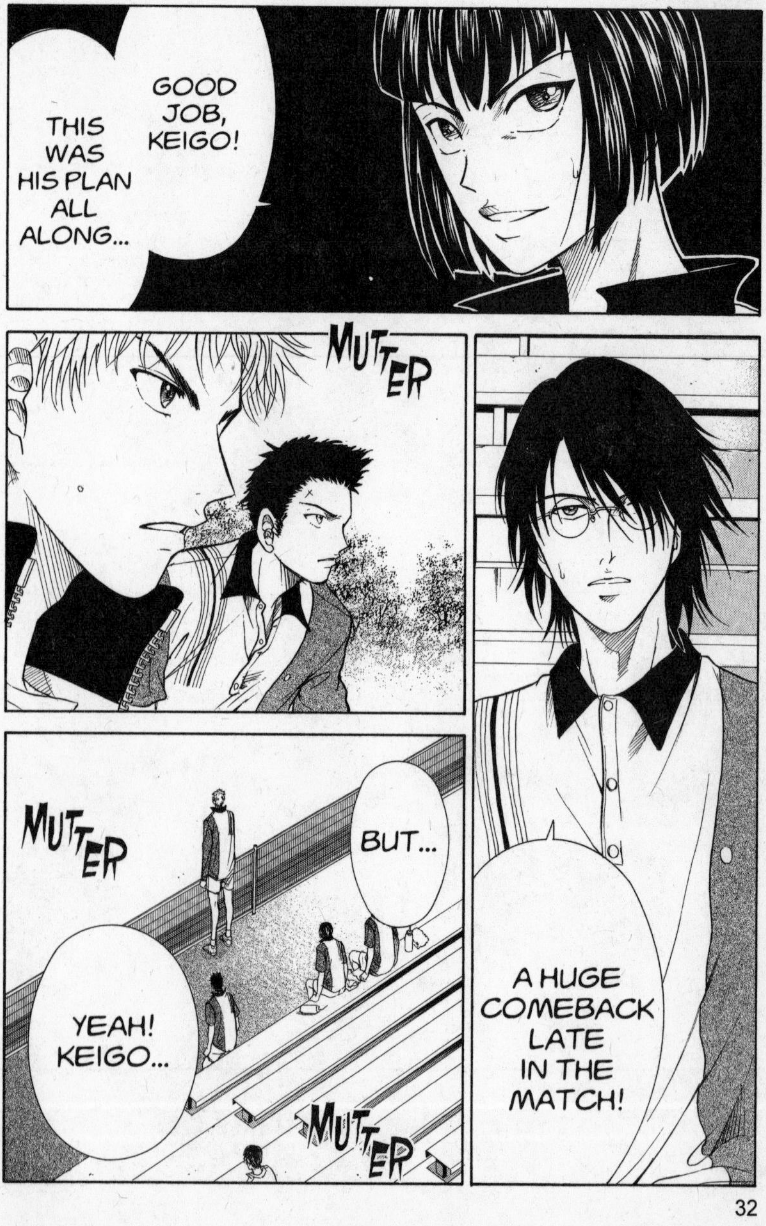
GOOD JOB, KEIGO!
THIS WAS HIS PLAN ALL ALONG...
A HUGE COMEBACK LATE IN THE MATCH!
MUTTER
BUT...
MUTTER
YEAH! KEIGO...
MUTTER

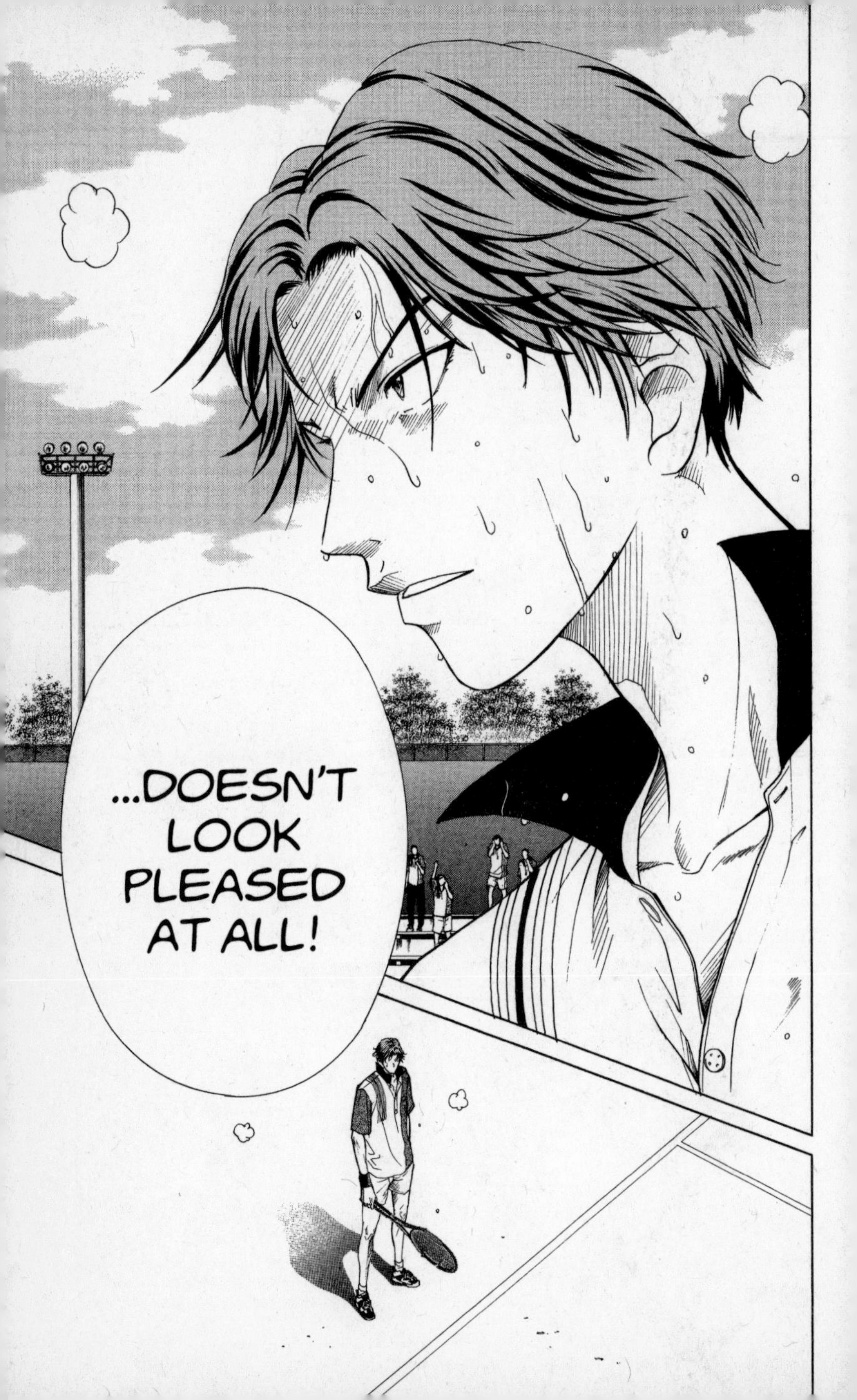
...DOESN'T LOOK PLEASED AT ALL!

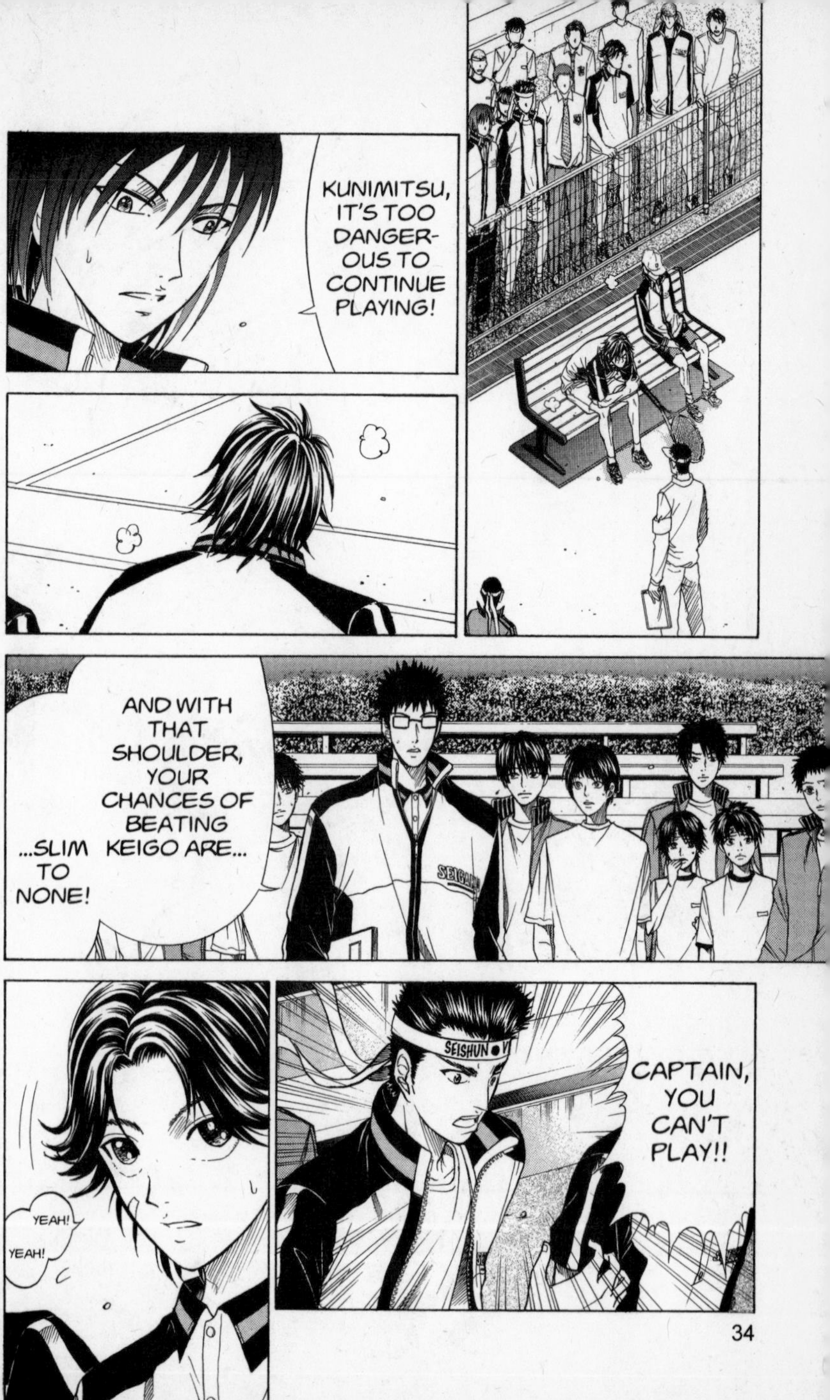
KUNIMITSU, IT'S TOO DANGER-OUS TO CONTINUE PLAYING!
AND WITH THAT SHOULDER, YOUR CHANCES OF BEATING KEIGO ARE...
...SLIM TO NONE!
SEIGAKU
SEISHUN
CAPTAIN, YOU CAN'T PLAY!!
YEAH!
YEAH!

READ THIS WAY

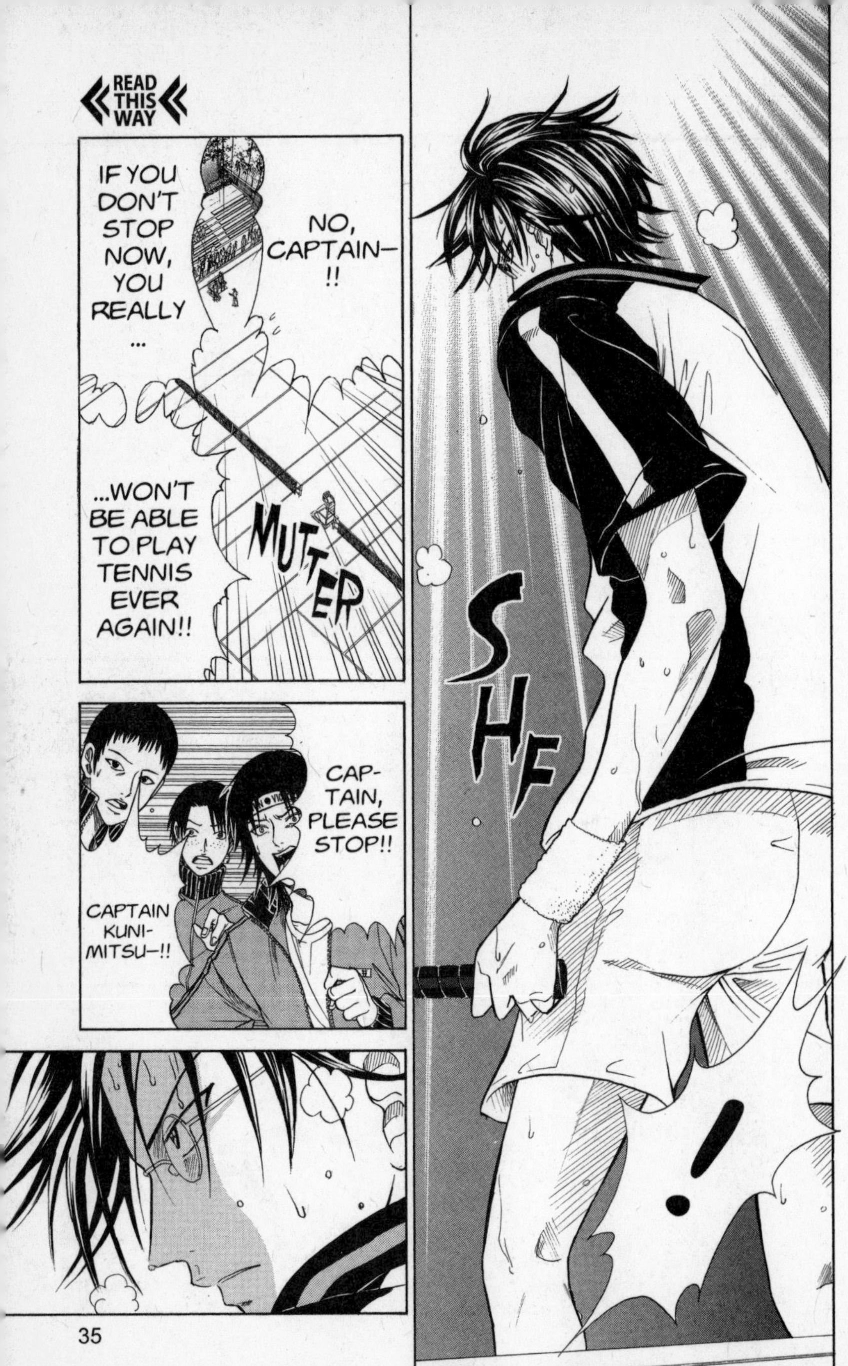
SHF
!
NO, CAPTAIN—!!
IF YOU DON'T STOP NOW, YOU REALLY ...
MUTTER
...WON'T BE ABLE TO PLAY TENNIS EVER AGAIN!!
CAP-TAIN, PLEASE STOP!!
CAPTAIN KUNI-MITSU—!!

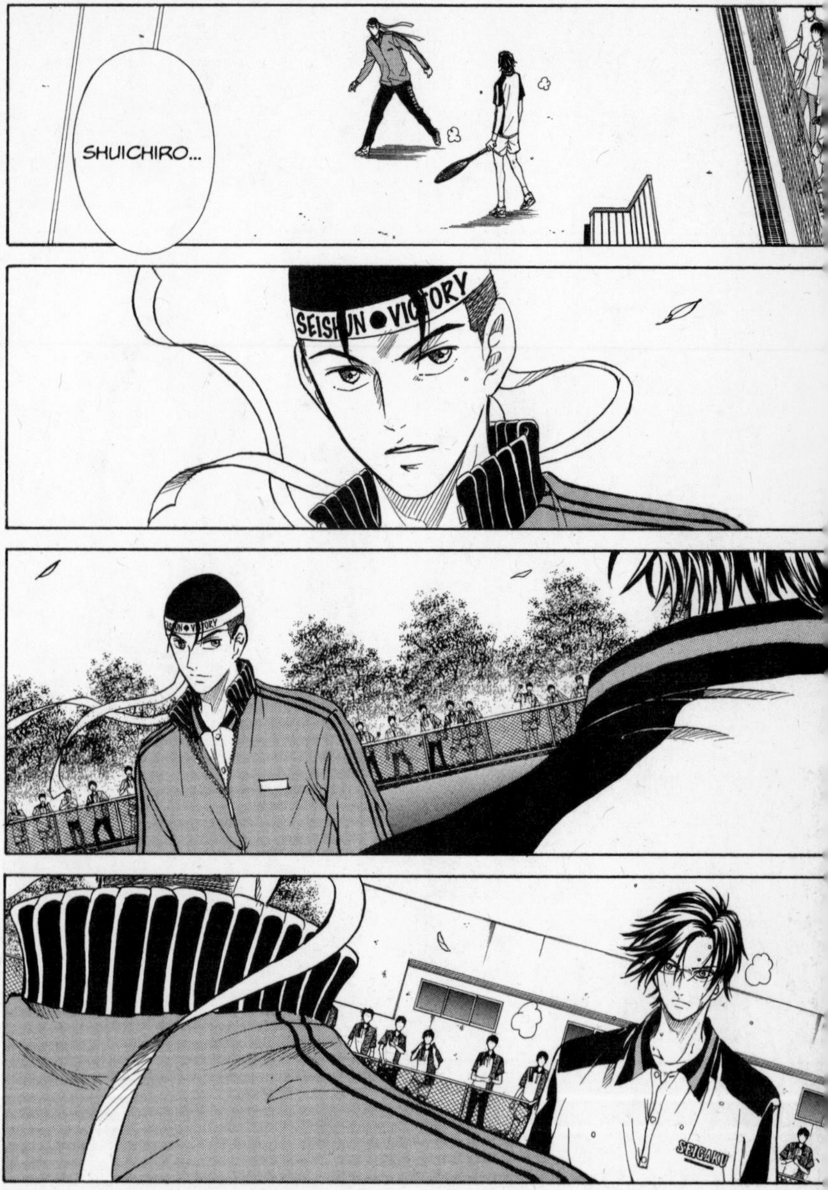
SHUICHIRO...
SEISHUN●VICTORY
SEIGAKU

READ THIS WAY

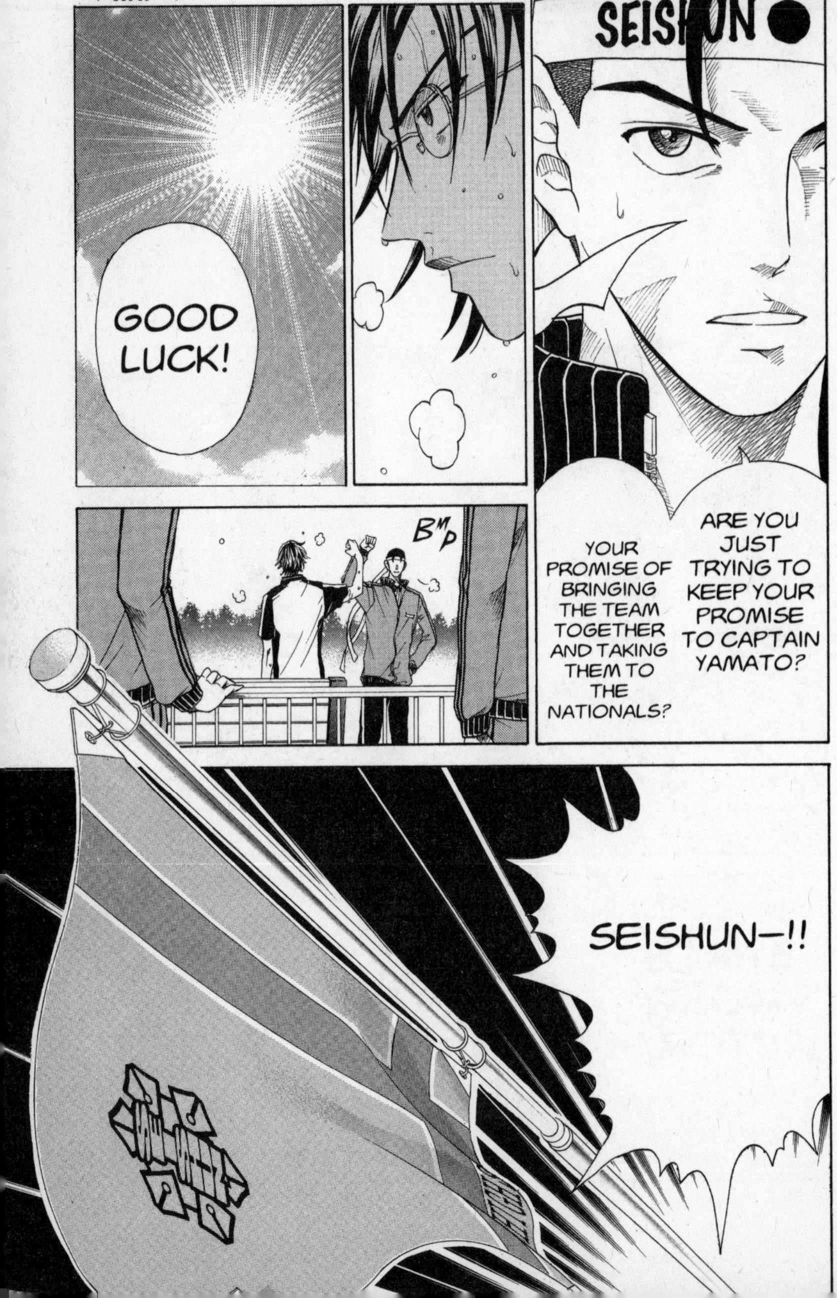
SEISHUN
ARE YOU JUST TRYING TO KEEP YOUR PROMISE TO CAPTAIN YAMATO?
YOUR PROMISE OF BRINGING THE TEAM TOGETHER AND TAKING THEM TO THE NATIONALS?
GOOD LUCK!
BMP
SEISHUN—!!

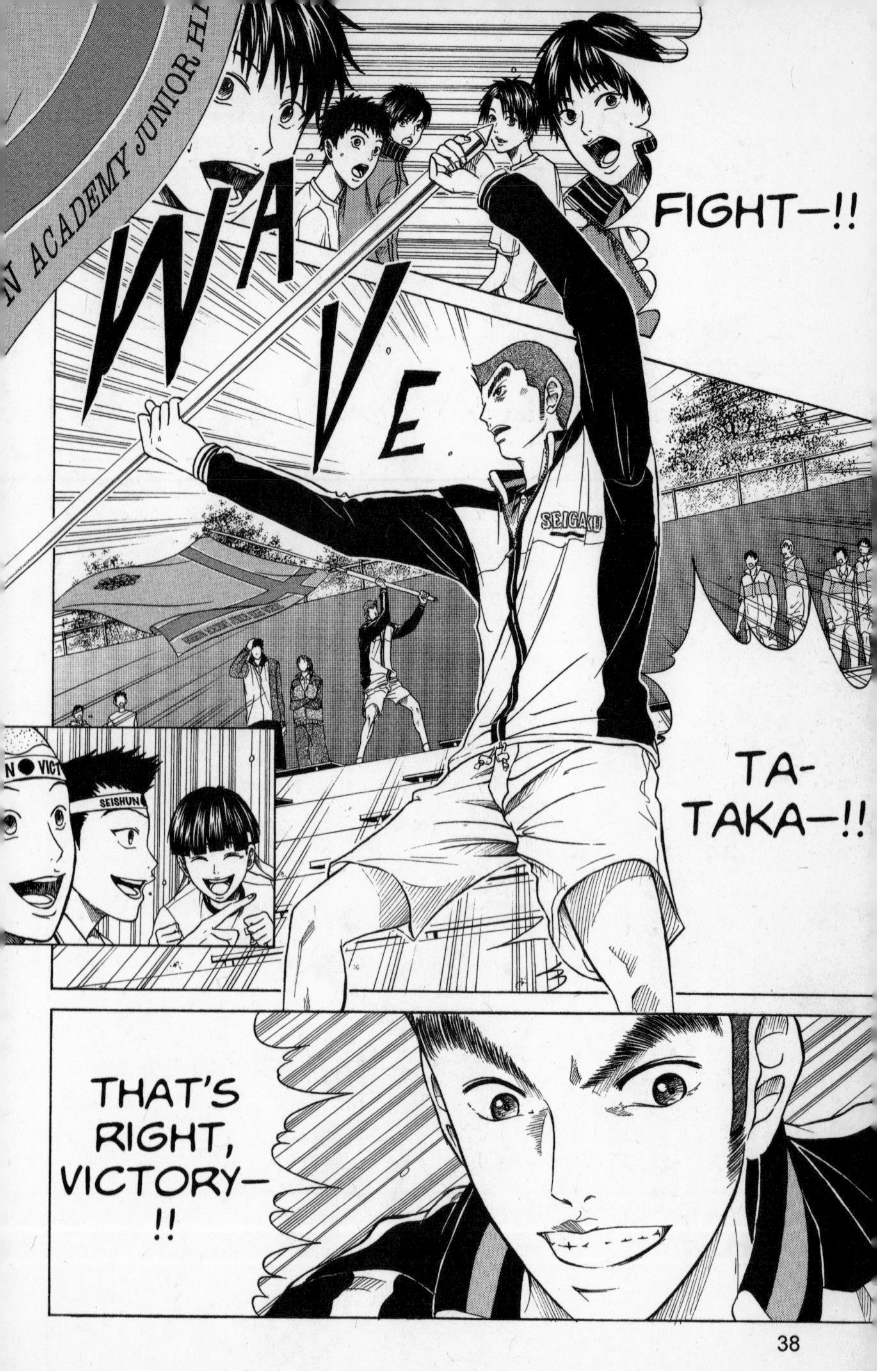
FIGHT—!!
WAVE
SEIGAKU
TA-
TAKA—!!
SEISHUN
THAT'S RIGHT, VICTORY—!!

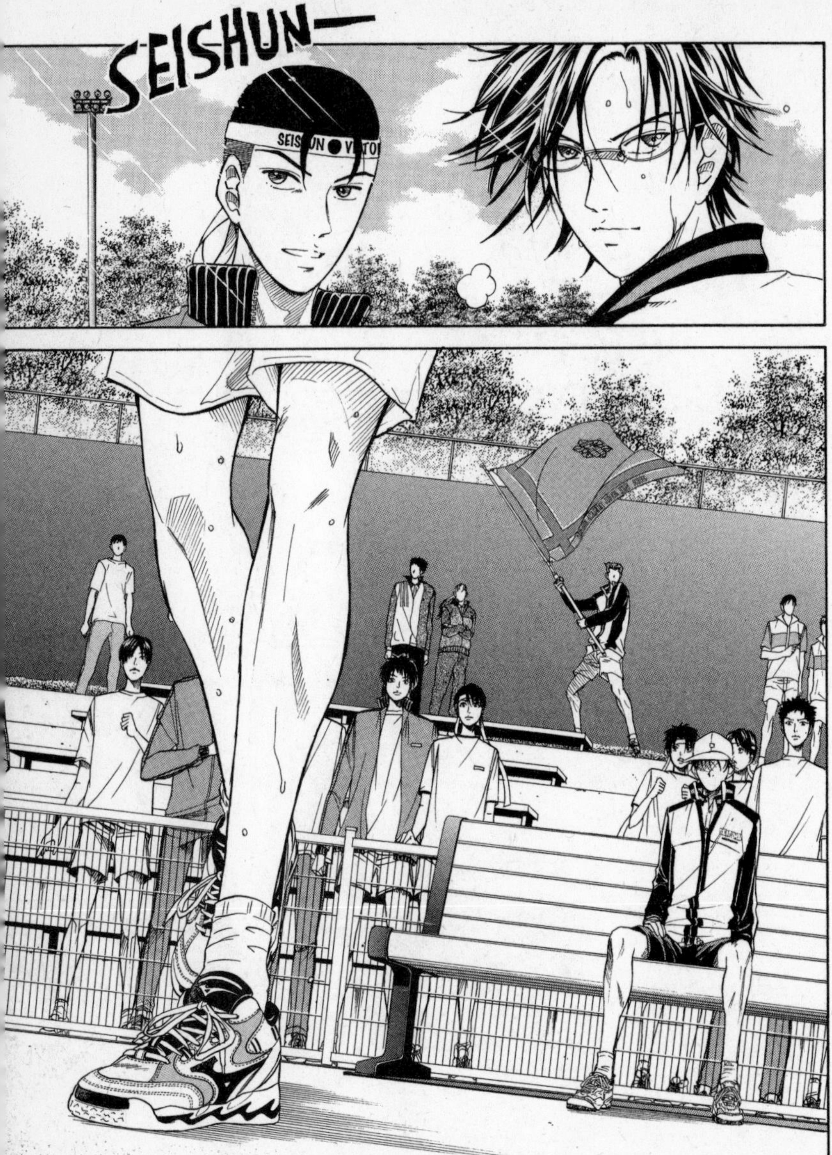
SEISHUN—

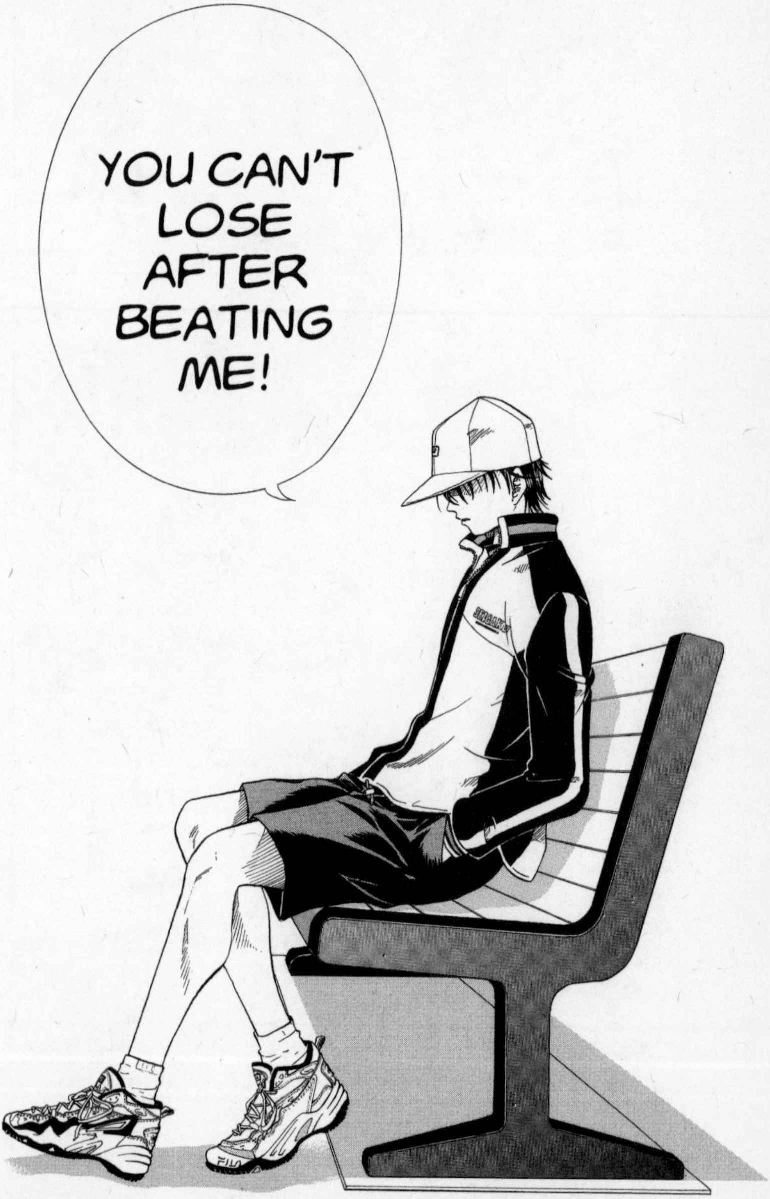
YOU CAN'T LOSE AFTER BEATING ME!

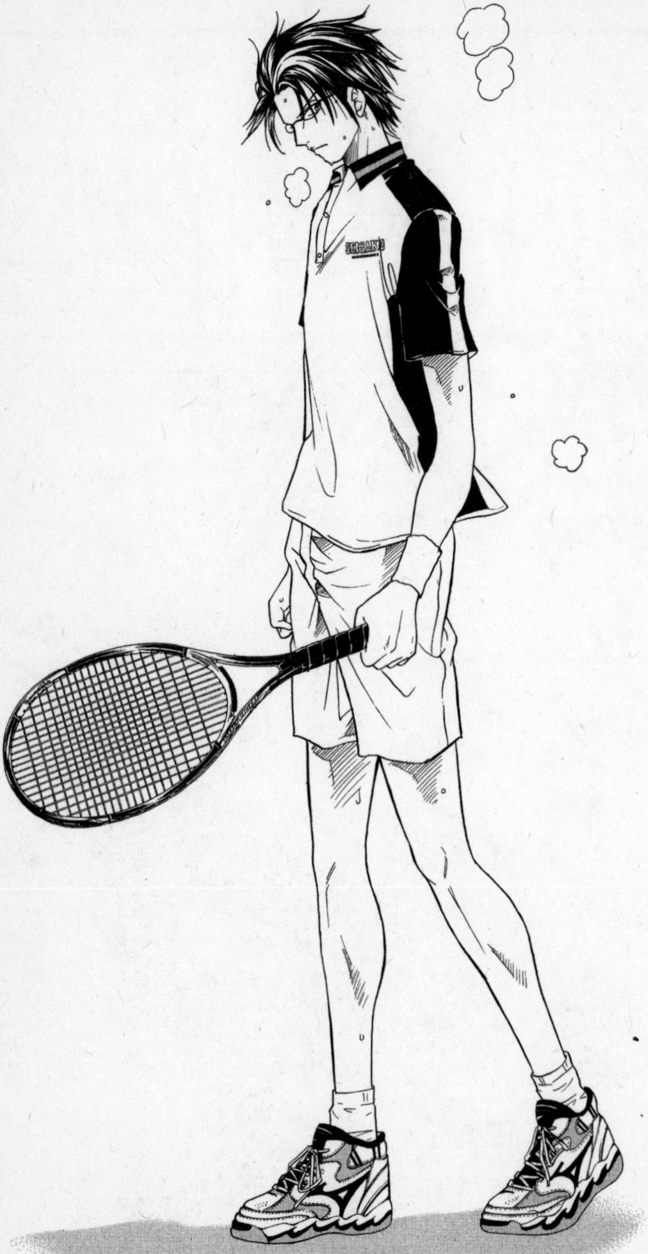
SEIGAKU

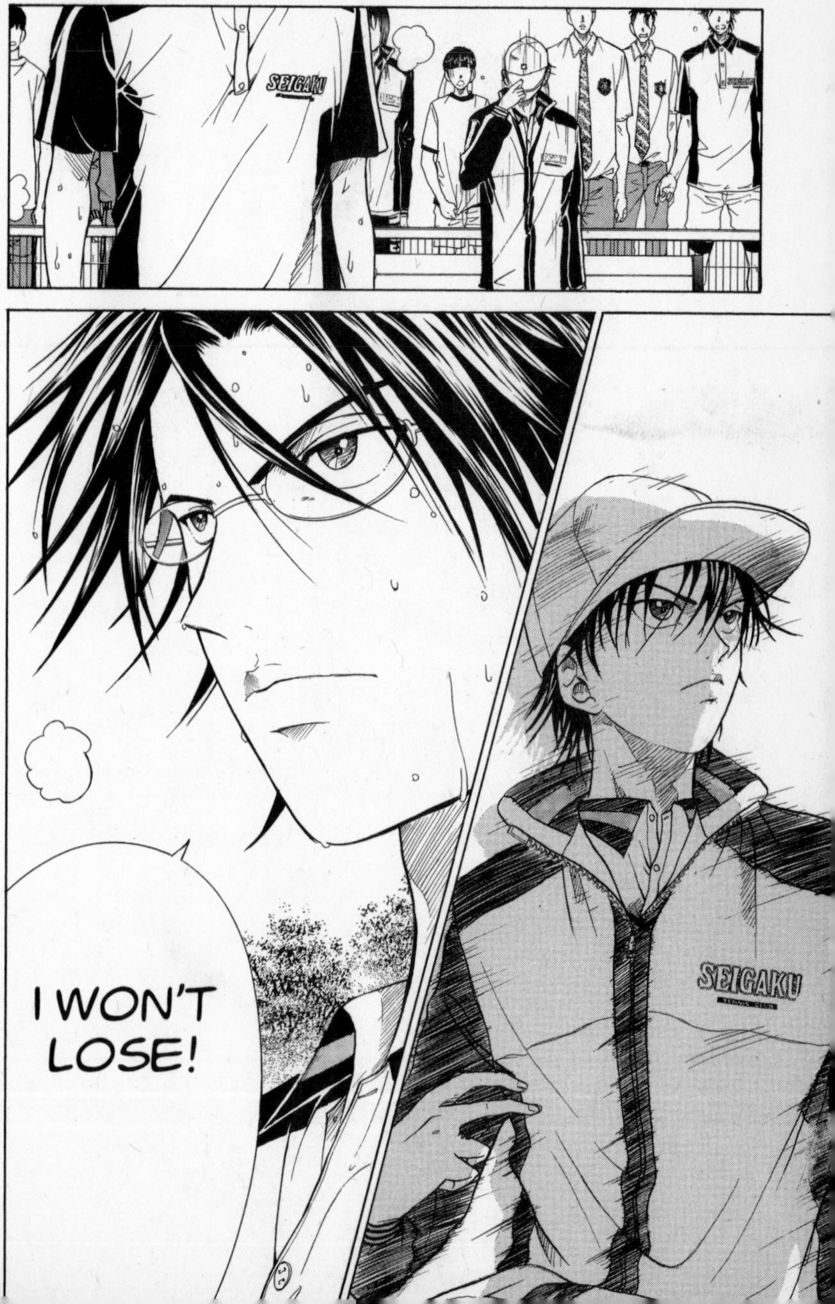

I WON'T LOSE!

READ THIS WAY

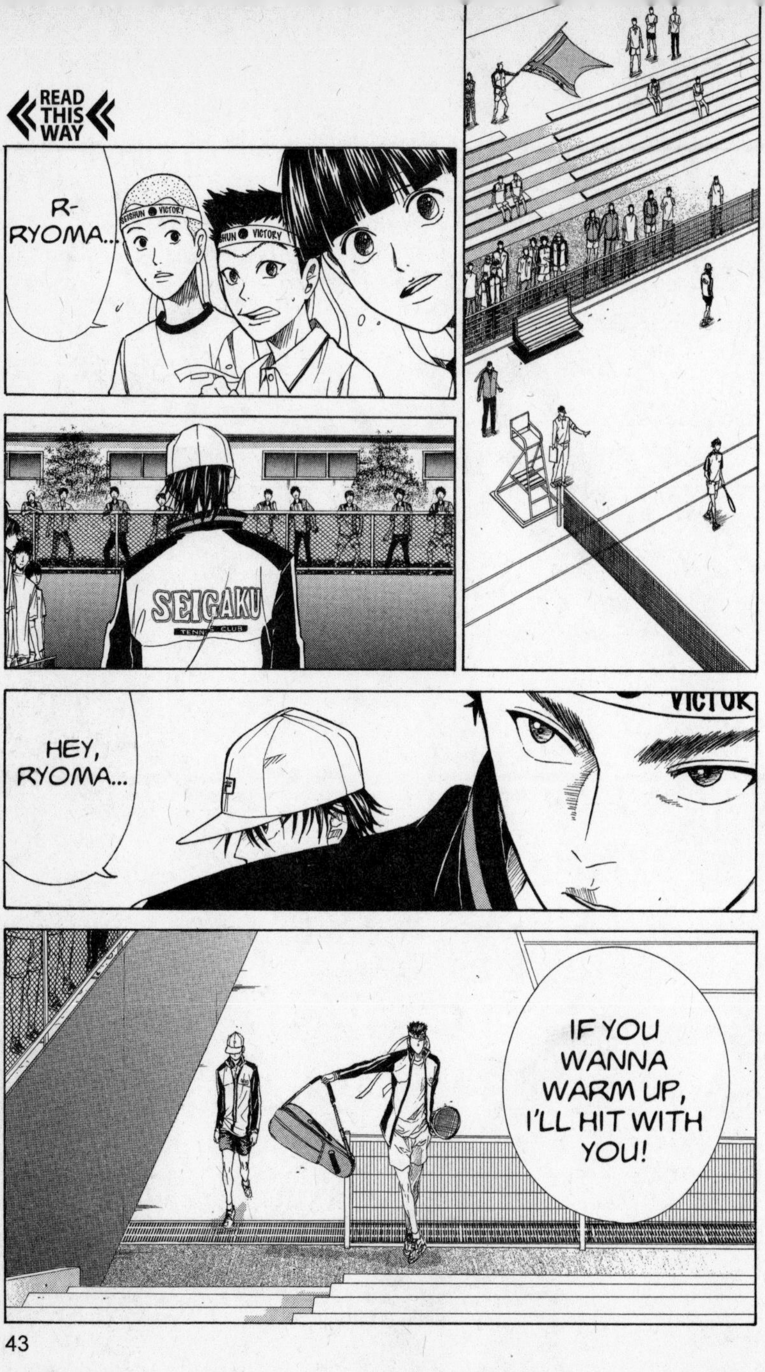
R-RYOMA...
SEIGAKU
HEY, RYOMA...
IF YOU WANNA WARM UP, I'LL HIT WITH YOU!

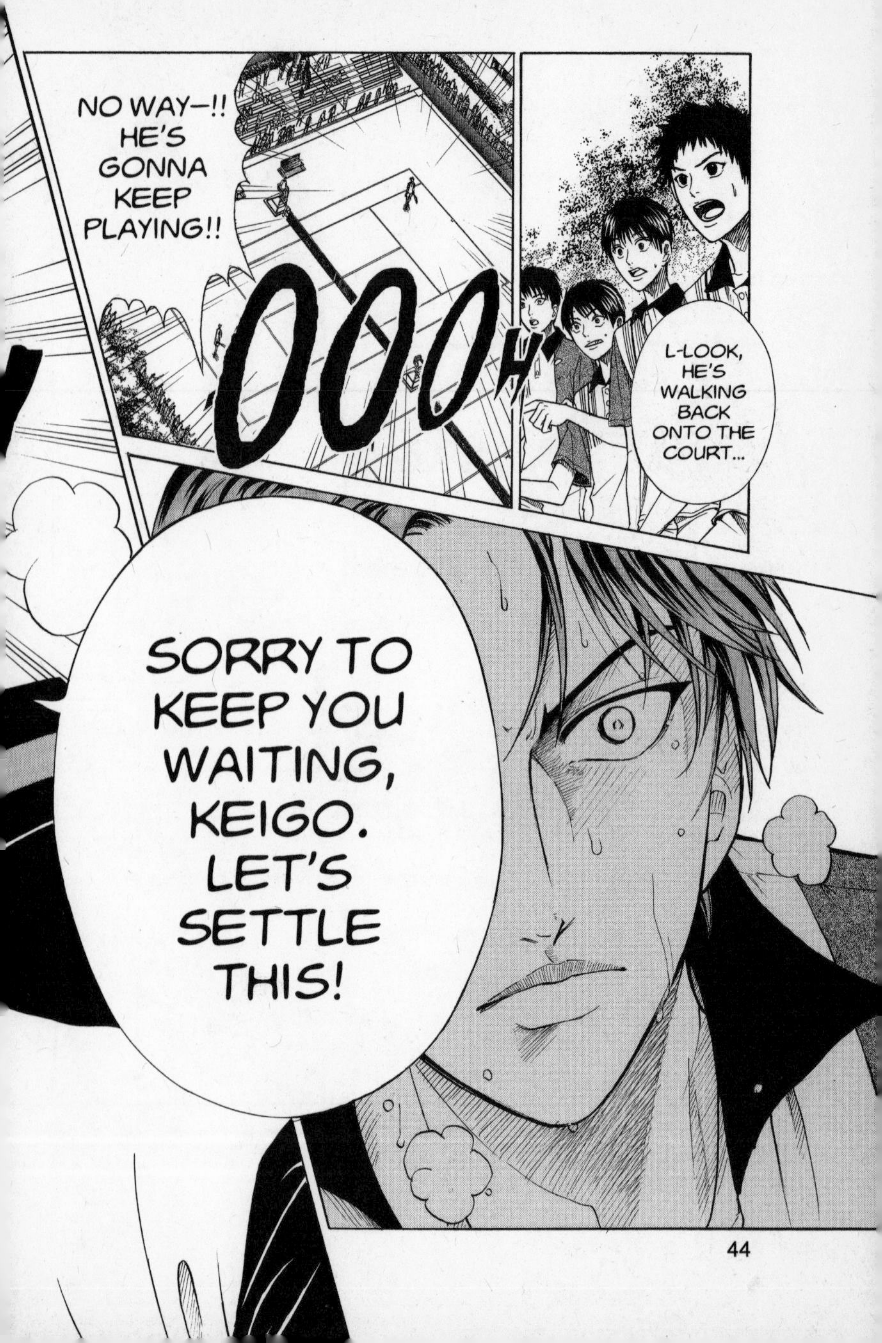

L-LOOK, HE'S WALKING BACK ONTO THE COURT...
NO WAY--!! HE'S GONNA KEEP PLAYING!!
OOOOH
SORRY TO KEEP YOU WAITING, KEIGO. LET'S SETTLE THIS!

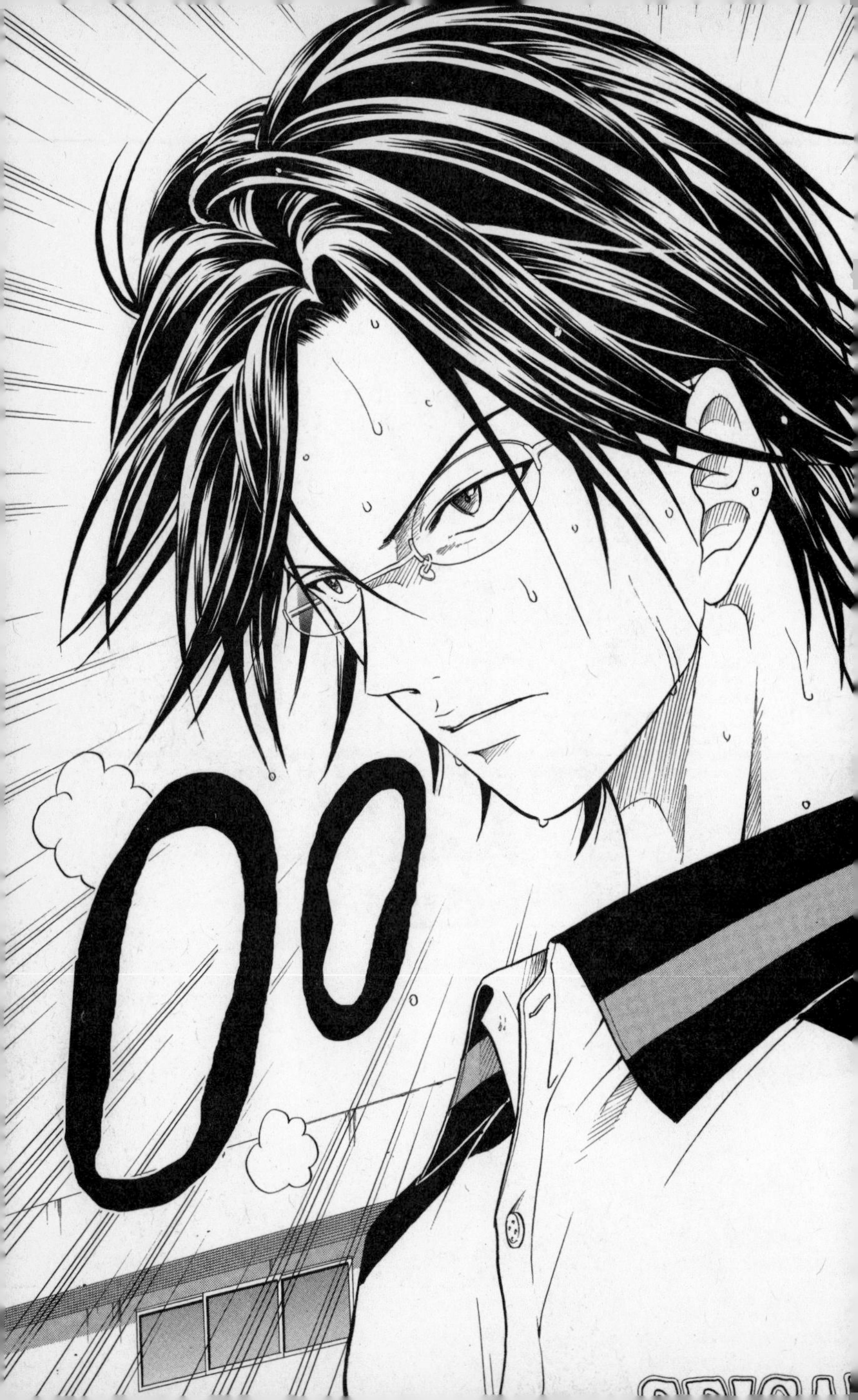

テニスの王子様

THE PRINCE OF TENNIS™

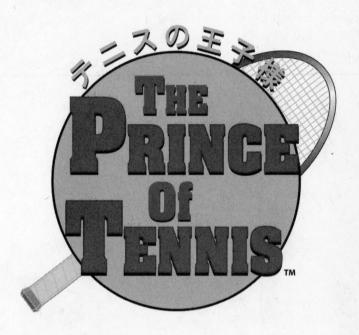

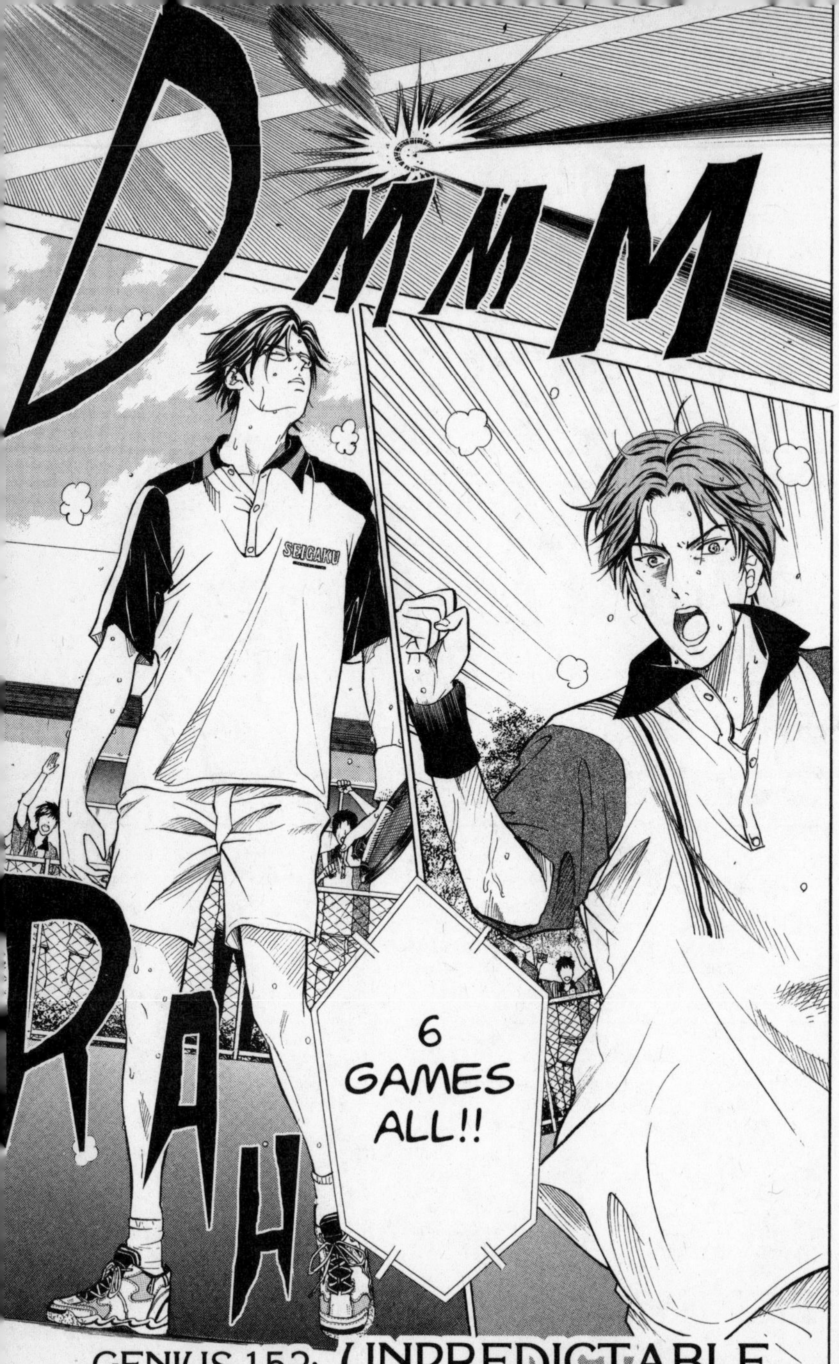
DMMM
6 GAMES ALL!!
RAH

GENIUS 152: UNPREDICTABLE

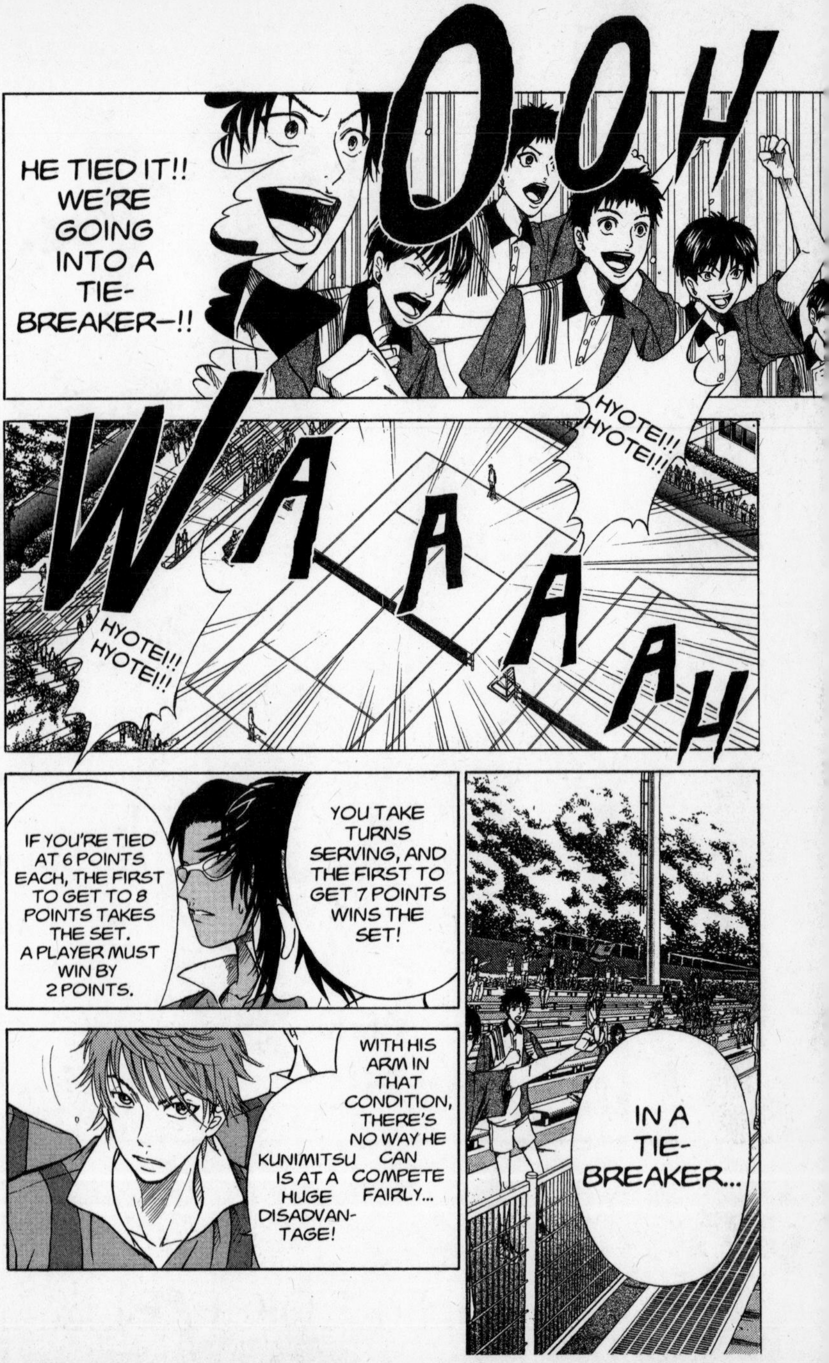
O-OH
HE TIED IT!! WE'RE GOING INTO A TIE-BREAKER—!!
HYOTE!!! HYOTE!!!
WAAAAH
HYOTE!!! HYOTE!!!
IN A TIE-BREAKER...
YOU TAKE TURNS SERVING, AND THE FIRST TO GET 7 POINTS WINS THE SET!
IF YOU'RE TIED AT 6 POINTS EACH, THE FIRST TO GET TO 8 POINTS TAKES THE SET. A PLAYER MUST WIN BY 2 POINTS.
WITH HIS ARM IN THAT CONDITION, THERE'S NO WAY HE CAN COMPETE FAIRLY...
KUNIMITSU IS AT A HUGE DISADVANTAGE!

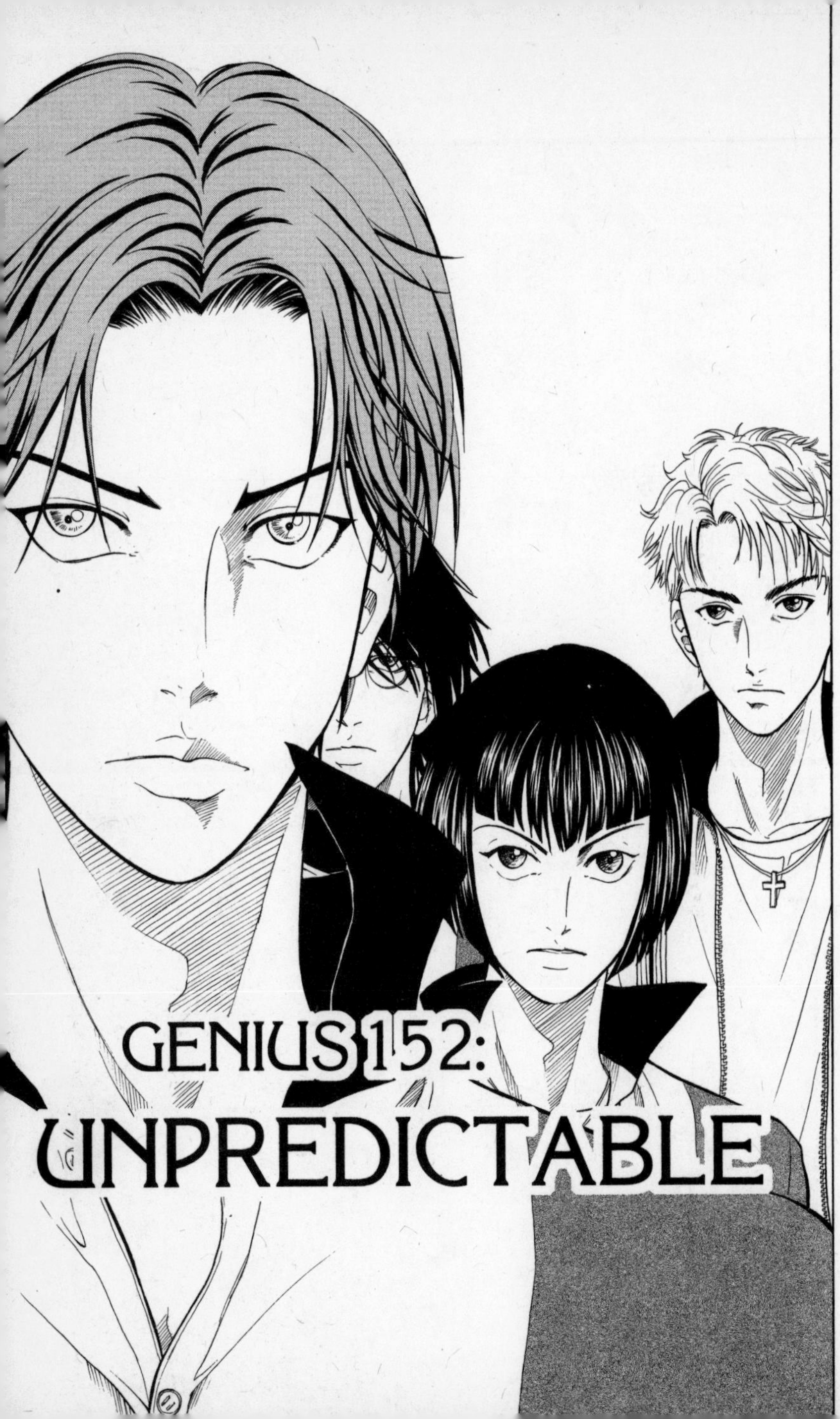
GENIUS 152:
UNPREDICTABLE

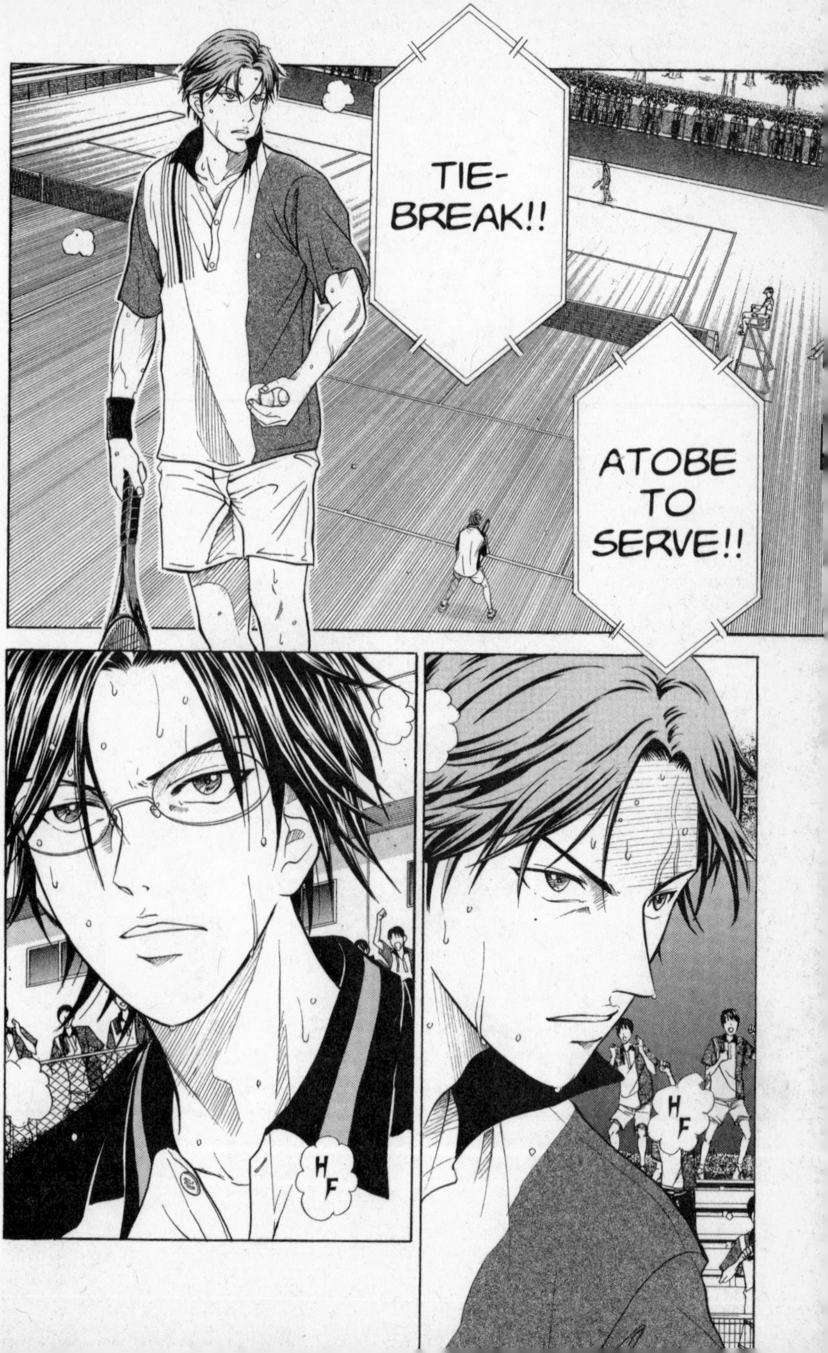
TIE-BREAK!!
ATOBE TO SERVE!!
HF
HF

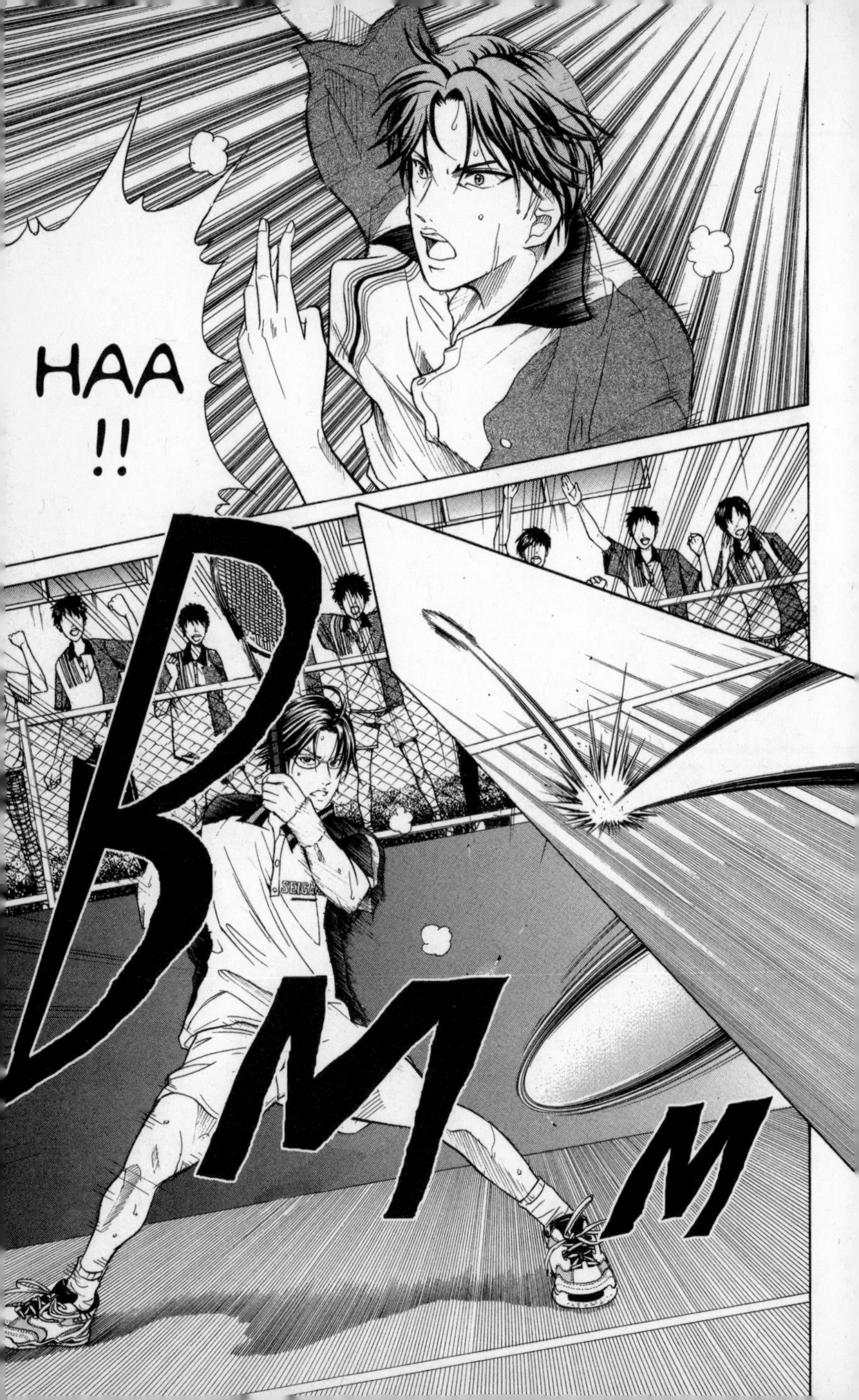
HAA
!!
BMM

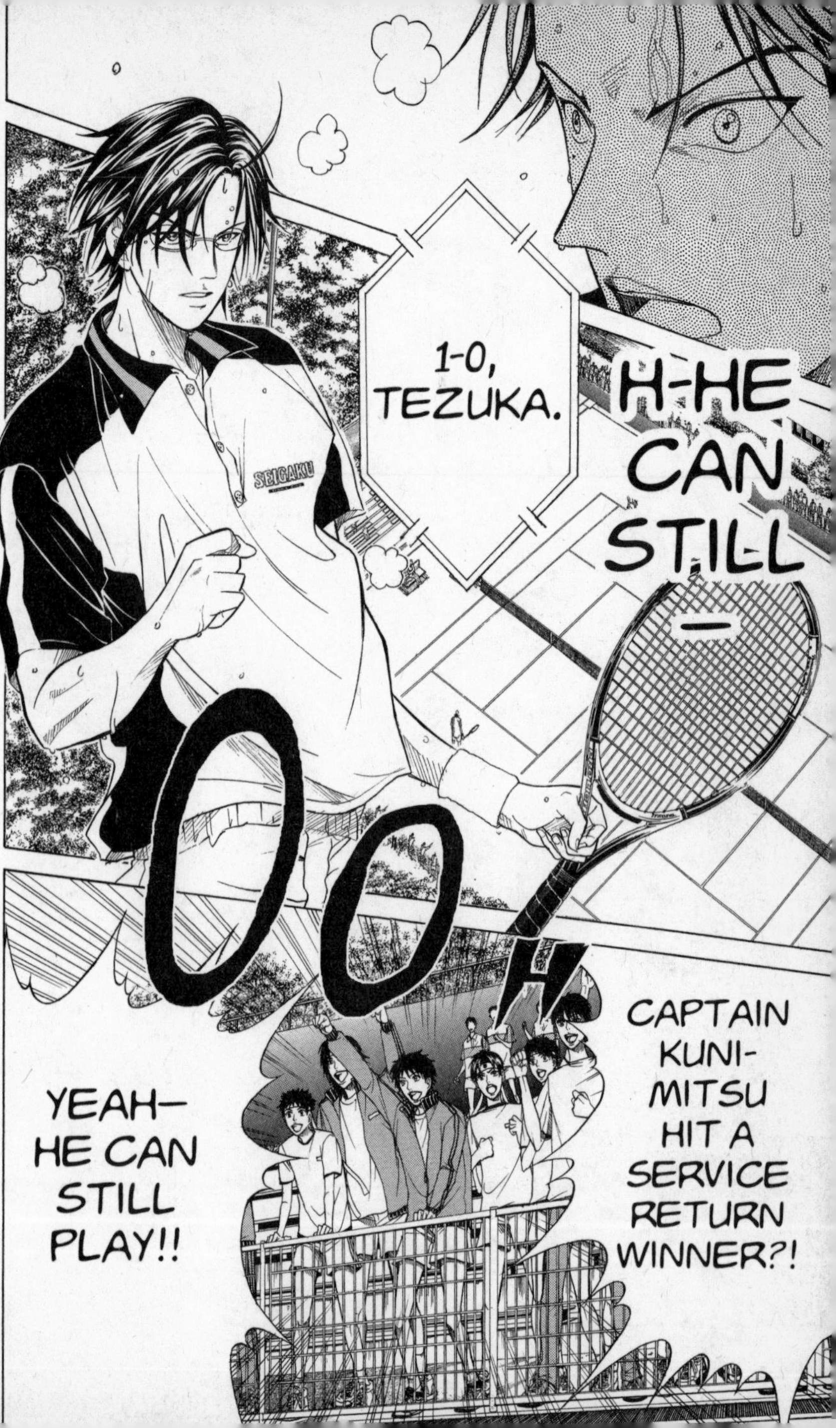
1-0, TEZUKA.
H-HE CAN STILL—
SEIGAKU
OOOH
CAPTAIN KUNIMITSU HIT A SERVICE RETURN WINNER?!
YEAH—HE CAN STILL PLAY!!

READ THIS WAY

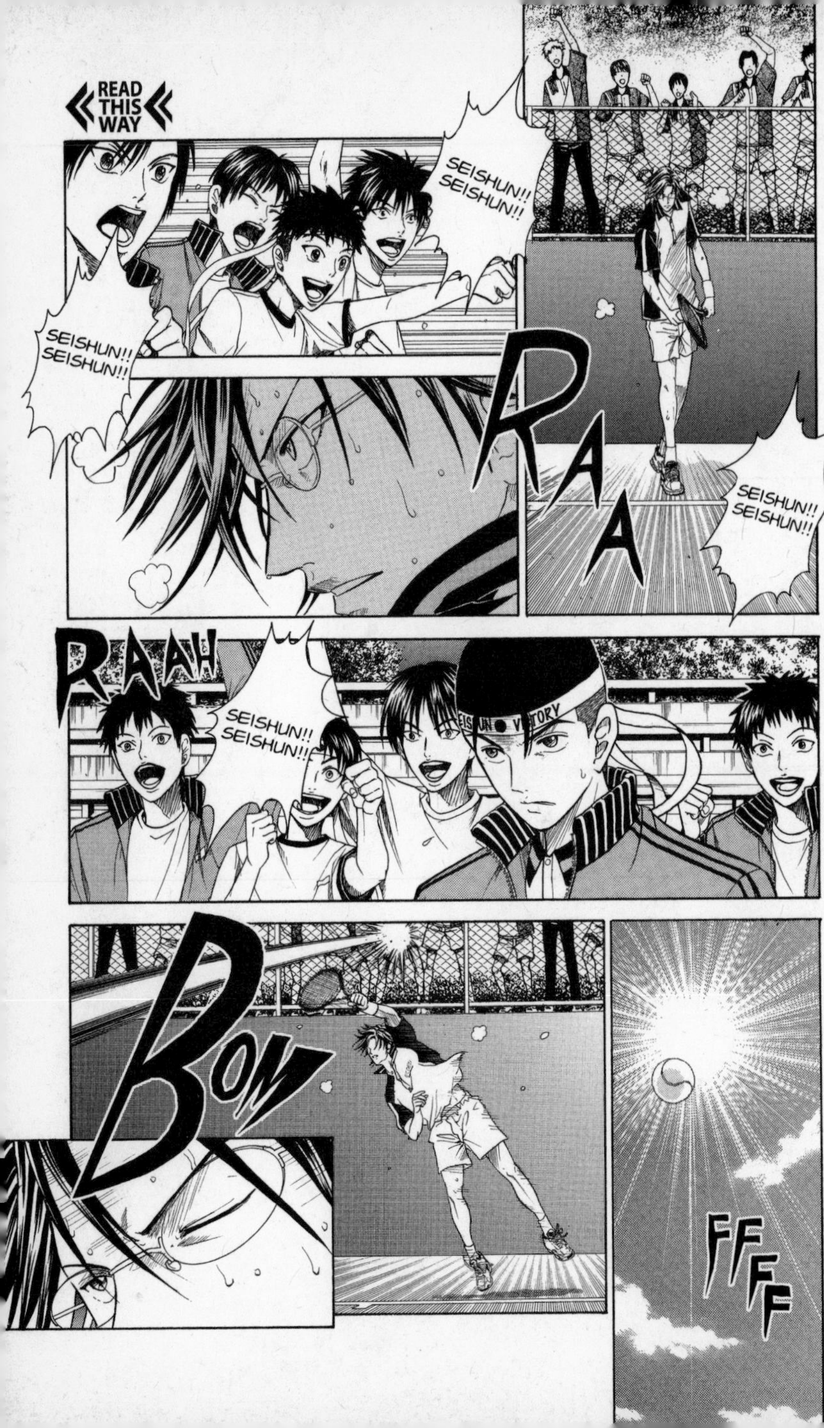
SEISHUN!! SEISHUN!!
RAA
SEISHUN!! SEISHUN!!
SEISHUN!! SEISHUN!!
RAAH
SEISHUN!! SEISHUN!!
SEISHUN VICTORY
FFFF
BOOM

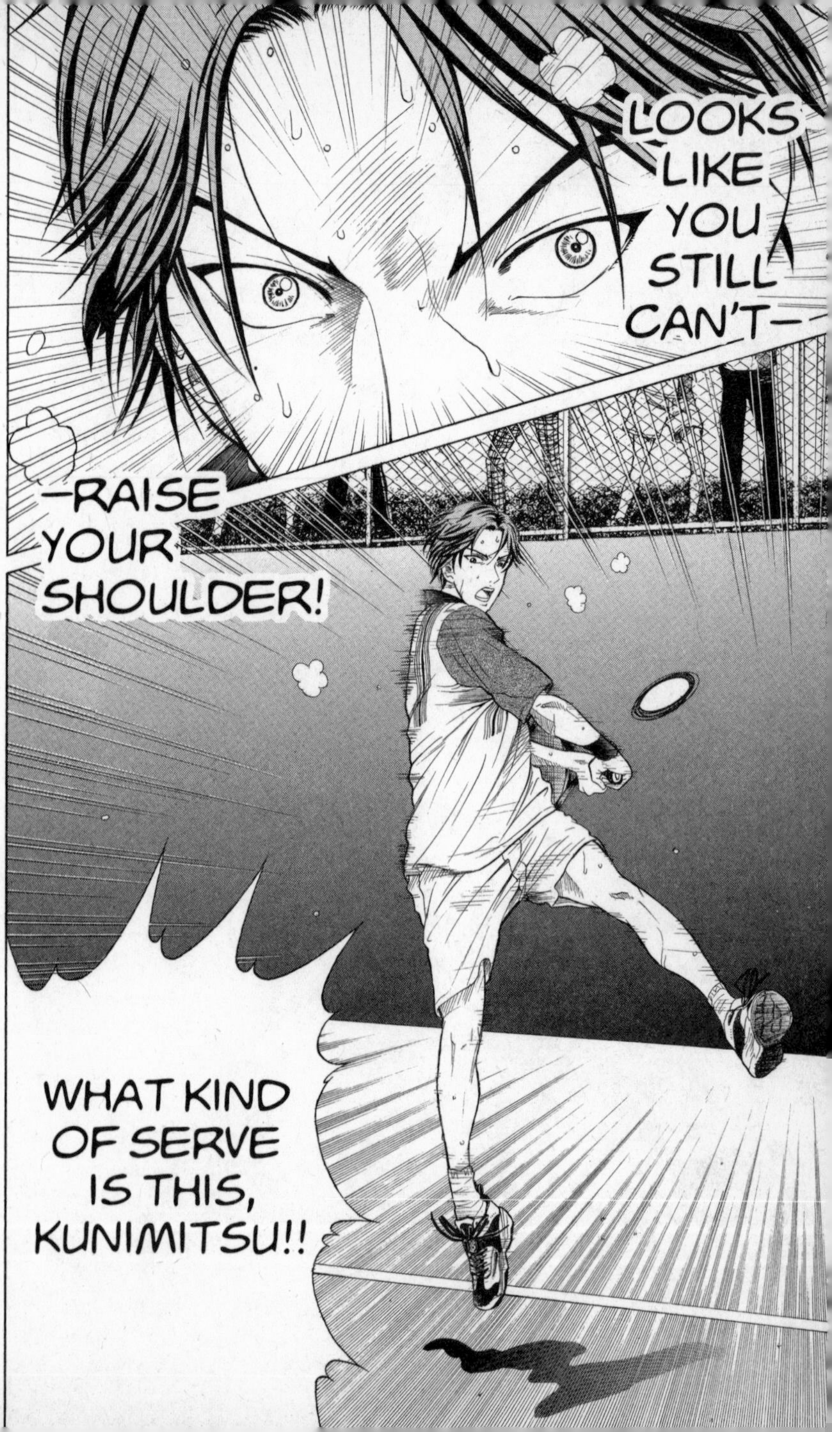
LOOKS LIKE YOU STILL CAN'T—
—RAISE YOUR SHOULDER!
WHAT KIND OF SERVE IS THIS, KUNIMITSU!!

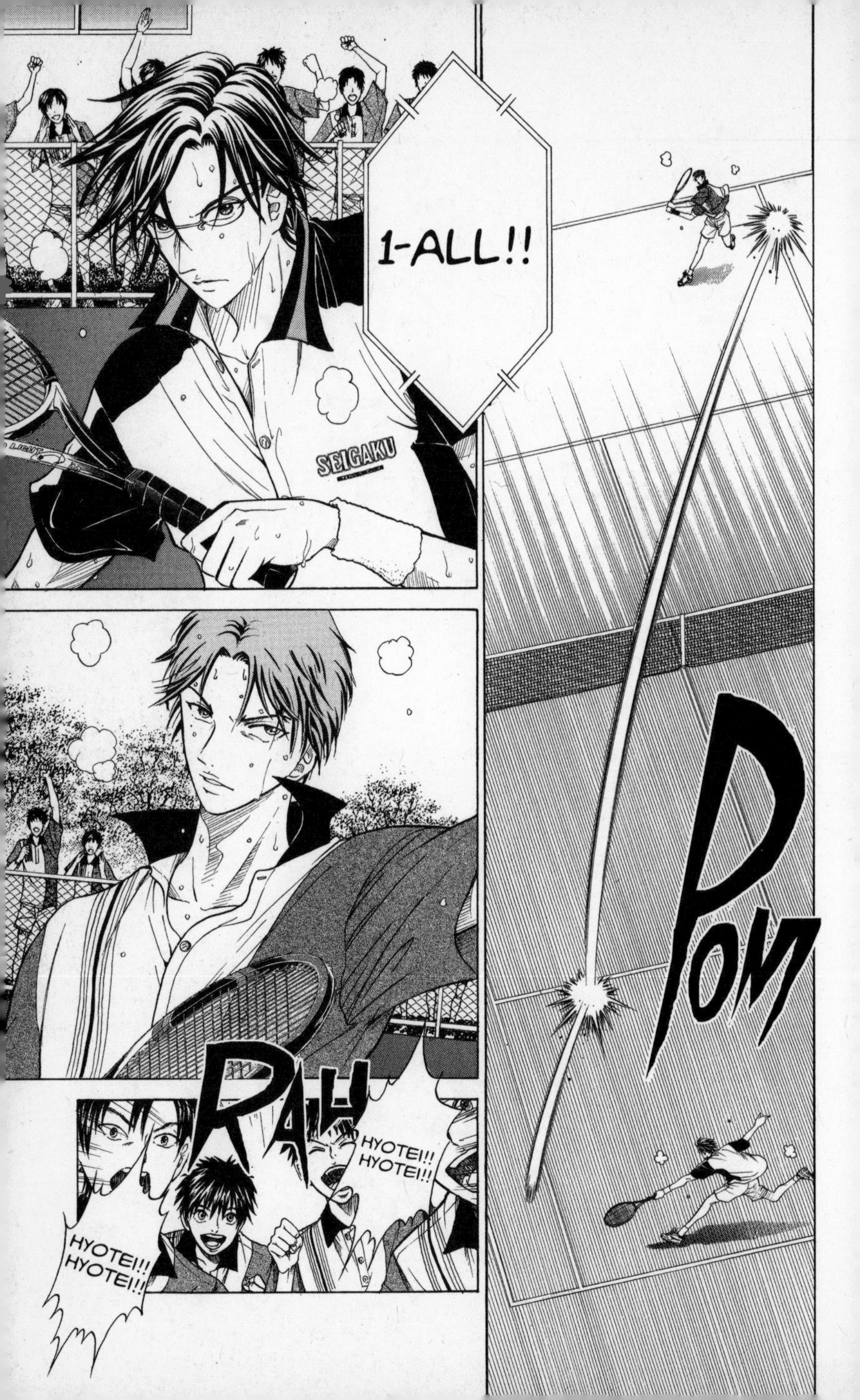
POM
1-ALL!!
RAH
HYOTEI!! HYOTEI!!
HYOTEI!! HYOTEI!!

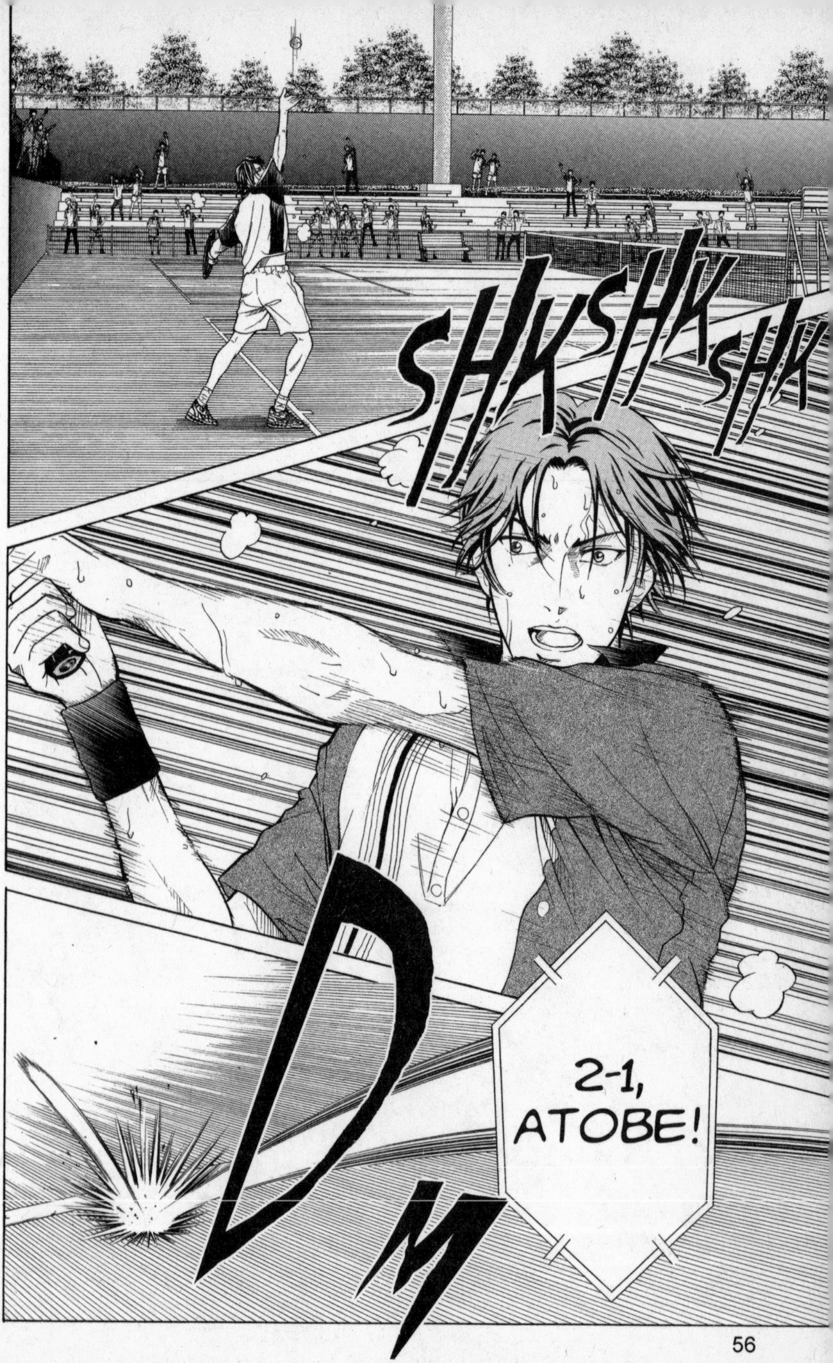
SHKSHKSHK
DM
2-1, ATOBE!

READ THIS WAY

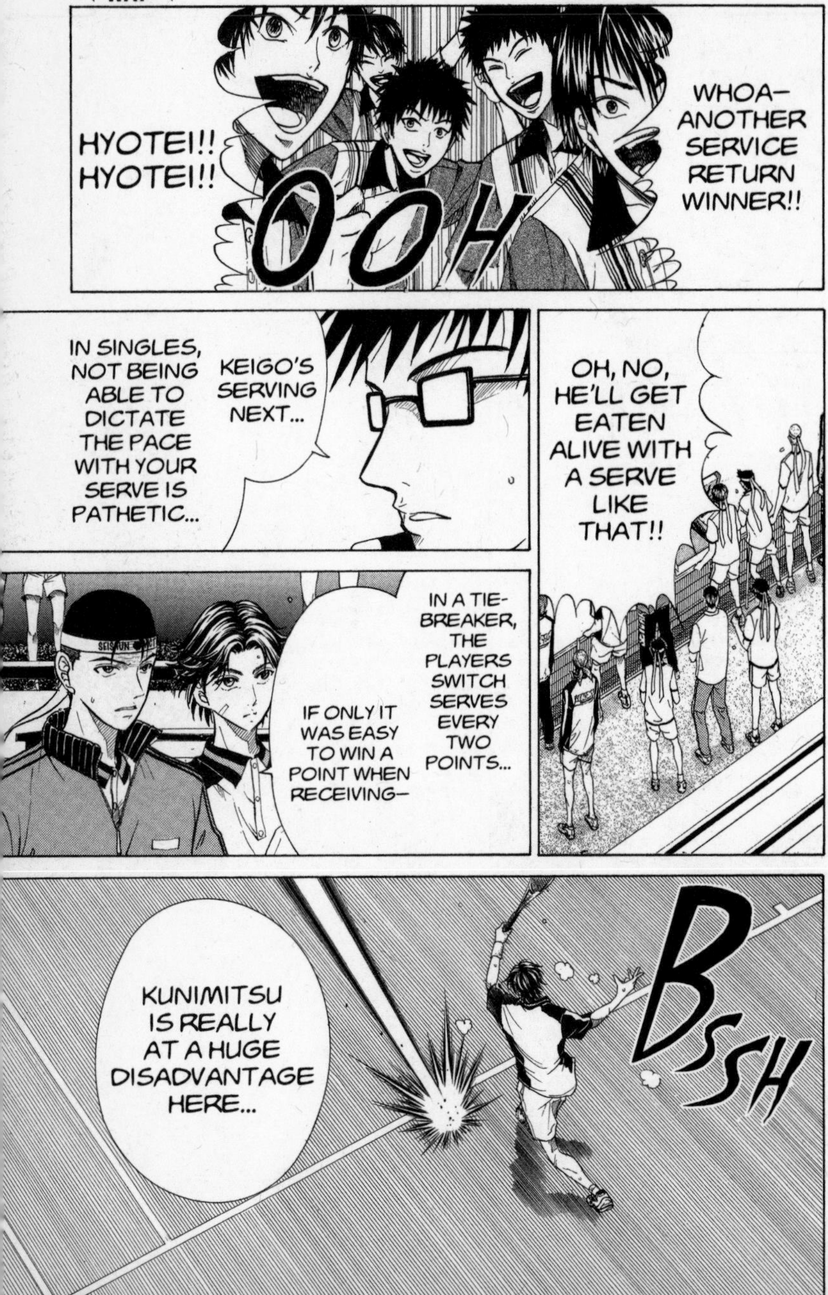
WHOA- ANOTHER SERVICE RETURN WINNER!!
OOH
HYOTEI!! HYOTEI!!
OH, NO, HE'LL GET EATEN ALIVE WITH A SERVE LIKE THAT!!
KEIGO'S SERVING NEXT...
IN SINGLES, NOT BEING ABLE TO DICTATE THE PACE WITH YOUR SERVE IS PATHETIC...
IN A TIE-BREAKER, THE PLAYERS SWITCH SERVES EVERY TWO POINTS...
IF ONLY IT WAS EASY TO WIN A POINT WHEN RECEIVING-
BSSH
KUNIMITSU IS REALLY AT A HUGE DISADVANTAGE HERE...

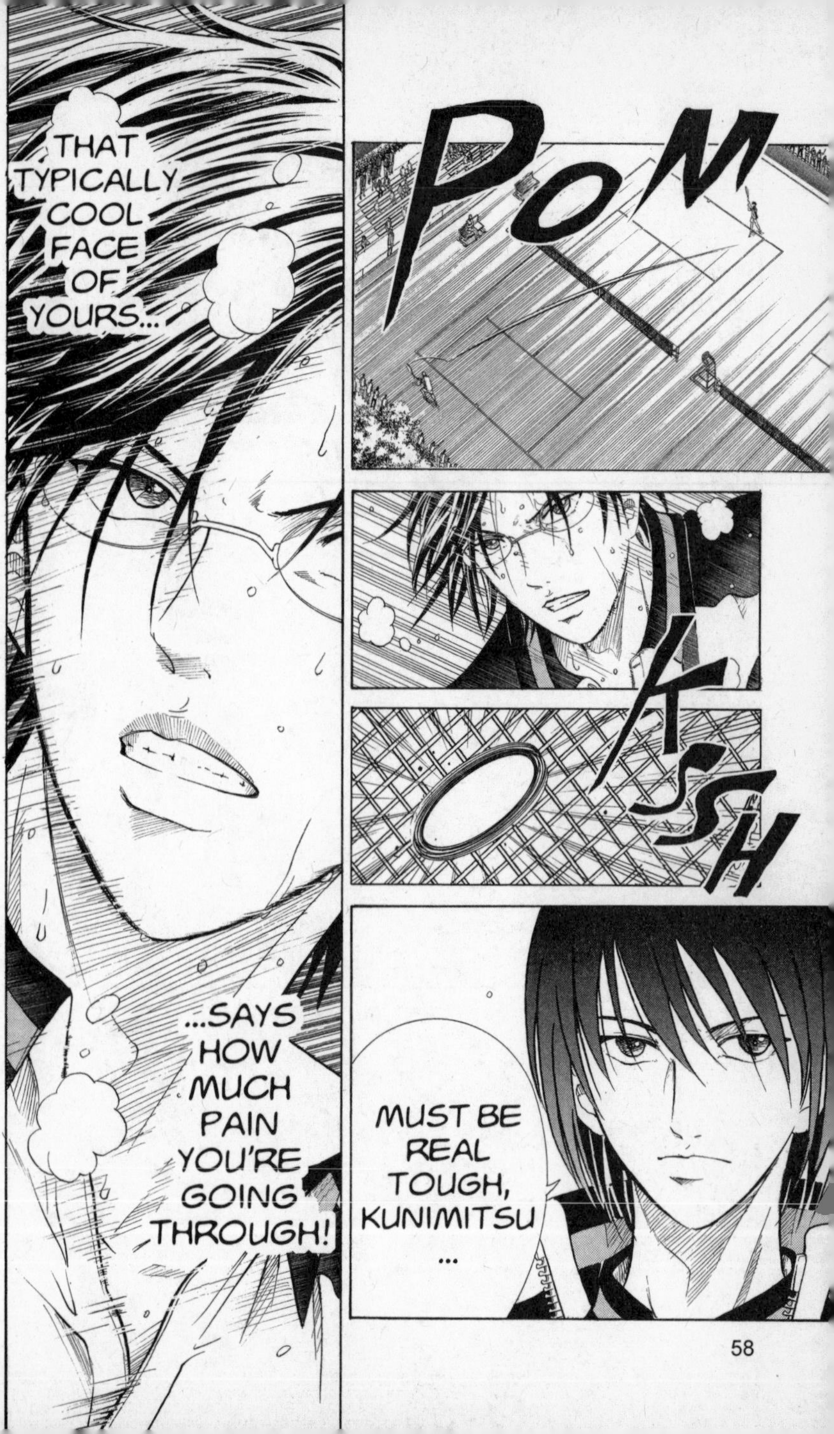
POM
KSH
MUST BE REAL TOUGH, KUNIMITSU ...
THAT TYPICALLY COOL FACE OF YOURS...
...SAYS HOW MUCH PAIN YOU'RE GOING THROUGH!

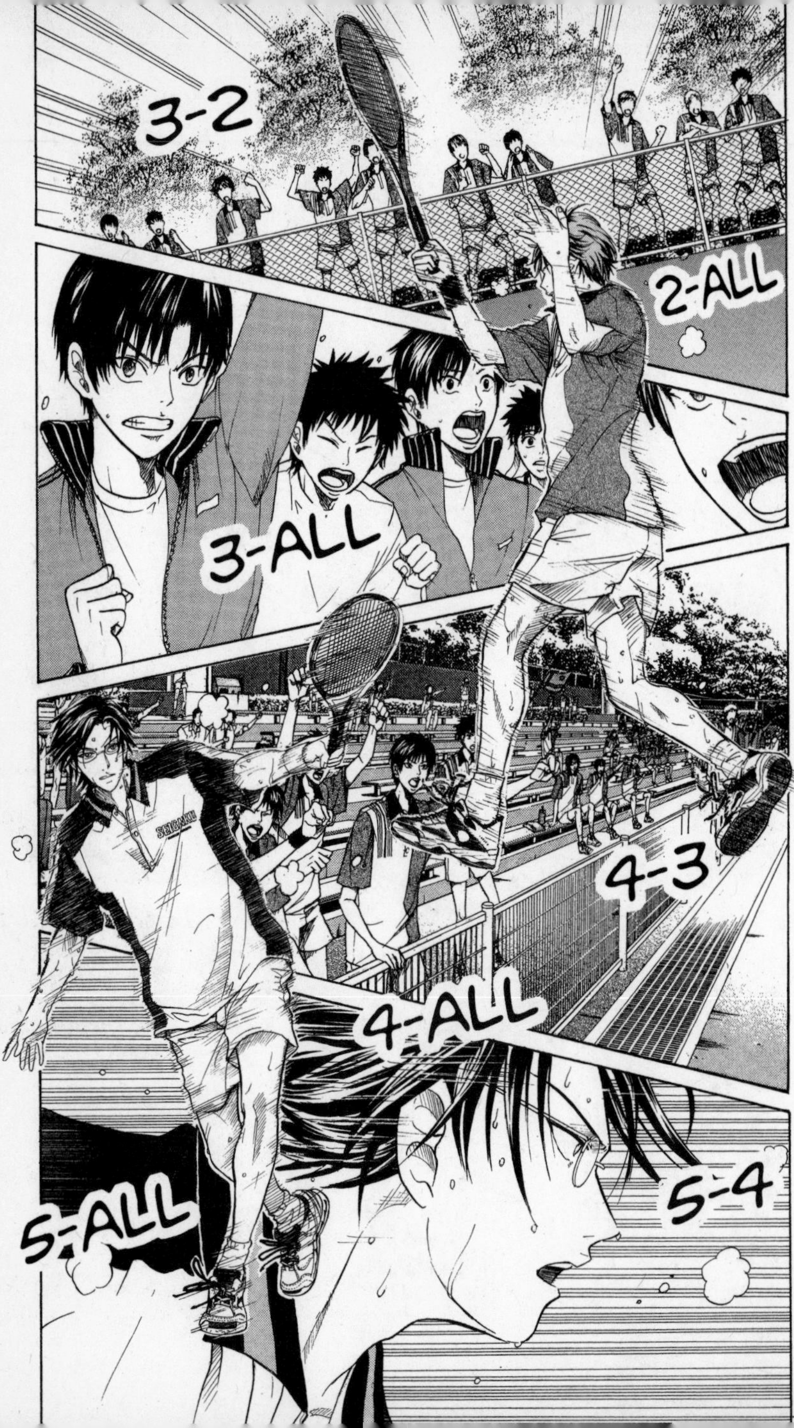
3-2
2-ALL
3-ALL
4-3
SEIGAKU
4-ALL
5-4
5-ALL

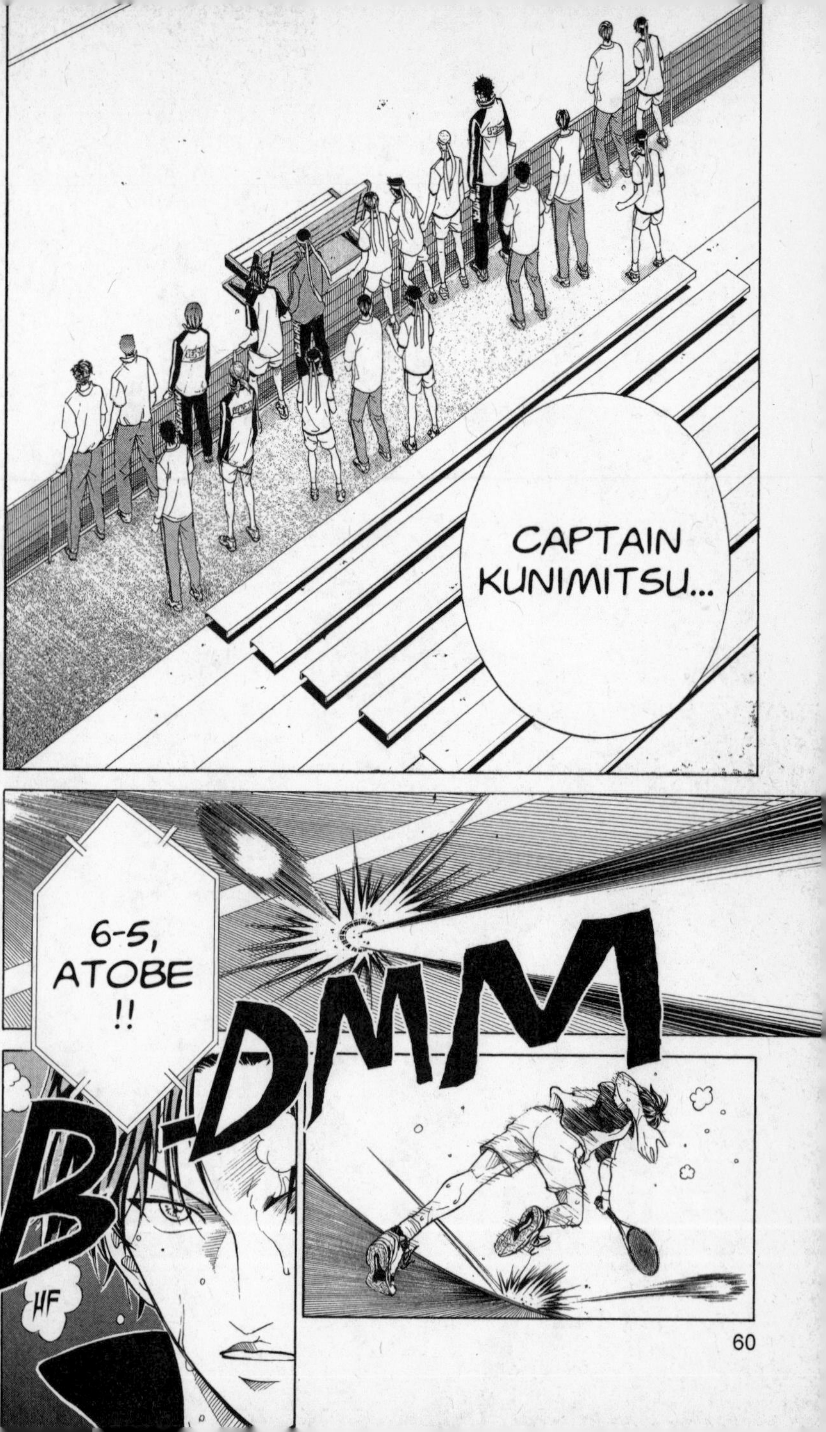
CAPTAIN KUNIMITSU...
6-5, ATOBE !!
B-DMM
HF

READ THIS WAY

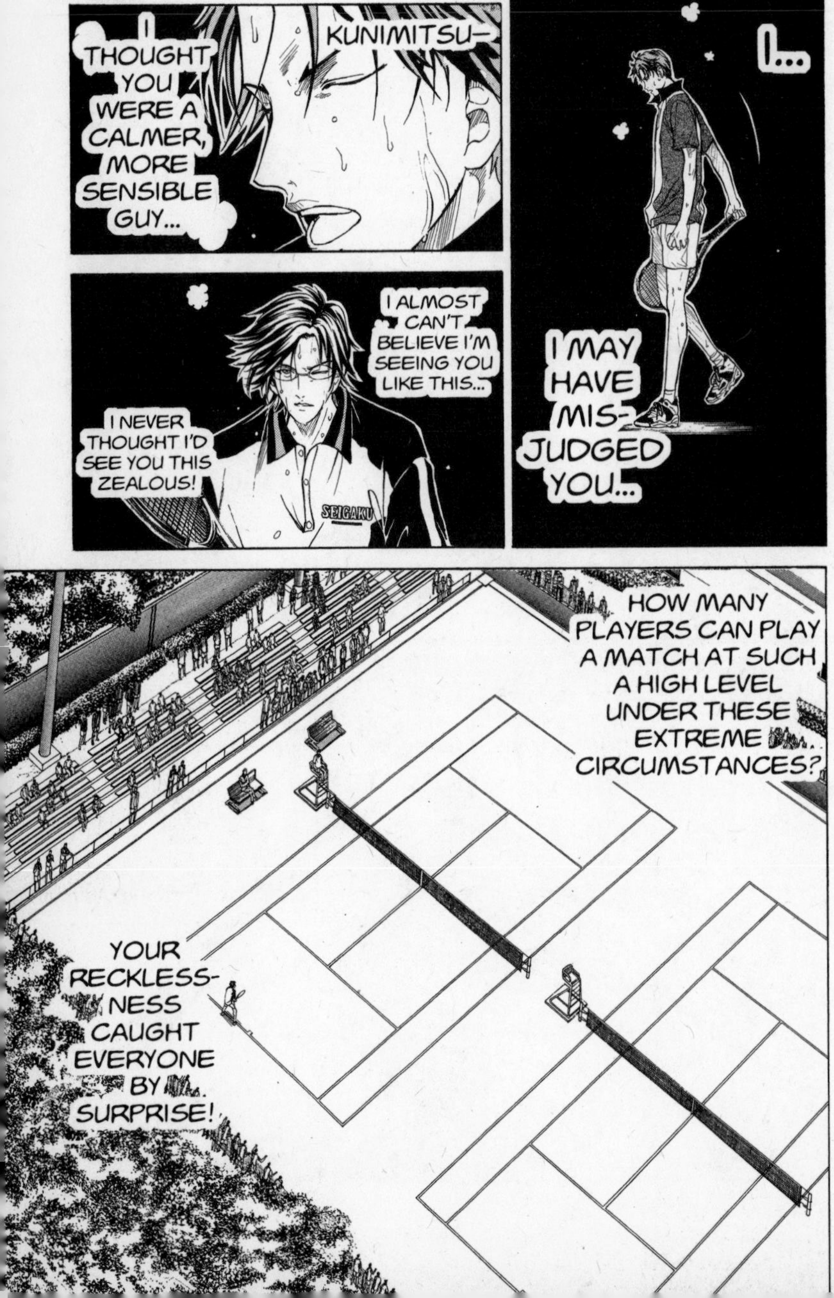
I...
I MAY HAVE MIS-JUDGED YOU...
KUNIMITSU–
I THOUGHT YOU WERE A CALMER, MORE SENSIBLE GUY...
I ALMOST CAN'T BELIEVE I'M SEEING YOU LIKE THIS...
I NEVER THOUGHT I'D SEE YOU THIS ZEALOUS!
SEIGAKU
HOW MANY PLAYERS CAN PLAY A MATCH AT SUCH A HIGH LEVEL UNDER THESE EXTREME CIRCUMSTANCES?
YOUR RECKLESS-NESS CAUGHT EVERYONE BY SURPRISE!

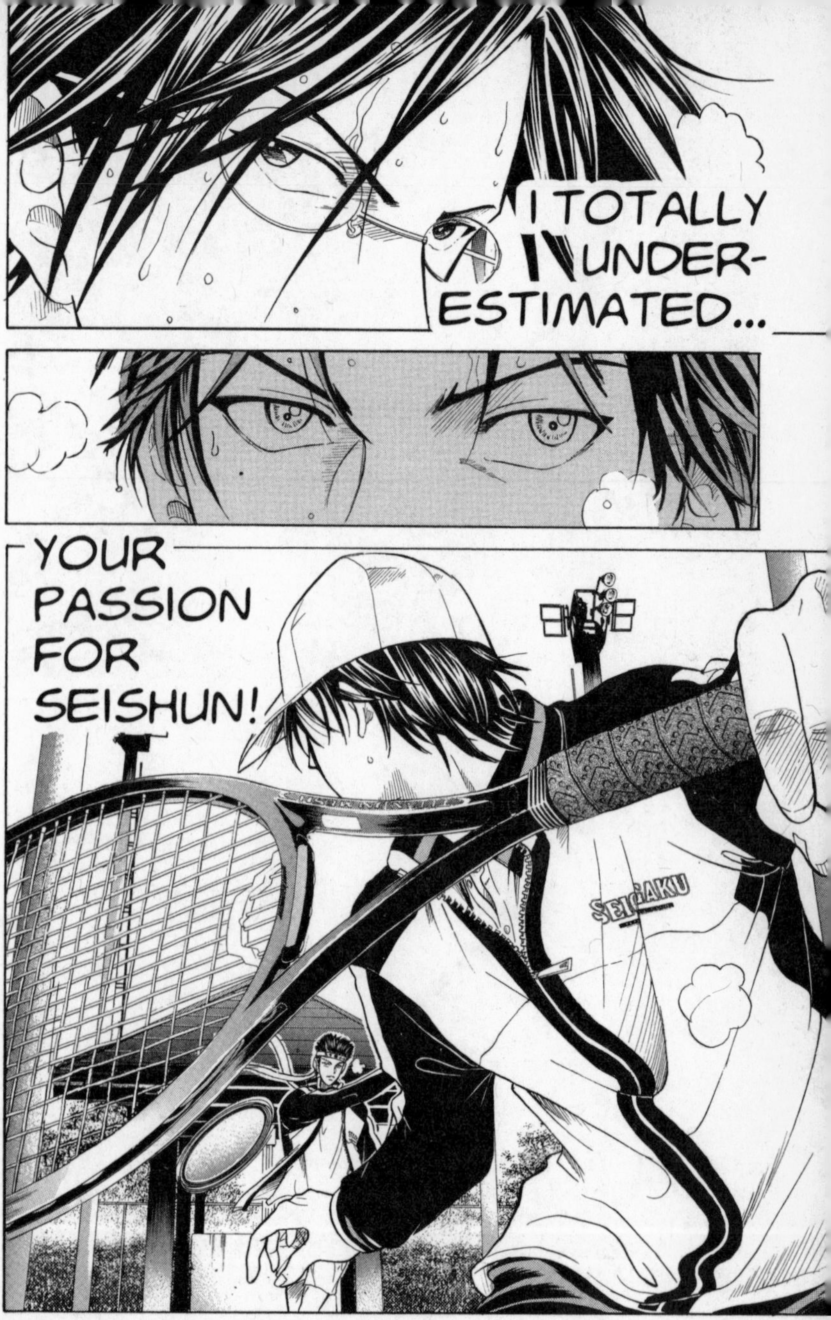
I TOTALLY UNDER-ESTIMATED...
YOUR PASSION FOR SEISHUN!
SEIGAKU

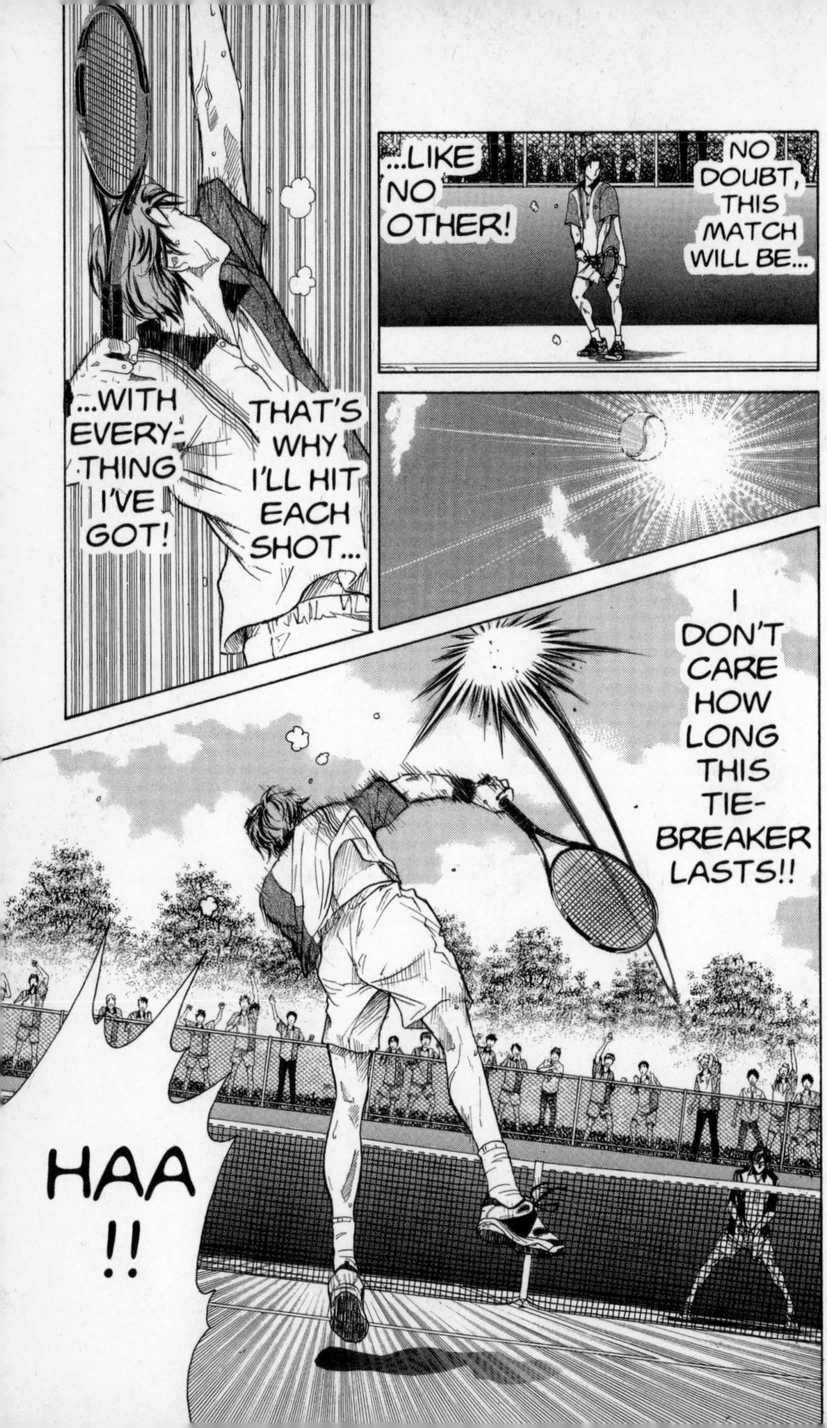

NO DOUBT, THIS MATCH WILL BE...
...LIKE NO OTHER!
THAT'S WHY I'LL HIT EACH SHOT...
...WITH EVERYTHING I'VE GOT!
I DON'T CARE HOW LONG THIS TIE-BREAKER LASTS!!
HAA !!

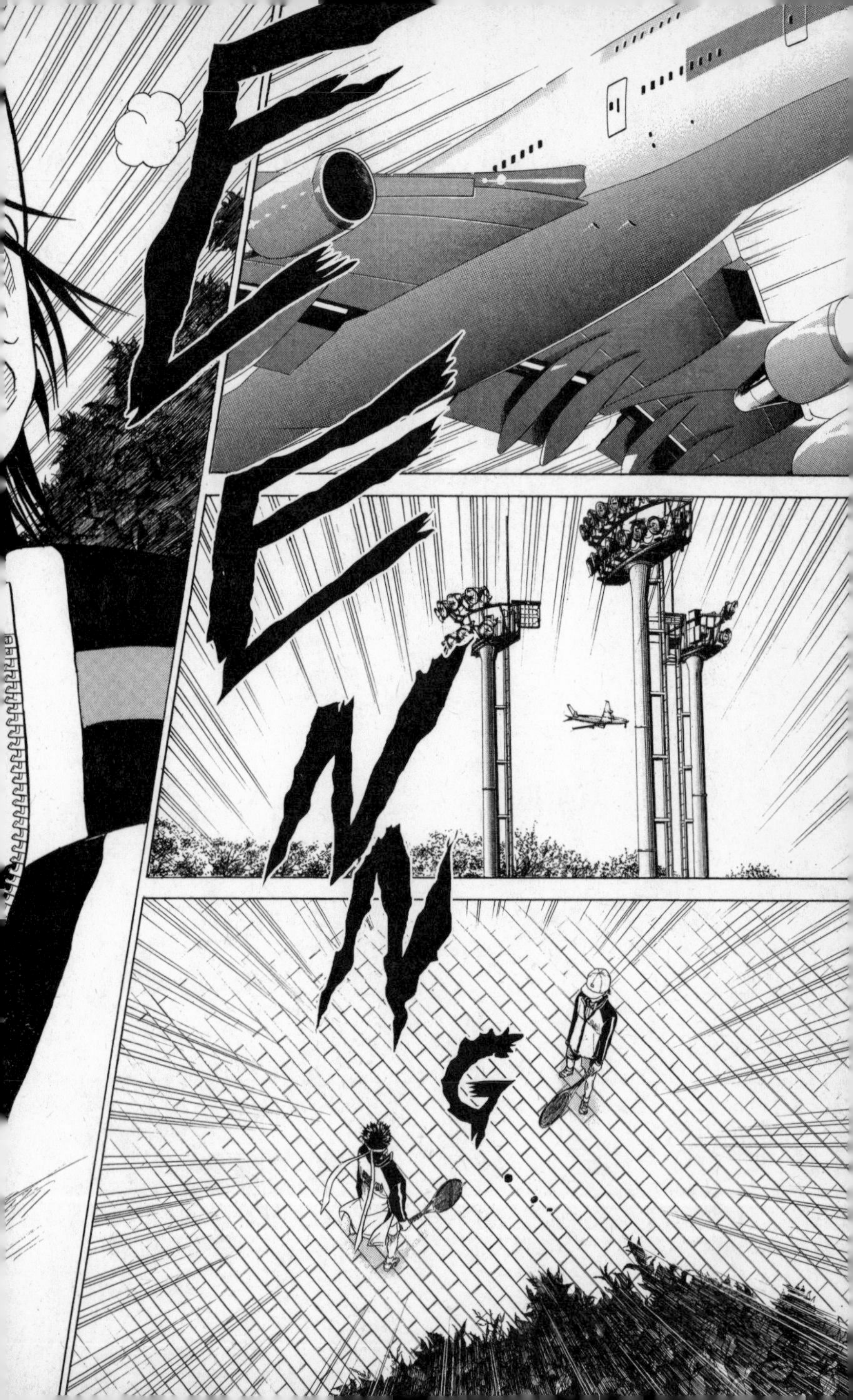
EENNG

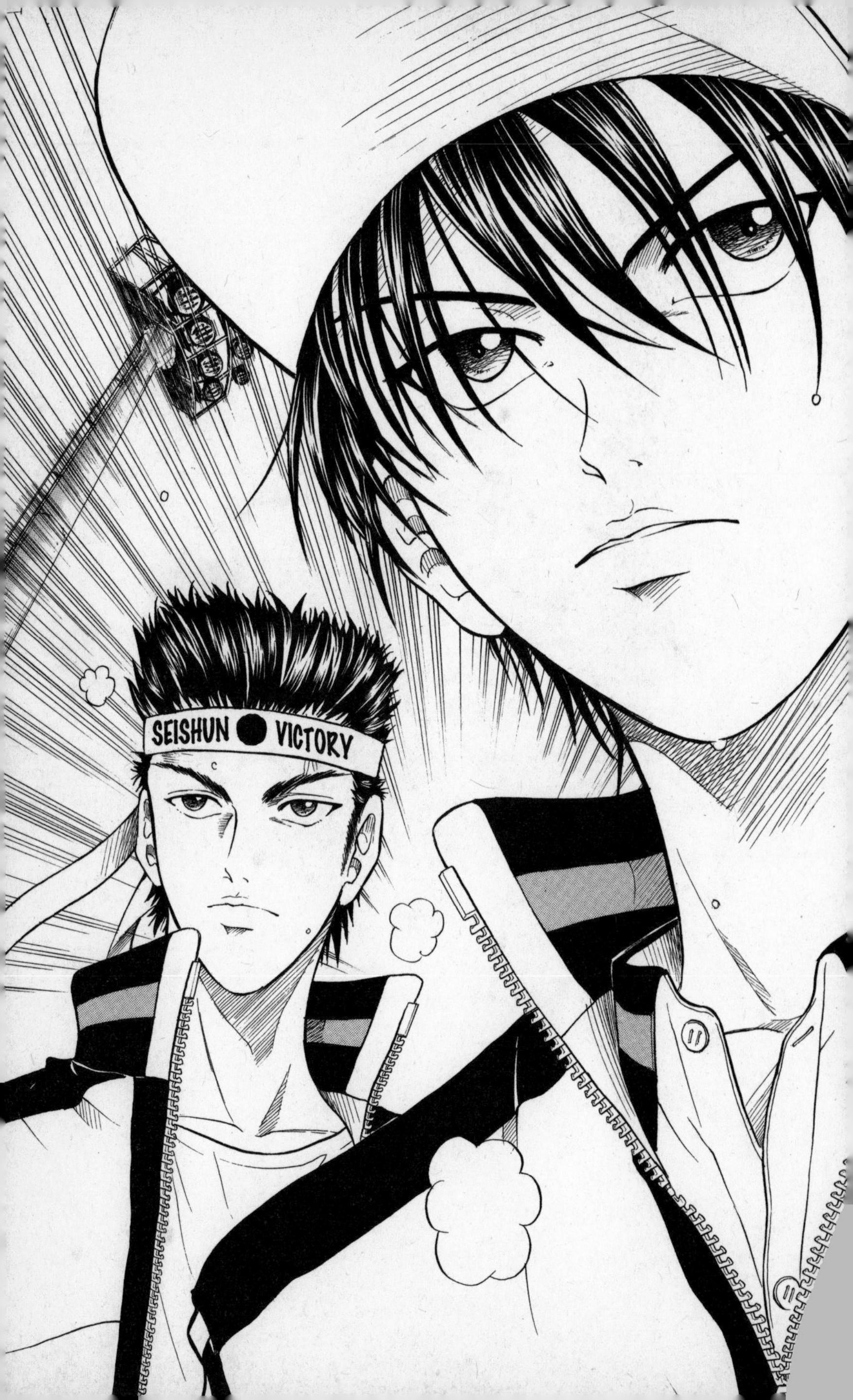
SEISHUN VICTORY

テニスの王子様

THE PRINCE OF TENNIS™

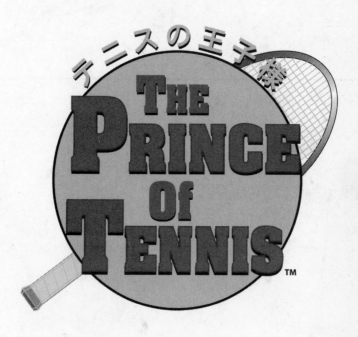

GENIUS 153: ILLUSION

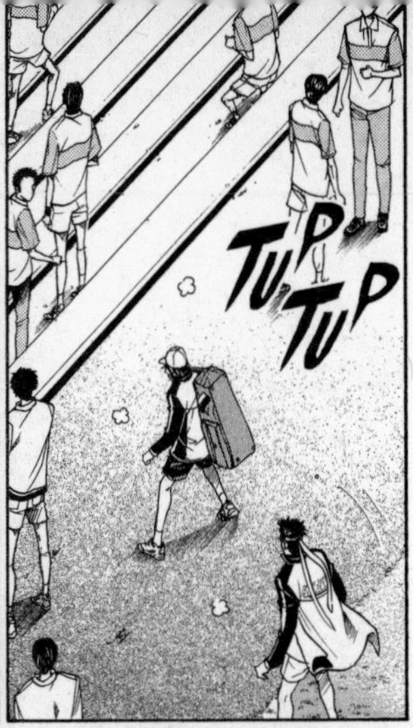
TUP TUP
TUP TUP

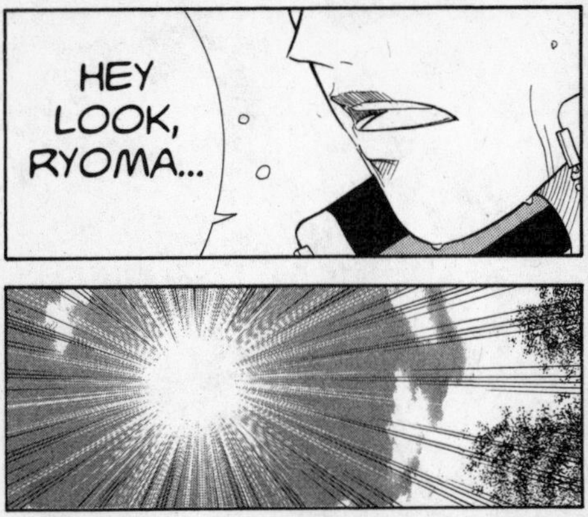
HEY LOOK, RYOMA...

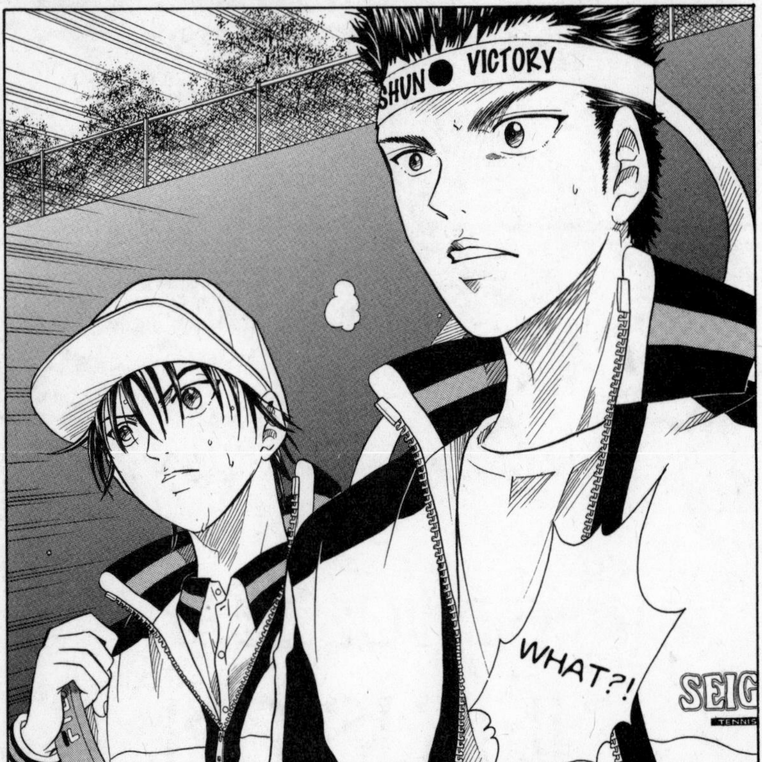
SHUN ● VICTORY
WHAT?!

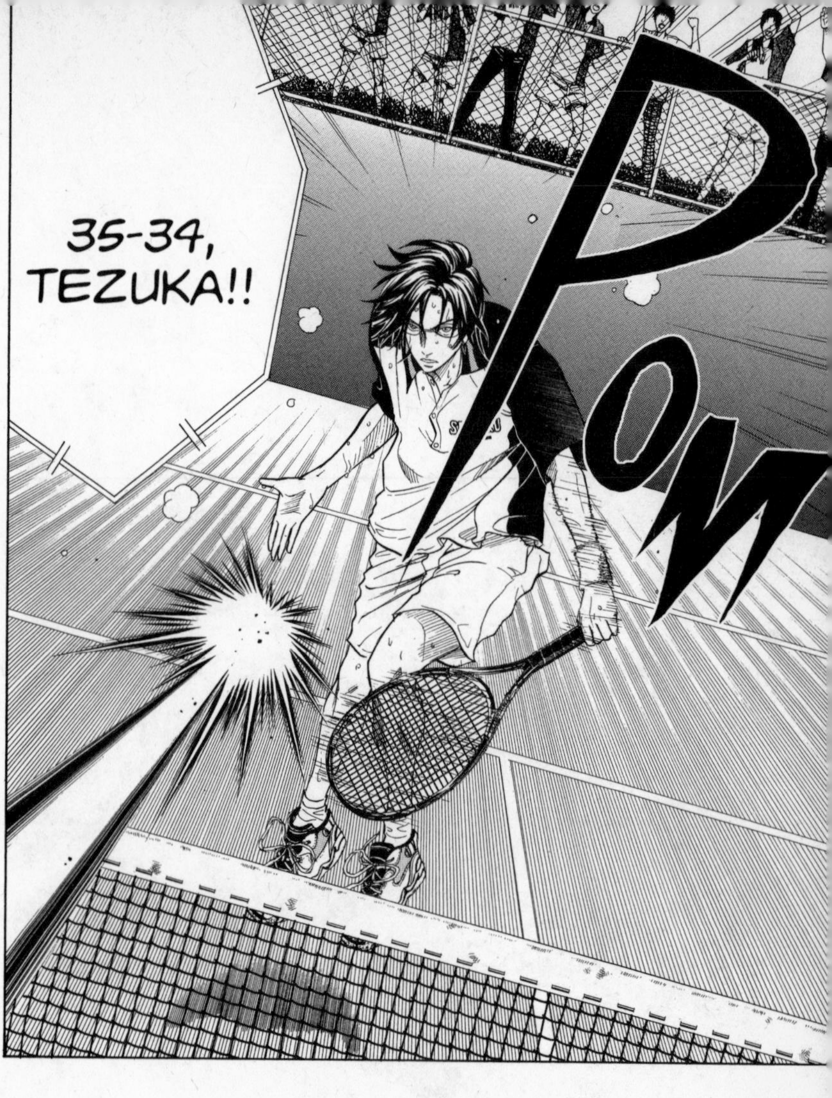
35-34, TEZUKA!!
POW

GENIUS 153: ILLUSION

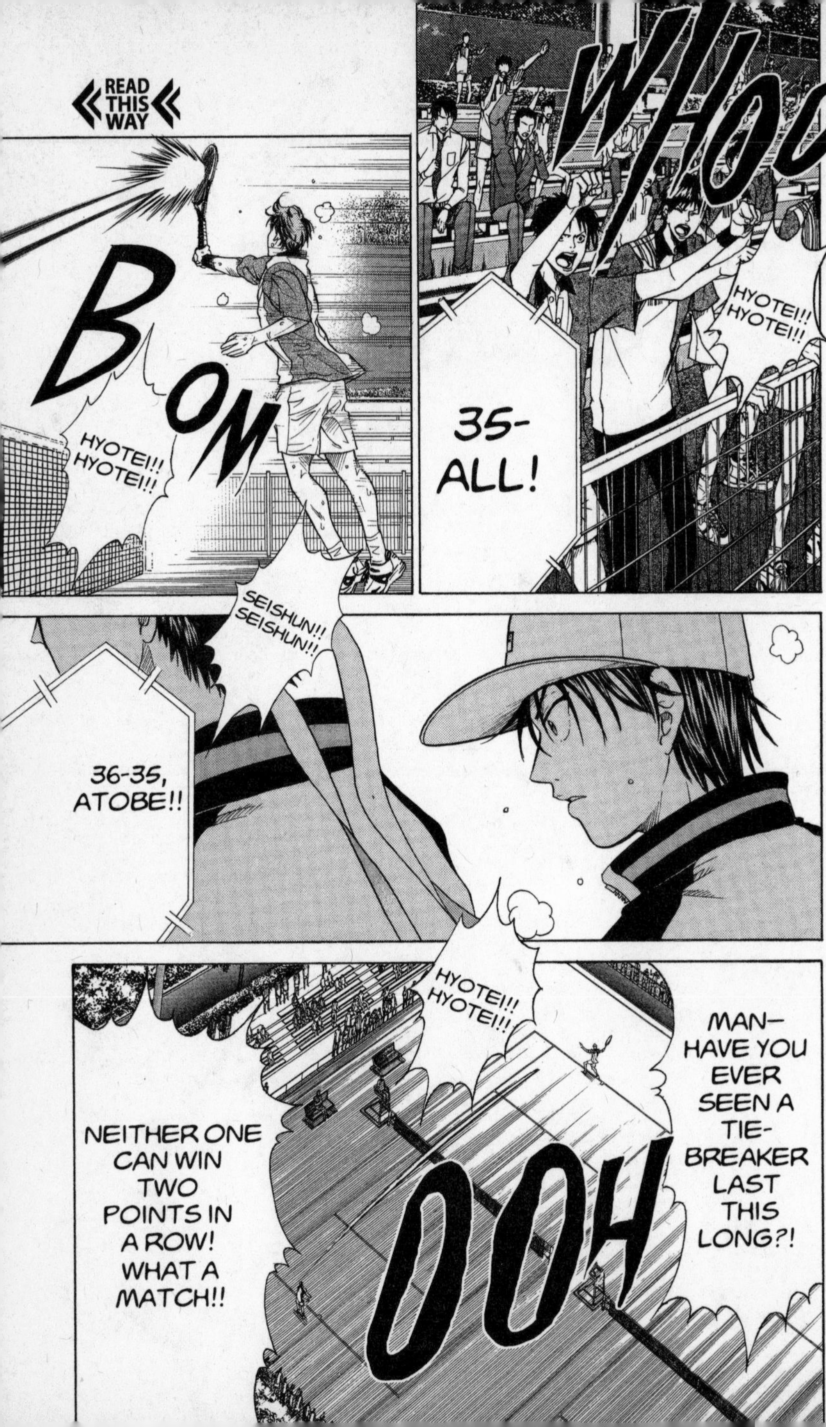
READ THIS WAY
WHOO
HYOTE!!! HYOTE!!!
35-ALL!
BOOM
HYOTEI!!! HYOTEI!!!
SEISHUN!! SEISHUN!!
36-35, ATOBE!!
MAN— HAVE YOU EVER SEEN A TIE-BREAKER LAST THIS LONG?!
HYOTEI!!! HYOTEI!!!
OOH
NEITHER ONE CAN WIN TWO POINTS IN A ROW! WHAT A MATCH!!

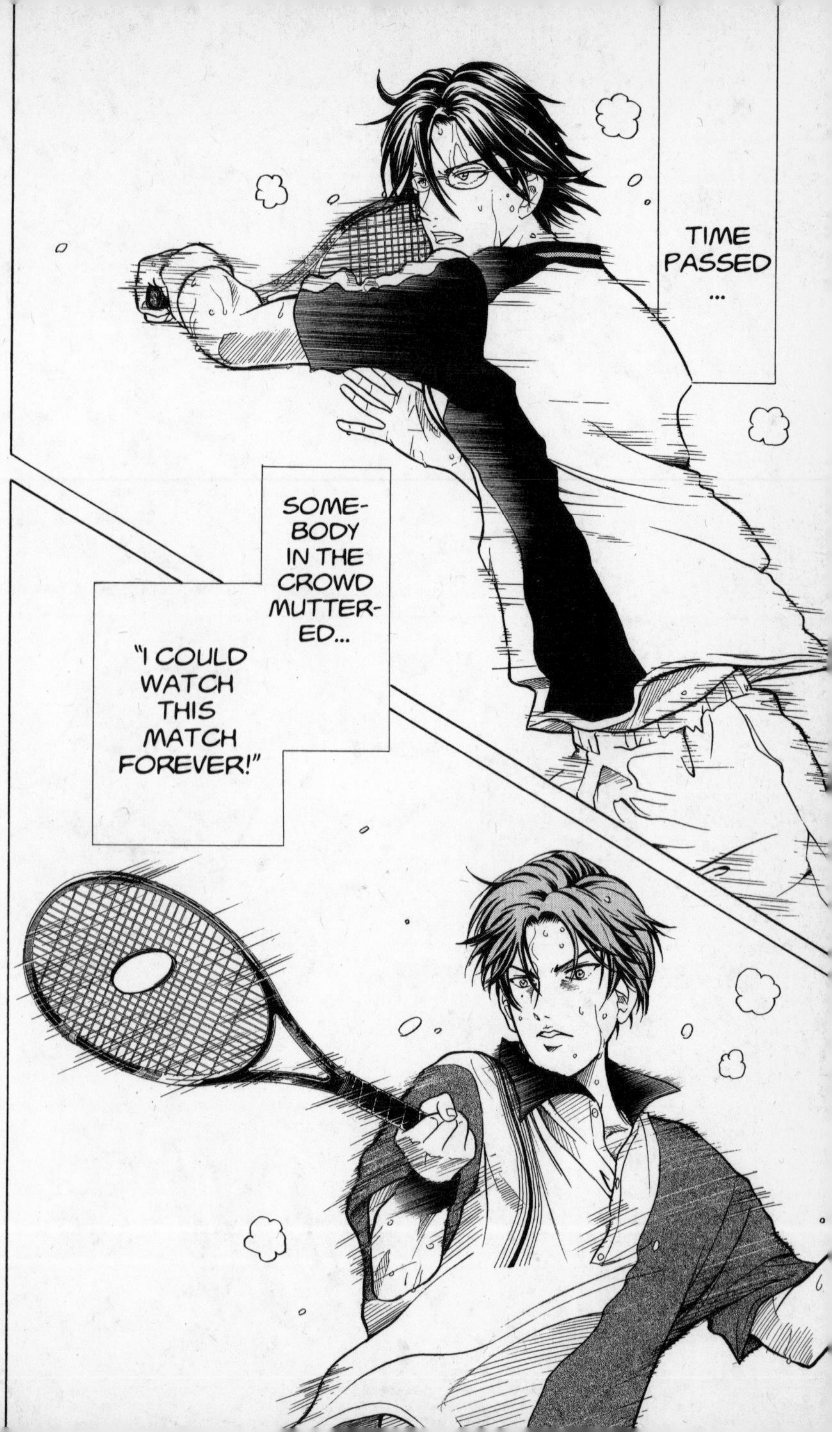
TIME PASSED ...
SOMEBODY IN THE CROWD MUTTERED...
"I COULD WATCH THIS MATCH FOREVER!"

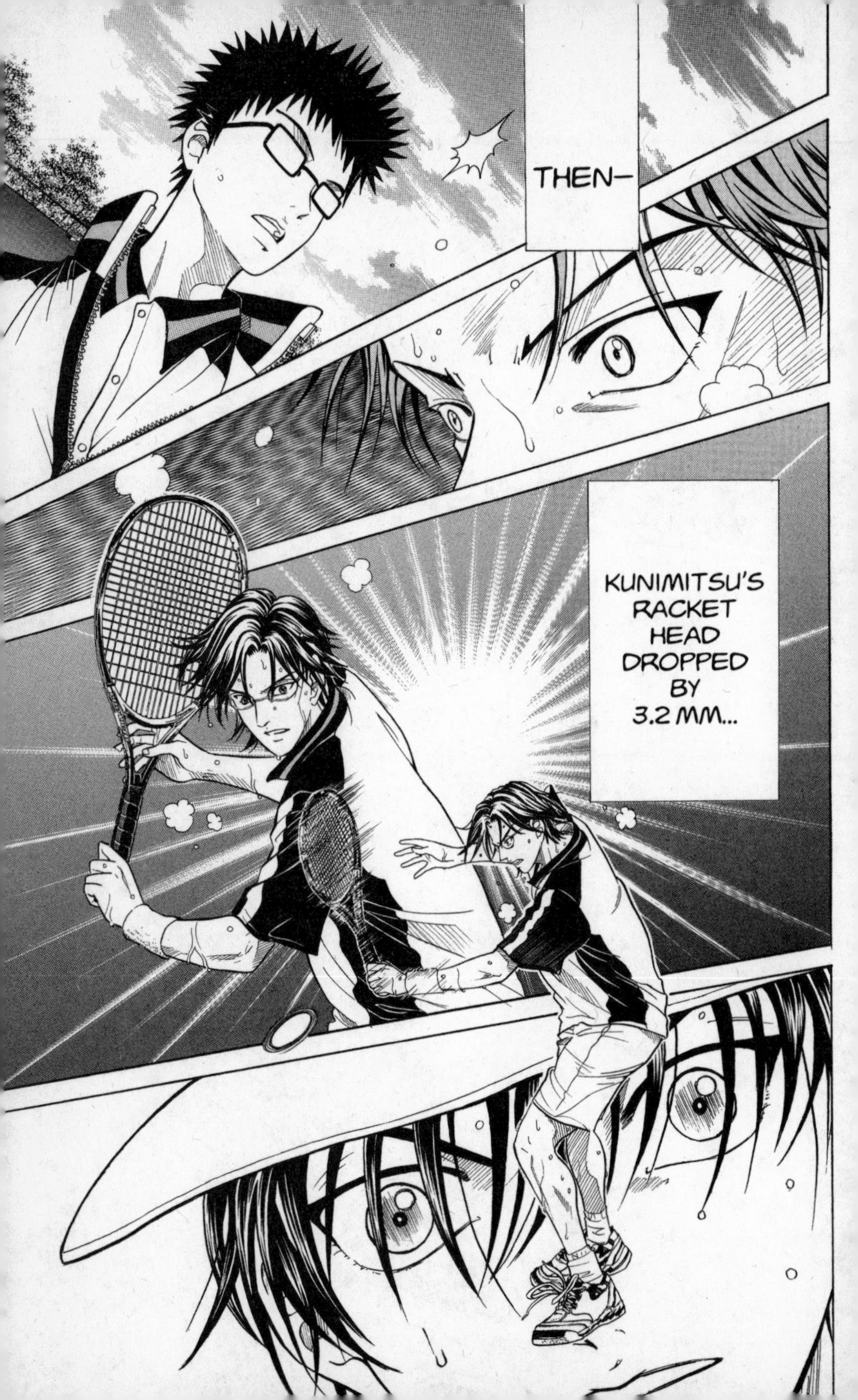
THEN–
KUNIMITSU'S RACKET HEAD DROPPED BY 3.2 MM...

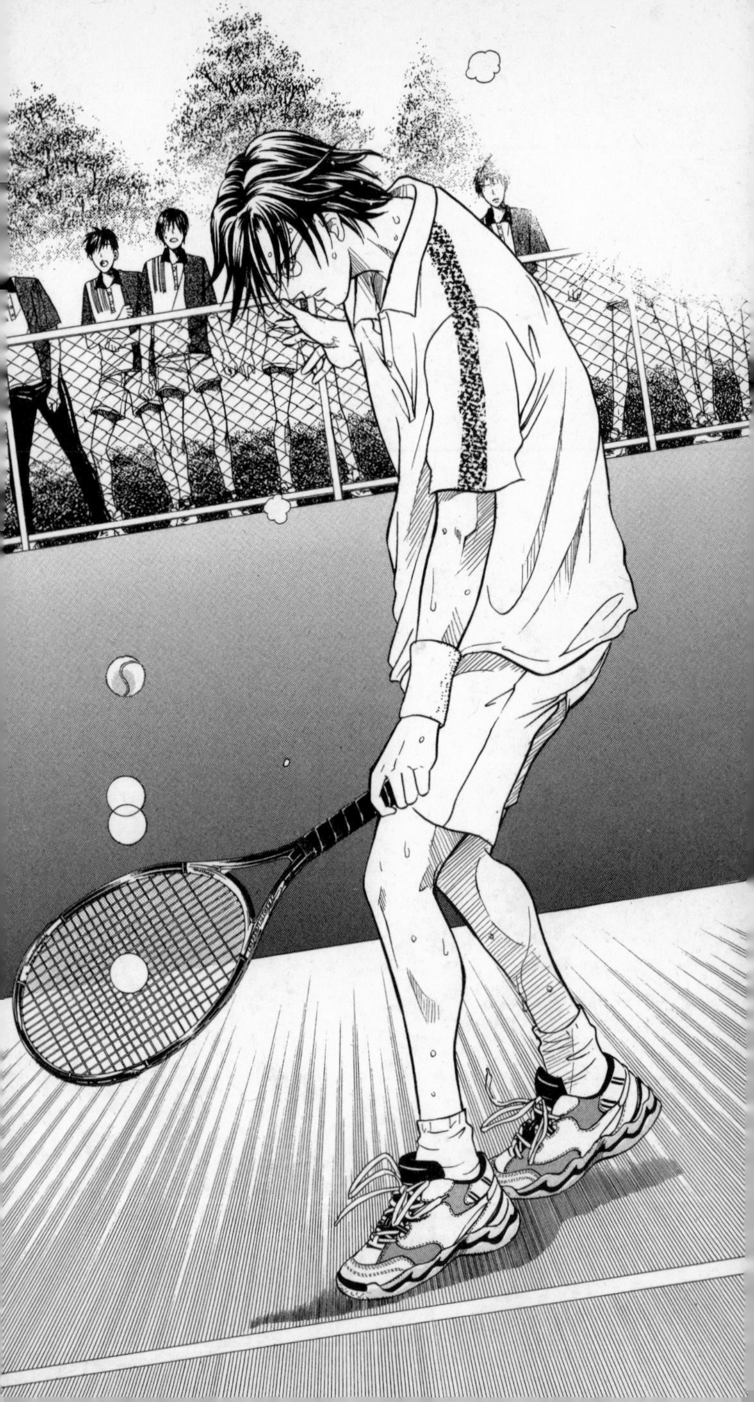

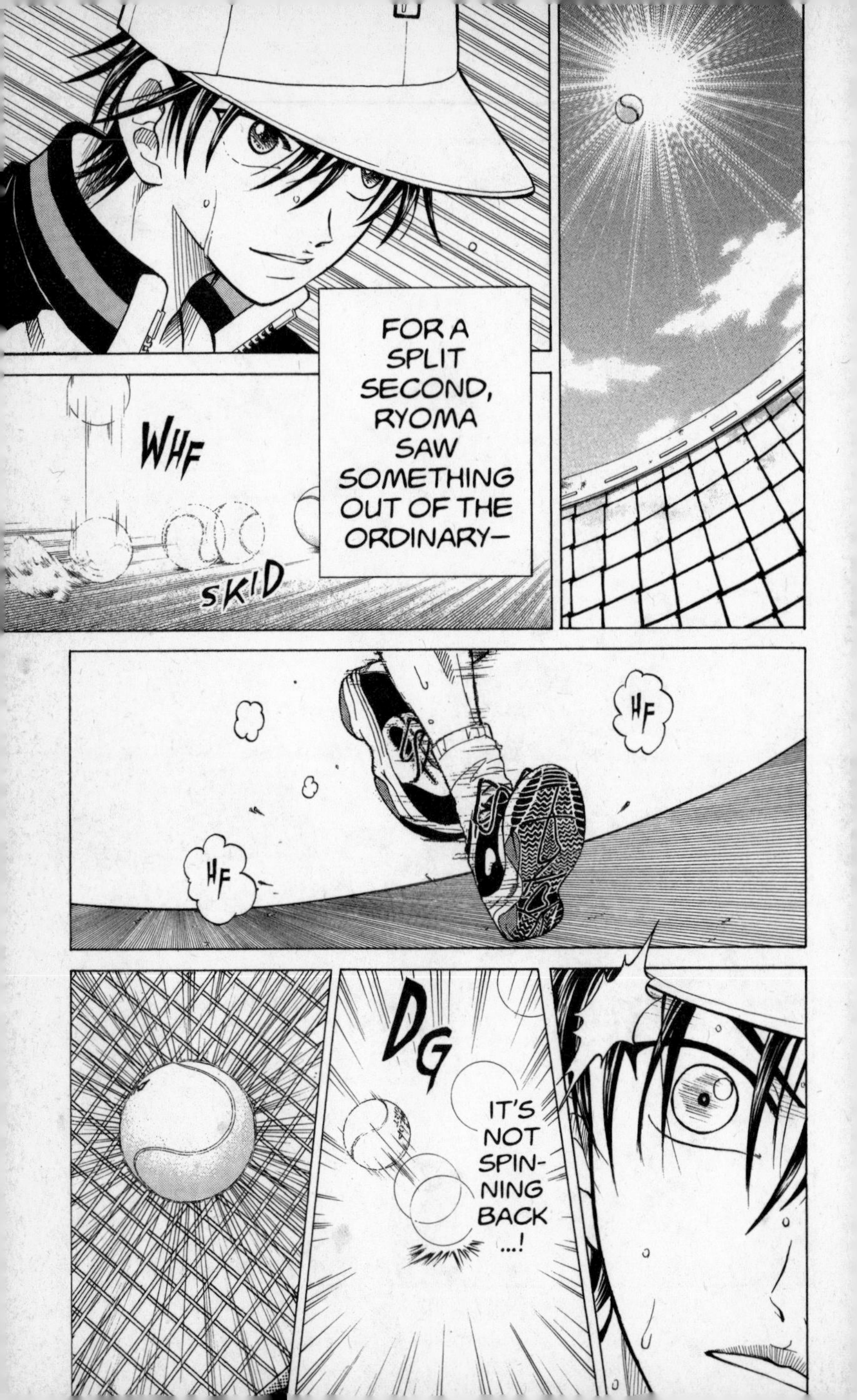
FOR A SPLIT SECOND, RYOMA SAW SOMETHING OUT OF THE ORDINARY—
WHF
SKID
HF
HF
DG
IT'S NOT SPIN-NING BACK ...!

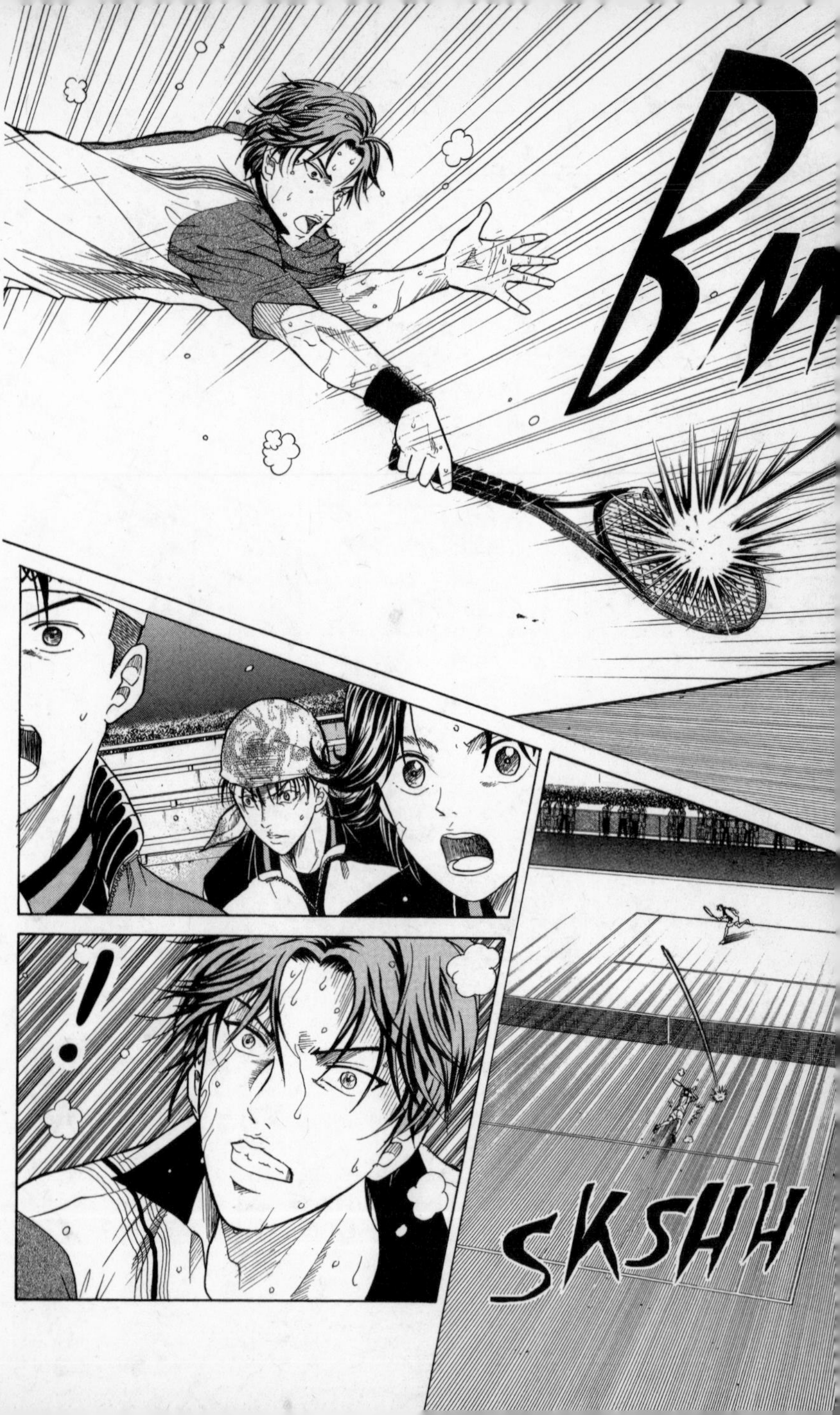

BM
!
SKSHH

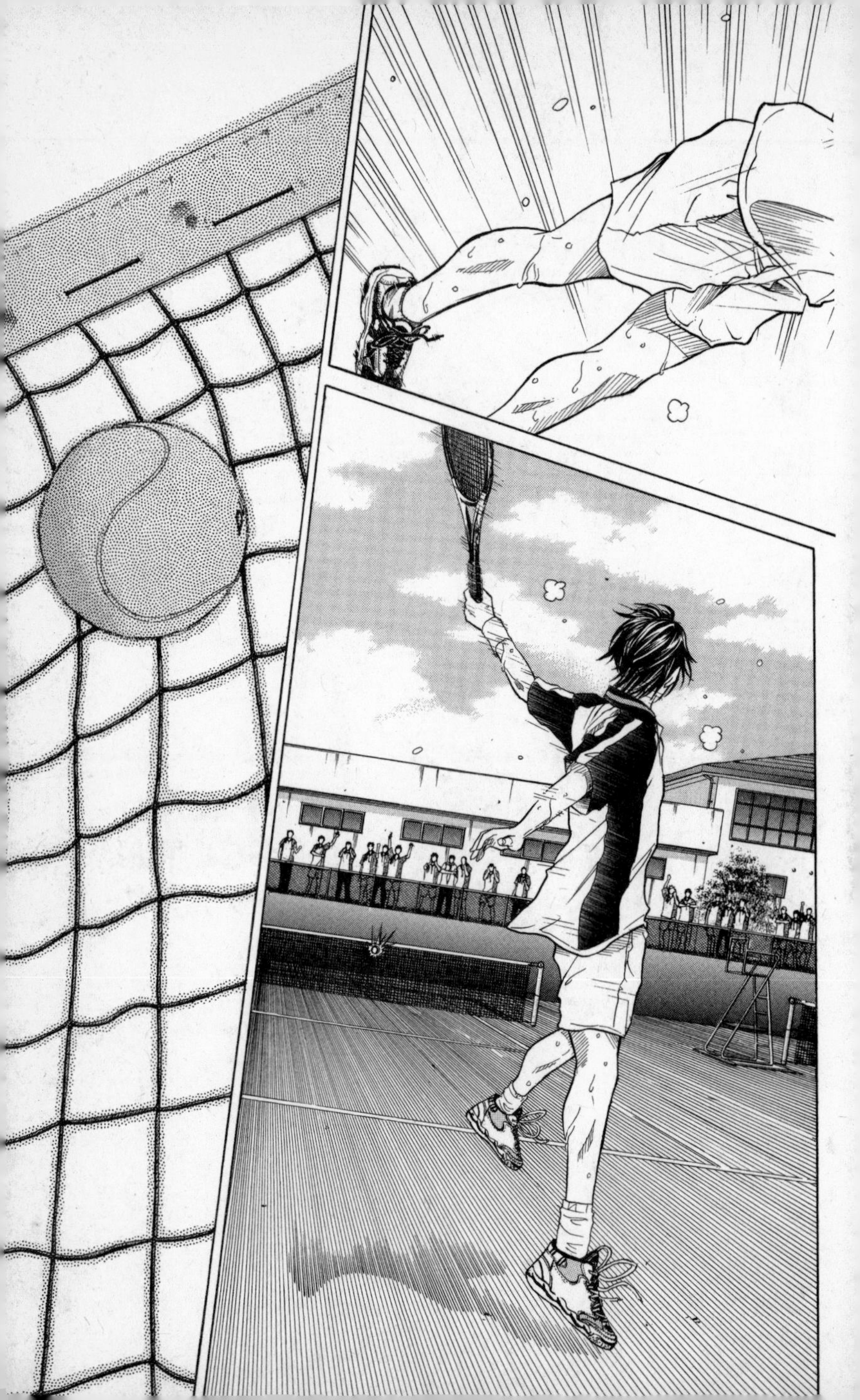

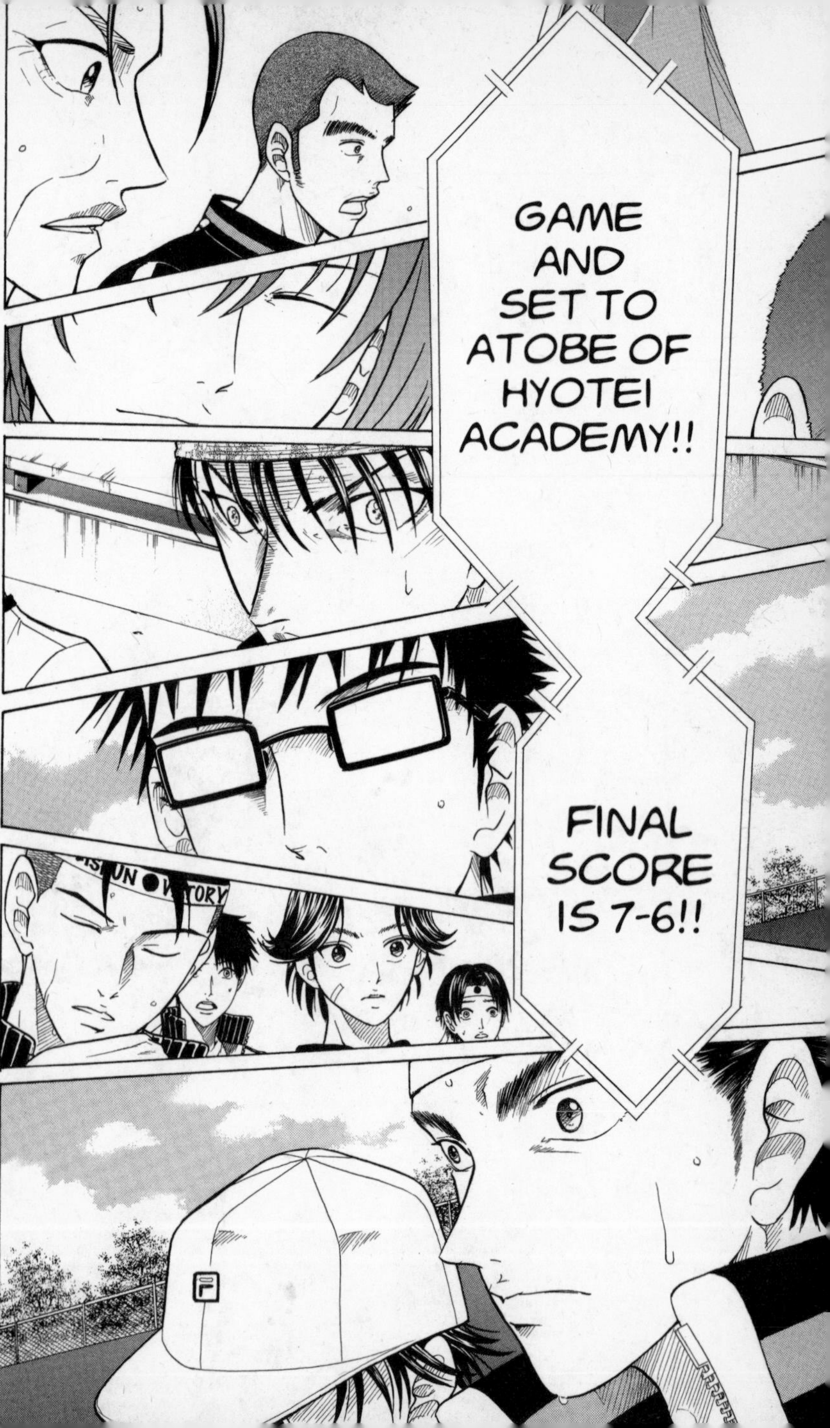
GAME AND SET TO ATOBE OF HYOTEI ACADEMY!!
FINAL SCORE IS 7-6!!

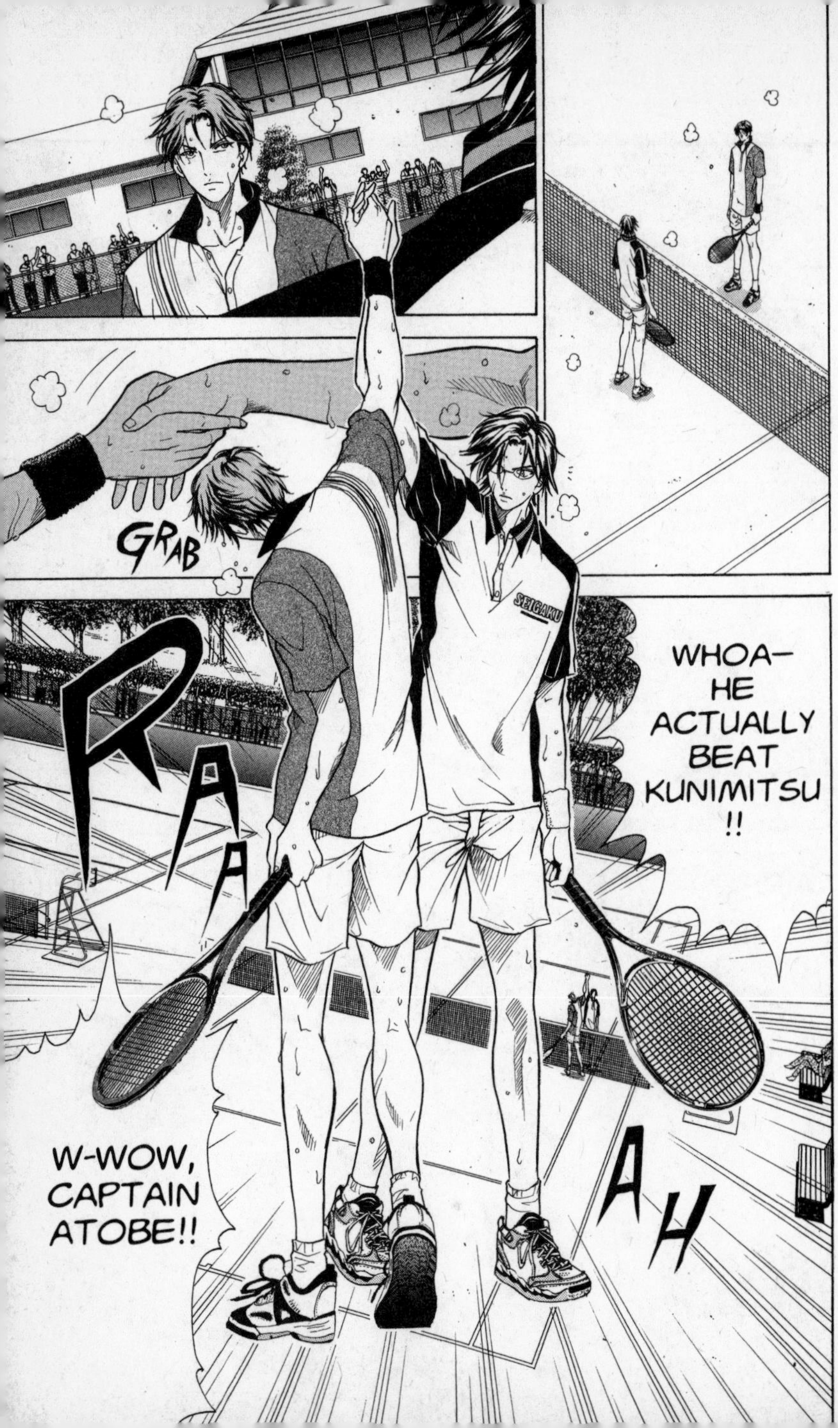
GRAB
WHOA-HE ACTUALLY BEAT KUNIMITSU!!
RAAA
AH
W-WOW, CAPTAIN ATOBE!!

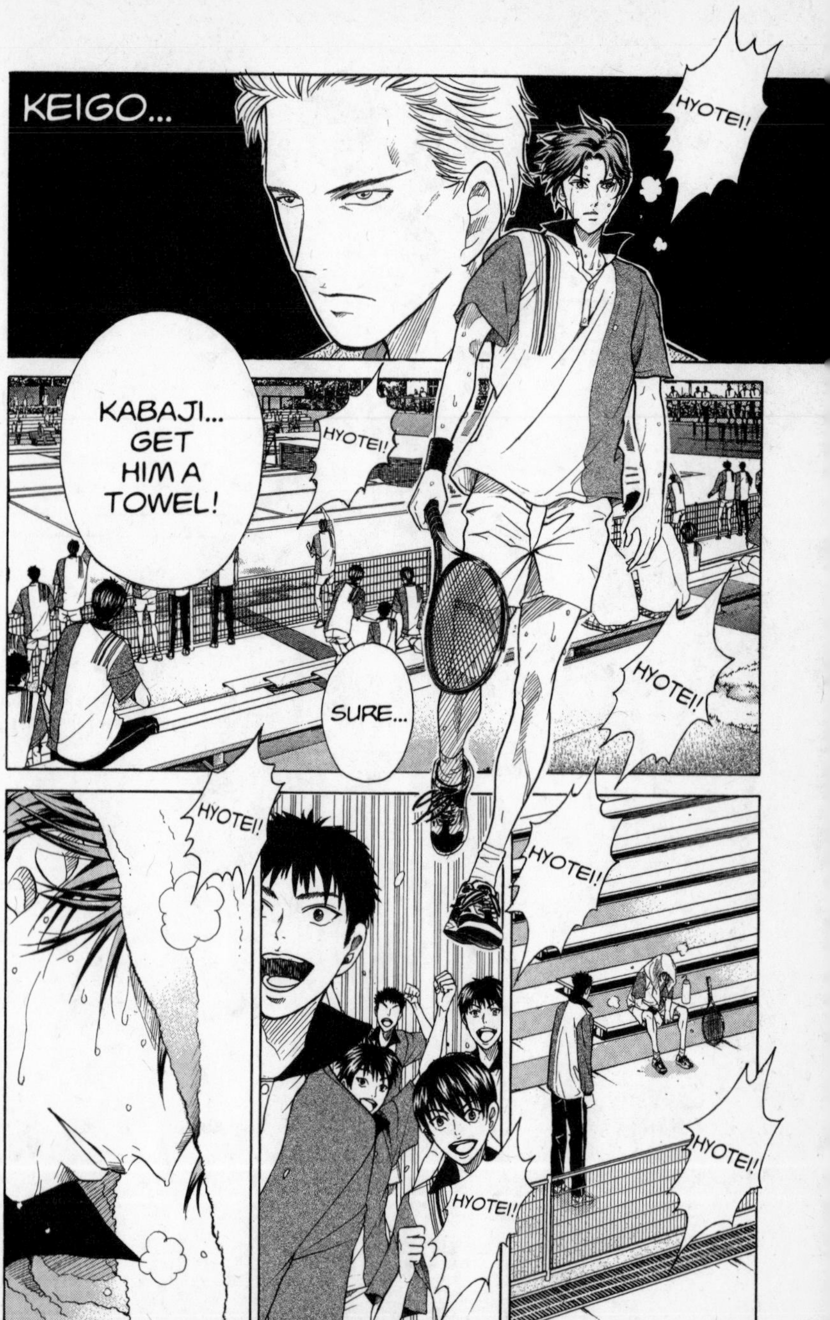
HYOTEI!
KEIGO...
HYOTEI!!
HYOTEI!!
KABAJI... GET HIM A TOWEL!
SURE...
HYOTEI!!
HYOTEI!!
HYOTEI!!
HYOTEI!!

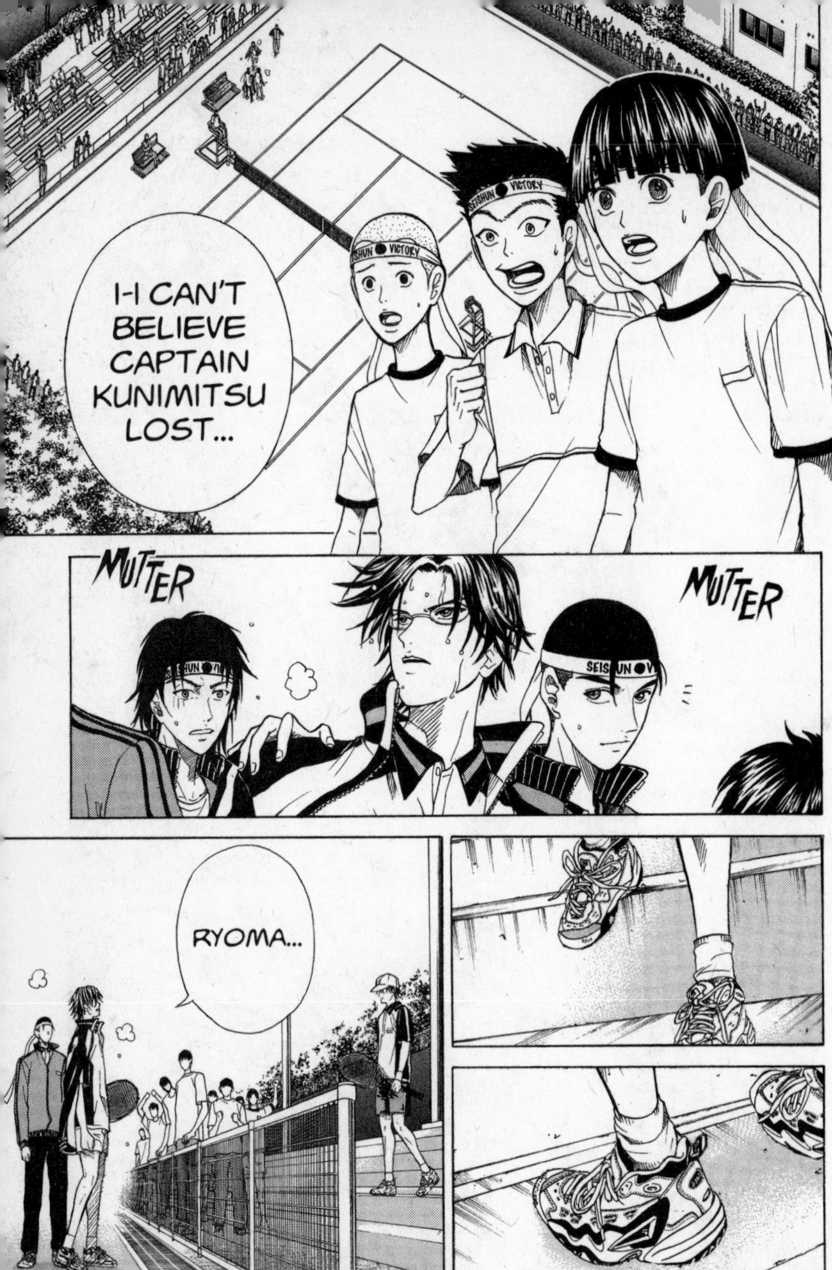
I-I CAN'T BELIEVE CAPTAIN KUNIMITSU LOST...
MUTTER
MUTTER
SEISHUN VICTORY
RYOMA...

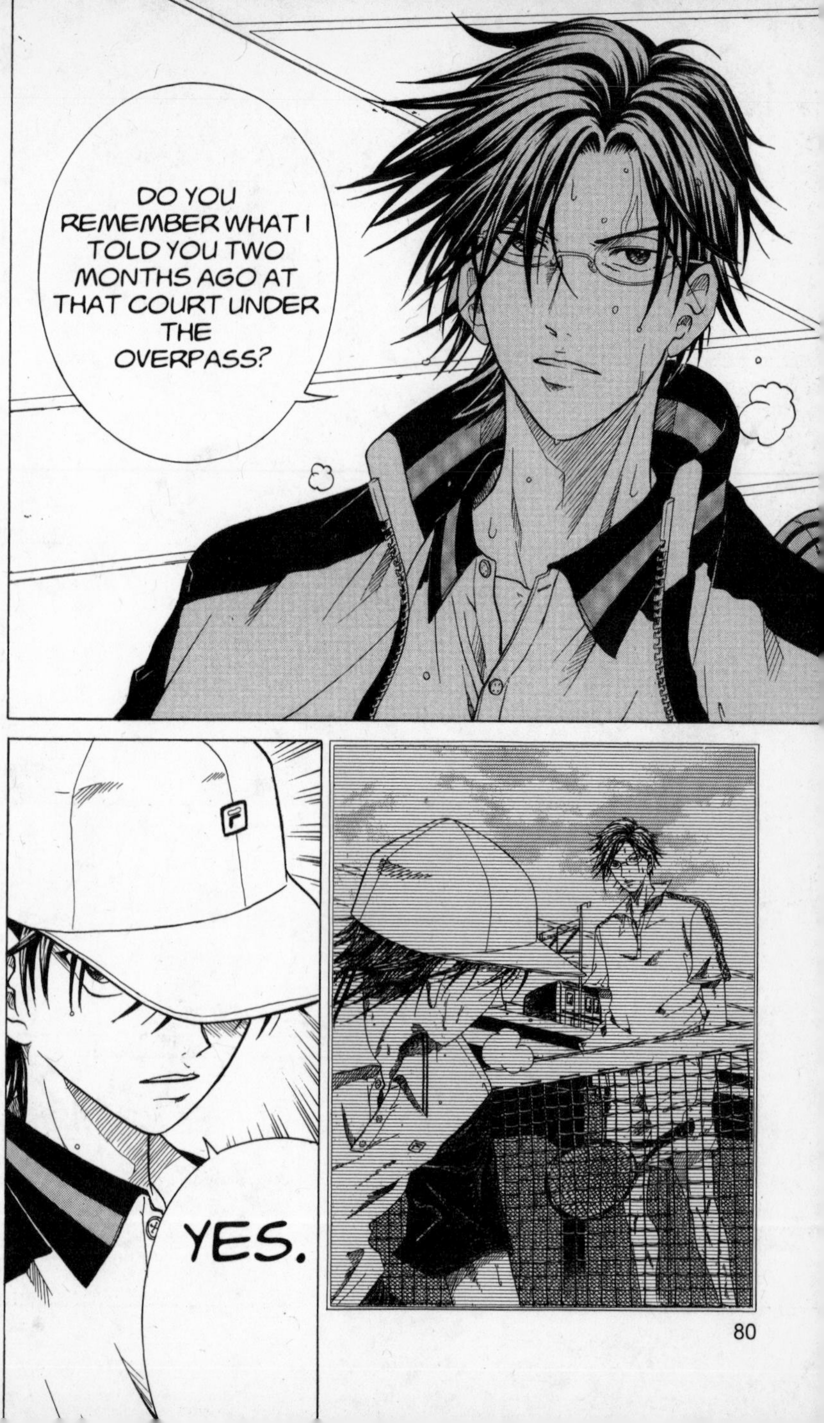
DO YOU REMEMBER WHAT I TOLD YOU TWO MONTHS AGO AT THAT COURT UNDER THE OVERPASS?
YES.

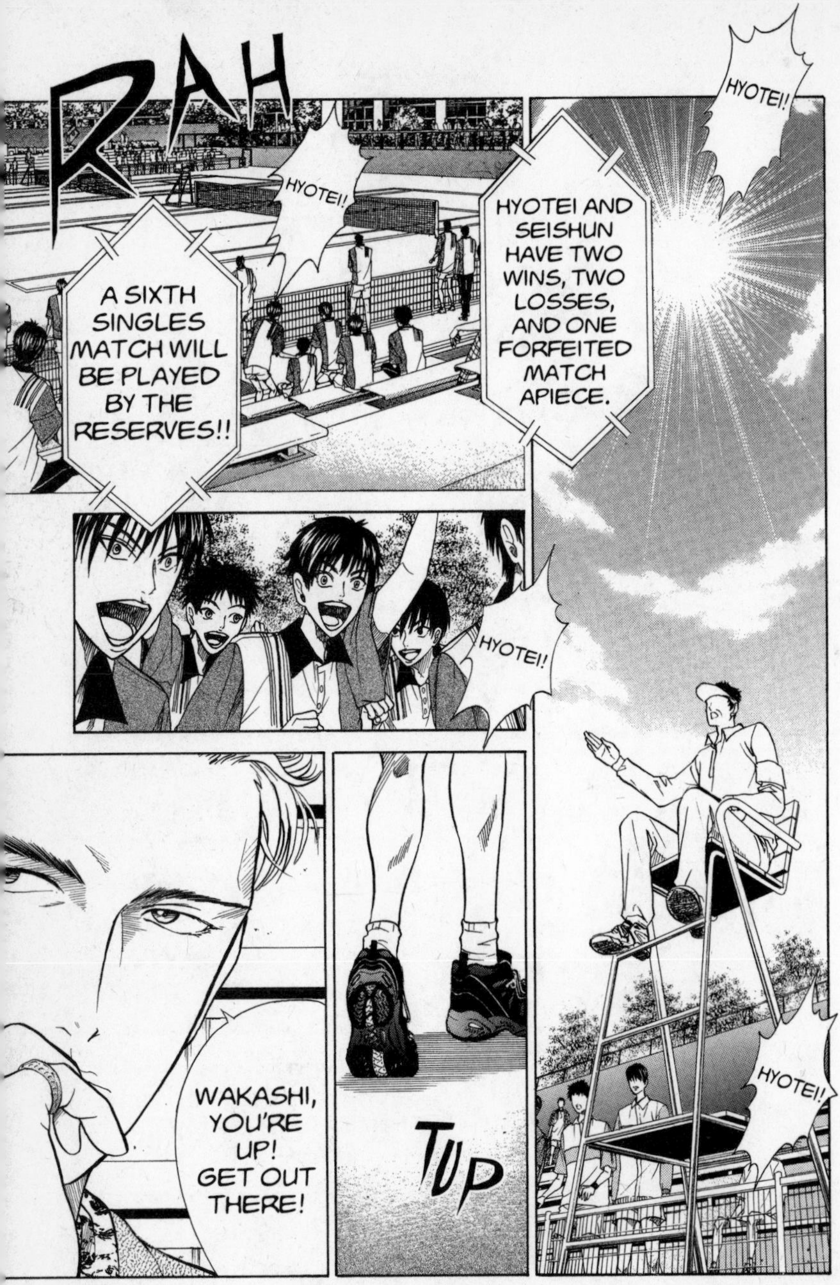
HYOTEI!!
HYOTEI AND SEISHUN HAVE TWO WINS, TWO LOSSES, AND ONE FORFEITED MATCH APIECE.
RAH
HYOTEI!!
A SIXTH SINGLES MATCH WILL BE PLAYED BY THE RESERVES!!
HYOTEI!!
HYOTEI!!
TUP
WAKASHI, YOU'RE UP! GET OUT THERE!

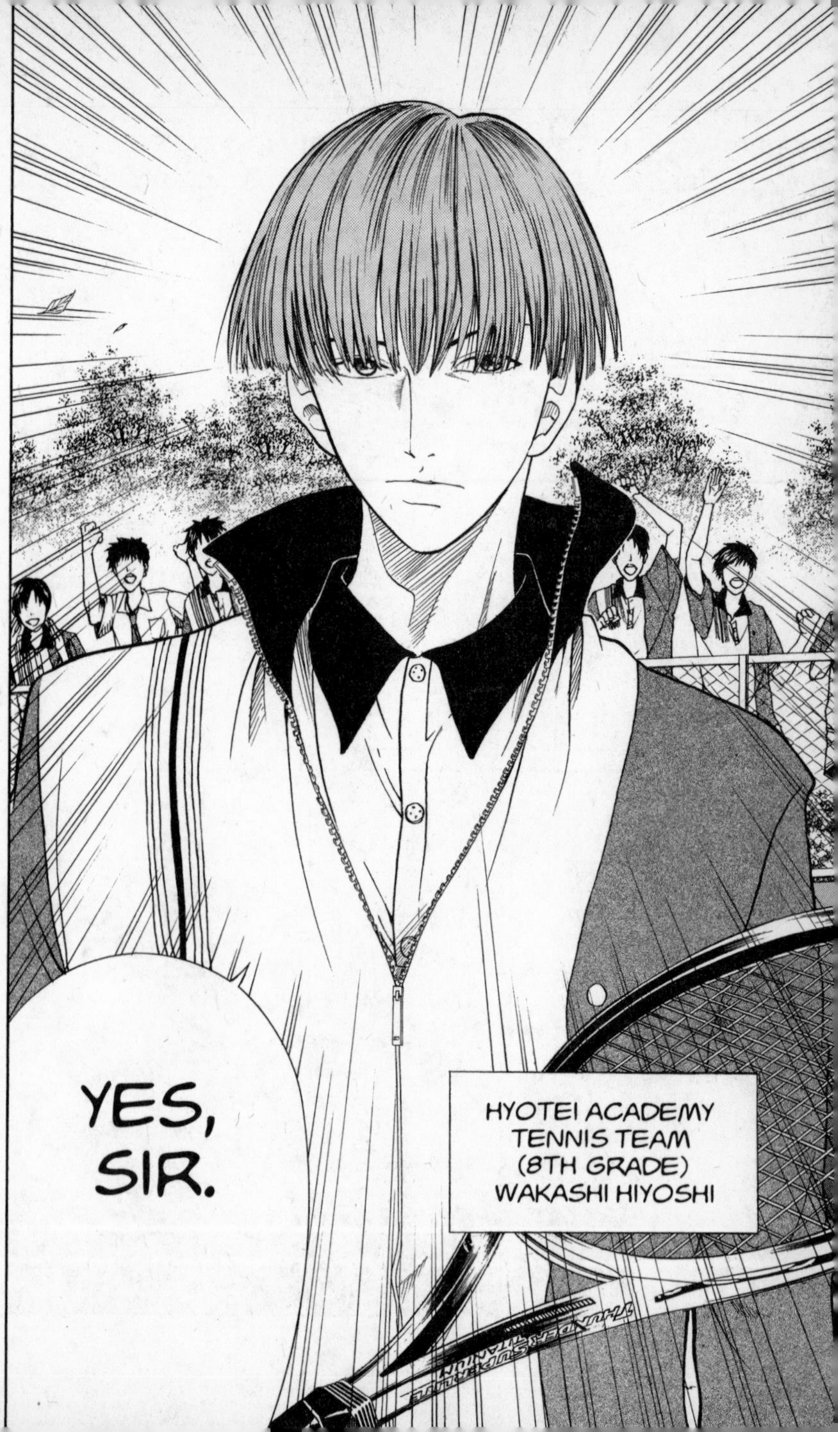
YES, SIR.
HYOTEI ACADEMY TENNIS TEAM (8TH GRADE) WAKASHI HIYOSHI

READ THIS WAY

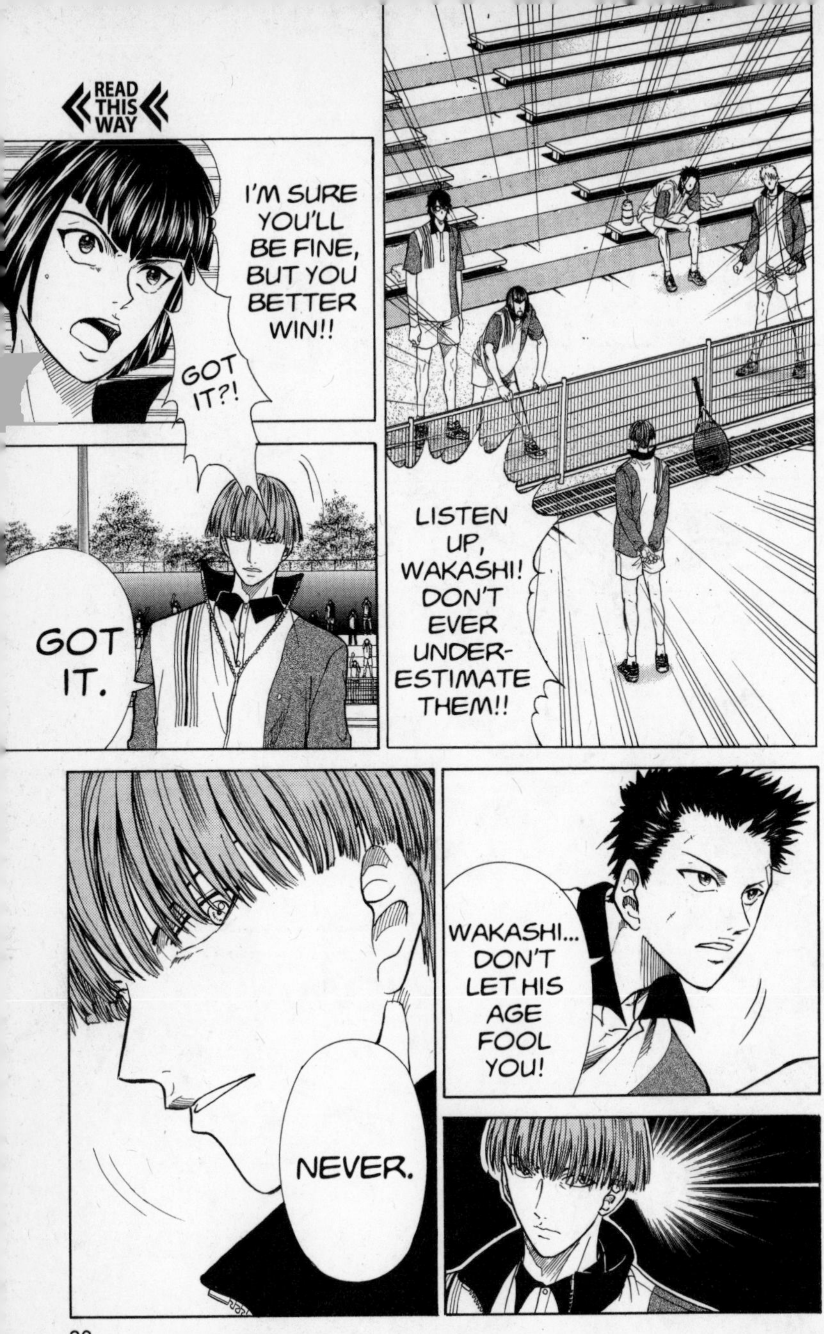
LISTEN UP, WAKASHI! DON'T EVER UNDER-ESTIMATE THEM!!
I'M SURE YOU'LL BE FINE, BUT YOU BETTER WIN!!
GOT IT?!
GOT IT.
WAKASHI... DON'T LET HIS AGE FOOL YOU!
NEVER.

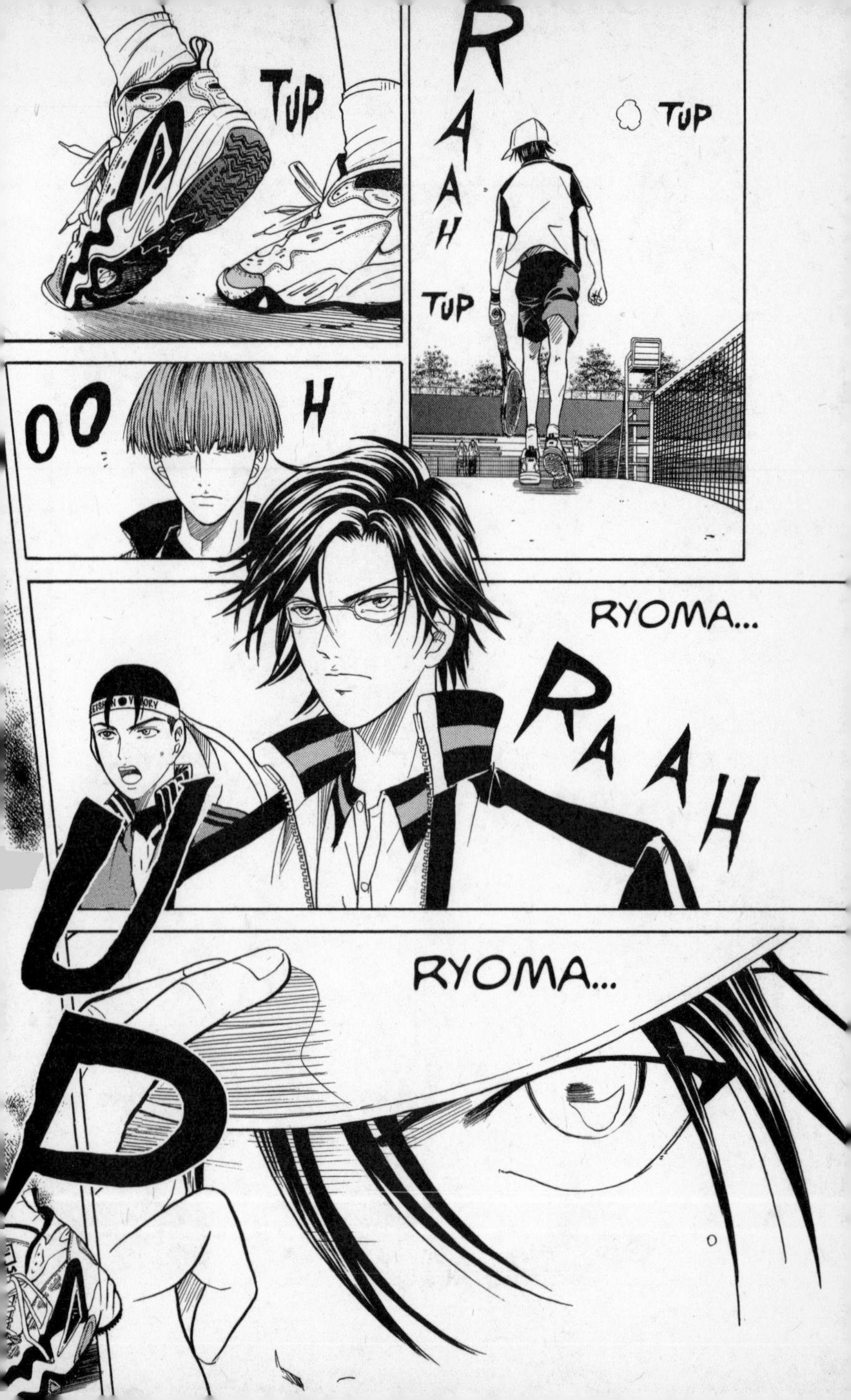
RAAH
TUP
TUP
TUP
OOH
RYOMA...
RAAH
RYOMA...
UP

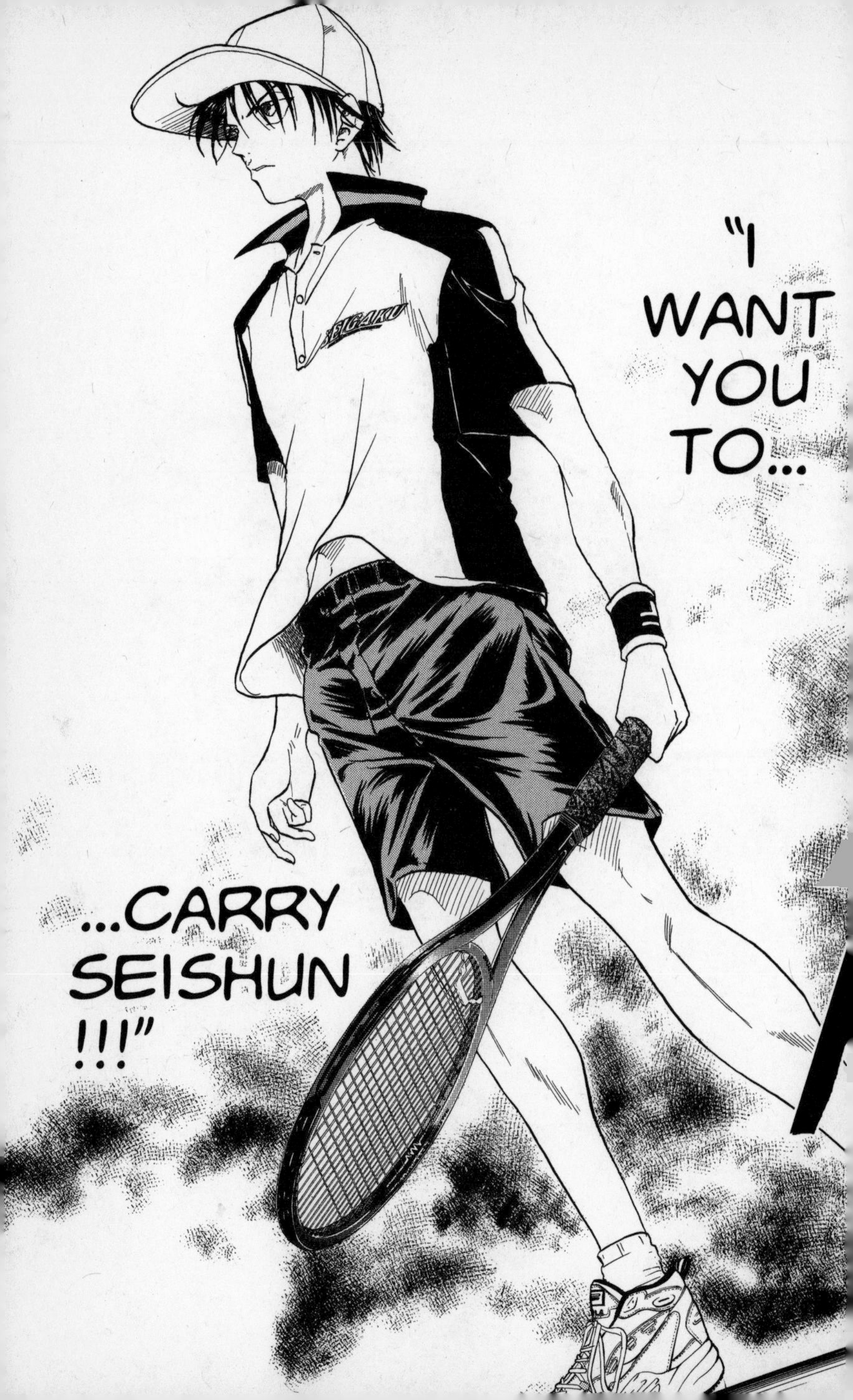
"I WANT YOU TO...
...CARRY SEISHUN!!!"

テニスの王子様

THE PRINCE OF TENNIS™

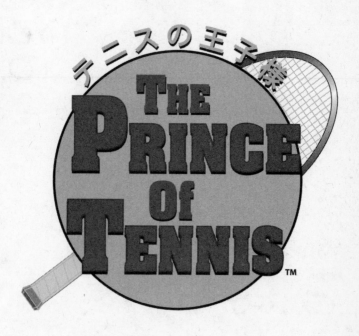

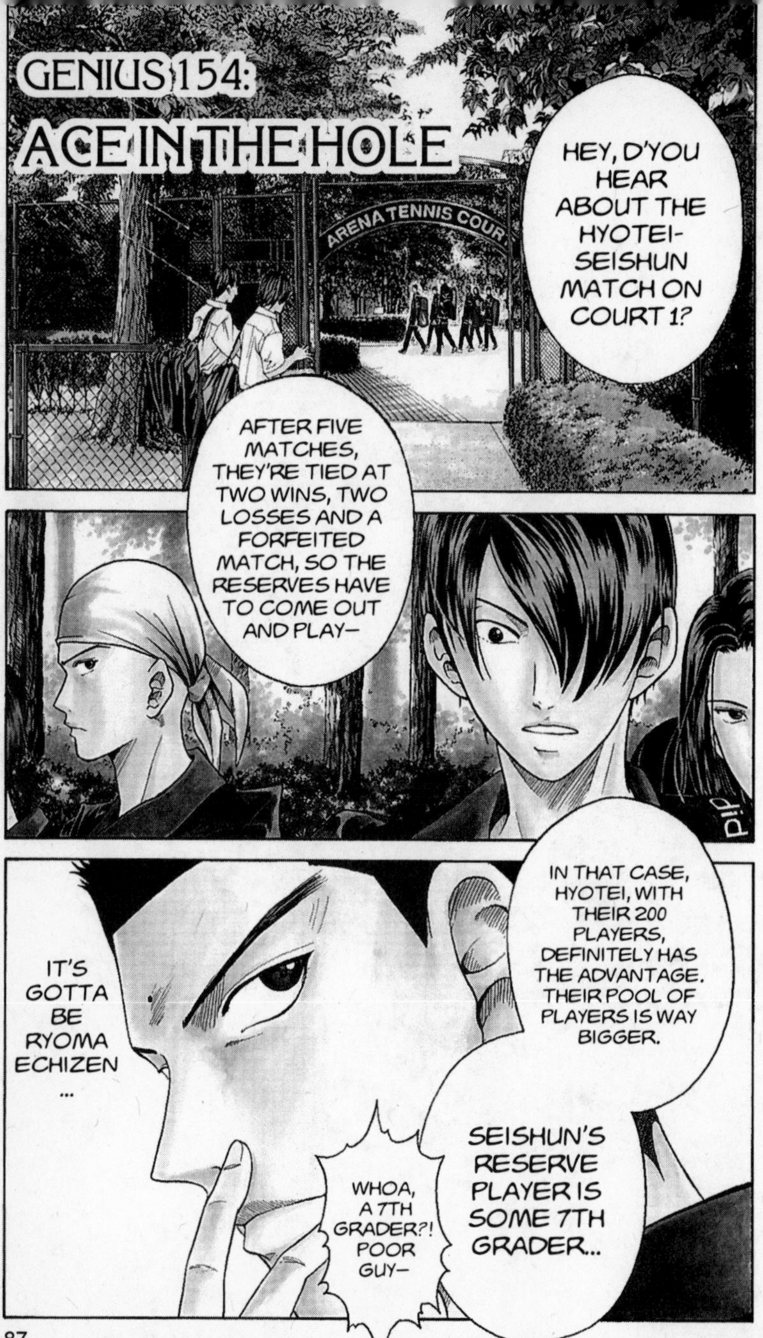
GENIUS 154:
ACE IN THE HOLE
ARENA TENNIS COUR
HEY, D'YOU HEAR ABOUT THE HYOTEI-SEISHUN MATCH ON COURT 1?
AFTER FIVE MATCHES, THEY'RE TIED AT TWO WINS, TWO LOSSES AND A FORFEITED MATCH, SO THE RESERVES HAVE TO COME OUT AND PLAY—
PIP
IN THAT CASE, HYOTEI, WITH THEIR 200 PLAYERS, DEFINITELY HAS THE ADVANTAGE. THEIR POOL OF PLAYERS IS WAY BIGGER.
SEISHUN'S RESERVE PLAYER IS SOME 7TH GRADER...
WHOA, A 7TH GRADER?! POOR GUY—
IT'S GOTTA BE RYOMA ECHIZEN ...

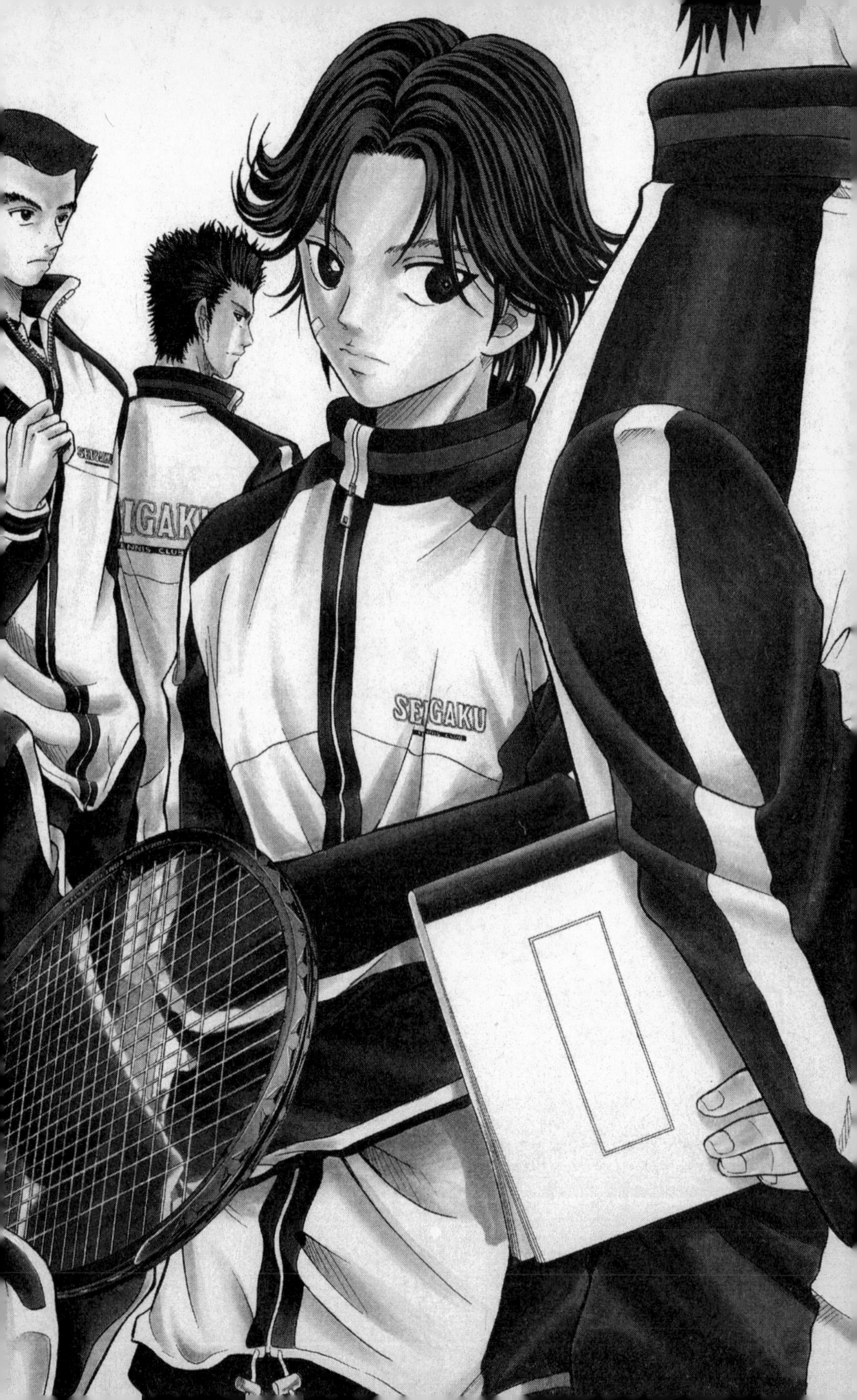
SEIGAKU

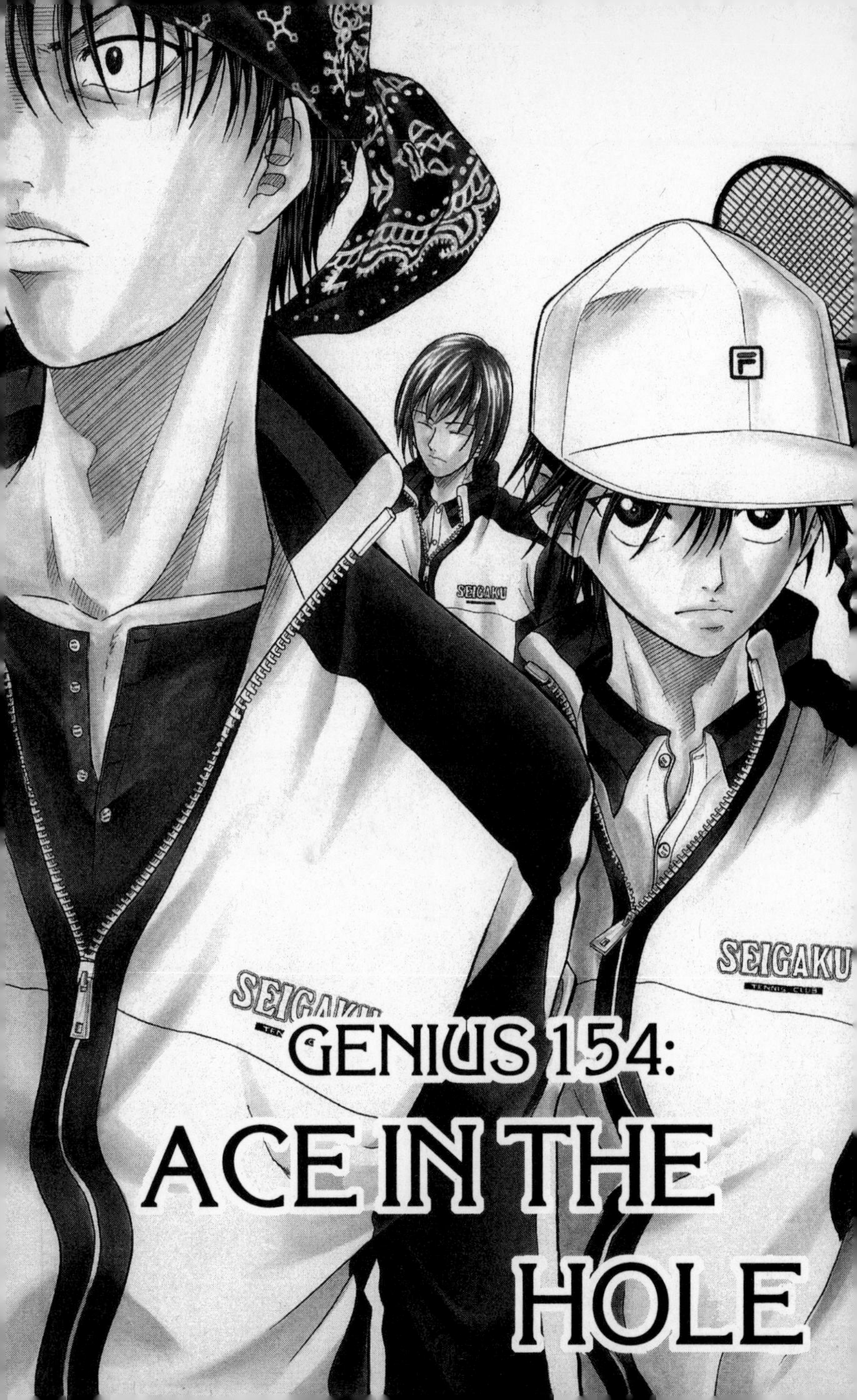
SEIGAKU
SEIGAKU
TENNIS CLUB
SEIGAKU
GENIUS 154:
ACE IN THE HOLE

テニスの王子様

THE PRINCE OF TENNIS™

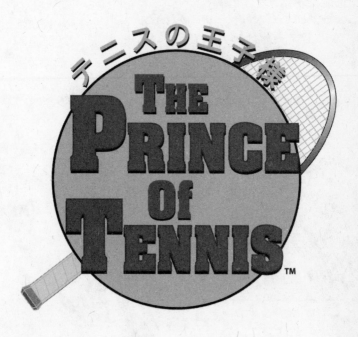

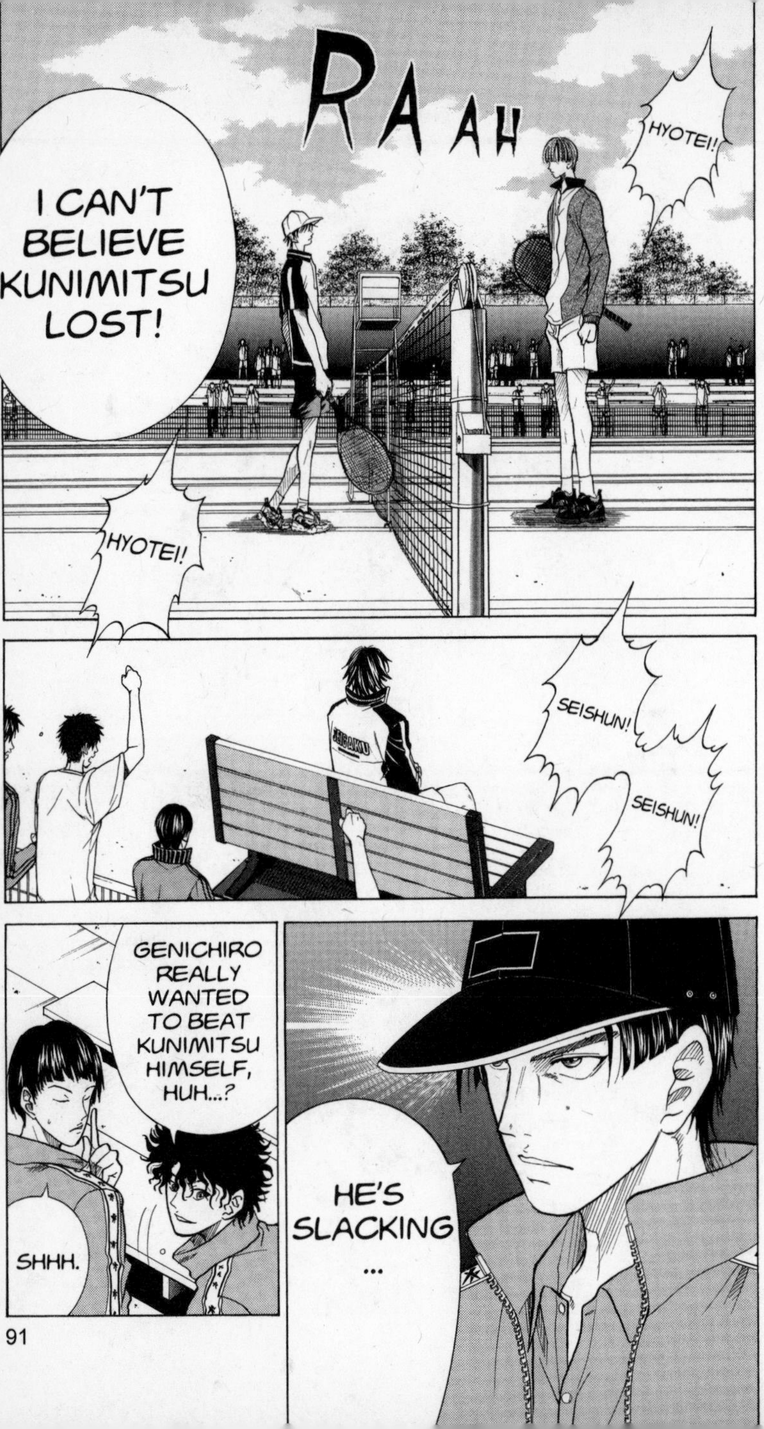
RAAH
HYOTEI!
I CAN'T BELIEVE KUNIMITSU LOST!
HYOTEI!
SEISHUN!
SEISHUN!
HE'S SLACKING ...
GENICHIRO REALLY WANTED TO BEAT KUNIMITSU HIMSELF, HUH...?
SHHH.

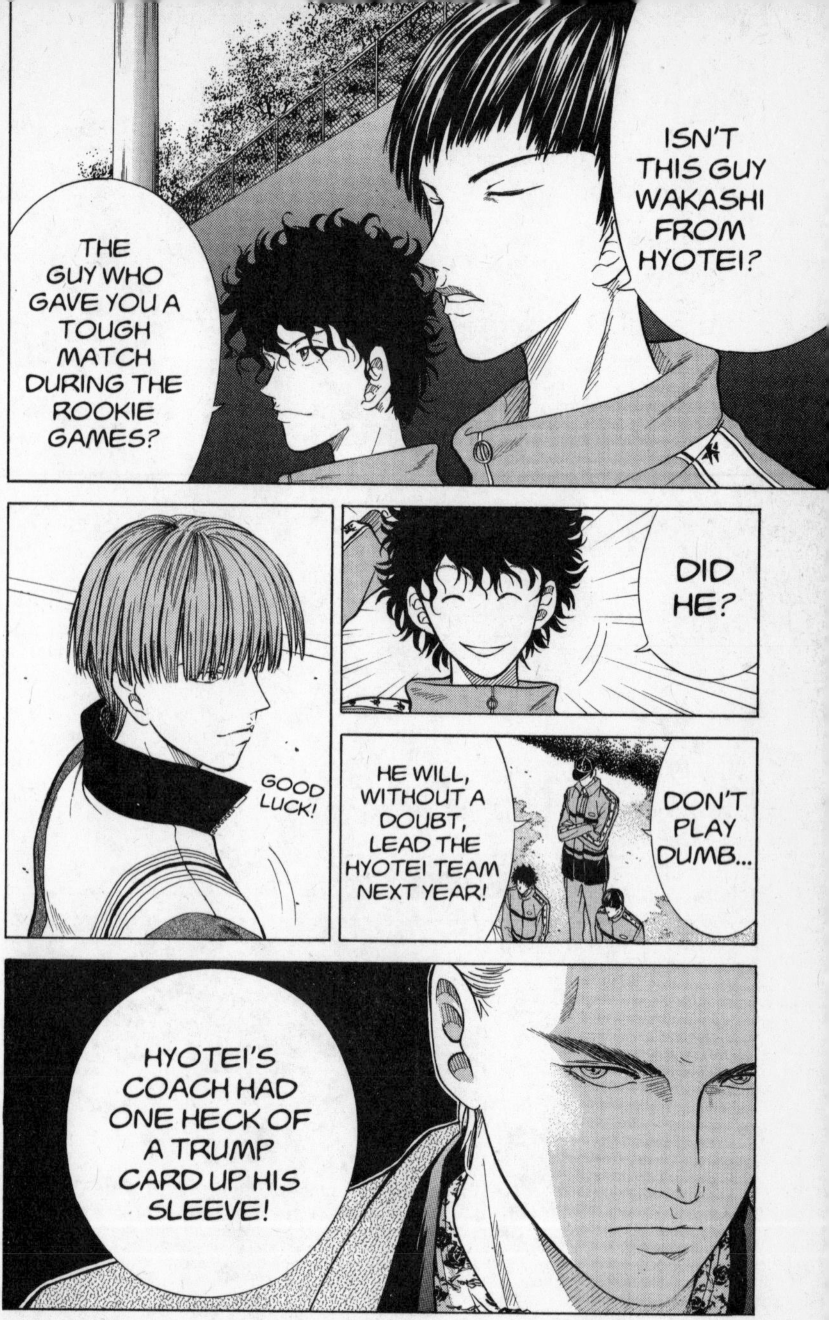
ISN'T THIS GUY WAKASHI FROM HYOTEI?
THE GUY WHO GAVE YOU A TOUGH MATCH DURING THE ROOKIE GAMES?
DID HE?
DON'T PLAY DUMB...
HE WILL, WITHOUT A DOUBT, LEAD THE HYOTEI TEAM NEXT YEAR!
GOOD LUCK!
HYOTEI'S COACH HAD ONE HECK OF A TRUMP CARD UP HIS SLEEVE!

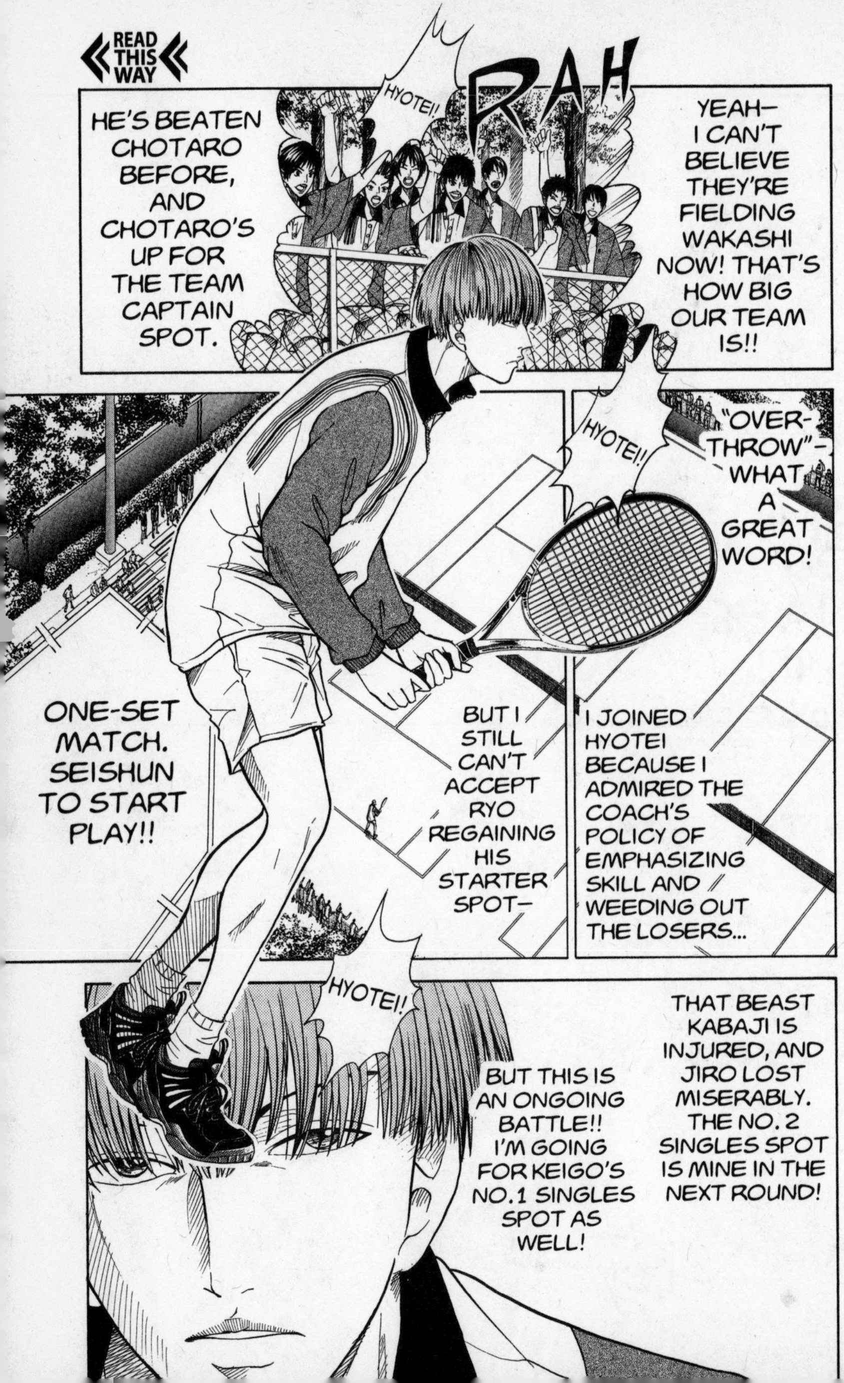
READ THIS WAY
YEAH— I CAN'T BELIEVE THEY'RE FIELDING WAKASHI NOW! THAT'S HOW BIG OUR TEAM IS!!
RAH
HYOTE!!
HE'S BEATEN CHOTARO BEFORE, AND CHOTARO'S UP FOR THE TEAM CAPTAIN SPOT.
"OVER-THROW"—WHAT A GREAT WORD!
HYOTE!!
I JOINED HYOTEI BECAUSE I ADMIRED THE COACH'S POLICY OF EMPHASIZING SKILL AND WEEDING OUT THE LOSERS...
BUT I STILL CAN'T ACCEPT RYO REGAINING HIS STARTER SPOT—
ONE-SET MATCH. SEISHUN TO START PLAY!!
THAT BEAST KABAJI IS INJURED, AND JIRO LOST MISERABLY. THE NO. 2 SINGLES SPOT IS MINE IN THE NEXT ROUND!
BUT THIS IS AN ONGOING BATTLE!! I'M GOING FOR KEIGO'S NO. 1 SINGLES SPOT AS WELL!
HYOTE!!

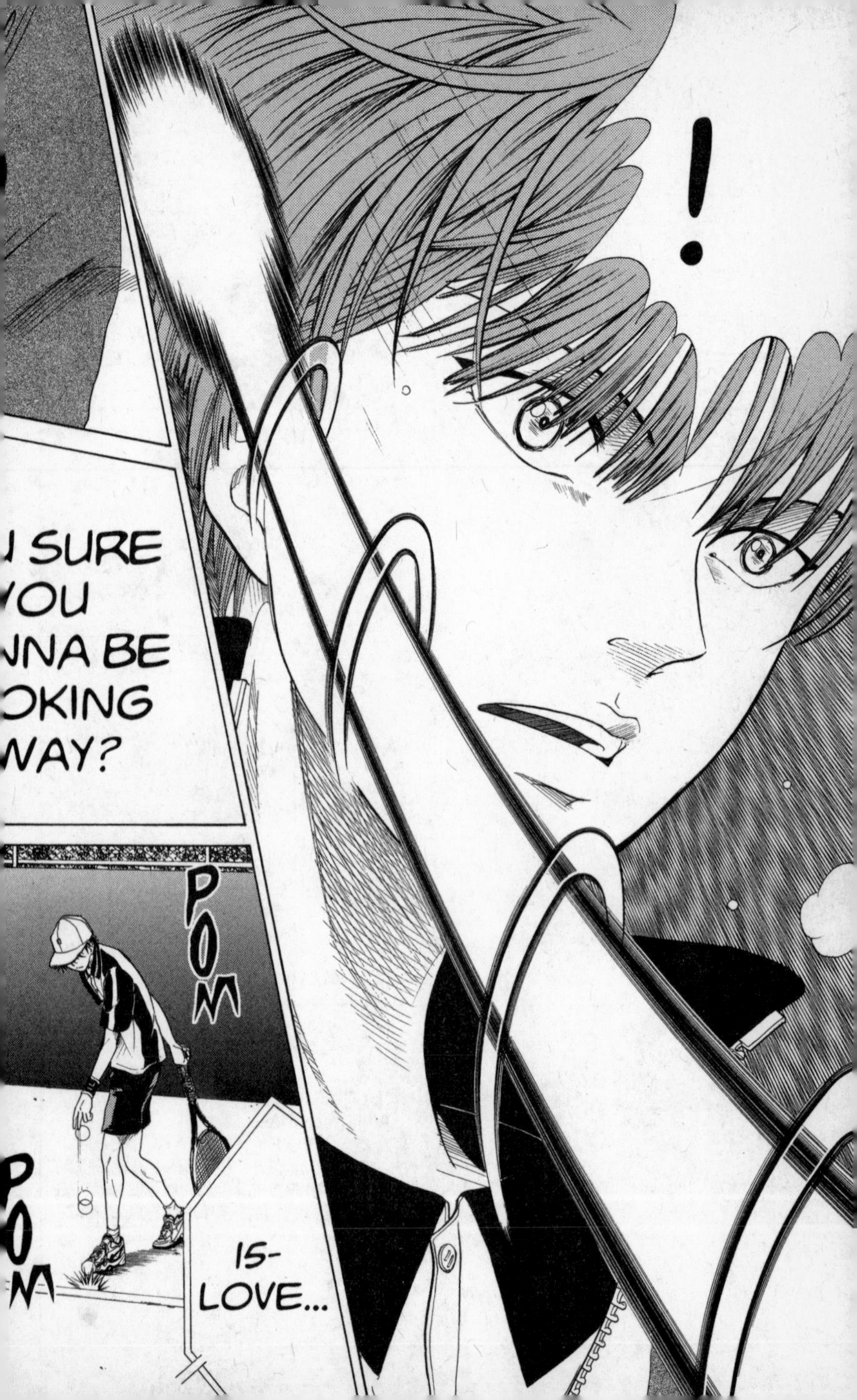
!
U SURE YOU NNA BE OKING WAY?
POM
POM
15-LOVE...

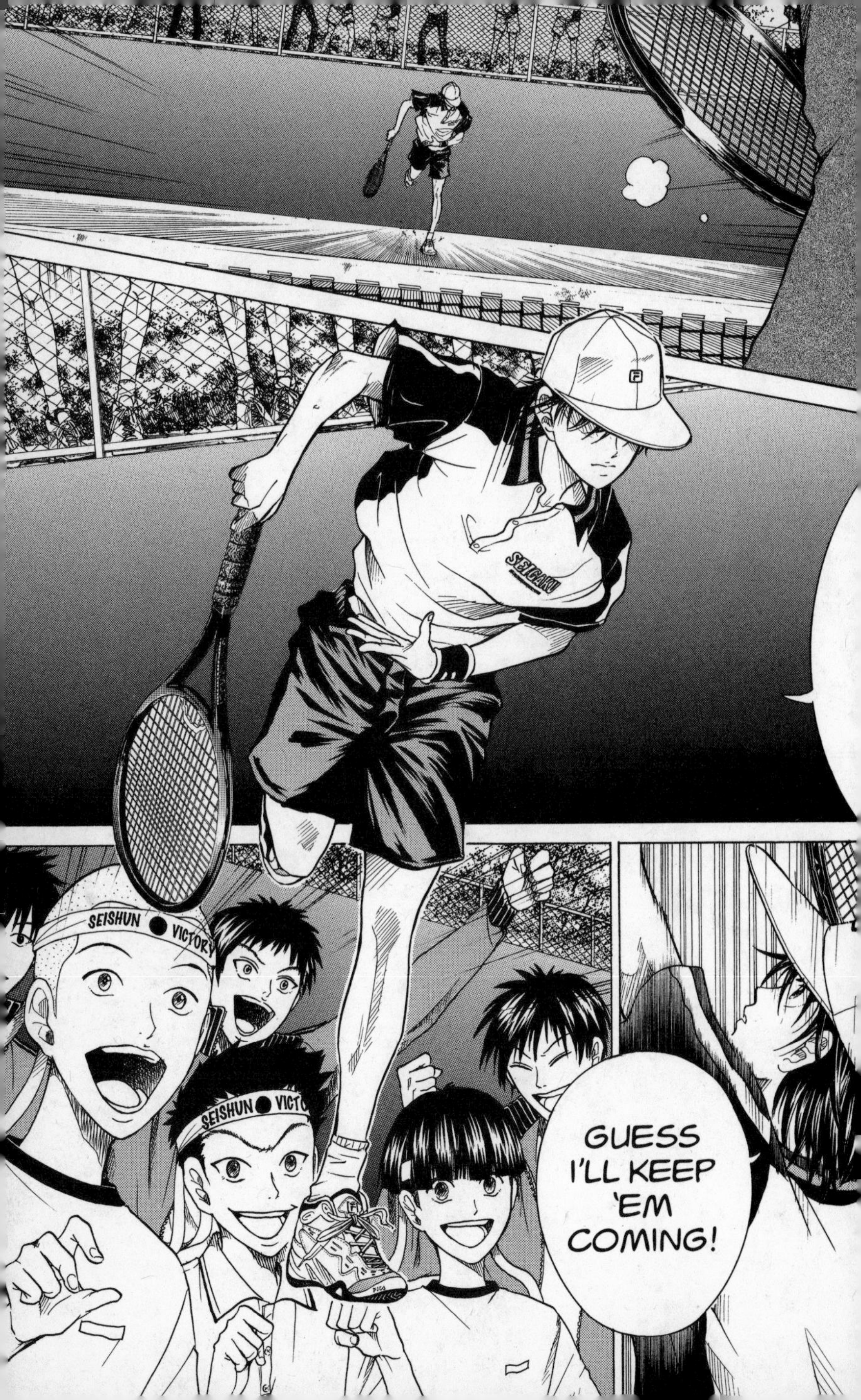
SEIGAKU
SEISHUN VICTORY
SEISHUN VICTORY
GUESS I'LL KEEP 'EM COMING!

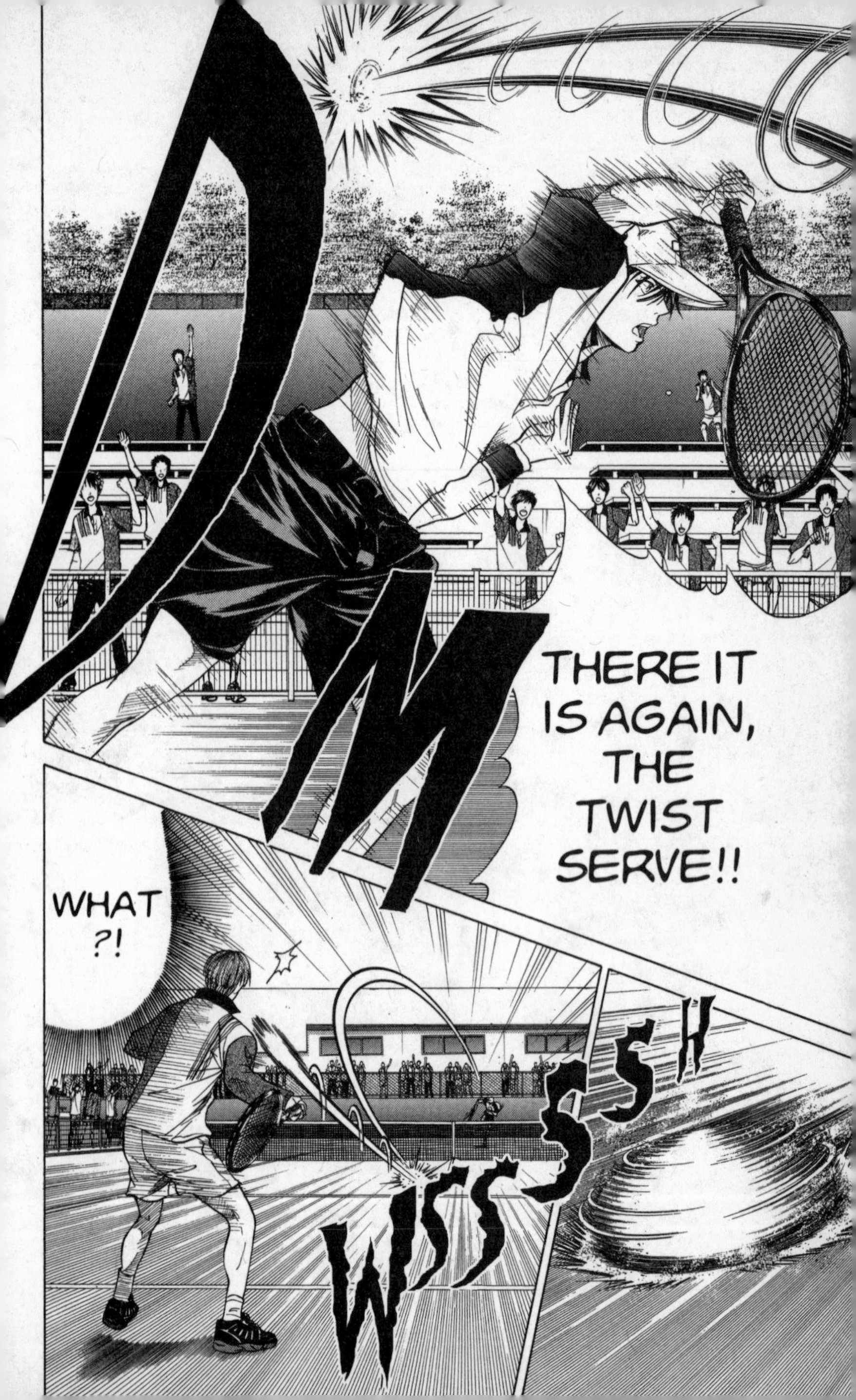
THERE IT IS AGAIN, THE TWIST SERVE!!
WHAT?!
WISSSSH

READ THIS WAY

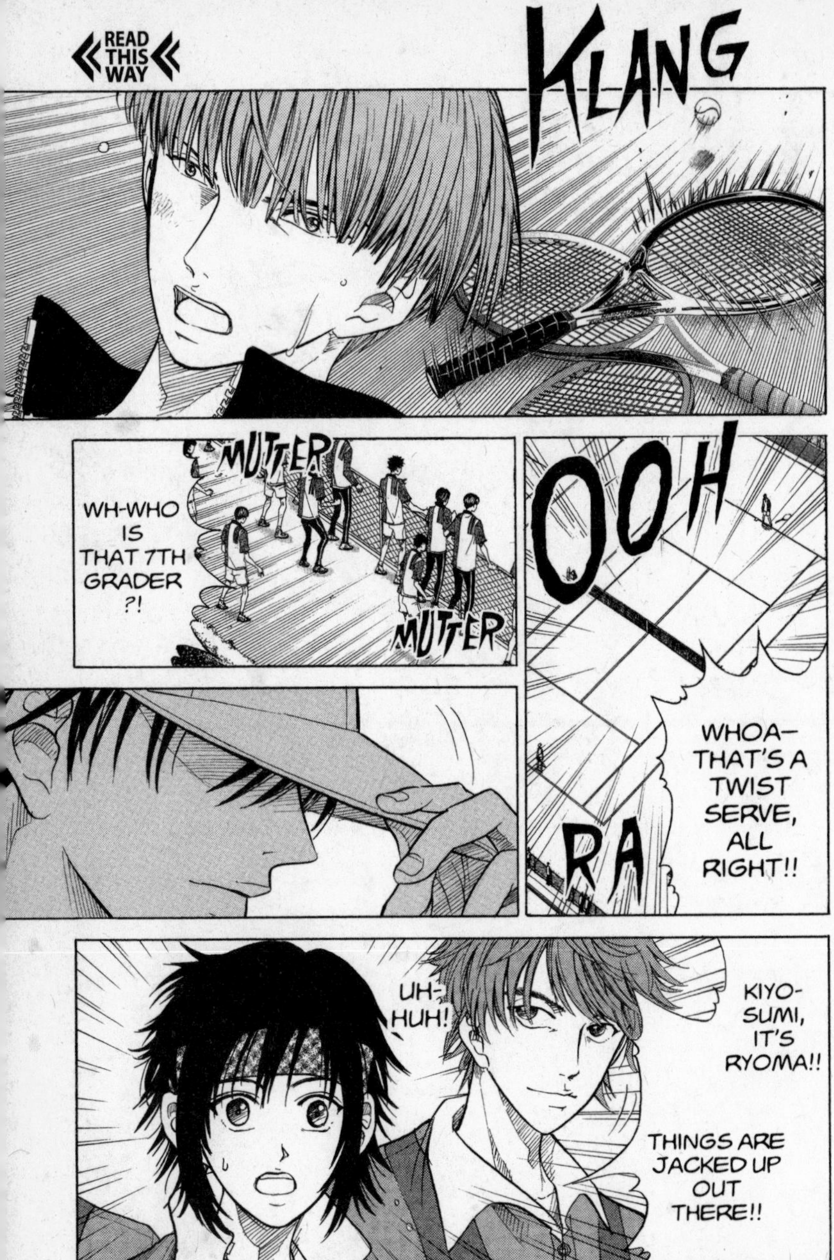

KLANG
OOH
RA
WHOA— THAT'S A TWIST SERVE, ALL RIGHT!!
MUTTER
WH-WHO IS THAT 7TH GRADER ?!
MUTTER
KIYO-SUMI, IT'S RYOMA!!
THINGS ARE JACKED UP OUT THERE!!
UH-HUH!

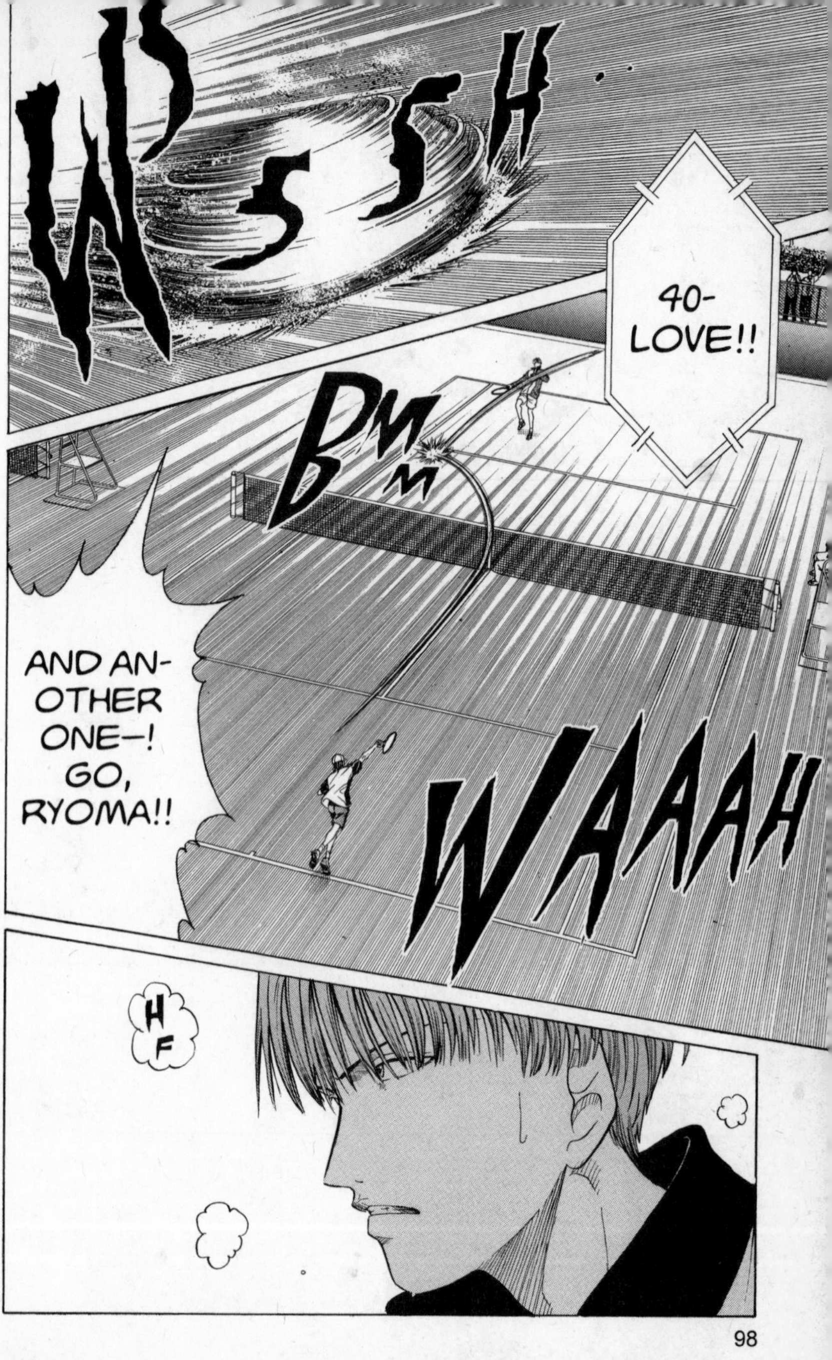

WSSH
40-LOVE!!
BMM
AND AN-OTHER ONE—! GO, RYOMA!!
WAAAH
HF

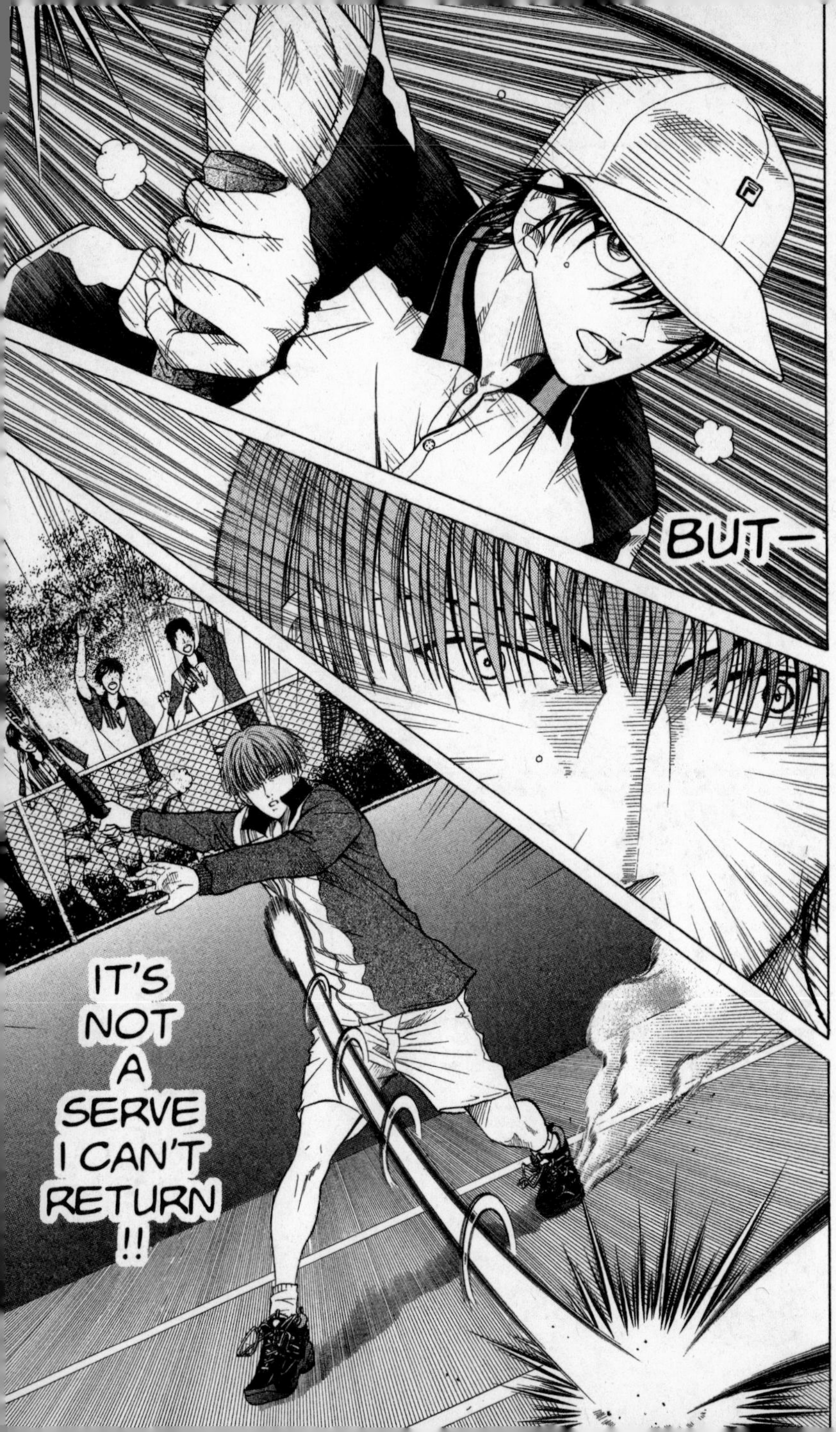
BUT—
IT'S NOT A SERVE I CAN'T RETURN!!

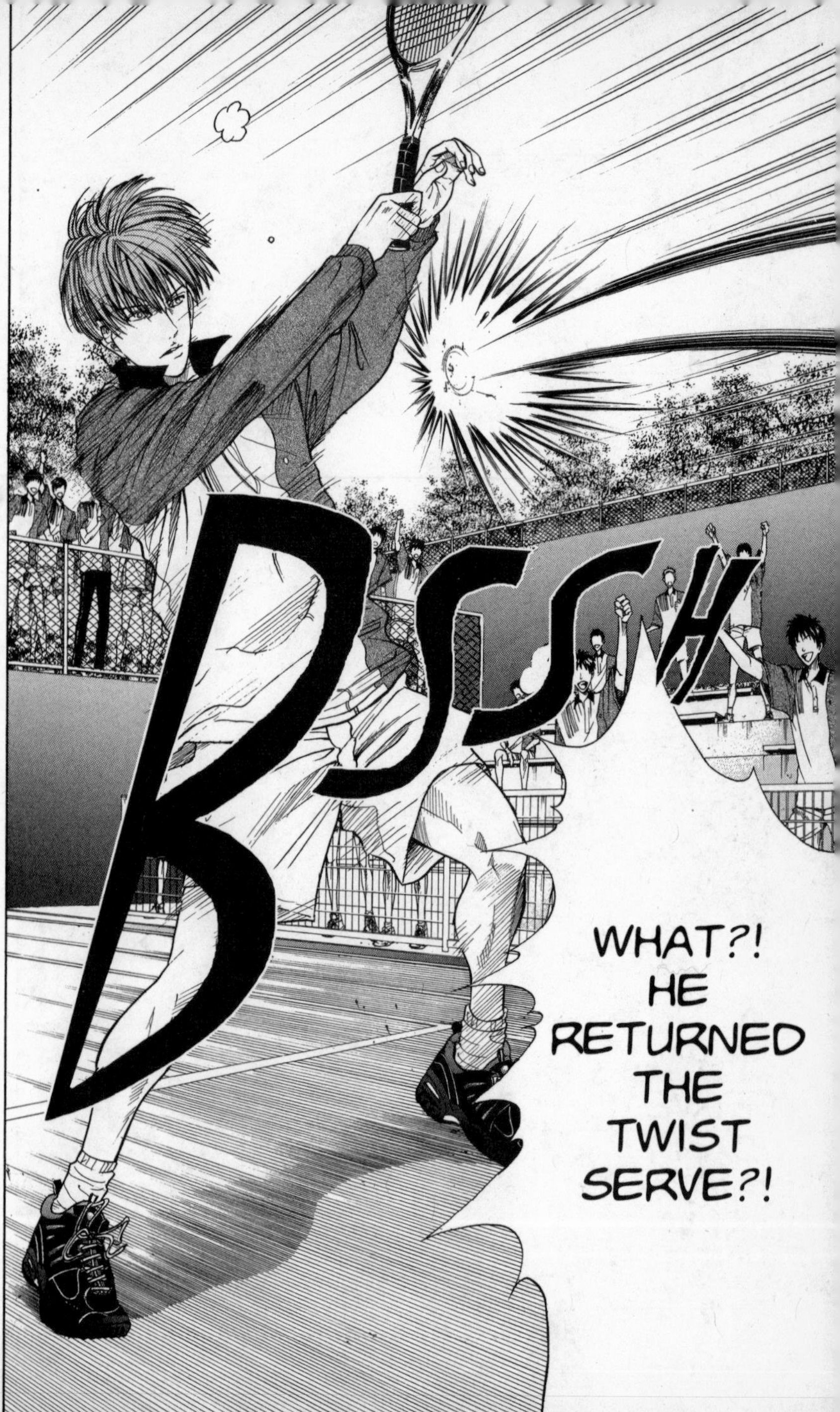
BSSH
WHAT?! HE RETURNED THE TWIST SERVE?!

READ THIS WAY

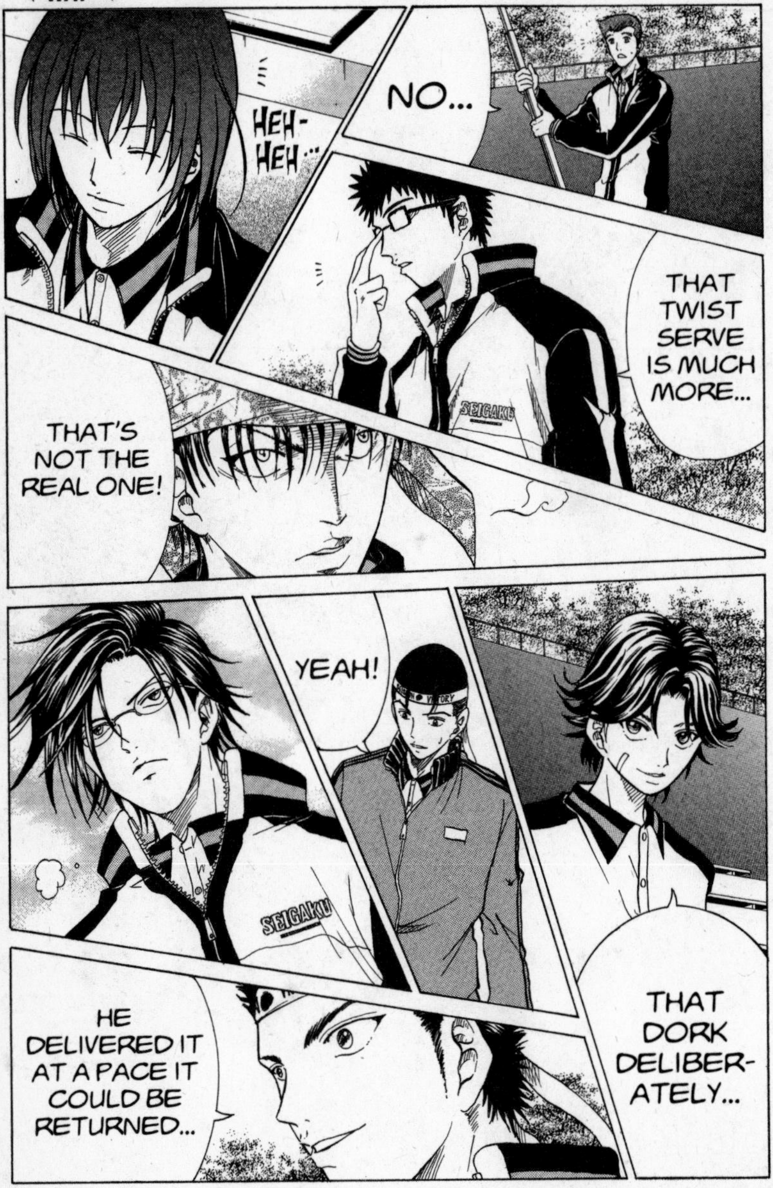
NO...
THAT TWIST SERVE IS MUCH MORE...
HEH-HEH...
THAT'S NOT THE REAL ONE!
THAT DORK DELIBER-ATELY...
YEAH!
HE DELIVERED IT AT A PACE IT COULD BE RETURNED...

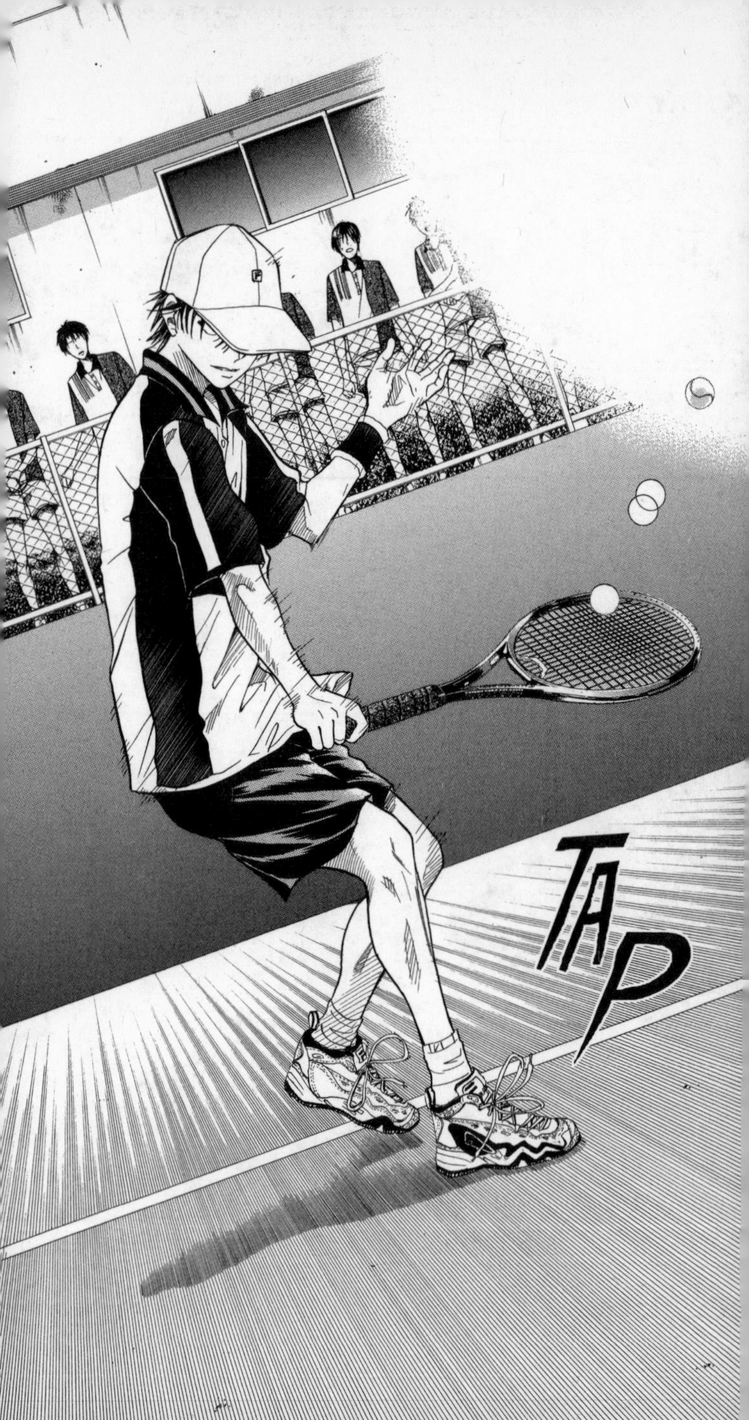
TAP

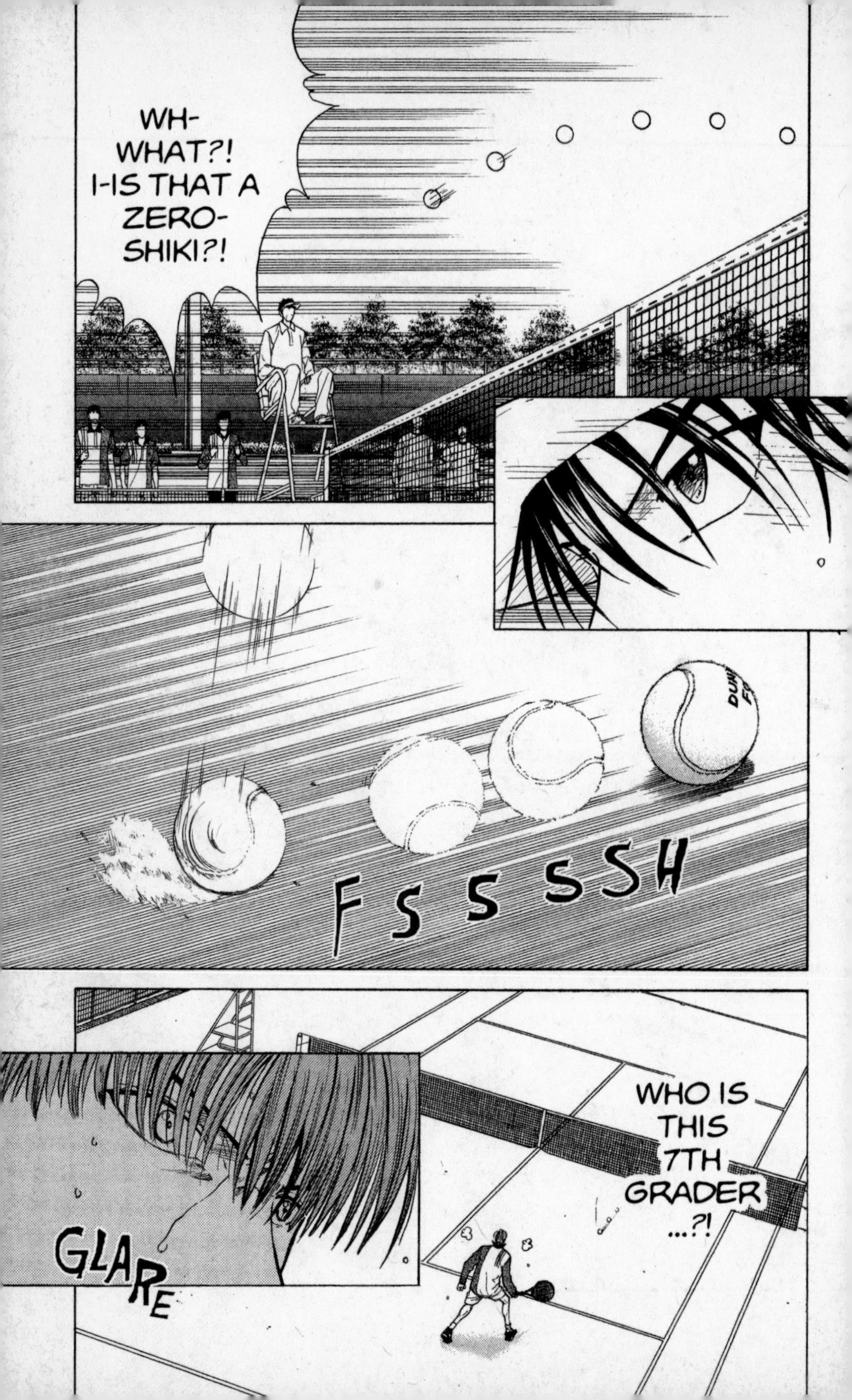
WH- WHAT?! I-IS THAT A ZERO-SHIKI?!
FSSSSH
WHO IS THIS 7TH GRADER ...?!
GLARE

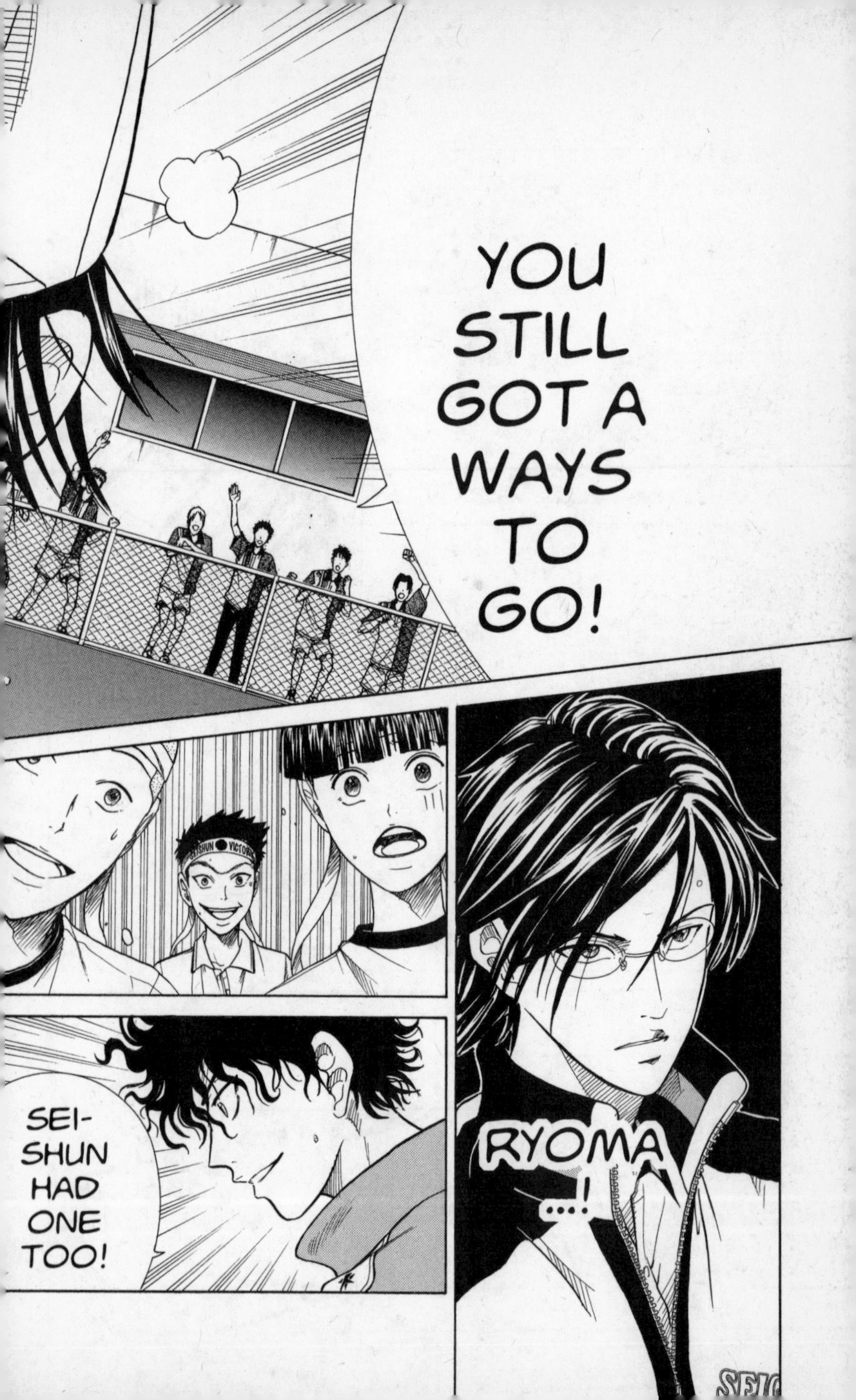
YOU STILL GOT A WAYS TO GO!
RYOMA ...!
SEI-SHUN HAD ONE TOO!

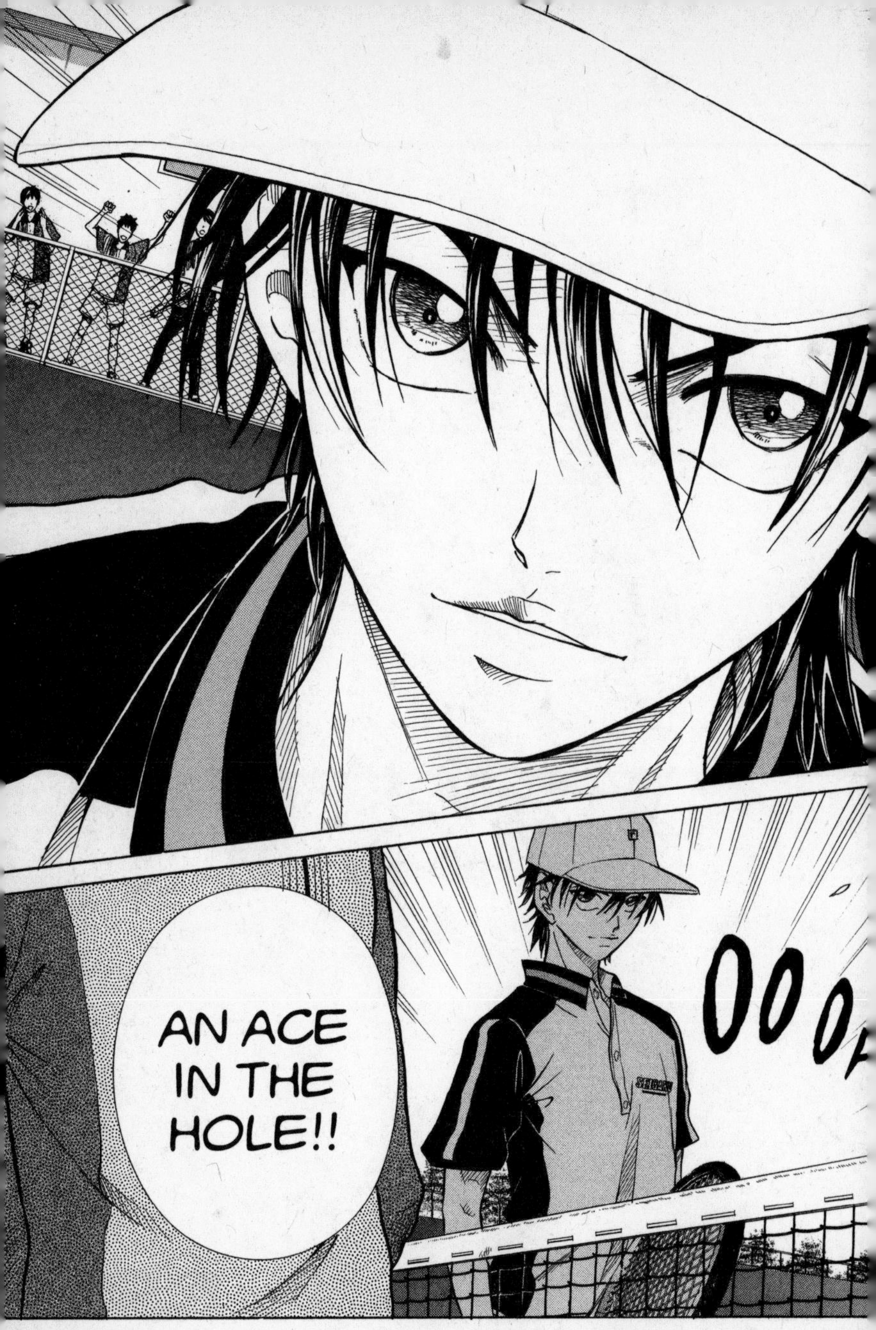
AN ACE IN THE HOLE!!

テニスの王子様

THE PRINCE OF TENNIS™

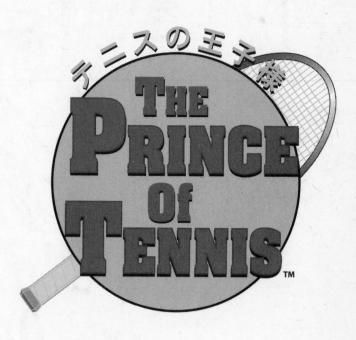

GENIUS 155: LOVE OVERTHROW

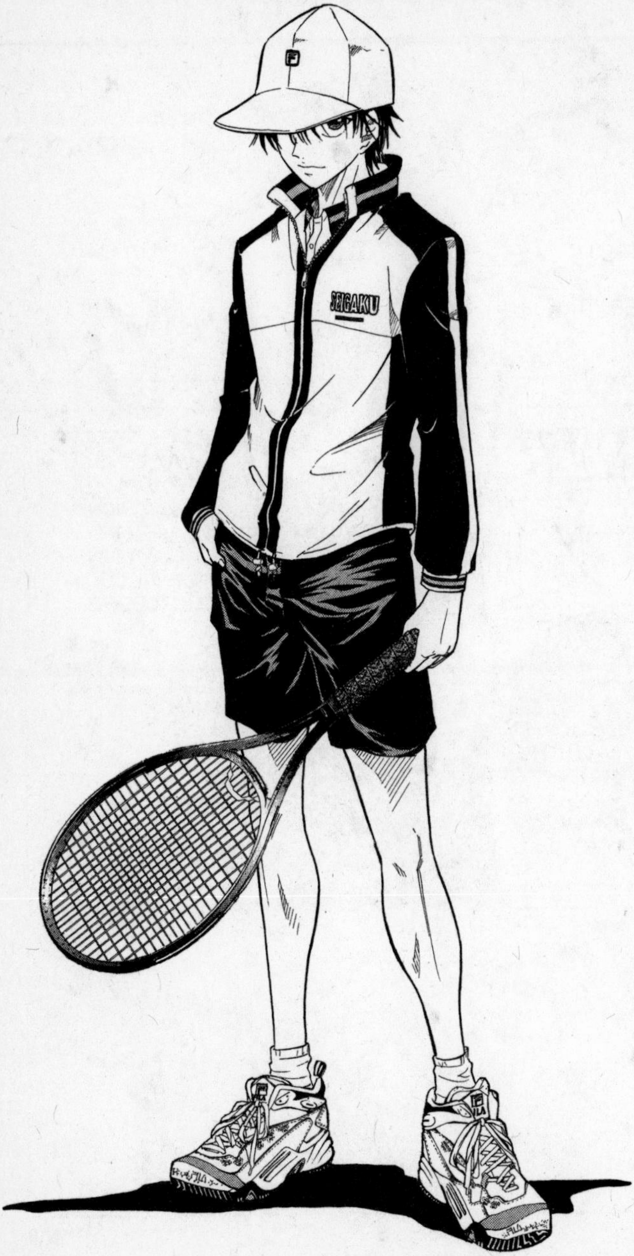
SEIGAKU

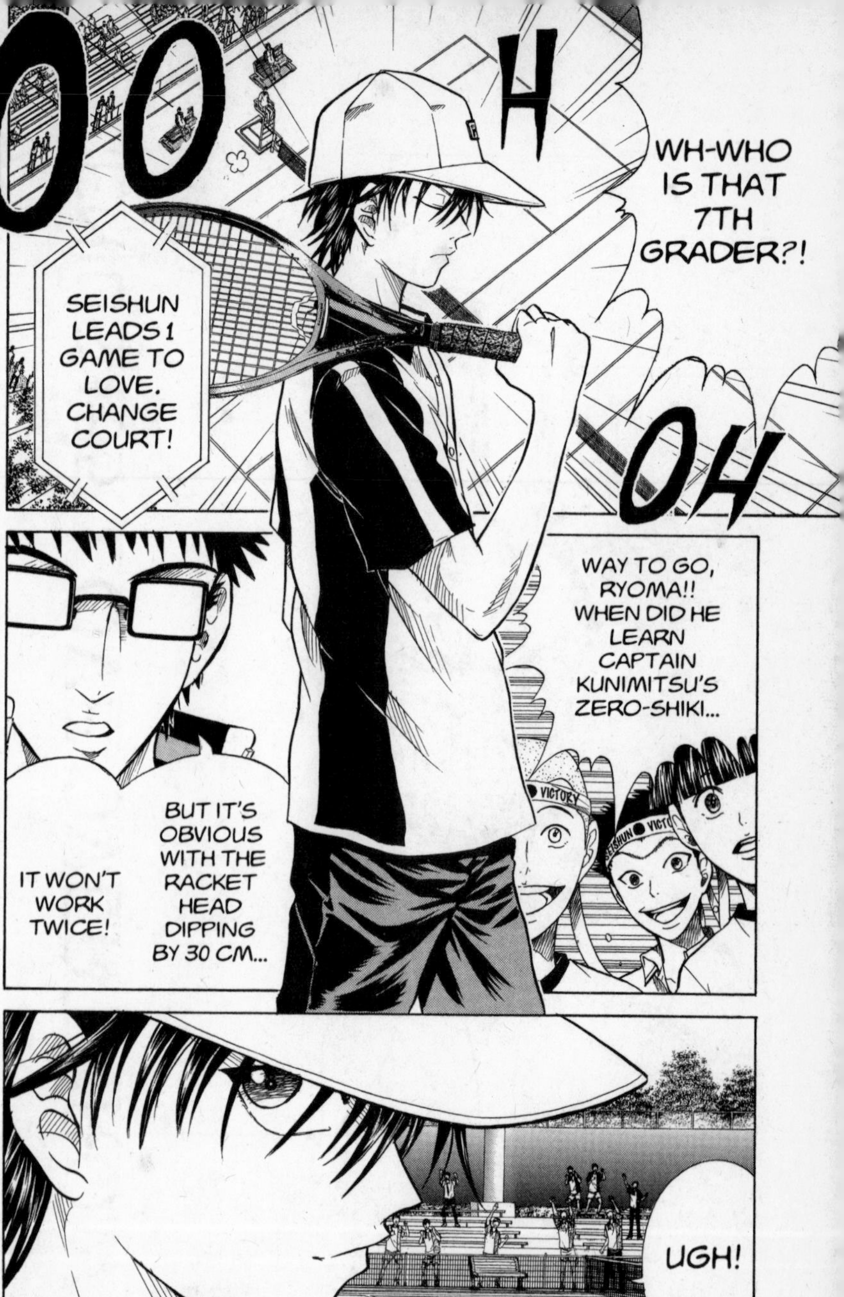
OOH
WH-WHO IS THAT 7TH GRADER?!
SEISHUN LEADS 1 GAME TO LOVE. CHANGE COURT!
OH
WAY TO GO, RYOMA!!
WHEN DID HE LEARN CAPTAIN KUNIMITSU'S ZERO-SHIKI...
VICTORY
SEISHUN VICTO
BUT IT'S OBVIOUS WITH THE RACKET HEAD DIPPING BY 30 CM...
IT WON'T WORK TWICE!
UGH!

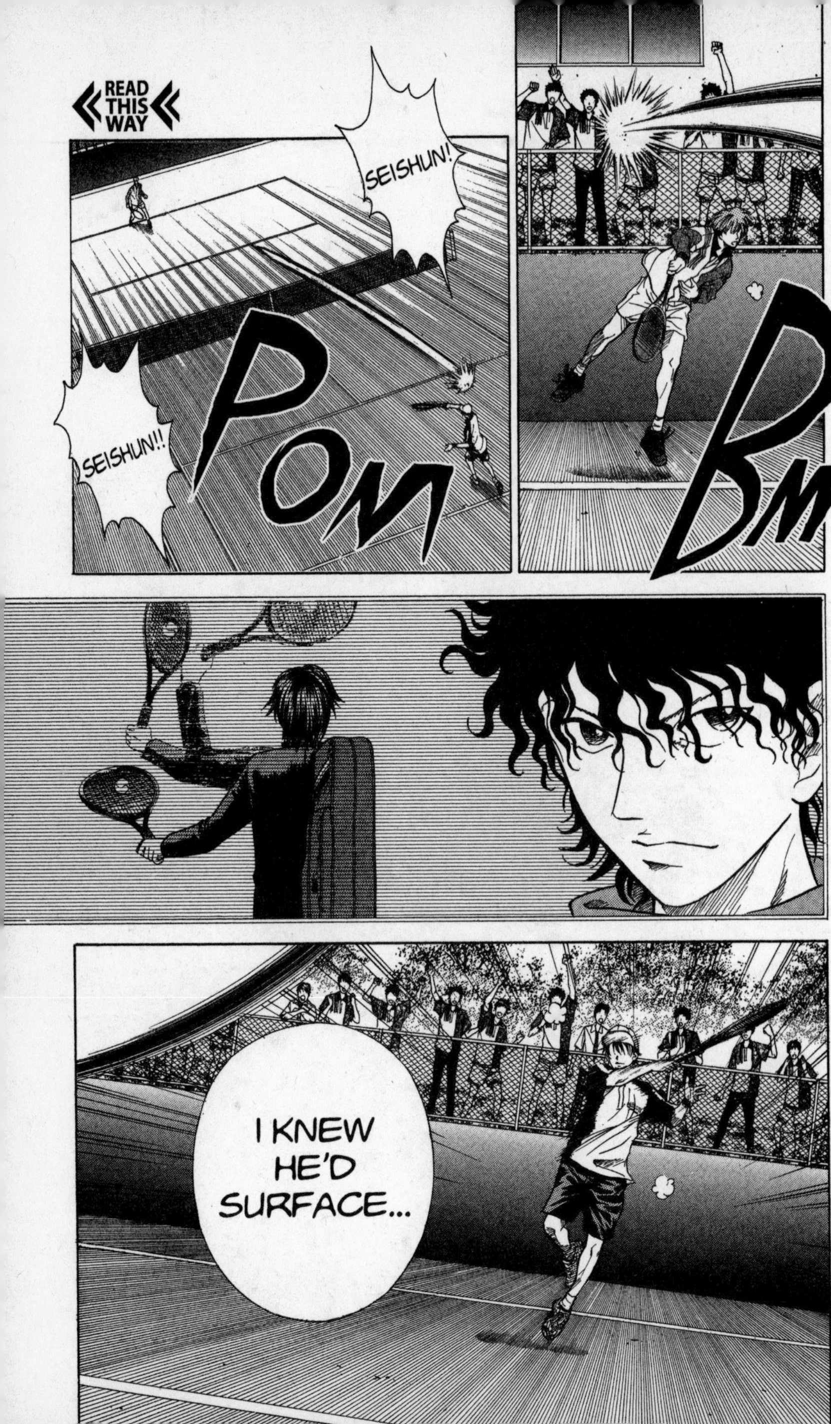
READ THIS WAY
BM
SEISHUN!
POM
SEISHUN!!
I KNEW HE'D SURFACE...

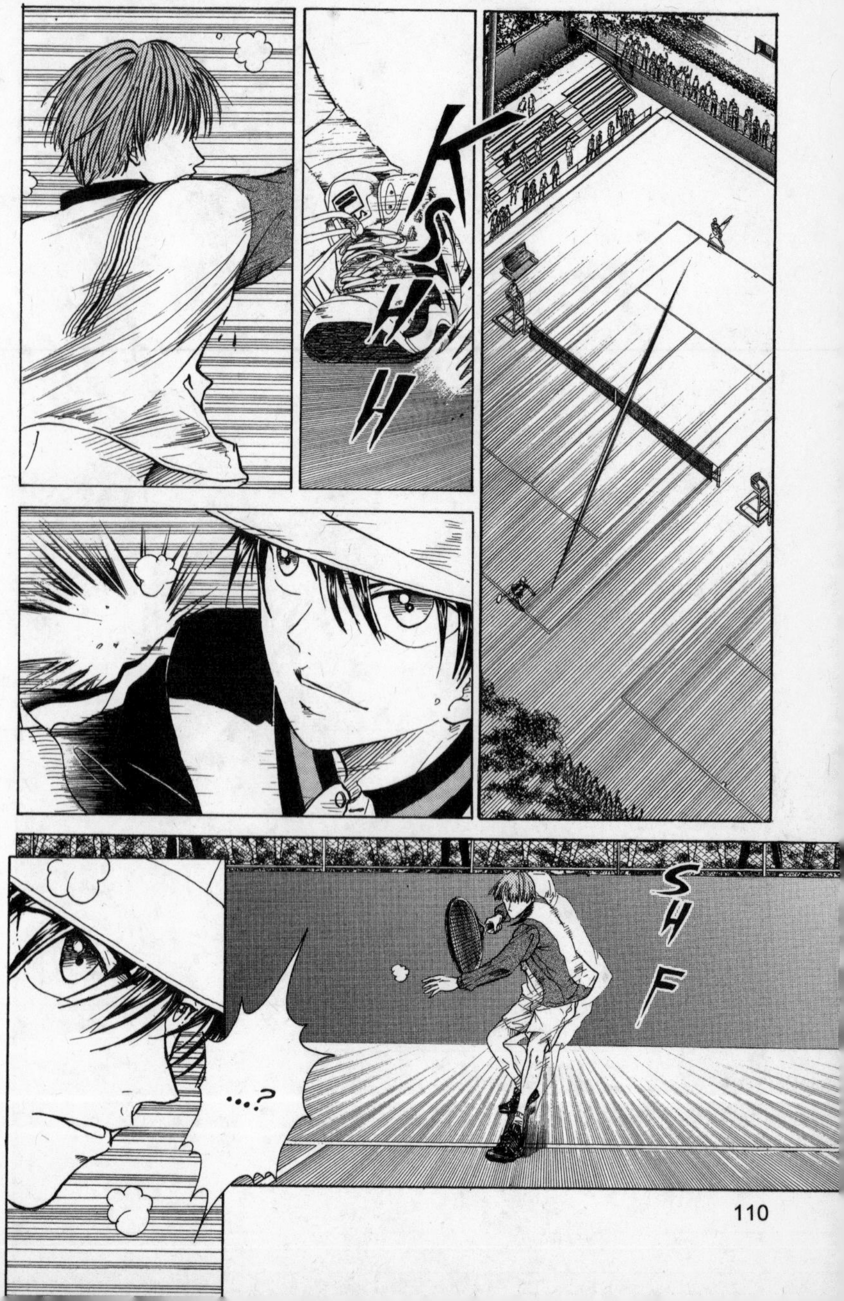
KSHHH
SHF
...?

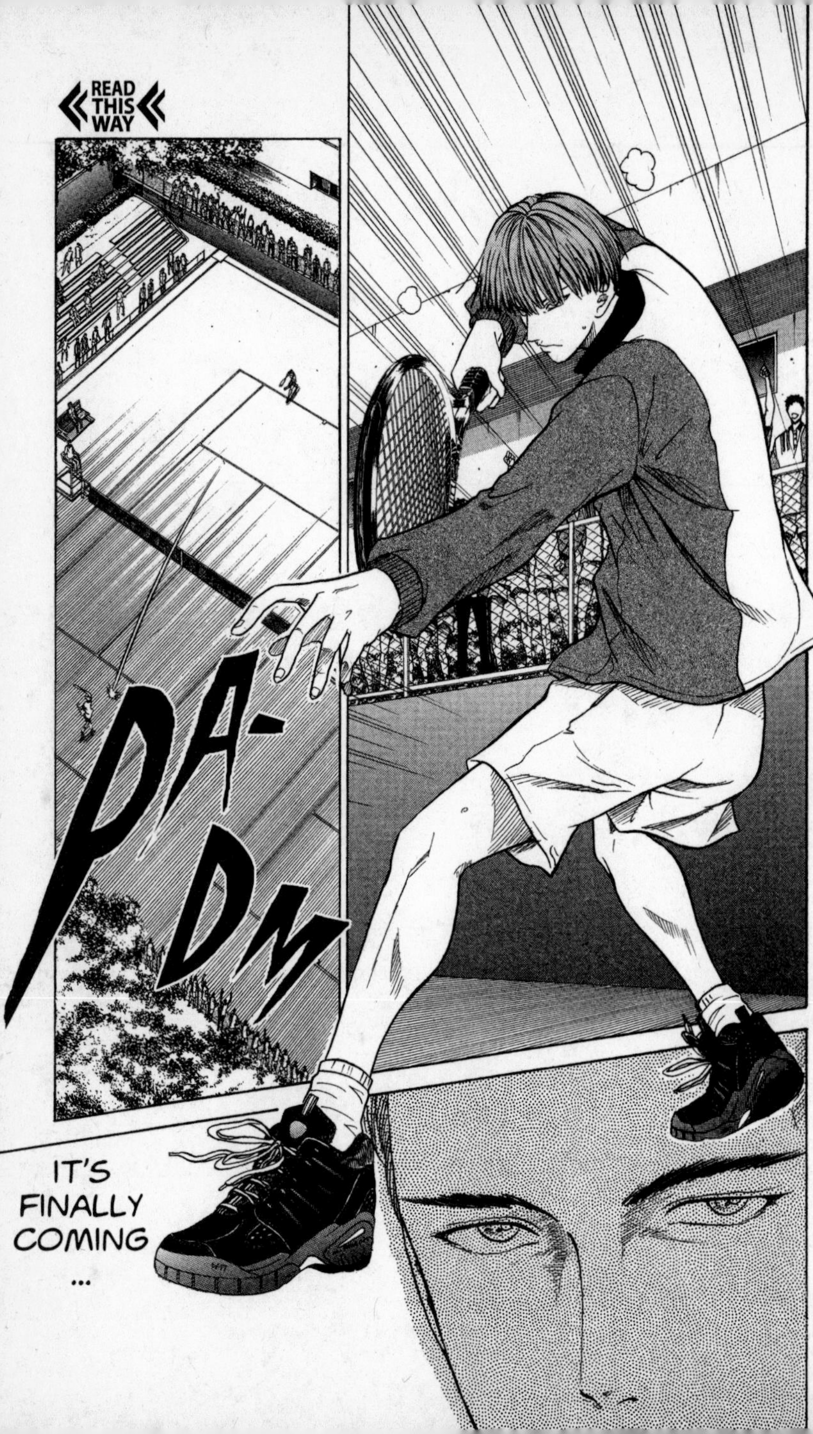
READ THIS WAY
DA-DM
IT'S FINALLY COMING ...

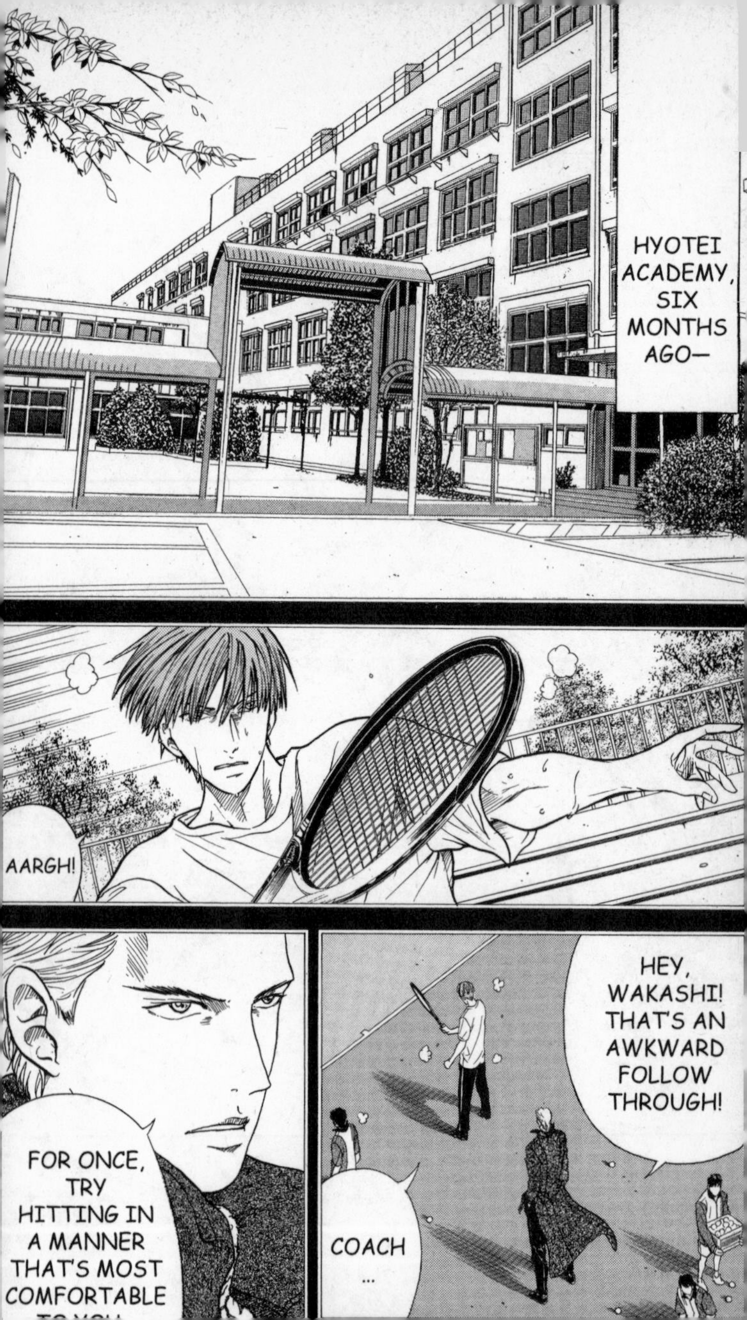
HYOTEI ACADEMY, SIX MONTHS AGO—
AARGH!
HEY, WAKASHI! THAT'S AN AWKWARD FOLLOW THROUGH!
COACH ...
FOR ONCE, TRY HITTING IN A MANNER THAT'S MOST COMFORTABLE

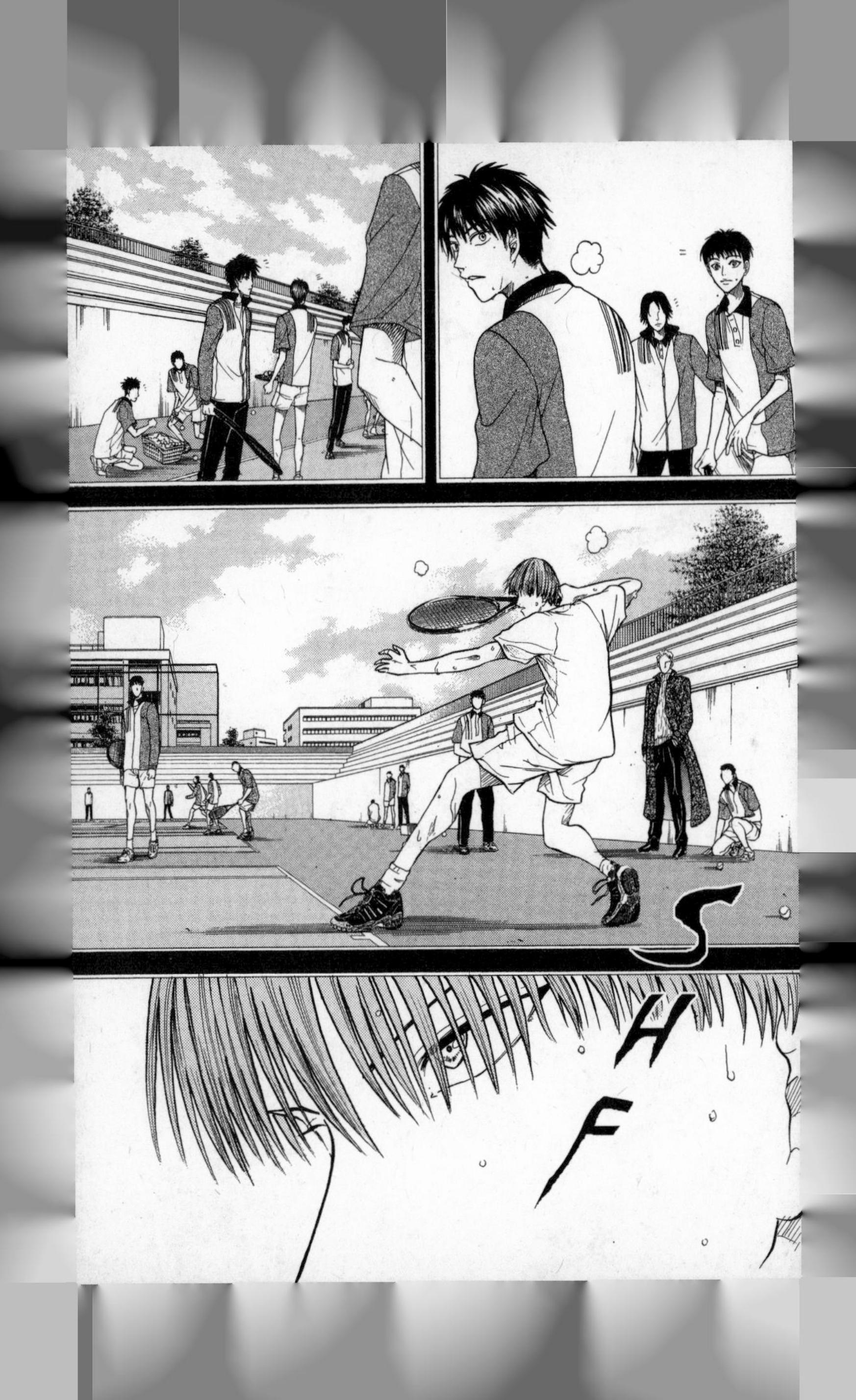
SHF

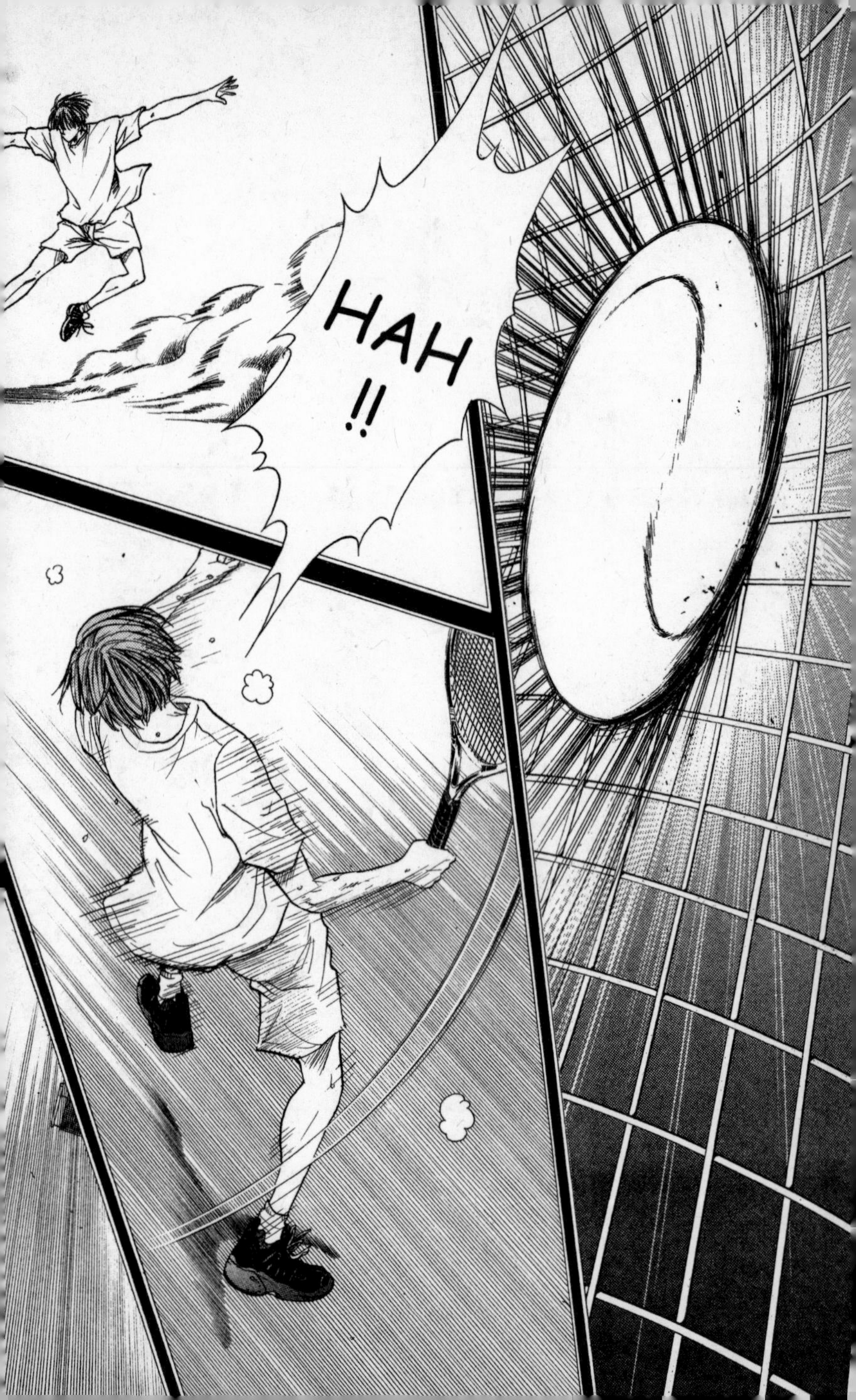
HAH !!

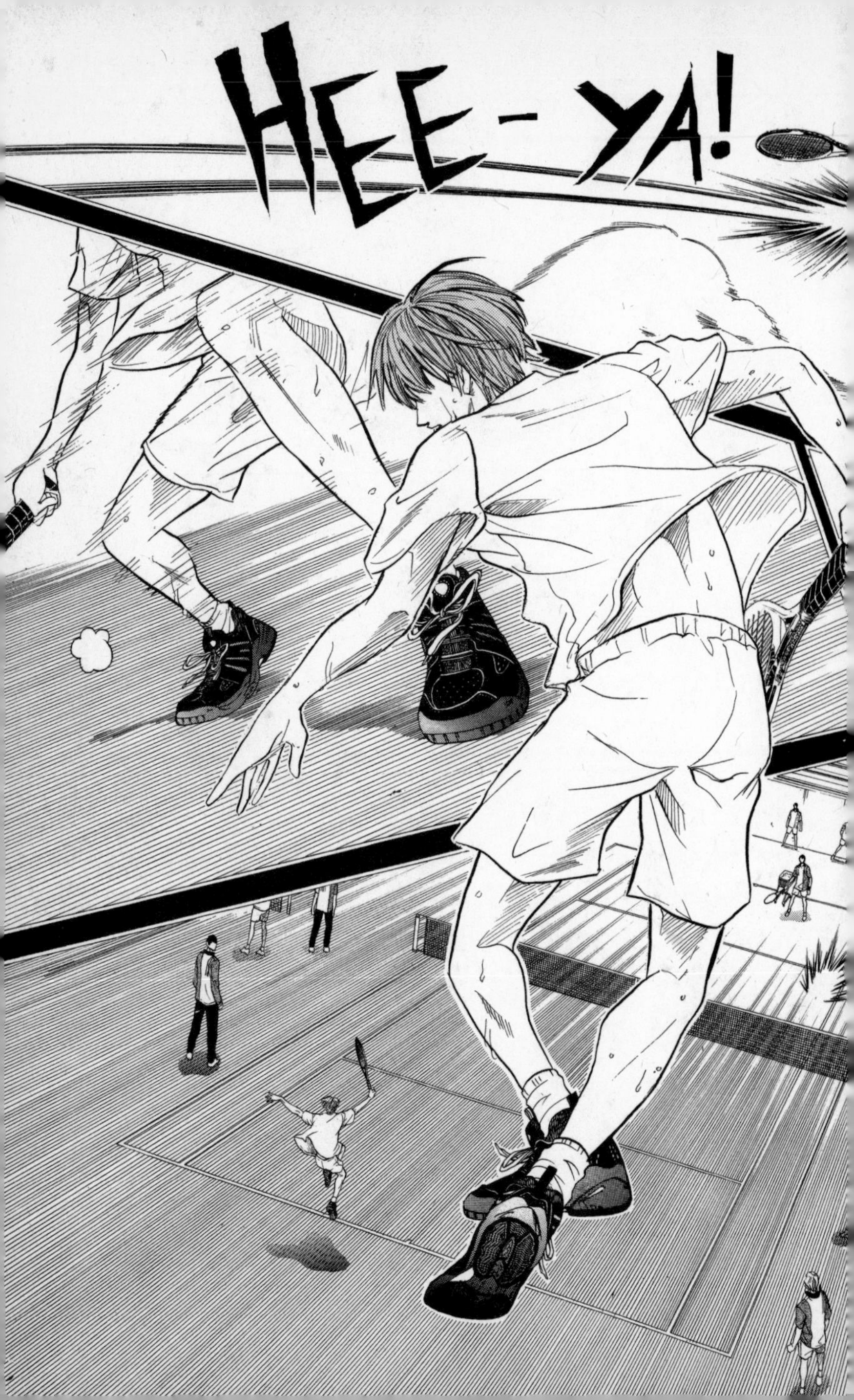
HEE-YA!

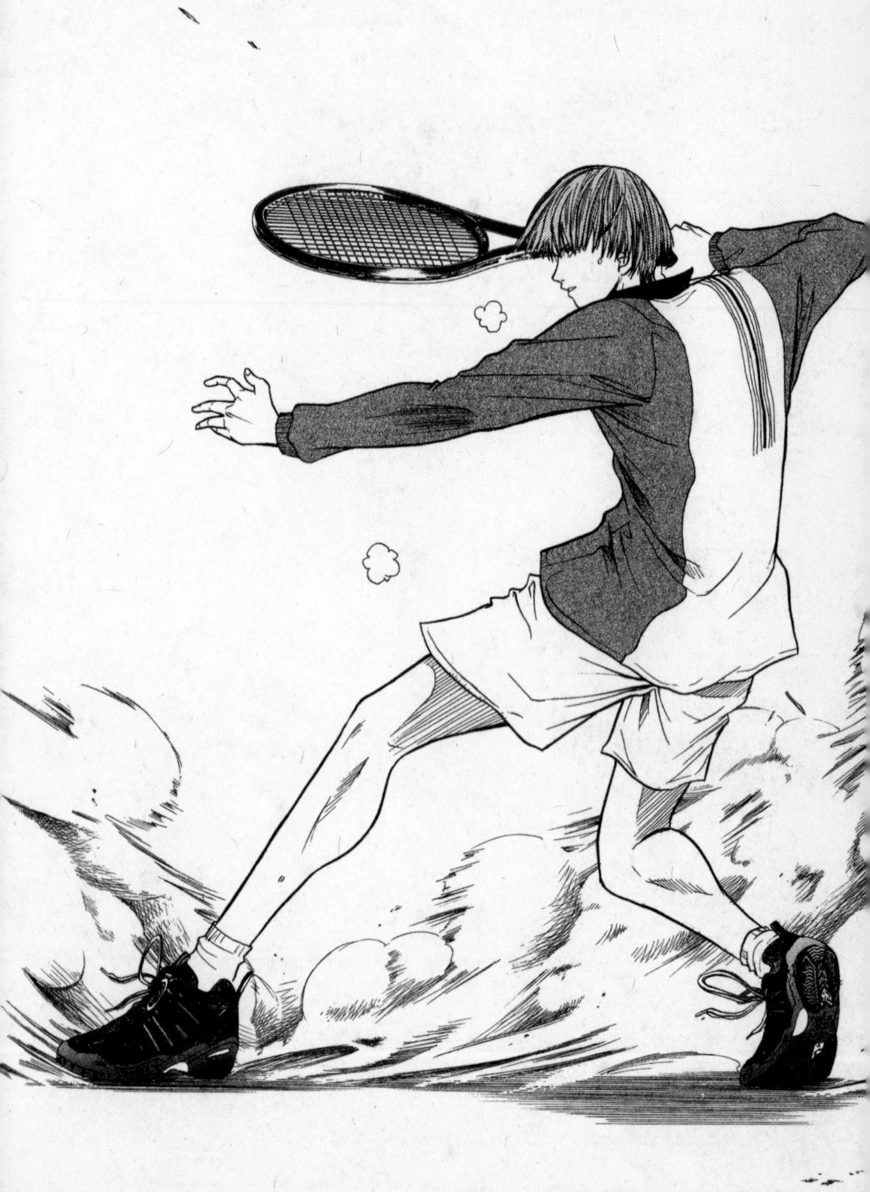

READ THIS WAY

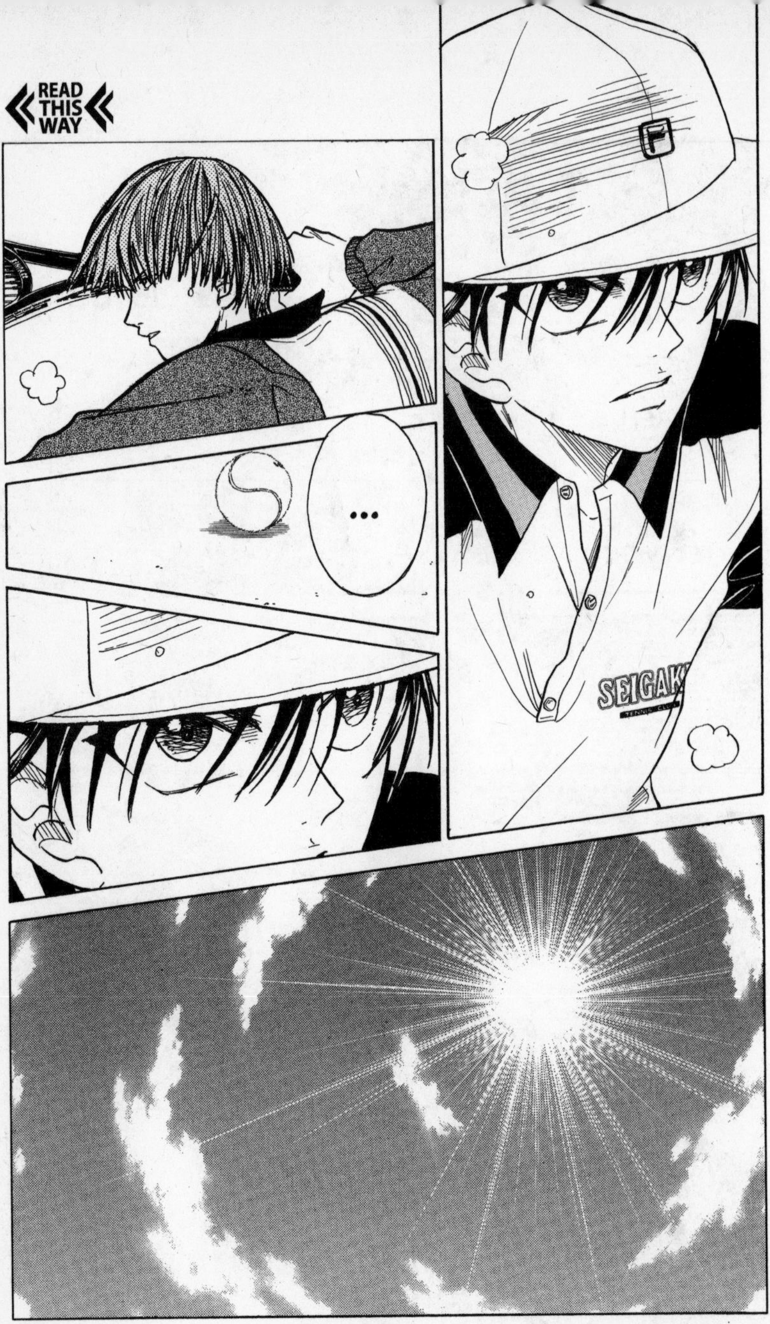
...

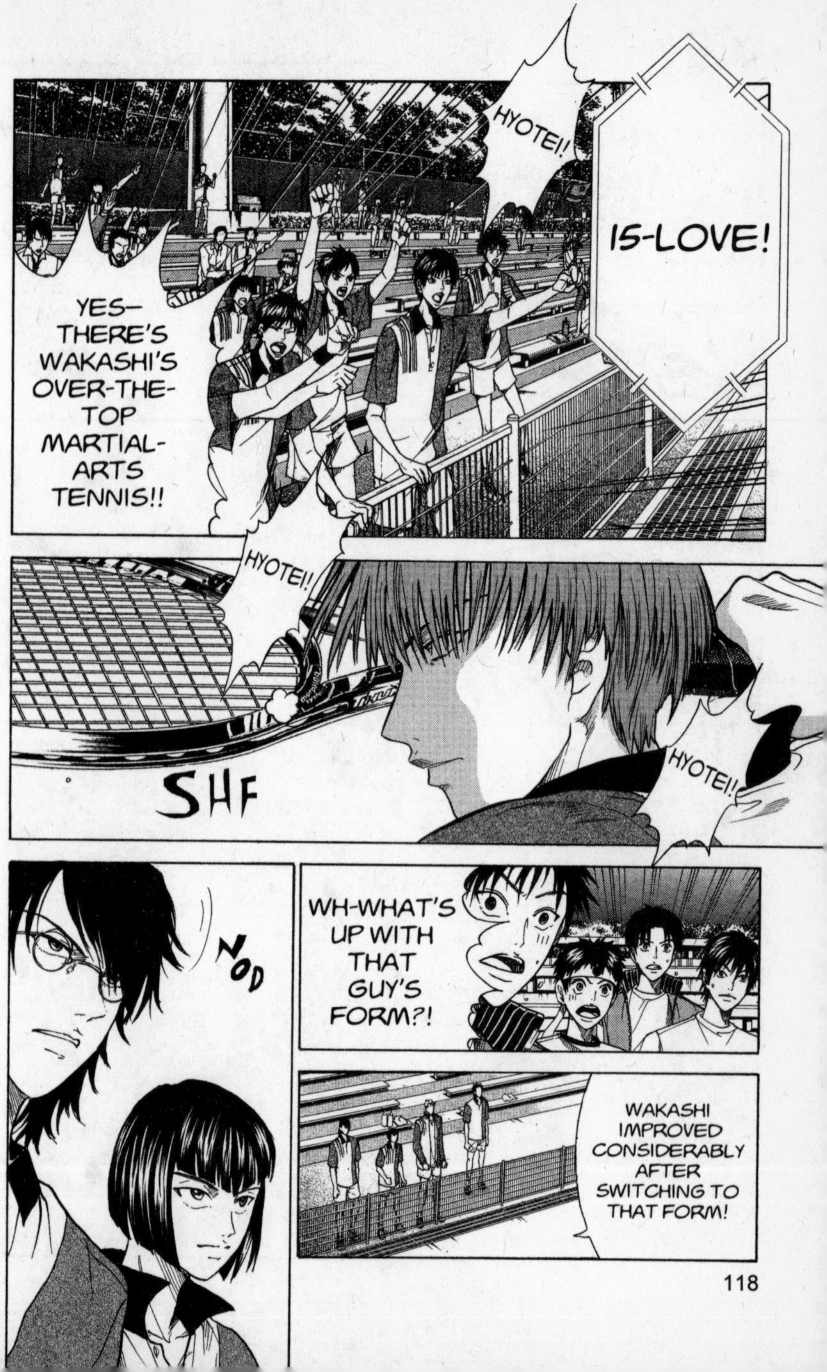
15-LOVE!
HYOTEI!!
YES— THERE'S WAKASHI'S OVER-THE-TOP MARTIAL-ARTS TENNIS!!
HYOTEI!!
HYOTEI!!
SHF
WH-WHAT'S UP WITH THAT GUY'S FORM?!
WAKASHI IMPROVED CONSIDERABLY AFTER SWITCHING TO THAT FORM!
NOD

READ THIS WAY

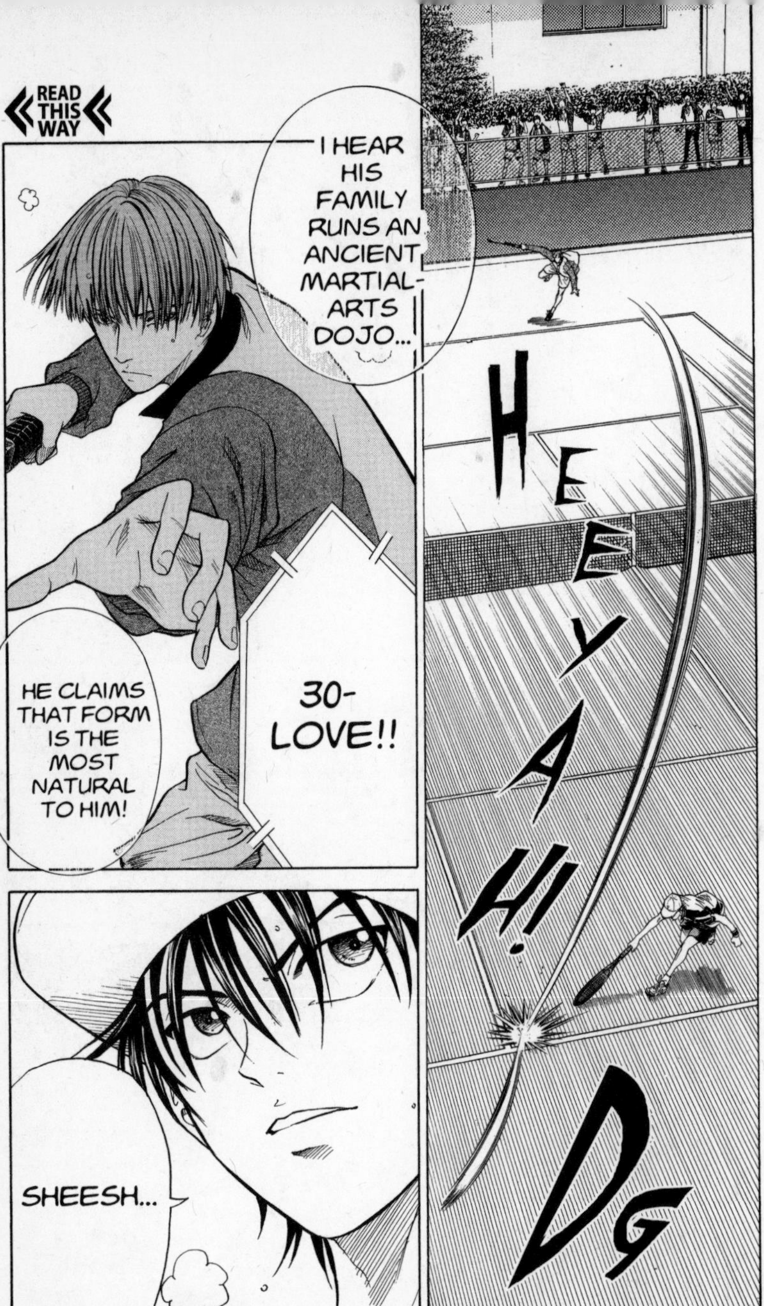
HEYAAH!!
Dg
I HEAR HIS FAMILY RUNS AN ANCIENT MARTIAL-ARTS DOJO...
30-LOVE!!
HE CLAIMS THAT FORM IS THE MOST NATURAL TO HIM!
SHEESH...

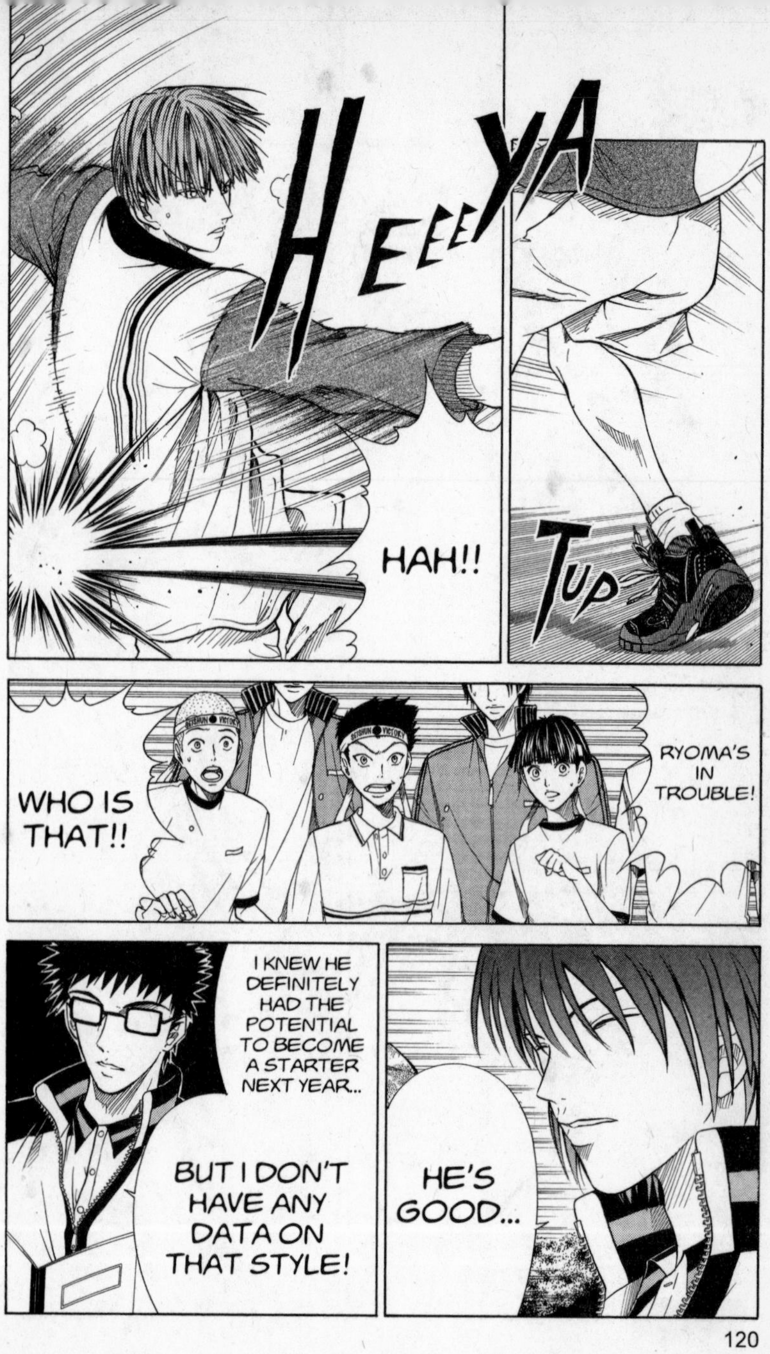
TUP
HEEEYA
HAH!!
RYOMA'S IN TROUBLE!
WHO IS THAT!!
HE'S GOOD...
I KNEW HE DEFINITELY HAD THE POTENTIAL TO BECOME A STARTER NEXT YEAR...
BUT I DON'T HAVE ANY DATA ON THAT STYLE!

READ THIS WAY

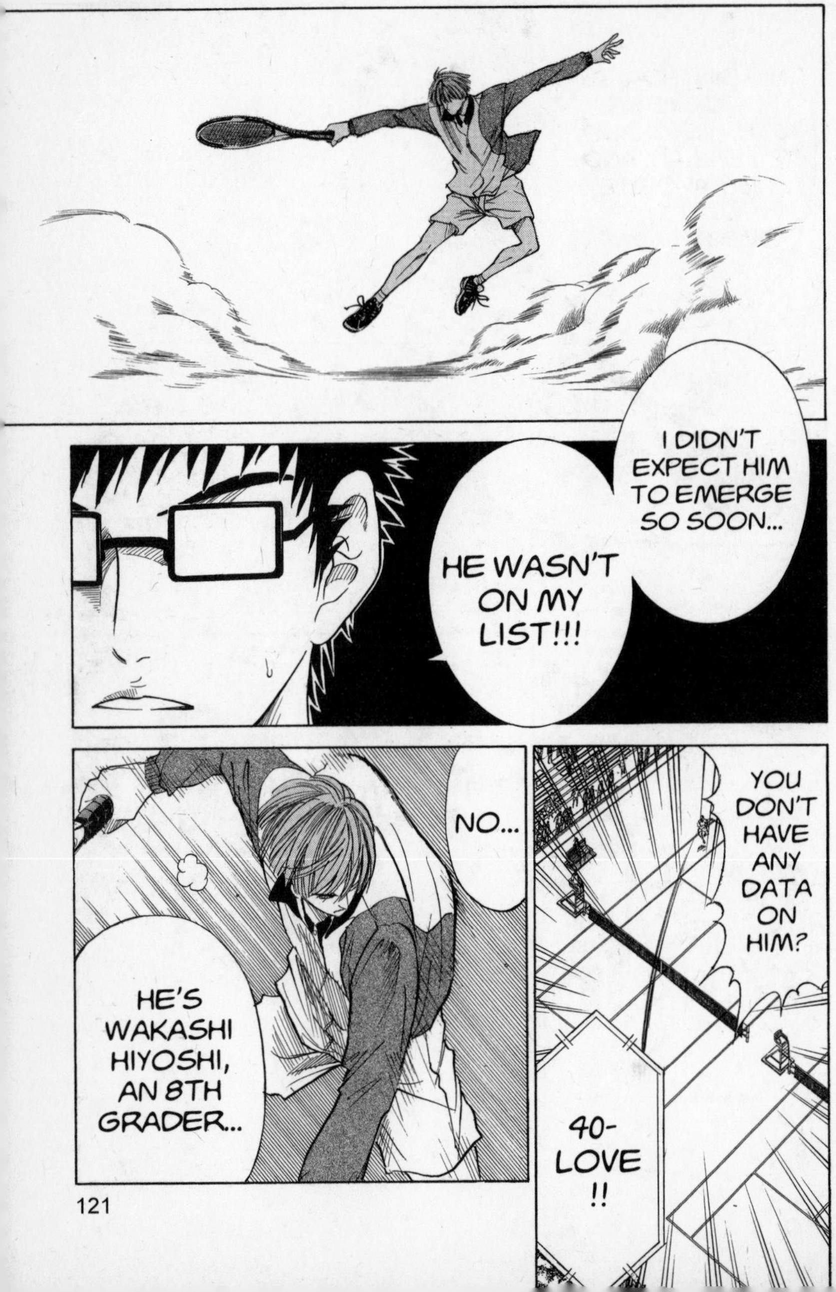

I DIDN'T EXPECT HIM TO EMERGE SO SOON...
HE WASN'T ON MY LIST!!!
YOU DON'T HAVE ANY DATA ON HIM?
40-LOVE !!
NO...
HE'S WAKASHI HIYOSHI, AN 8TH GRADER...

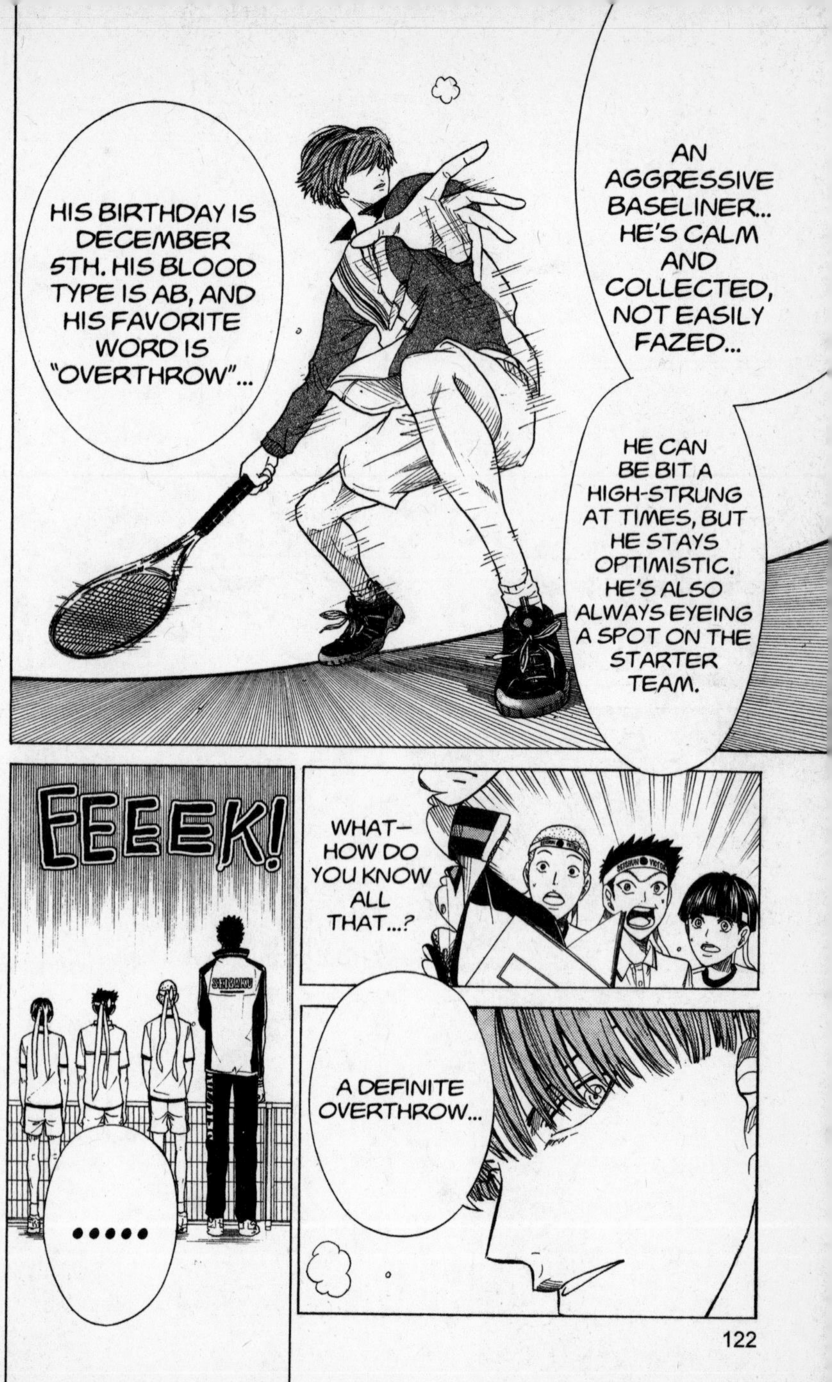
AN AGGRESSIVE BASELINER... HE'S CALM AND COLLECTED, NOT EASILY FAZED...
HE CAN BE BIT A HIGH-STRUNG AT TIMES, BUT HE STAYS OPTIMISTIC. HE'S ALSO ALWAYS EYEING A SPOT ON THE STARTER TEAM.
HIS BIRTHDAY IS DECEMBER 5TH. HIS BLOOD TYPE IS AB, AND HIS FAVORITE WORD IS "OVERTHROW"...
WHAT— HOW DO YOU KNOW ALL THAT...?
A DEFINITE OVERTHROW...
EEEEK!
.....

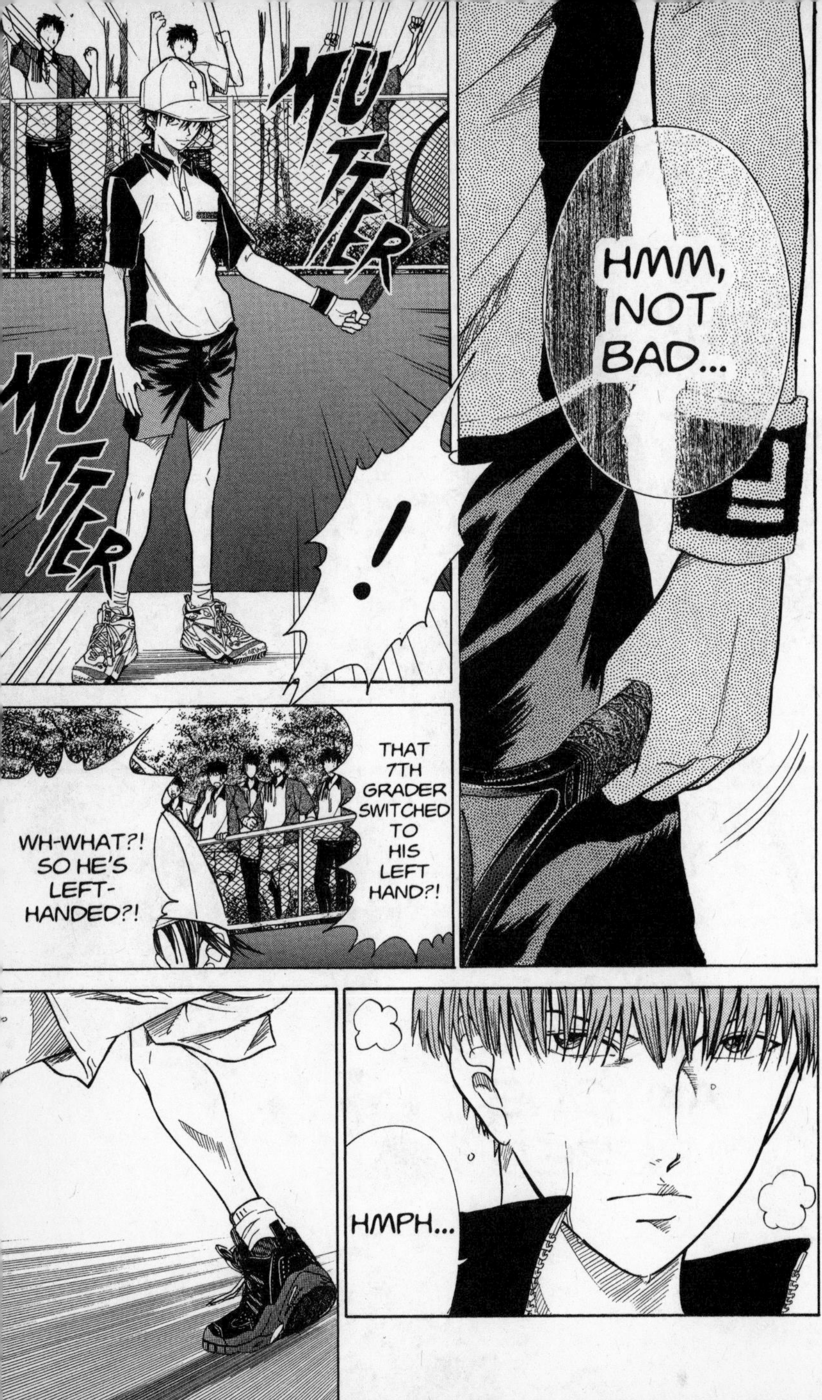
HMM, NOT BAD...
MUTTER
MUTTER
!
THAT 7TH GRADER SWITCHED TO HIS LEFT HAND?!
WH-WHAT?! SO HE'S LEFT-HANDED?!
HMPH...

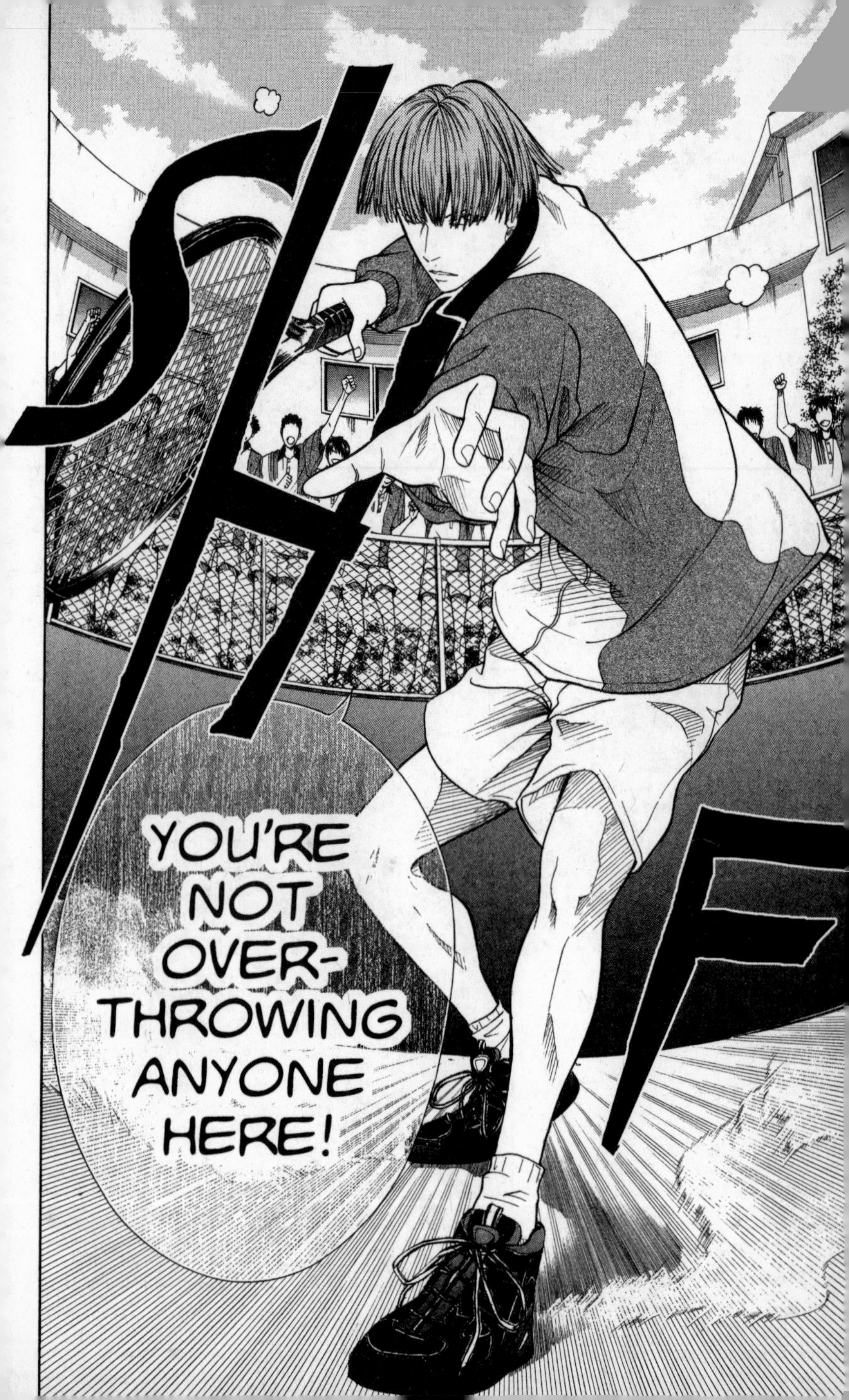
SHF
YOU'RE NOT OVER-THROWING ANYONE HERE!

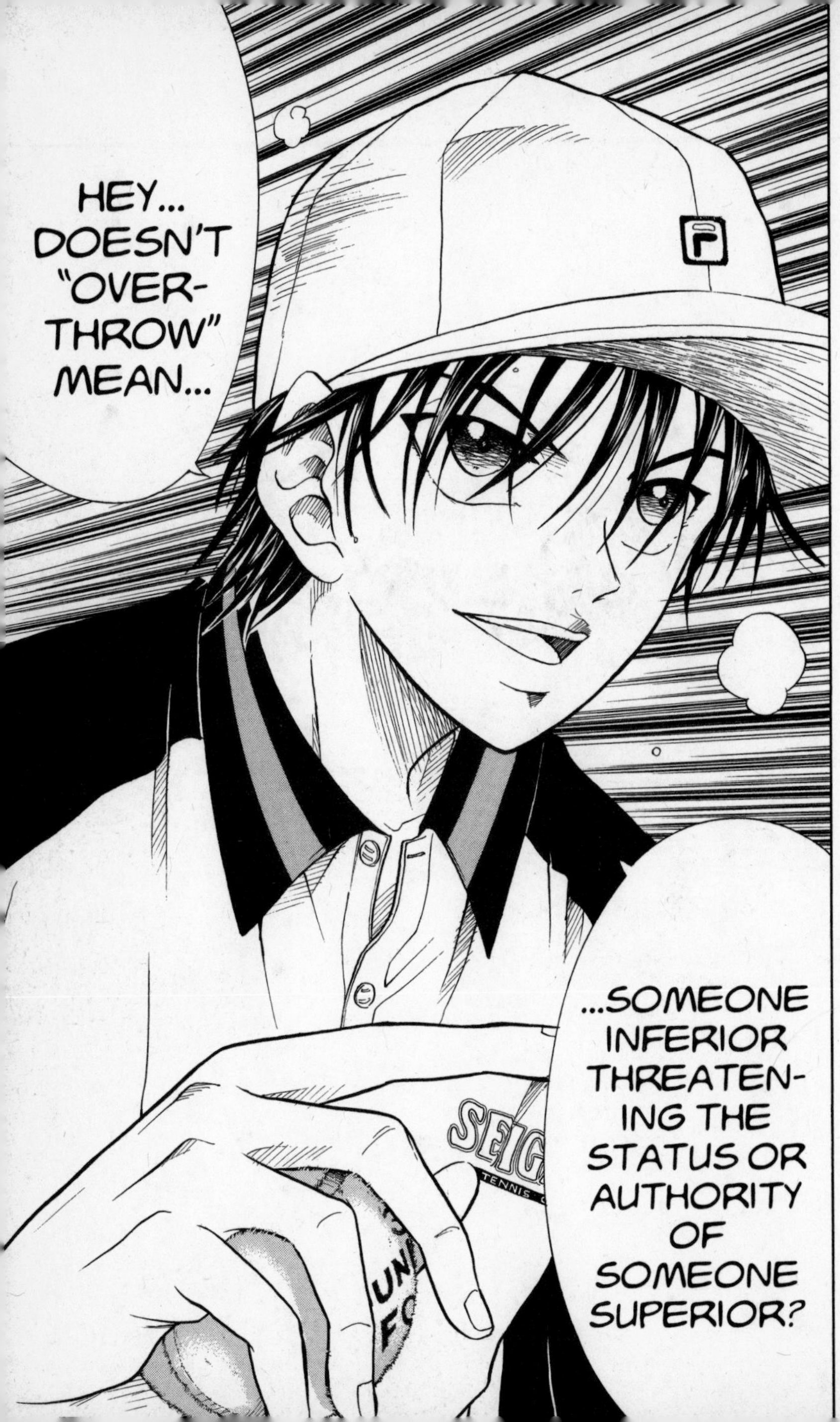
HEY... DOESN'T "OVER-THROW" MEAN...
...SOMEONE INFERIOR THREATEN-ING THE STATUS OR AUTHORITY OF SOMEONE SUPERIOR?

テニスの王子様

THE PRINCE OF TENNIS™

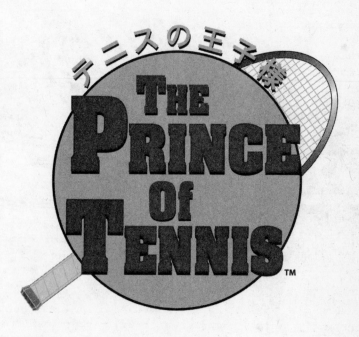

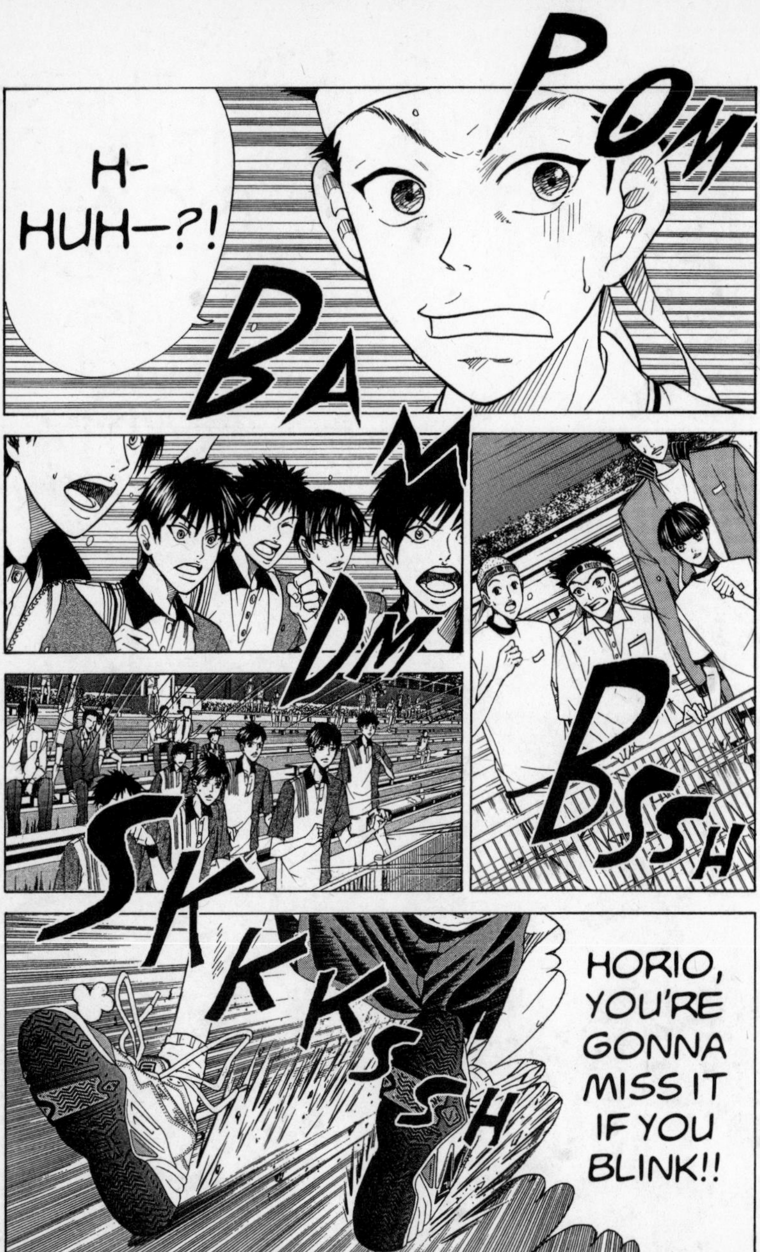
POM
H-
HUH—?!
BAM
BSSH
DM
SKKKSSH
HORIO, YOU'RE GONNA MISS IT IF YOU BLINK!!

GENIUS 156: OPTIMUM PACE

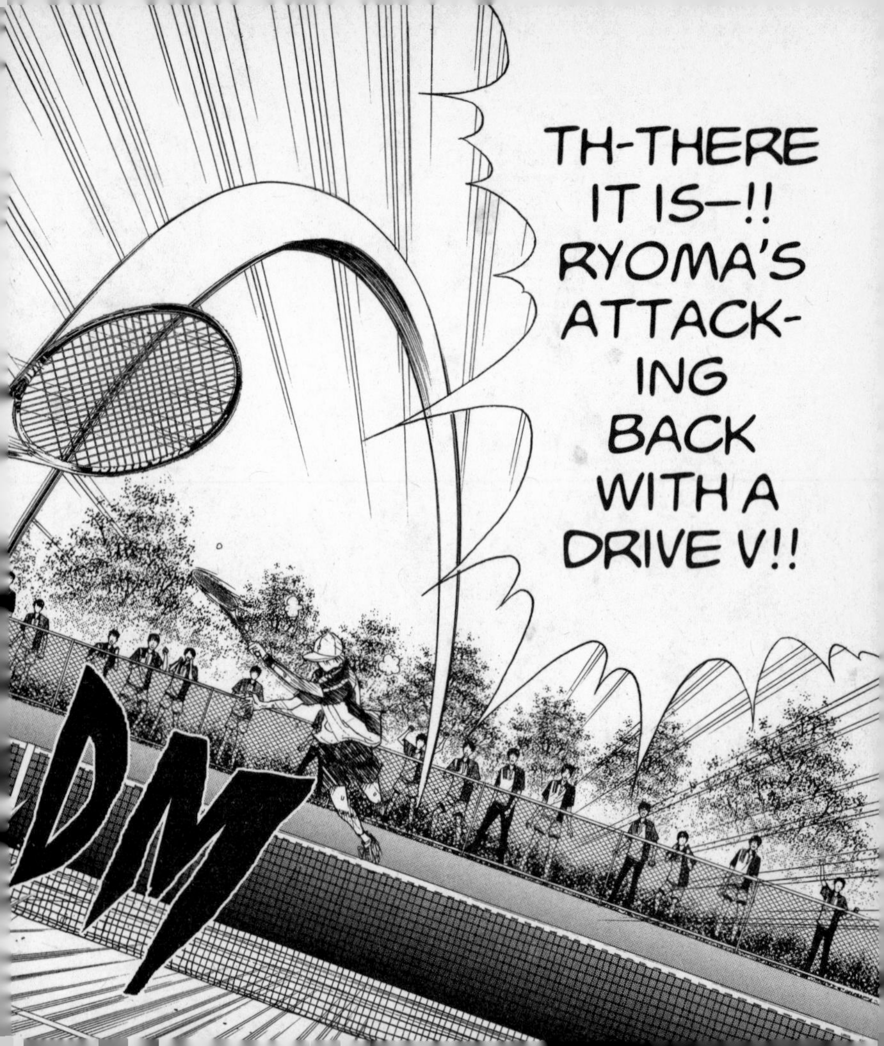
TH-THERE IT IS—!! RYOMA'S ATTACKING BACK WITH A DRIVE V!!
DM

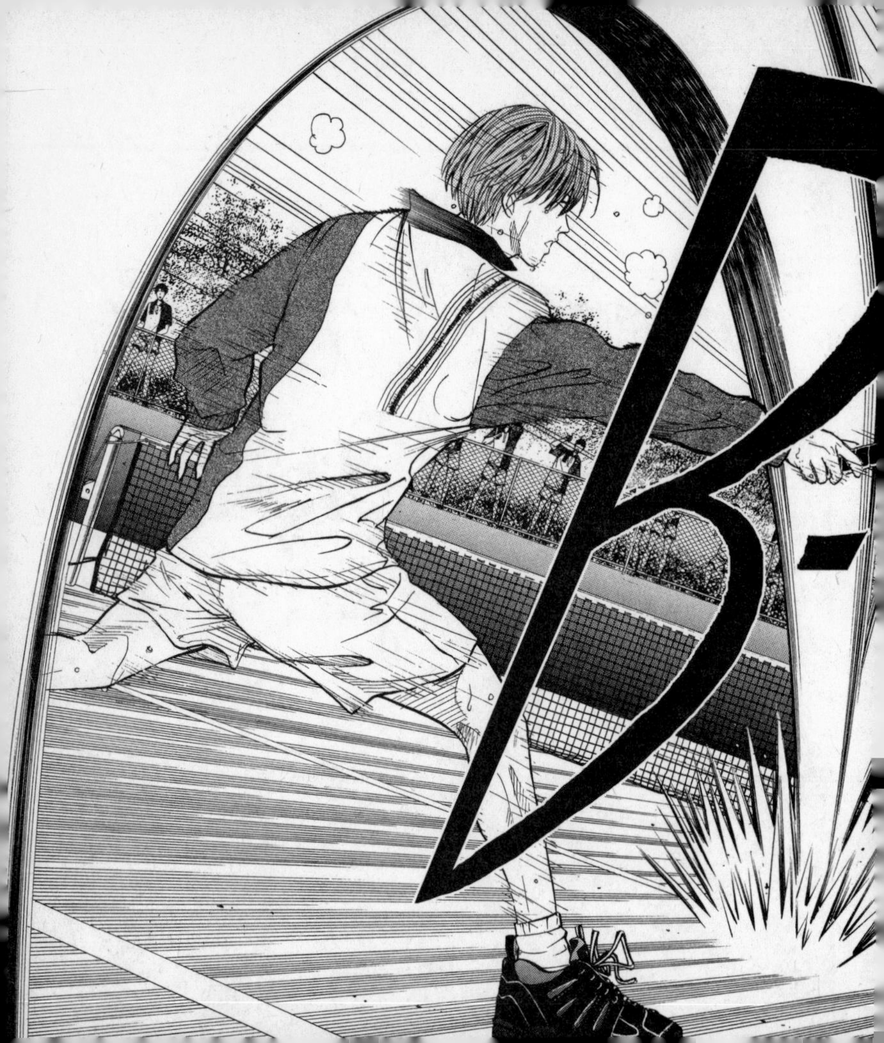

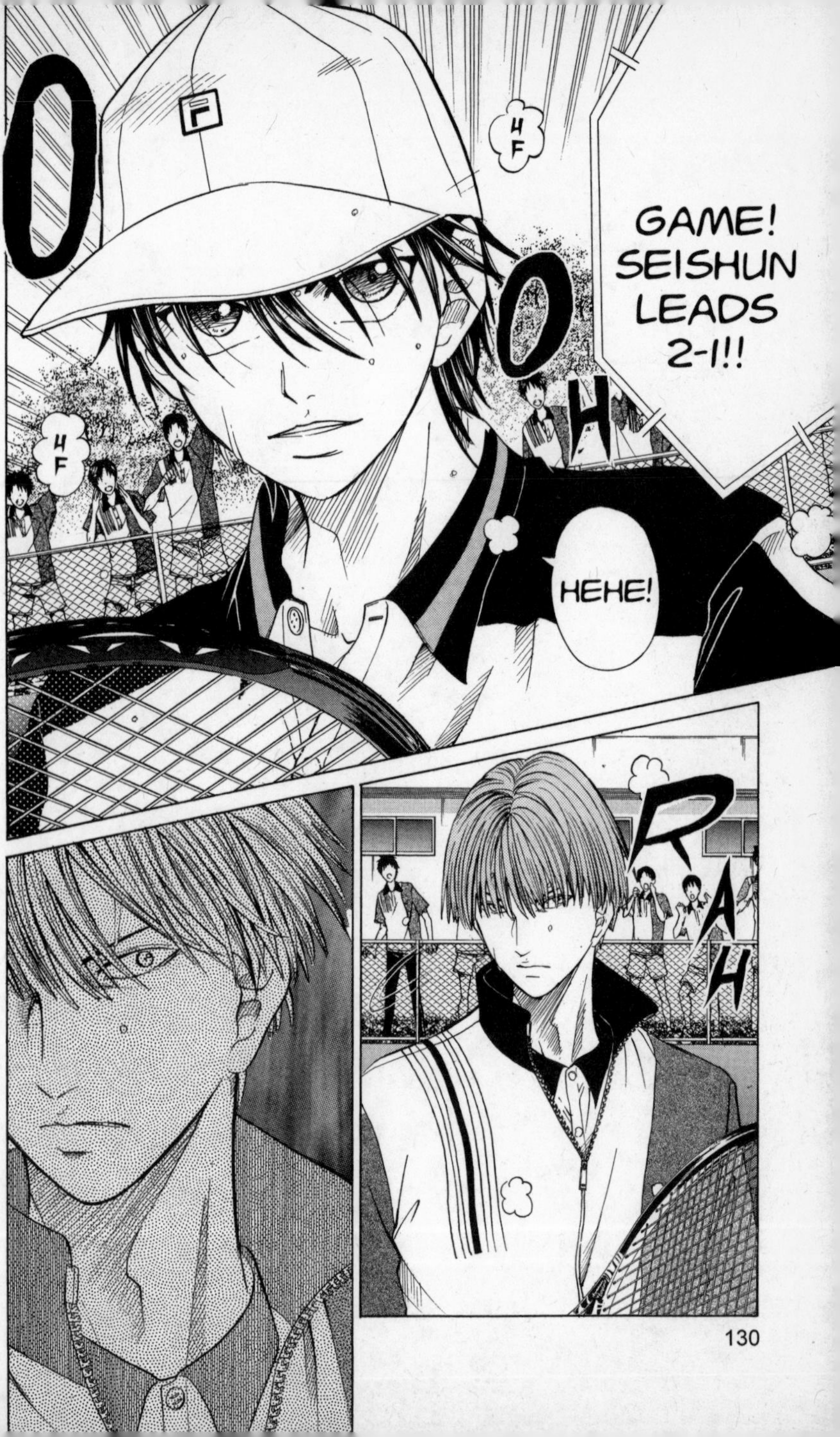
GAME! SEISHUN LEADS 2-1!!
OOH
HEHE!
RAH

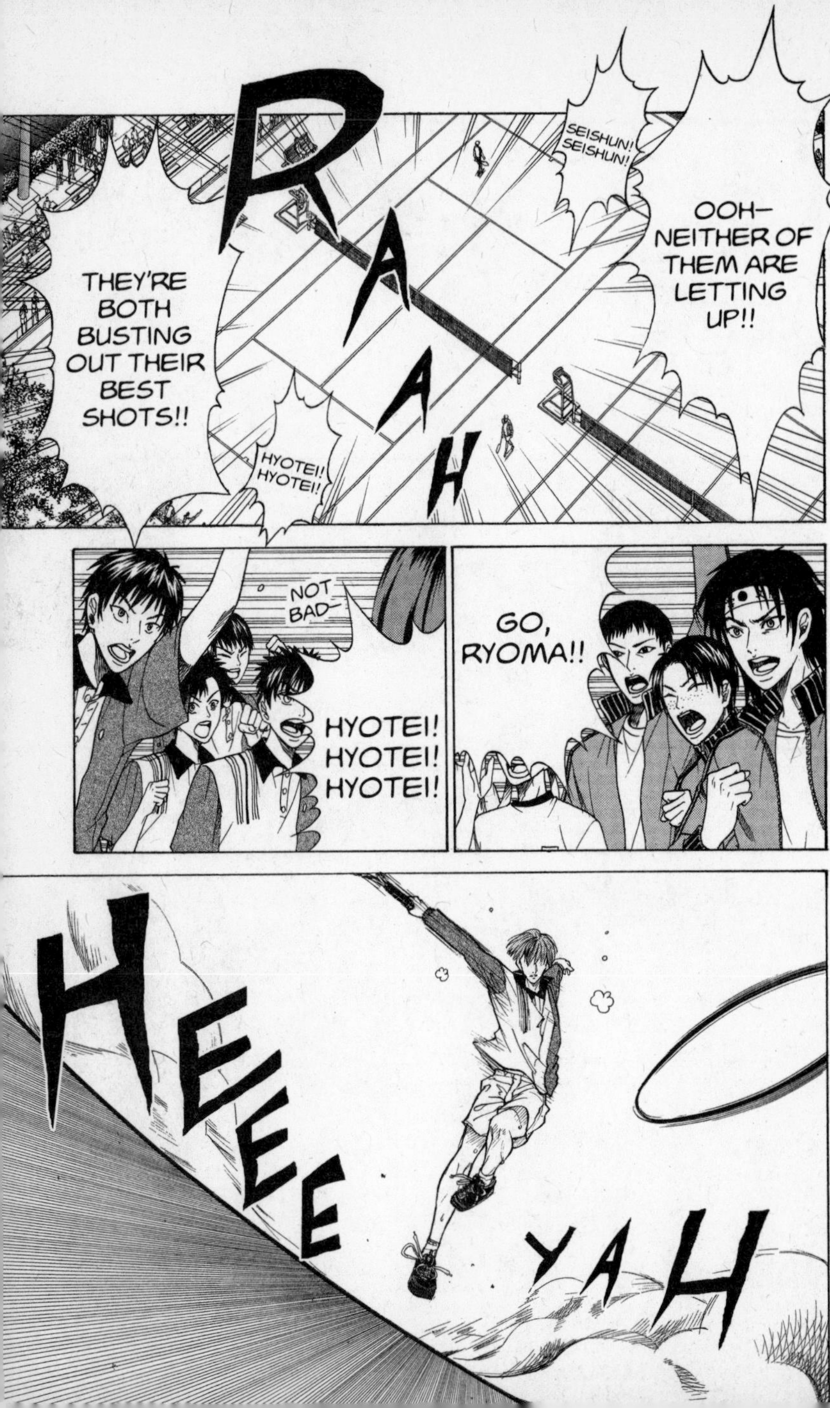
SEISHUN! SEISHUN!
OOH— NEITHER OF THEM ARE LETTING UP!!
RAAH
HYOTEI!! HYOTEI!!
THEY'RE BOTH BUSTING OUT THEIR BEST SHOTS!!
GO, RYOMA!!
NOT BAD—
HYOTEI! HYOTEI! HYOTEI!
HEEEE YAH

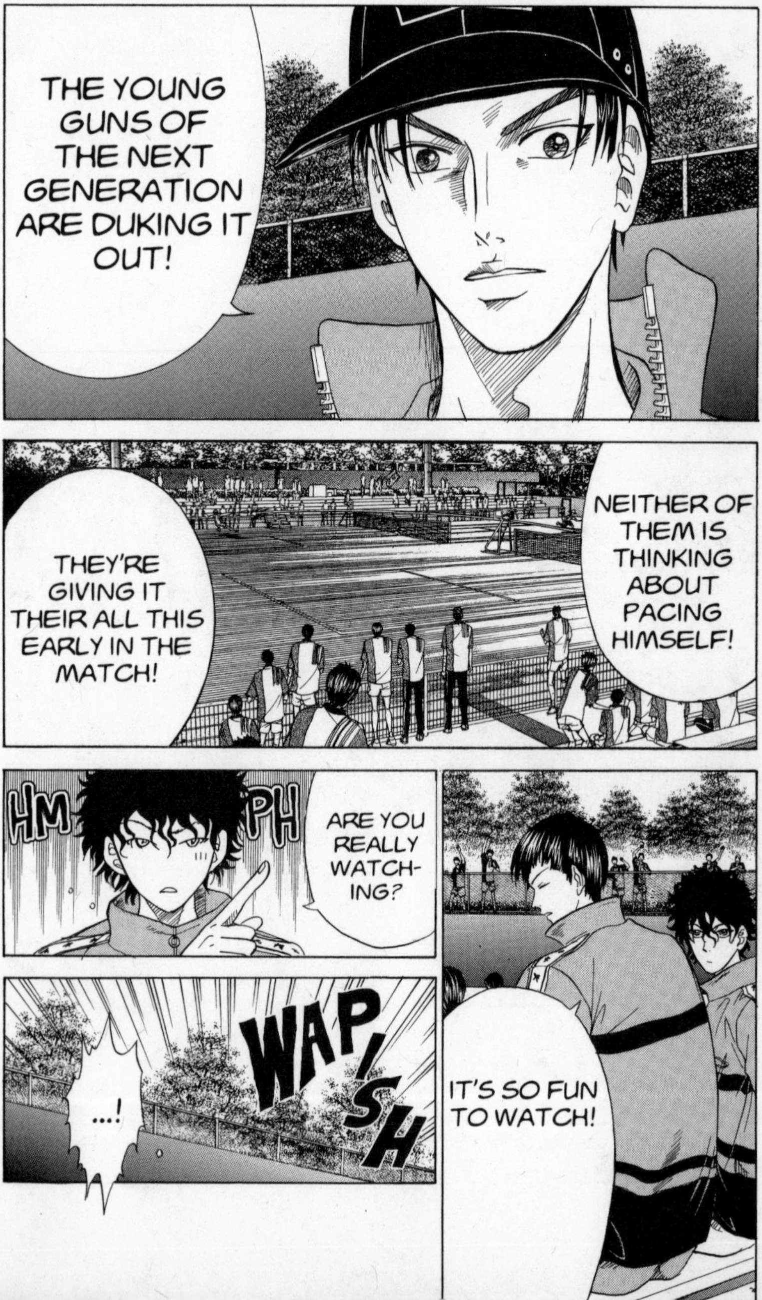
THE YOUNG GUNS OF THE NEXT GENERATION ARE DUKING IT OUT!
NEITHER OF THEM IS THINKING ABOUT PACING HIMSELF!
THEY'RE GIVING IT THEIR ALL THIS EARLY IN THE MATCH!
IT'S SO FUN TO WATCH!
HMPH
ARE YOU REALLY WATCH-ING?
WAPISH
...!

READ THIS WAY

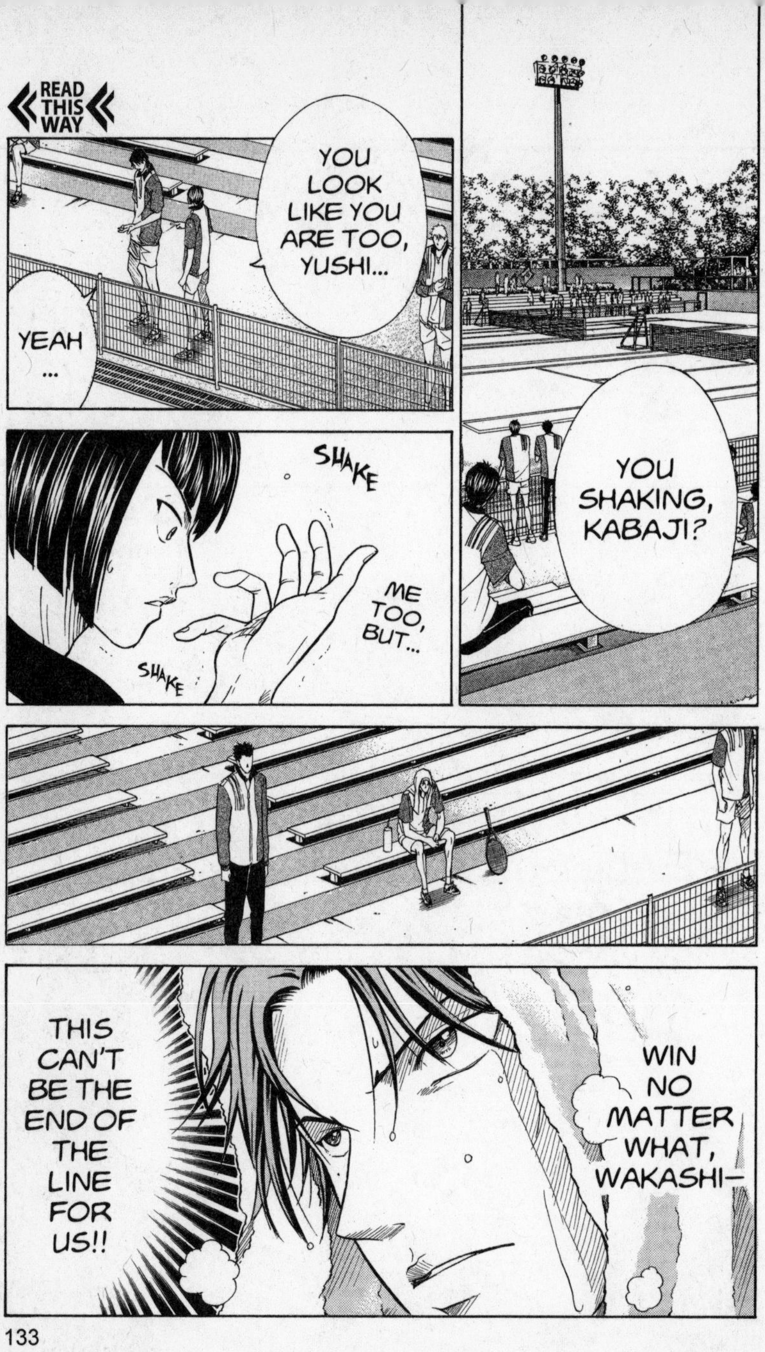

YOU SHAKING, KABAJI?
YOU LOOK LIKE YOU ARE TOO, YUSHI...
YEAH ...
SHAKE
ME TOO, BUT...
SHAKE
WIN NO MATTER WHAT, WAKASHI—
THIS CAN'T BE THE END OF THE LINE FOR US!!

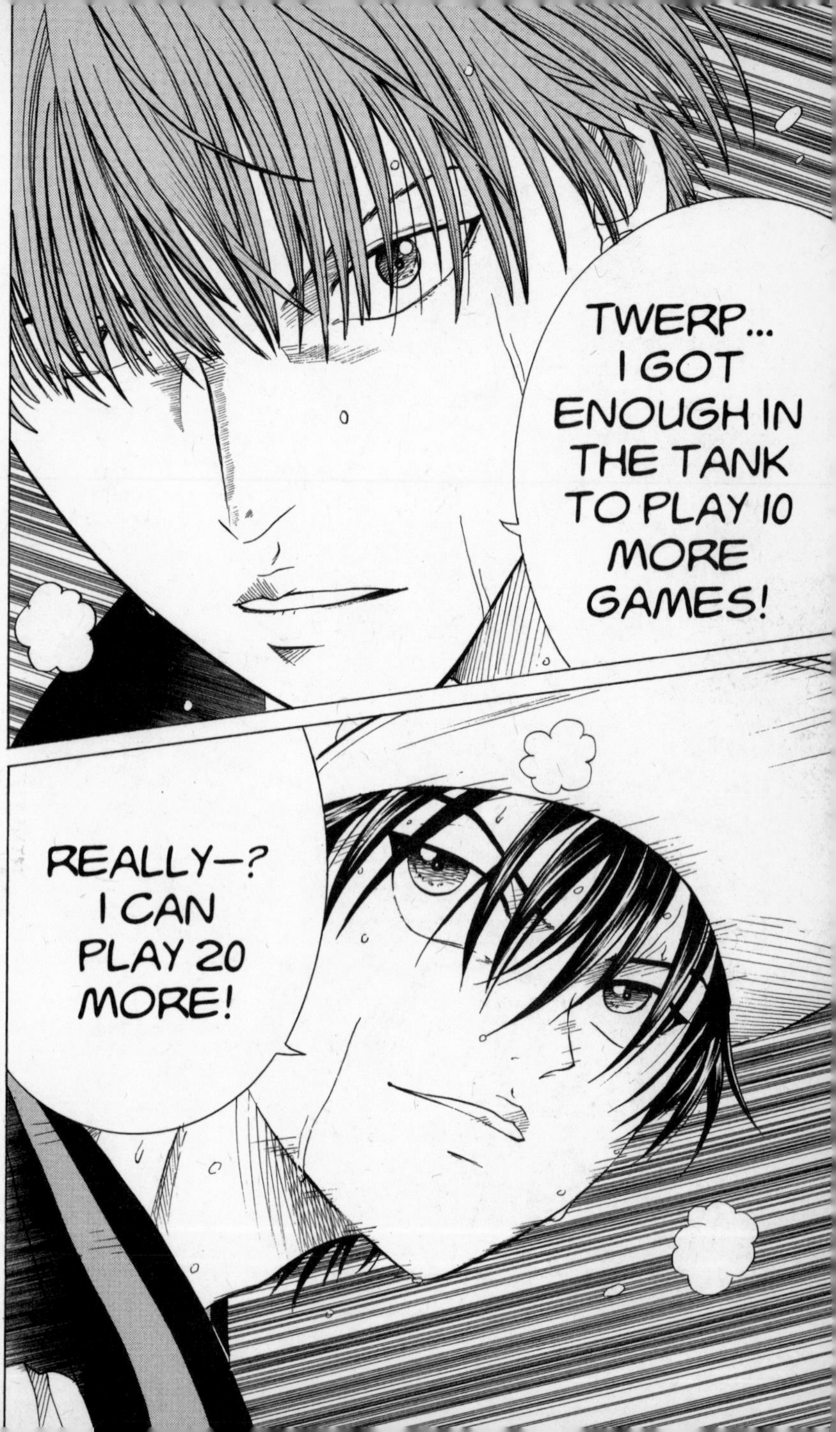
TWERP... I GOT ENOUGH IN THE TANK TO PLAY 10 MORE GAMES!
REALLY—? I CAN PLAY 20 MORE!

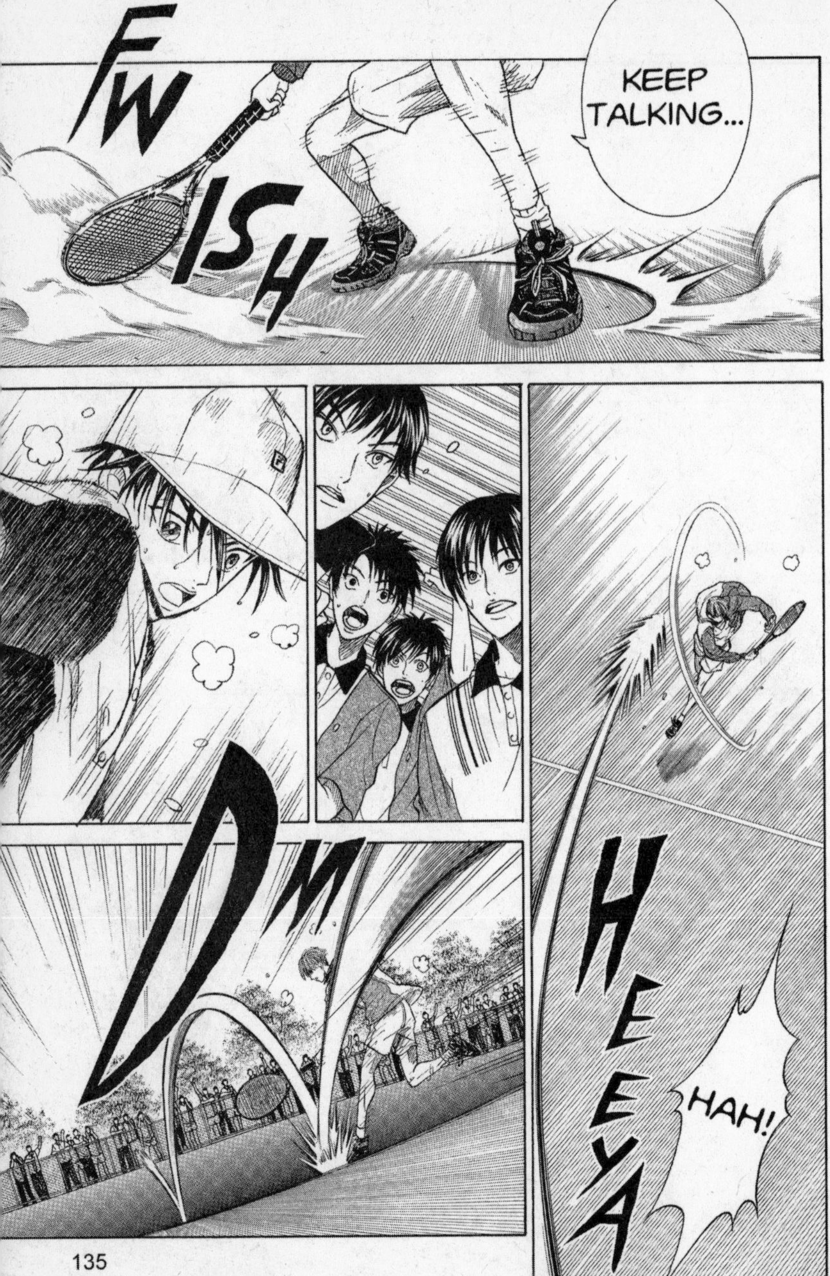
KEEP TALKING...
FWISH
HEEYA
HAH!
DMM

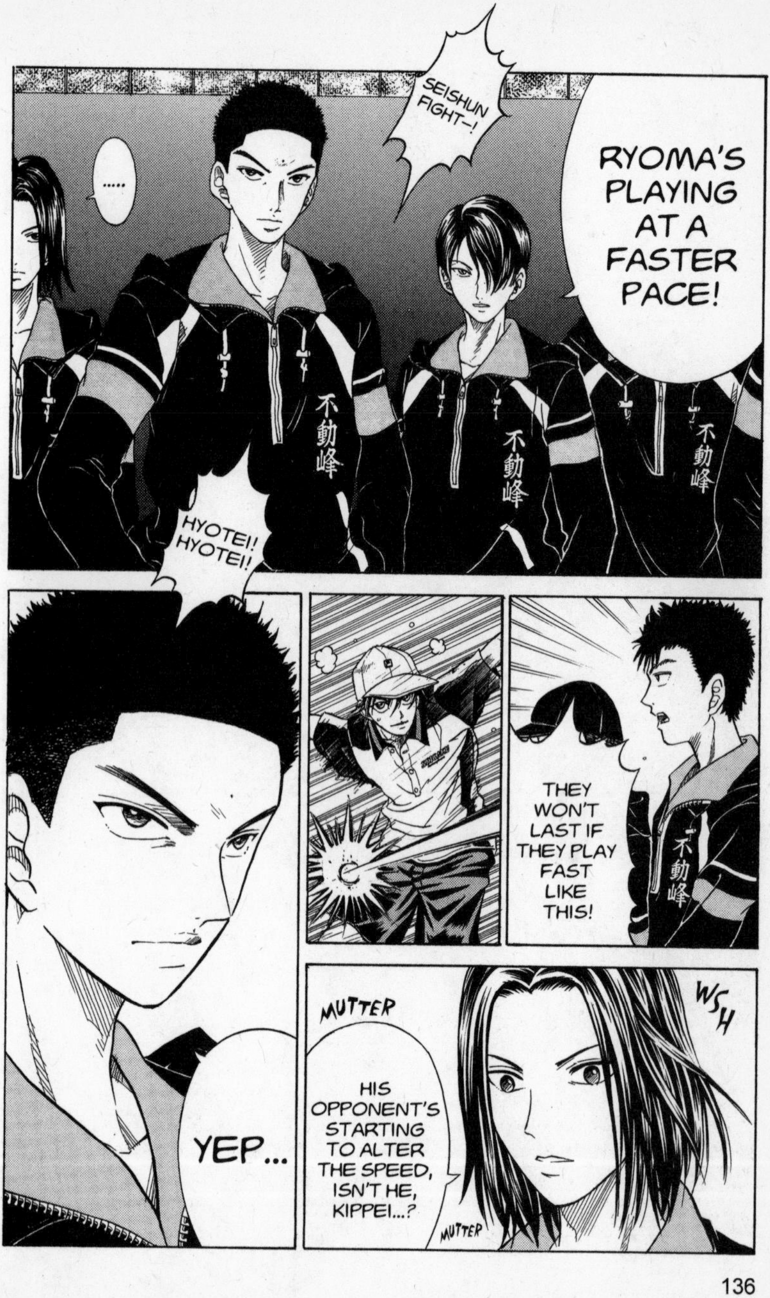
RYOMA'S PLAYING AT A FASTER PACE!
SEISHUN FIGHT-!
.....
HYOTEI! HYOTEI!
THEY WON'T LAST IF THEY PLAY FAST LIKE THIS!
WSH
MUTTER
HIS OPPONENT'S STARTING TO ALTER THE SPEED, ISN'T HE, KIPPEI...?
MUTTER
YEP...

READ THIS WAY

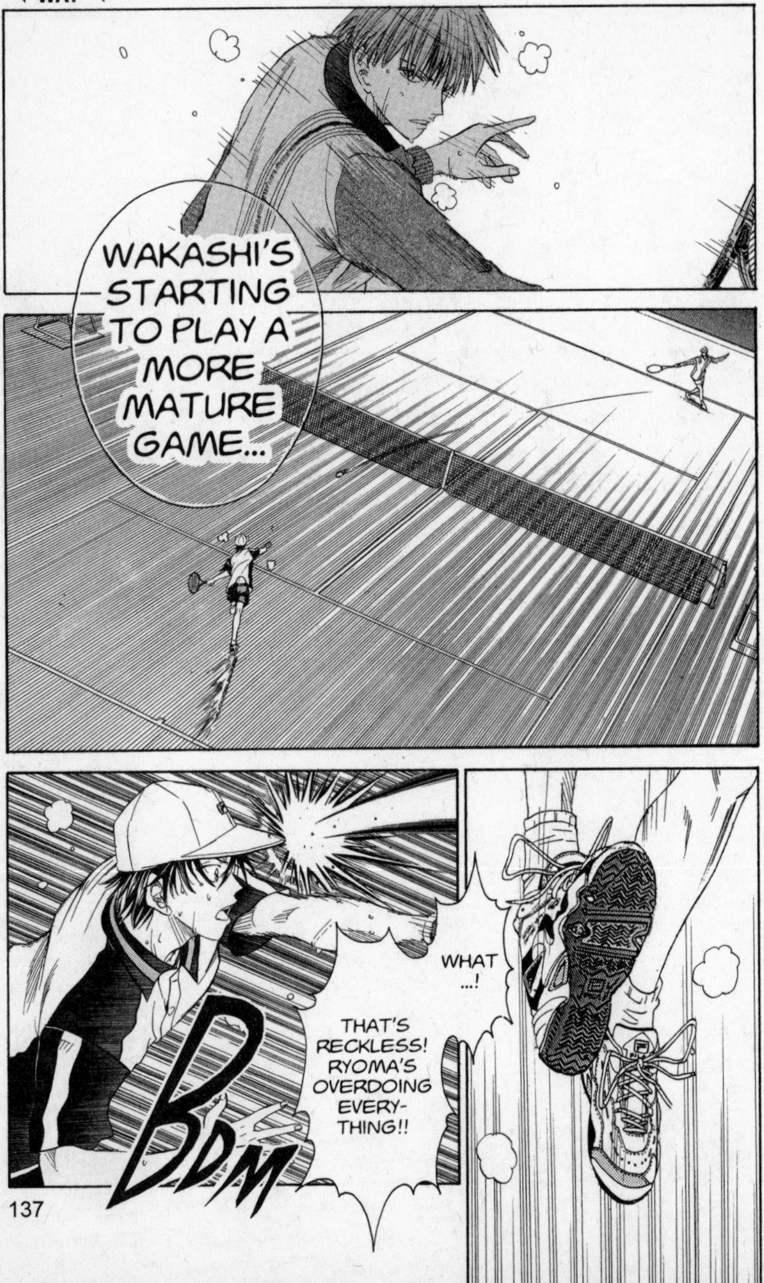
WAKASHI'S STARTING TO PLAY A MORE MATURE GAME...
WHAT ...!
THAT'S RECKLESS! RYOMA'S OVERDOING EVERY-THING!!
BDM

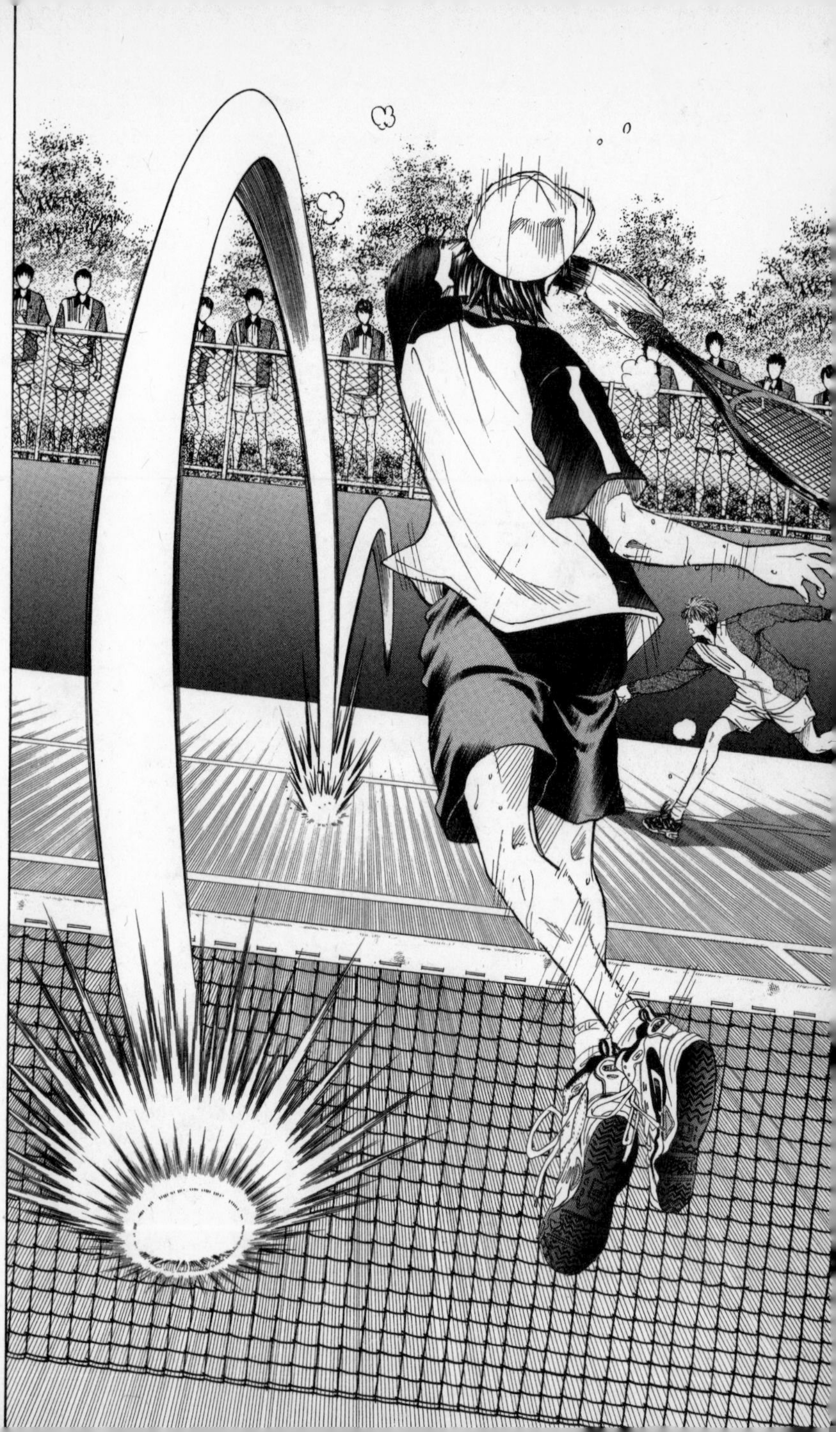

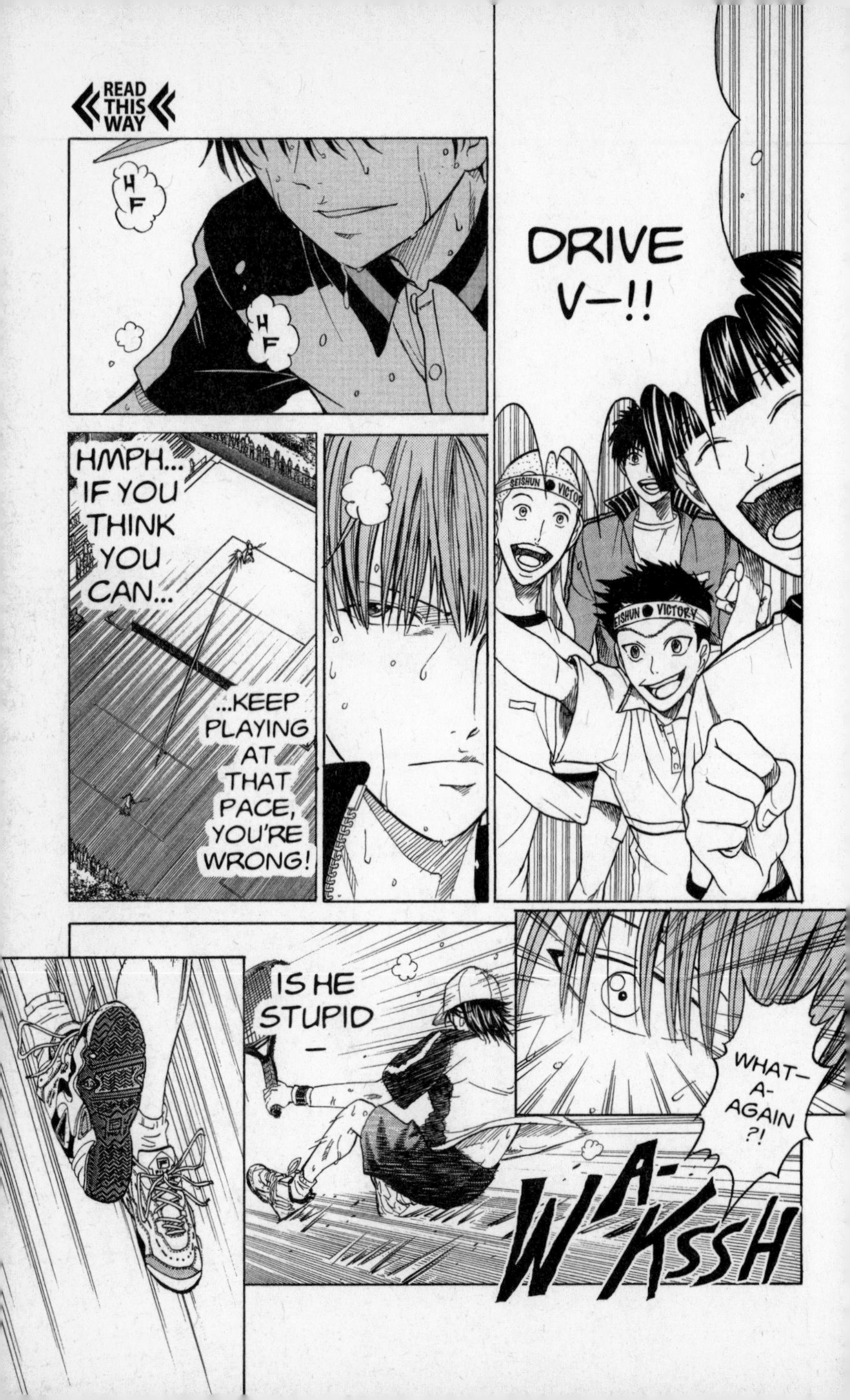
READ THIS WAY
DRIVE V—!!
HF
HF
HMPH... IF YOU THINK YOU CAN...
...KEEP PLAYING AT THAT PACE, YOU'RE WRONG!
WHAT-A-AGAIN?!
IS HE STUPID —
WA-KSSH

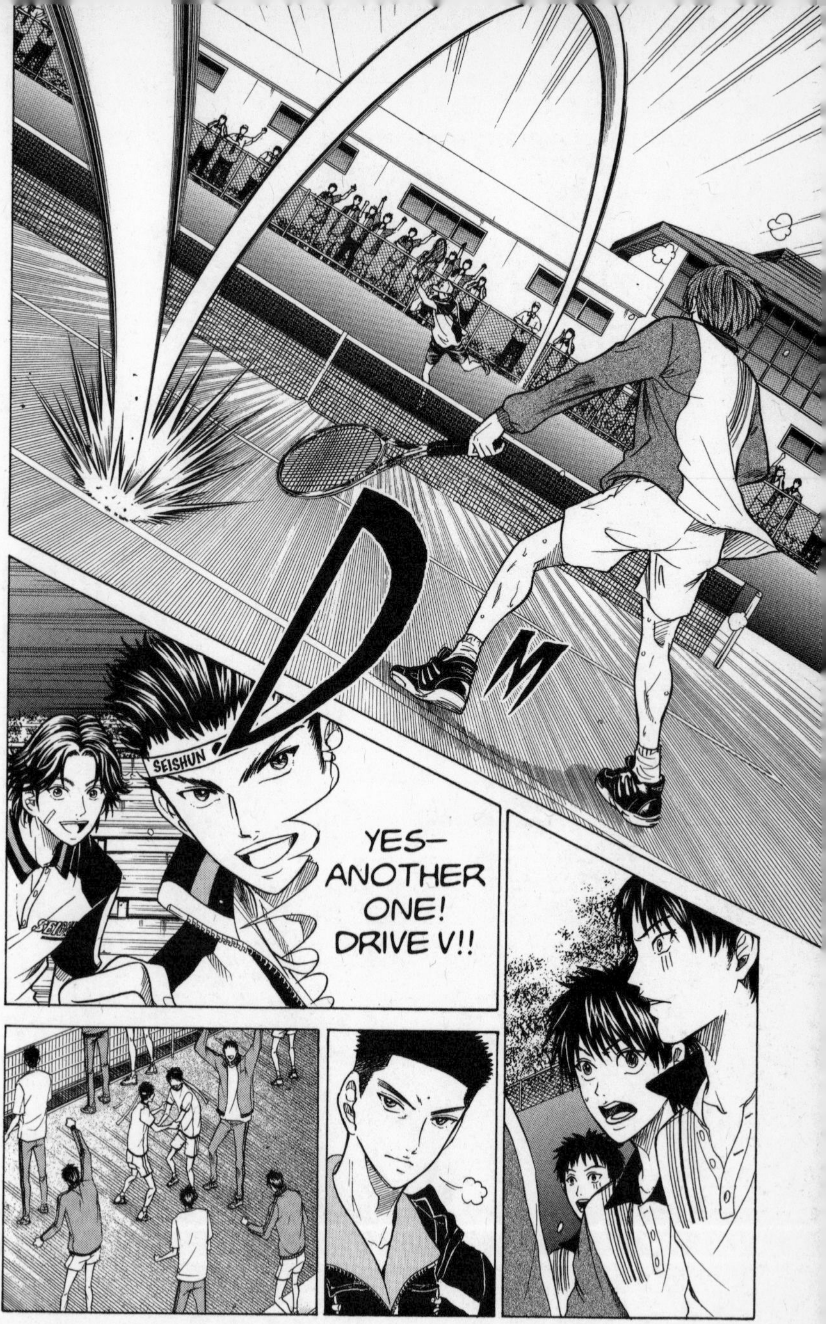
DM
SEISHUN
YES—ANOTHER ONE! DRIVE V!!

READ THIS WAY

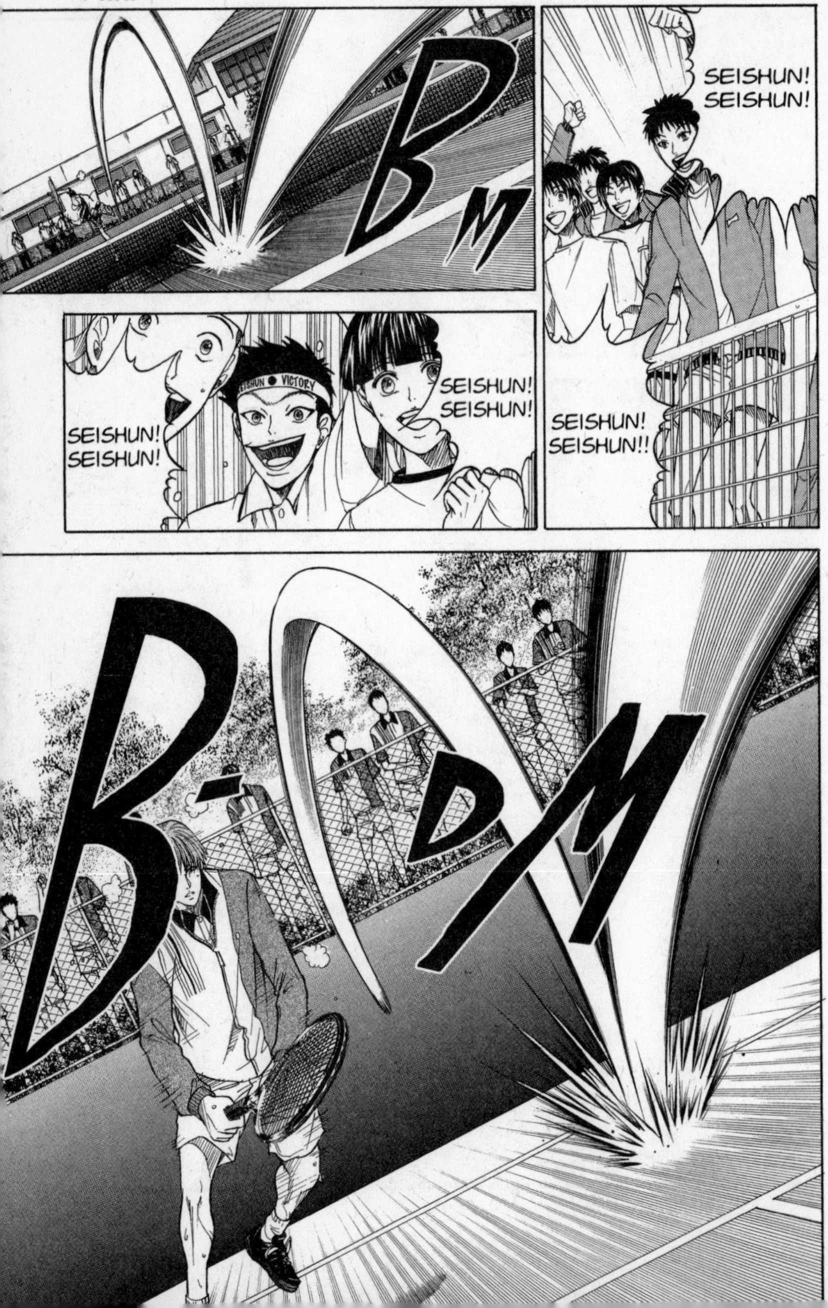
SEISHUN! SEISHUN!
SEISHUN! SEISHUN!!
BM
SEISHUN! SEISHUN!
SEISHUN! SEISHUN!
B-DM

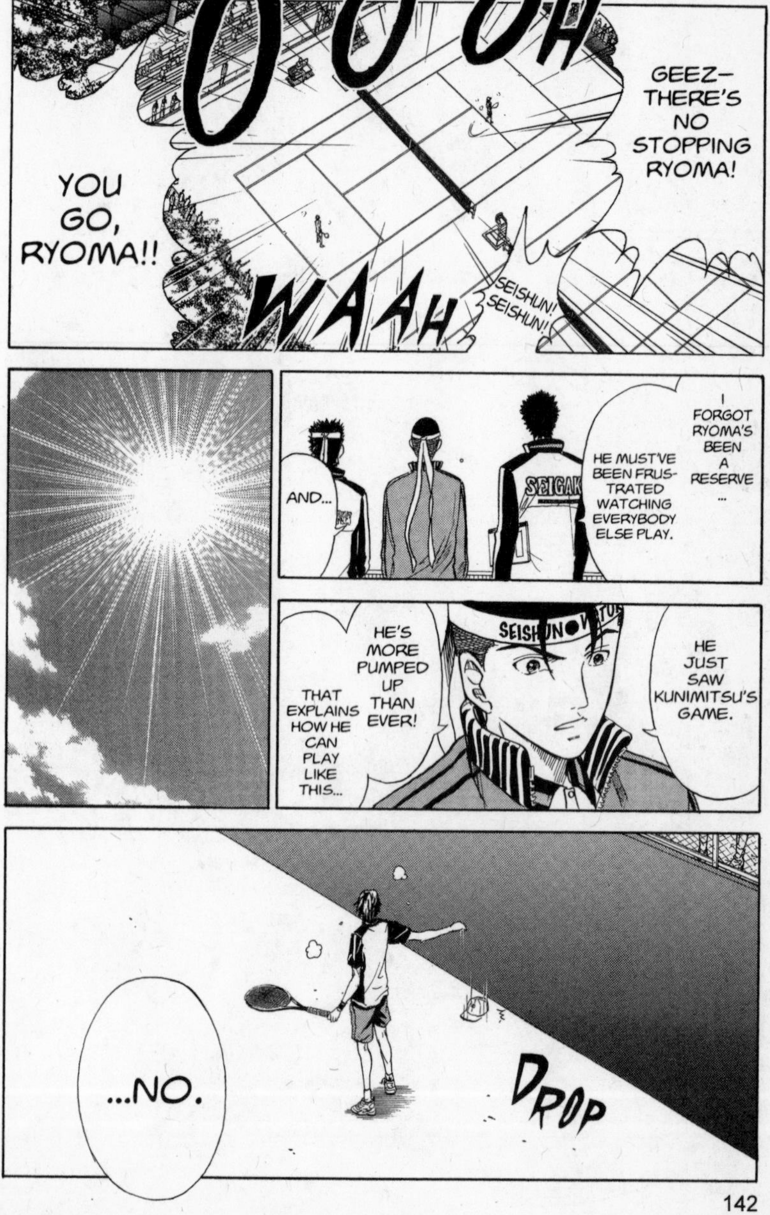
GEEZ—THERE'S NO STOPPING RYOMA!
OOOH
SEISHUN! SEISHUN!
WAAH
YOU GO, RYOMA!!
I FORGOT RYOMA'S BEEN A RESERVE ...
HE MUST'VE BEEN FRUS-TRATED WATCHING EVERYBODY ELSE PLAY.
AND...
HE JUST SAW KUNIMITSU'S GAME.
HE'S MORE PUMPED UP THAN EVER!
THAT EXPLAINS HOW HE CAN PLAY LIKE THIS...
DROP
...NO.

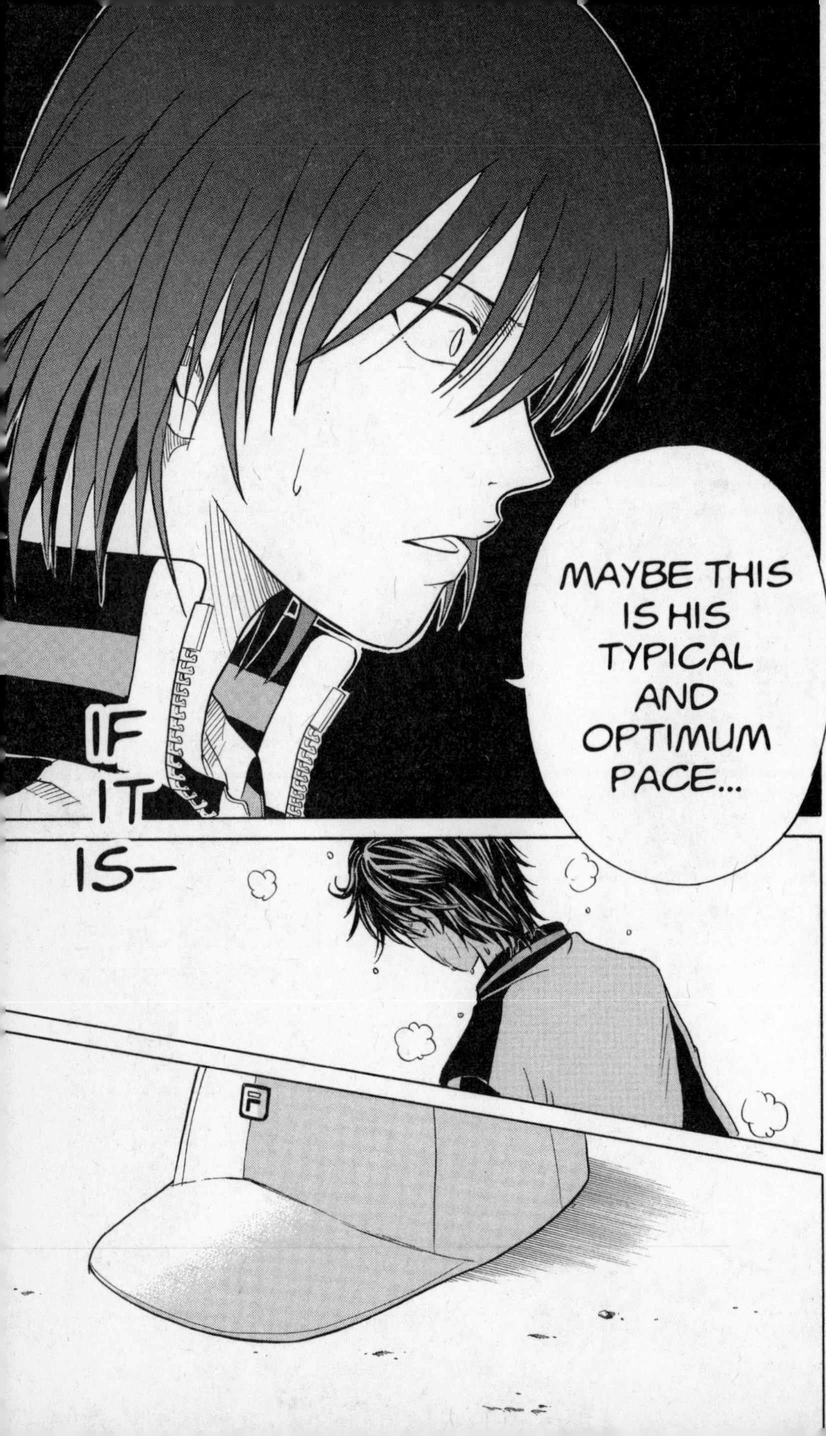
MAYBE THIS IS HIS TYPICAL AND OPTIMUM PACE...
IF IT IS—

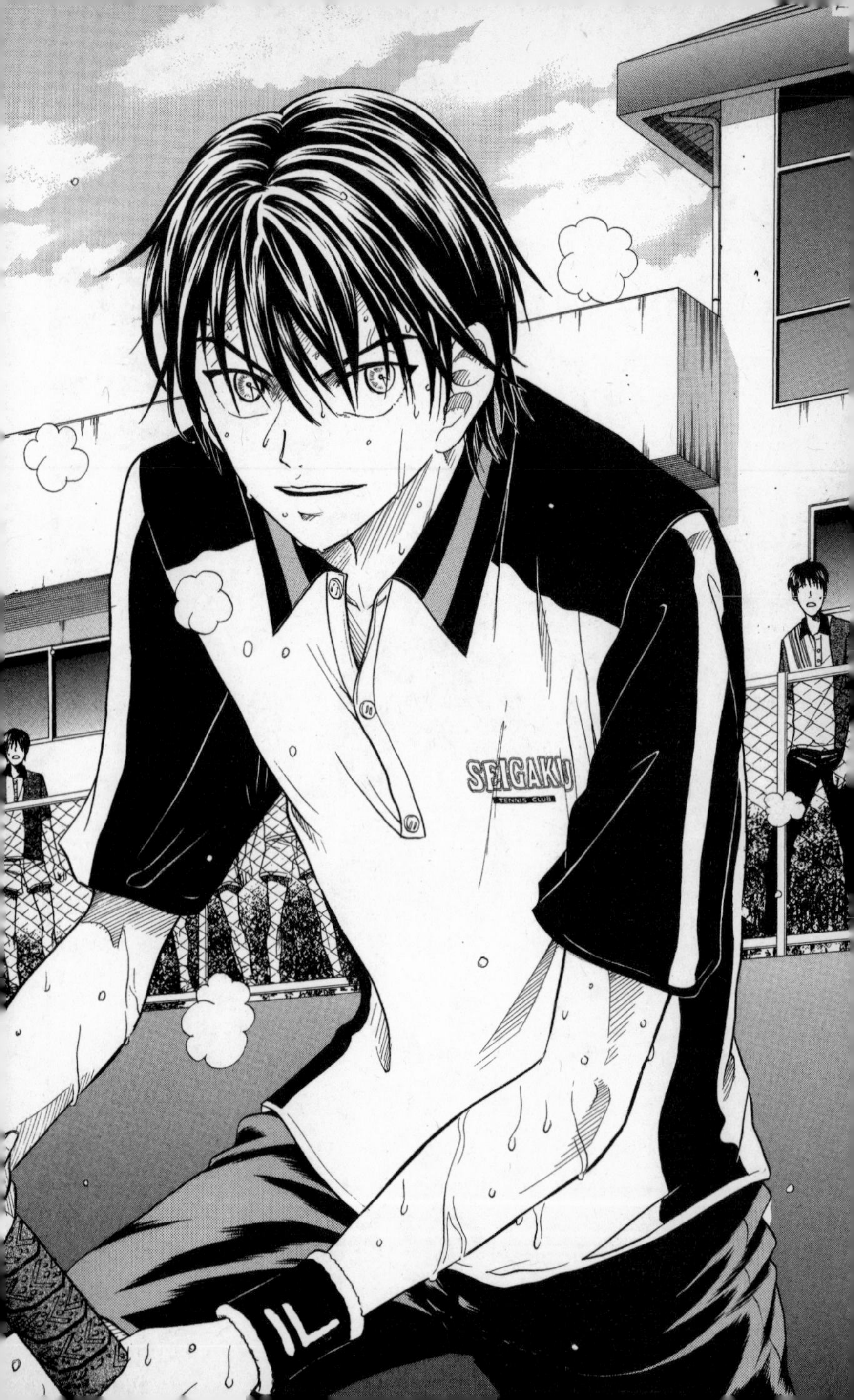
SEIGAKU
TENNIS CLUB

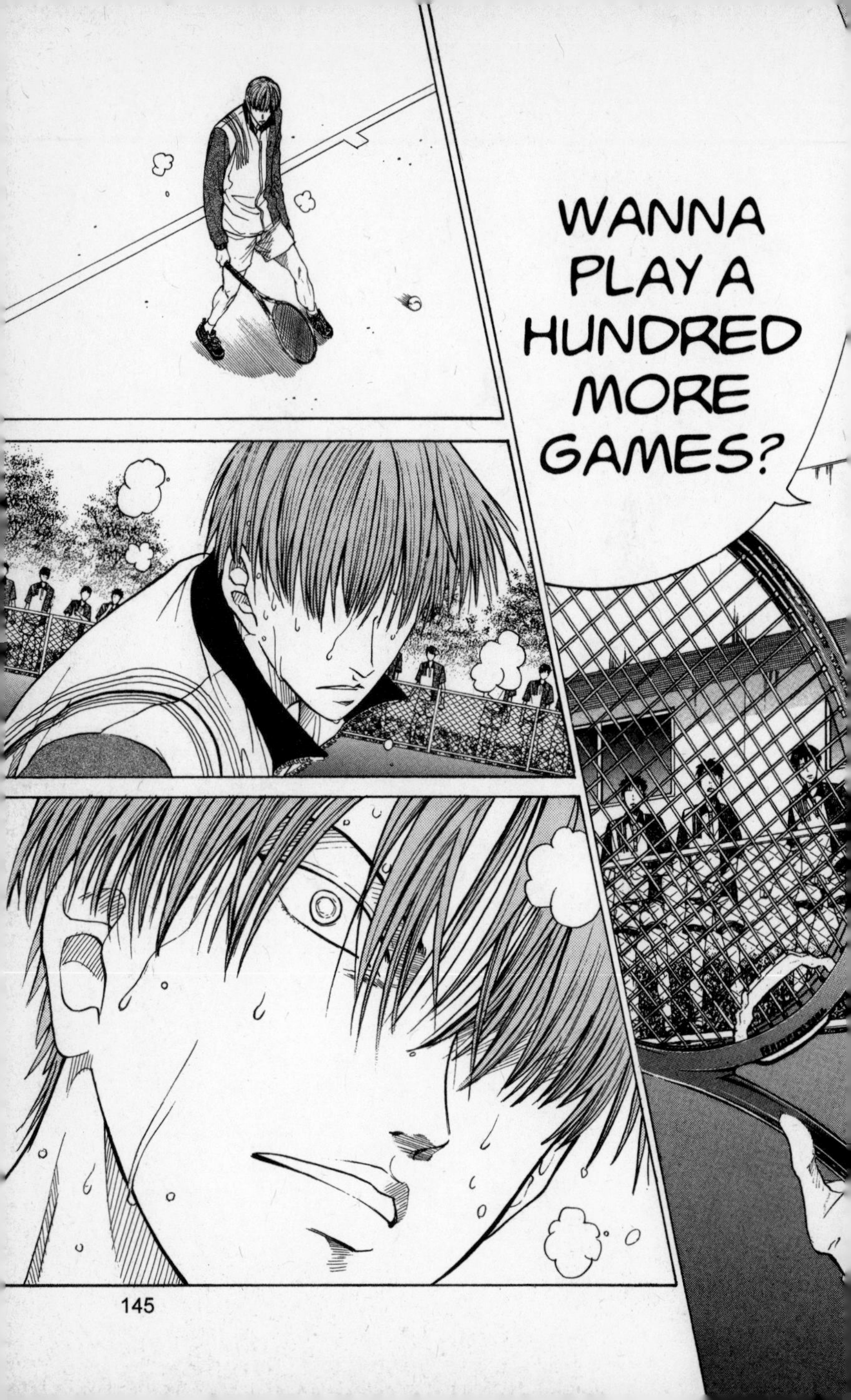
WANNA PLAY A HUNDRED MORE GAMES?

テニスの王子様

THE PRINCE OF TENNIS™

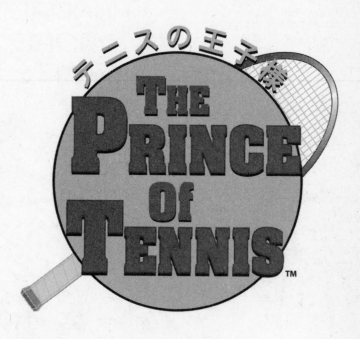

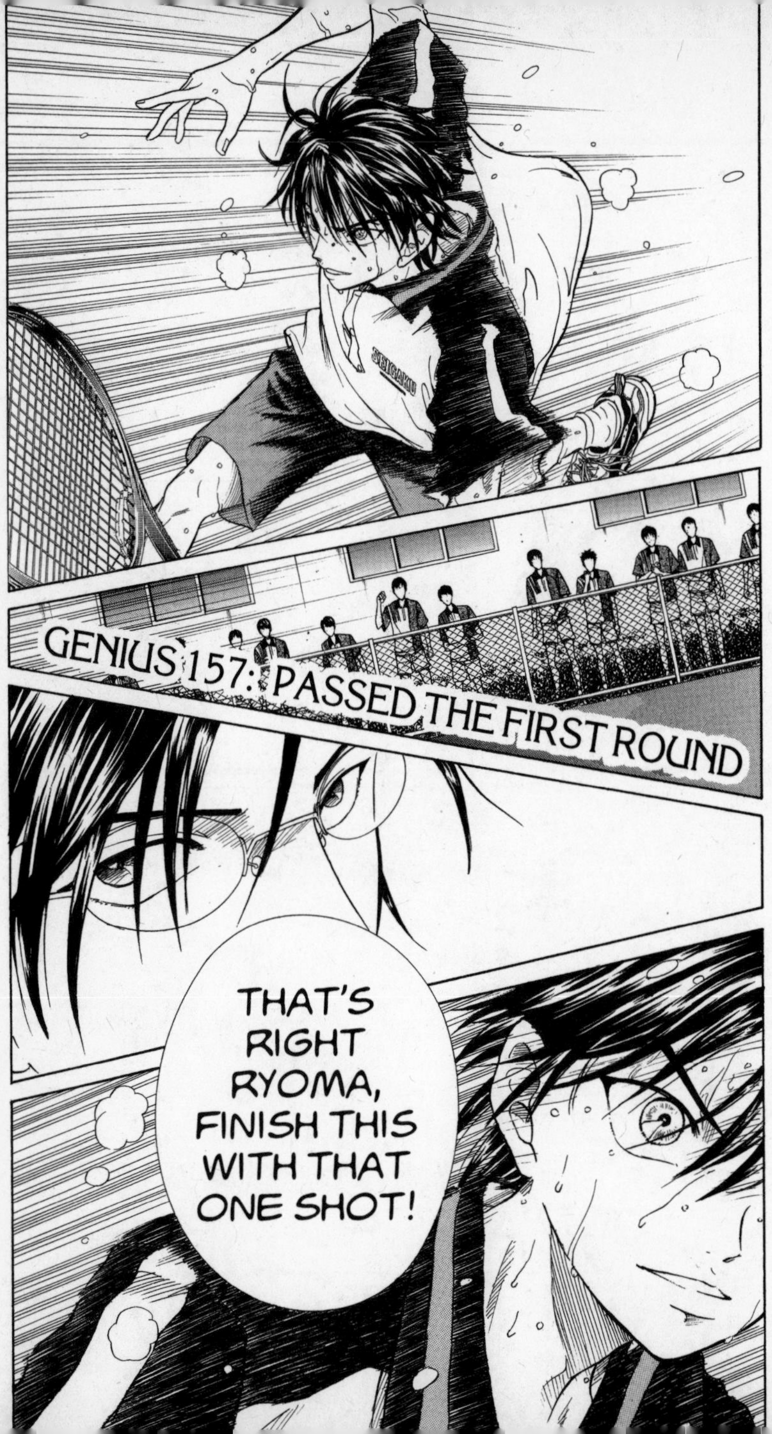
SEIGAKU
GENIUS 157: PASSED THE FIRST ROUND
THAT'S RIGHT RYOMA, FINISH THIS WITH THAT ONE SHOT!

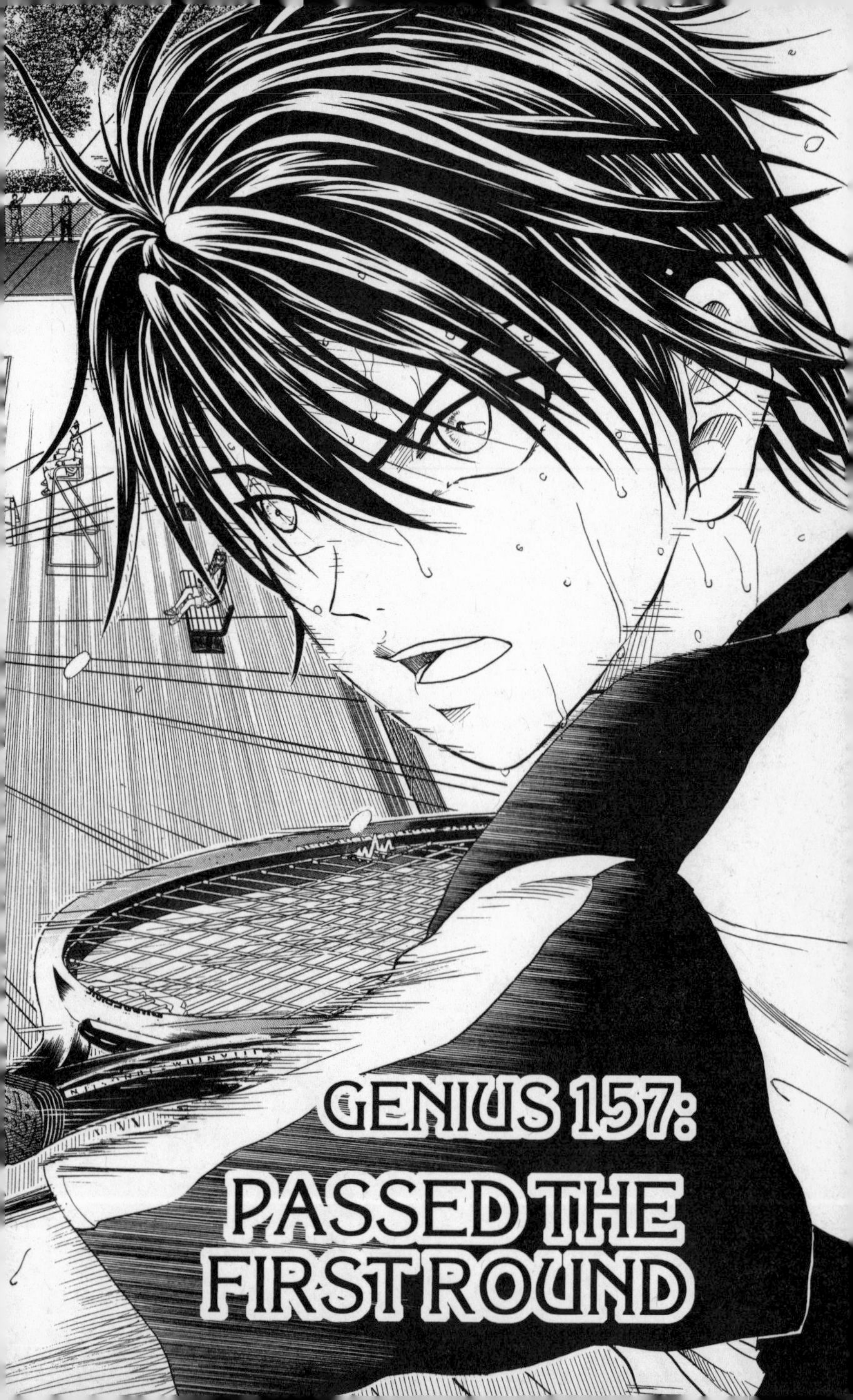
GENIUS 157:
PASSED THE FIRST ROUND

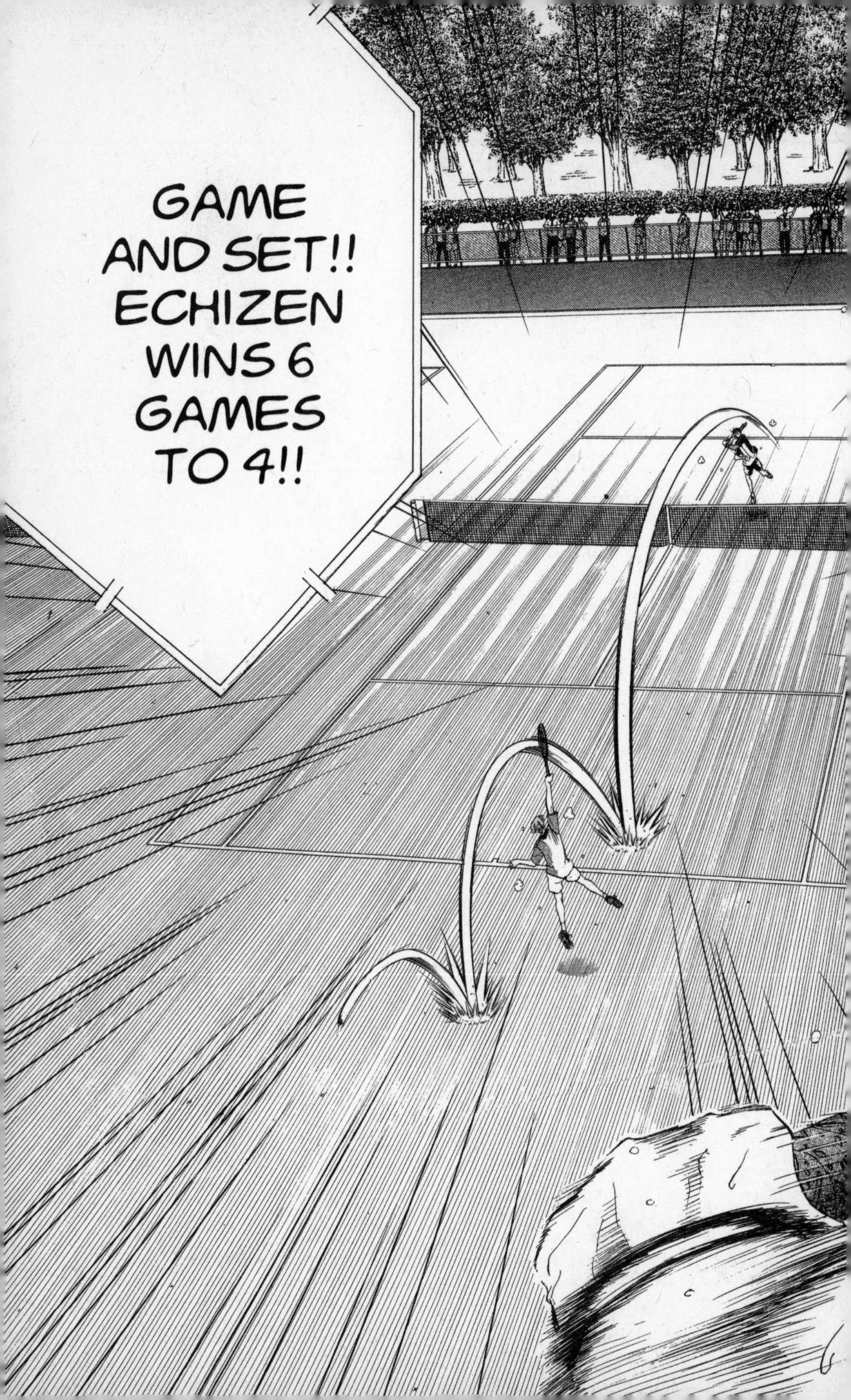
GAME AND SET!! ECHIZEN WINS 6 GAMES TO 4!!

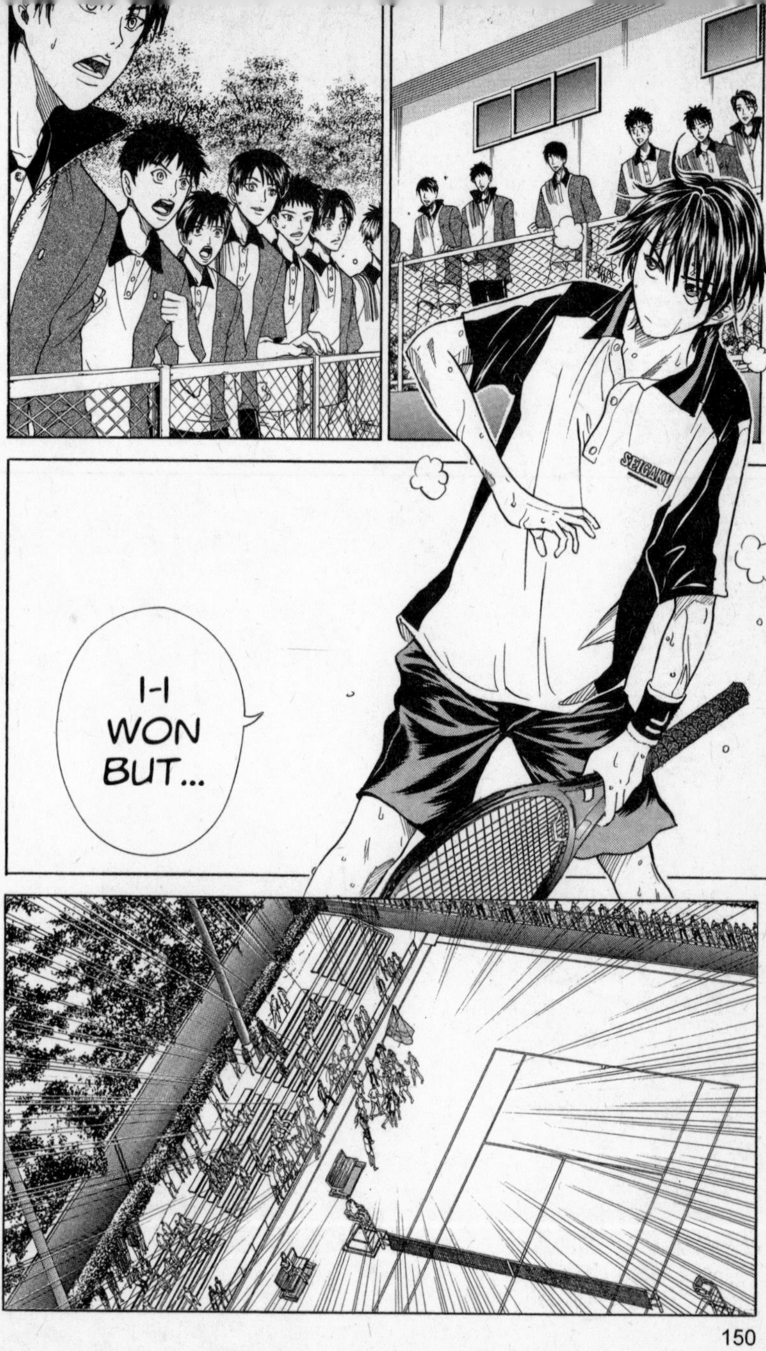
I-I WON BUT...

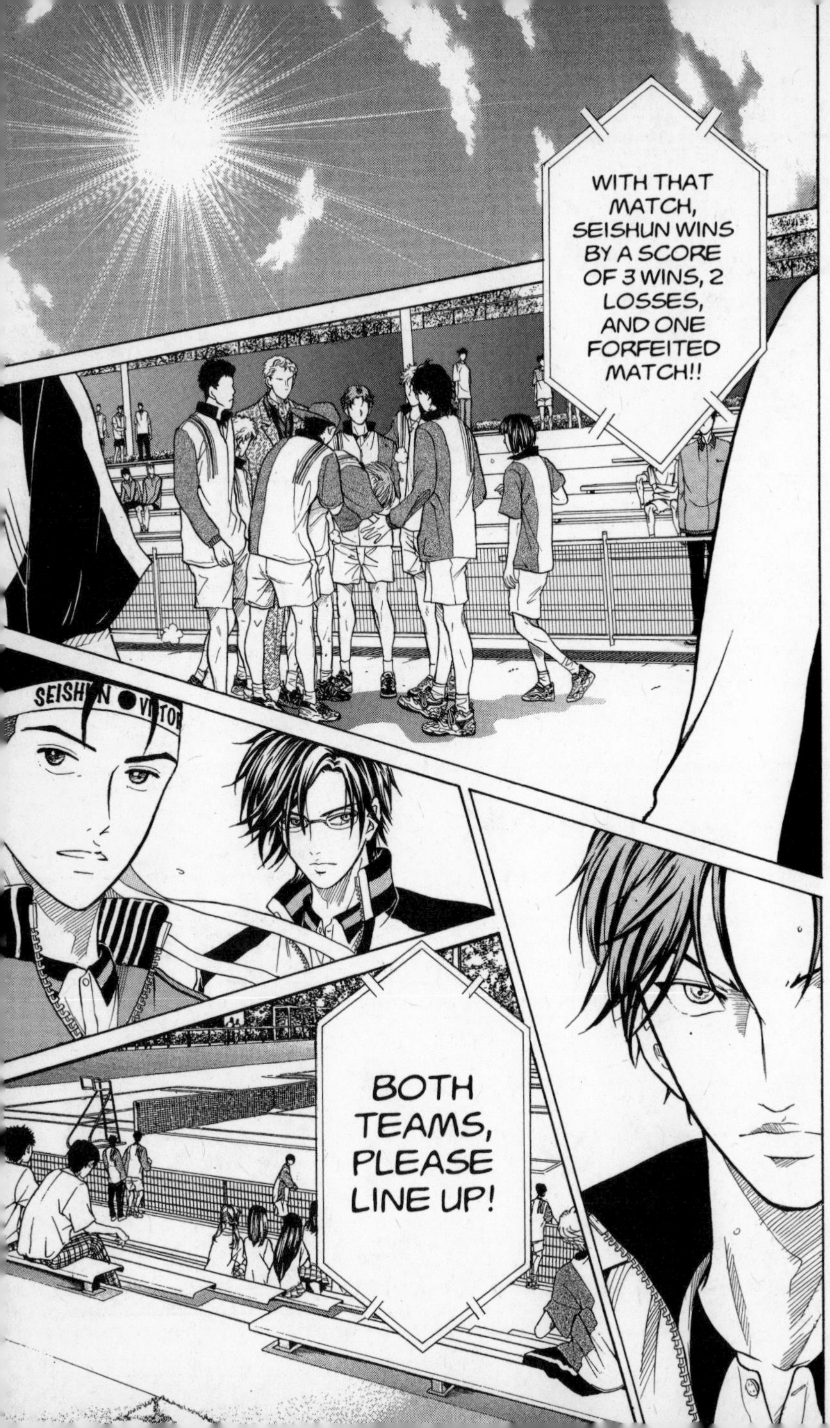
WITH THAT MATCH, SEISHUN WINS BY A SCORE OF 3 WINS, 2 LOSSES, AND ONE FORFEITED MATCH!!
BOTH TEAMS, PLEASE LINE UP!

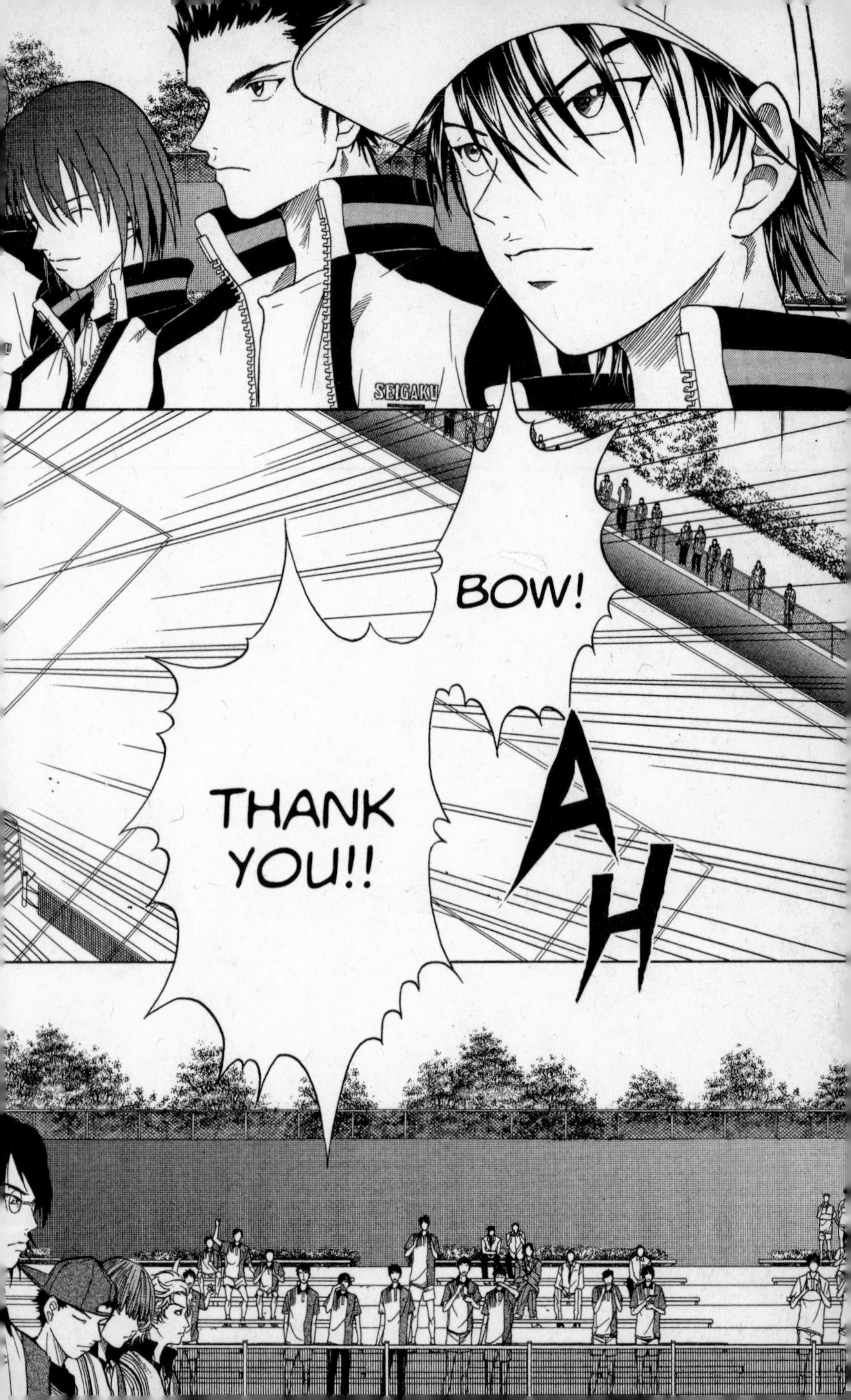
SEIGAKU
BOW!
THANK YOU!!
AH

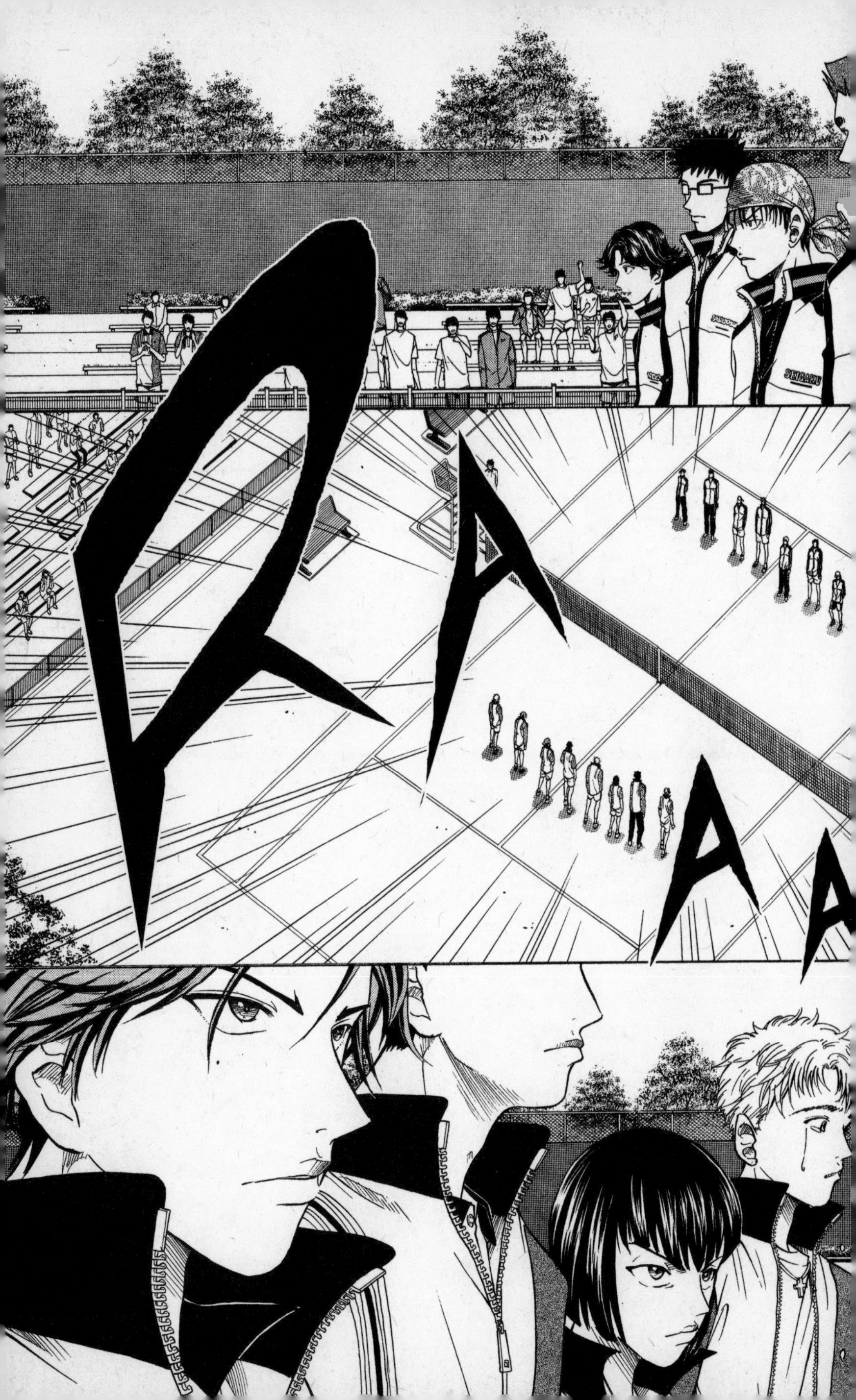
SEIGAKU
WAAA

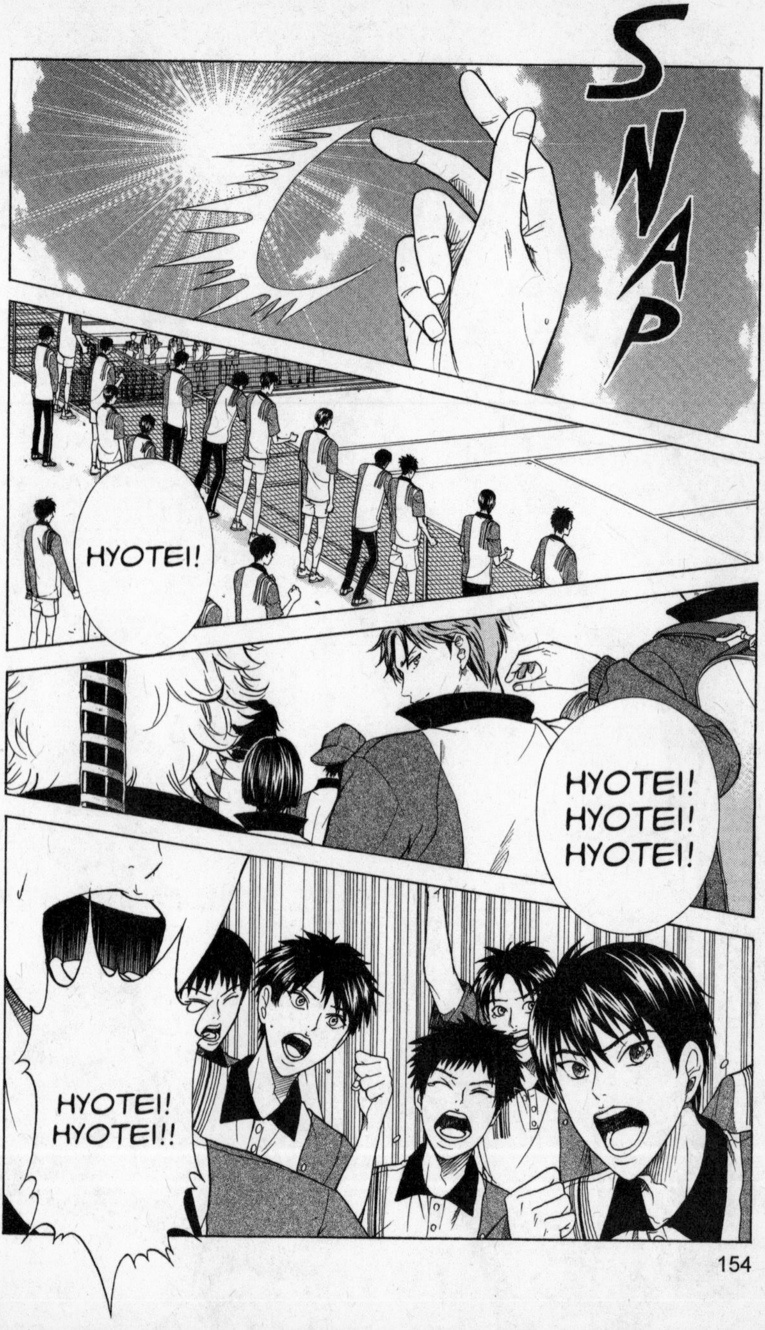
SNAP
HYOTEI!
HYOTEI! HYOTEI! HYOTEI!
HYOTEI! HYOTEI!!

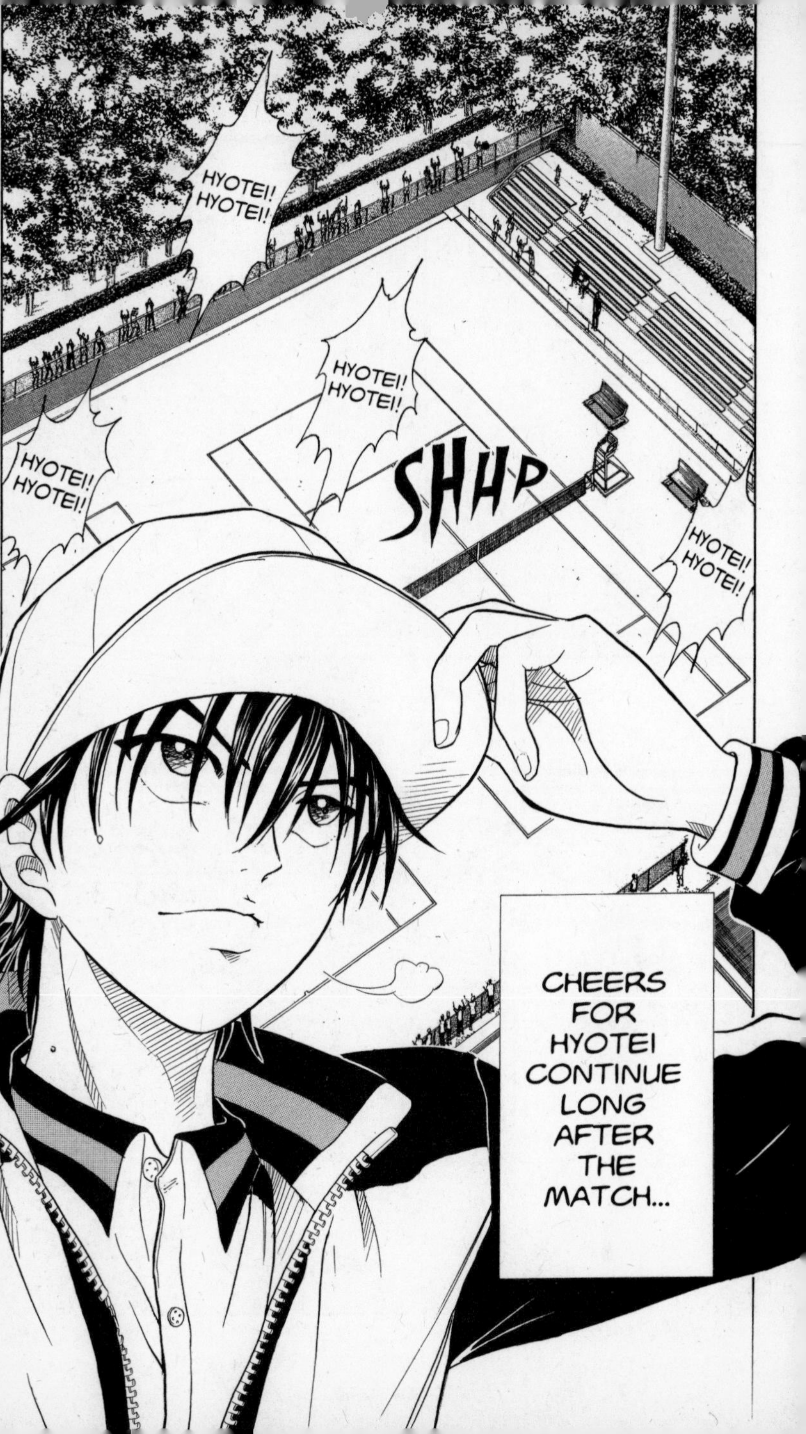
HYOTEI! HYOTEI!
HYOTEI! HYOTEI!
HYOTEI! HYOTEI!
SHHP
HYOTEI! HYOTEI!
CHEERS FOR HYOTEI CONTINUE LONG AFTER THE MATCH...

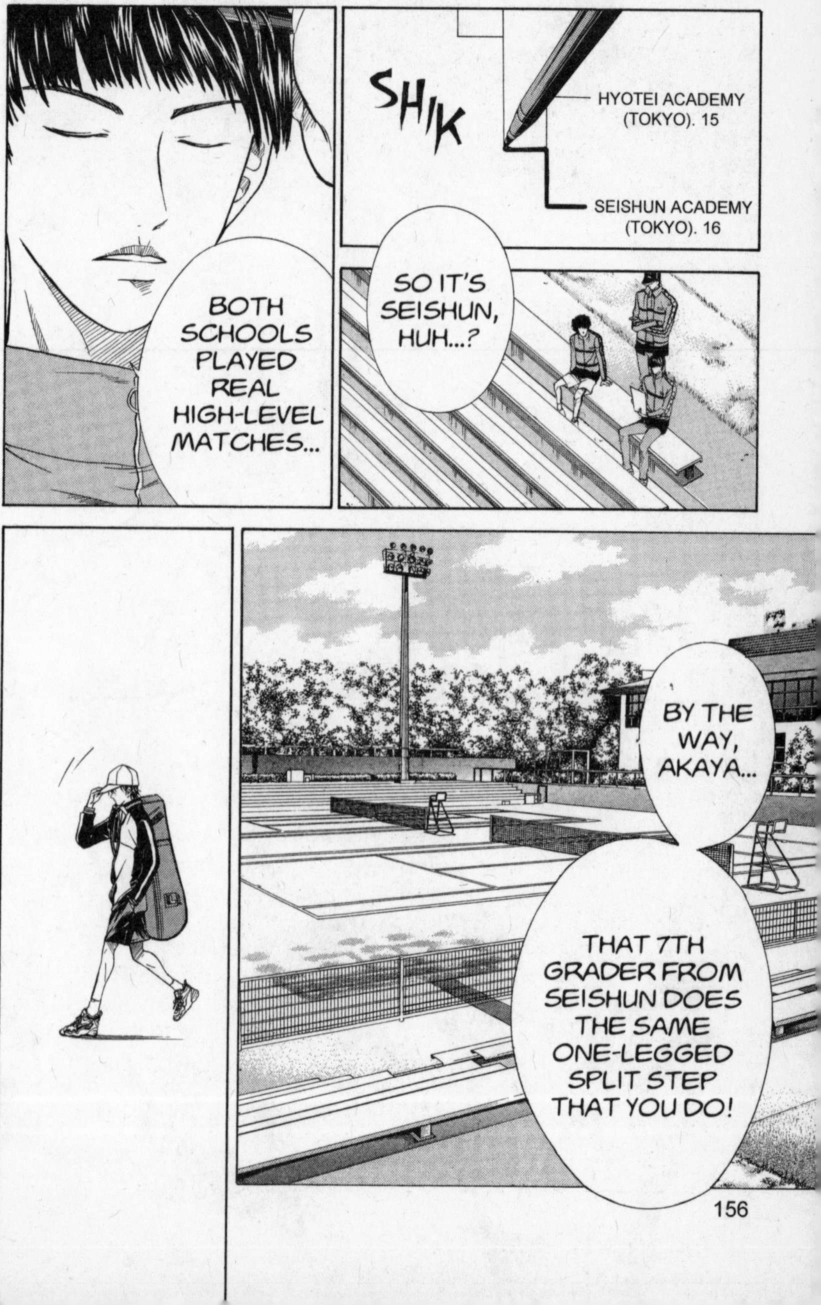
SHIK
HYOTEI ACADEMY (TOKYO). 15
SEISHUN ACADEMY (TOKYO). 16
SO IT'S SEISHUN, HUH...?
BOTH SCHOOLS PLAYED REAL HIGH-LEVEL MATCHES...
BY THE WAY, AKAYA...
THAT 7TH GRADER FROM SEISHUN DOES THE SAME ONE-LEGGED SPLIT STEP THAT YOU DO!

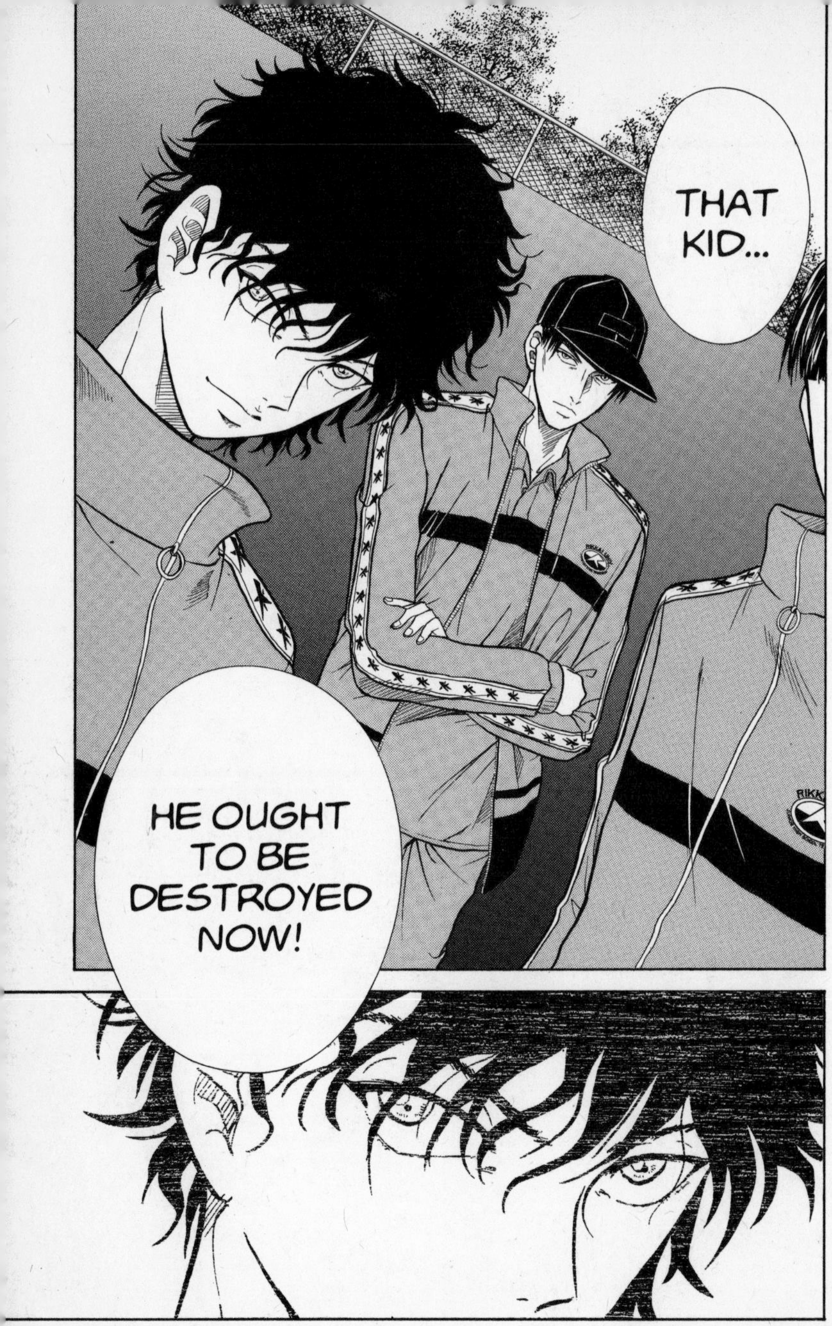
THAT KID...
HE OUGHT TO BE DESTROYED NOW!

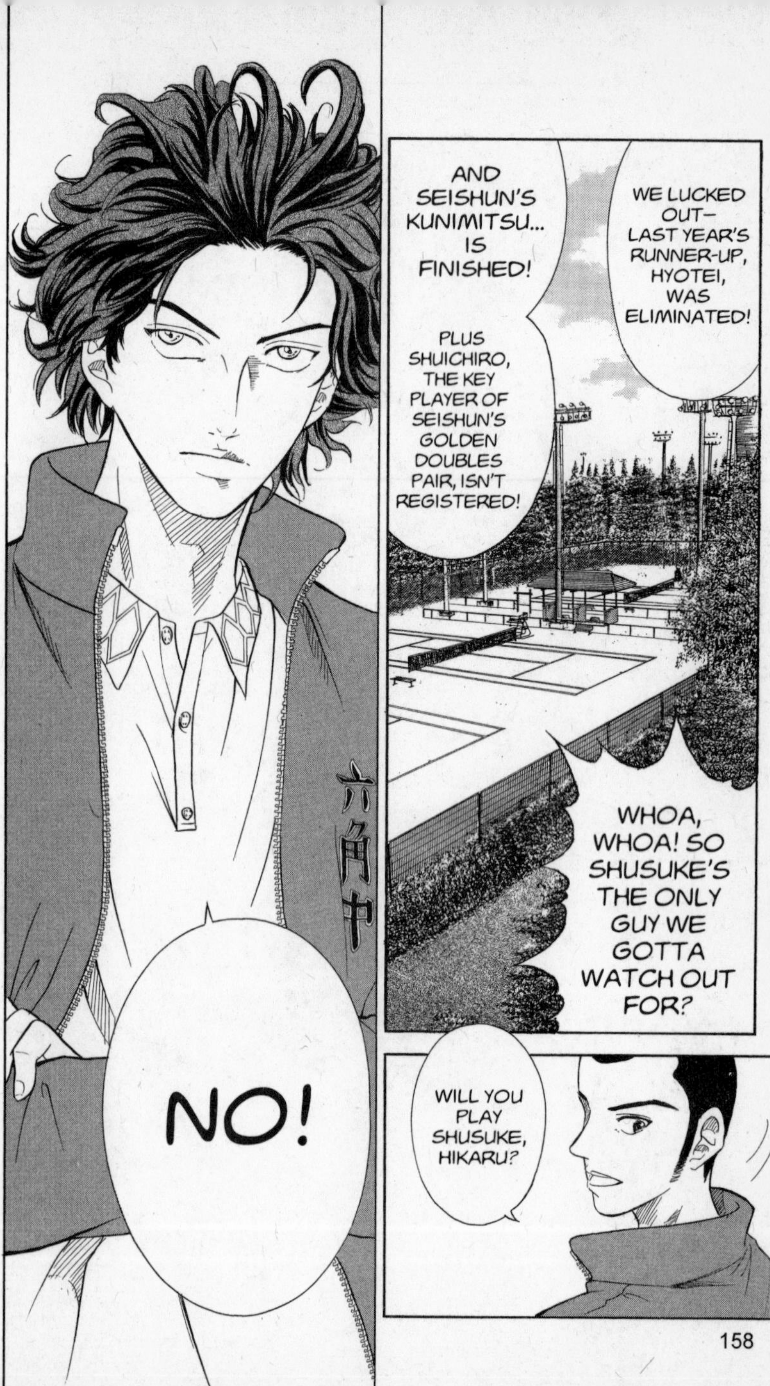
WE LUCKED OUT— LAST YEAR'S RUNNER-UP, HYOTEI, WAS ELIMINATED!
AND SEISHUN'S KUNIMITSU... IS FINISHED!
PLUS SHUICHIRO, THE KEY PLAYER OF SEISHUN'S GOLDEN DOUBLES PAIR, ISN'T REGISTERED!
WHOA, WHOA! SO SHUSUKE'S THE ONLY GUY WE GOTTA WATCH OUT FOR?
WILL YOU PLAY SHUSUKE, HIKARU?
NO!

READ THIS WAY

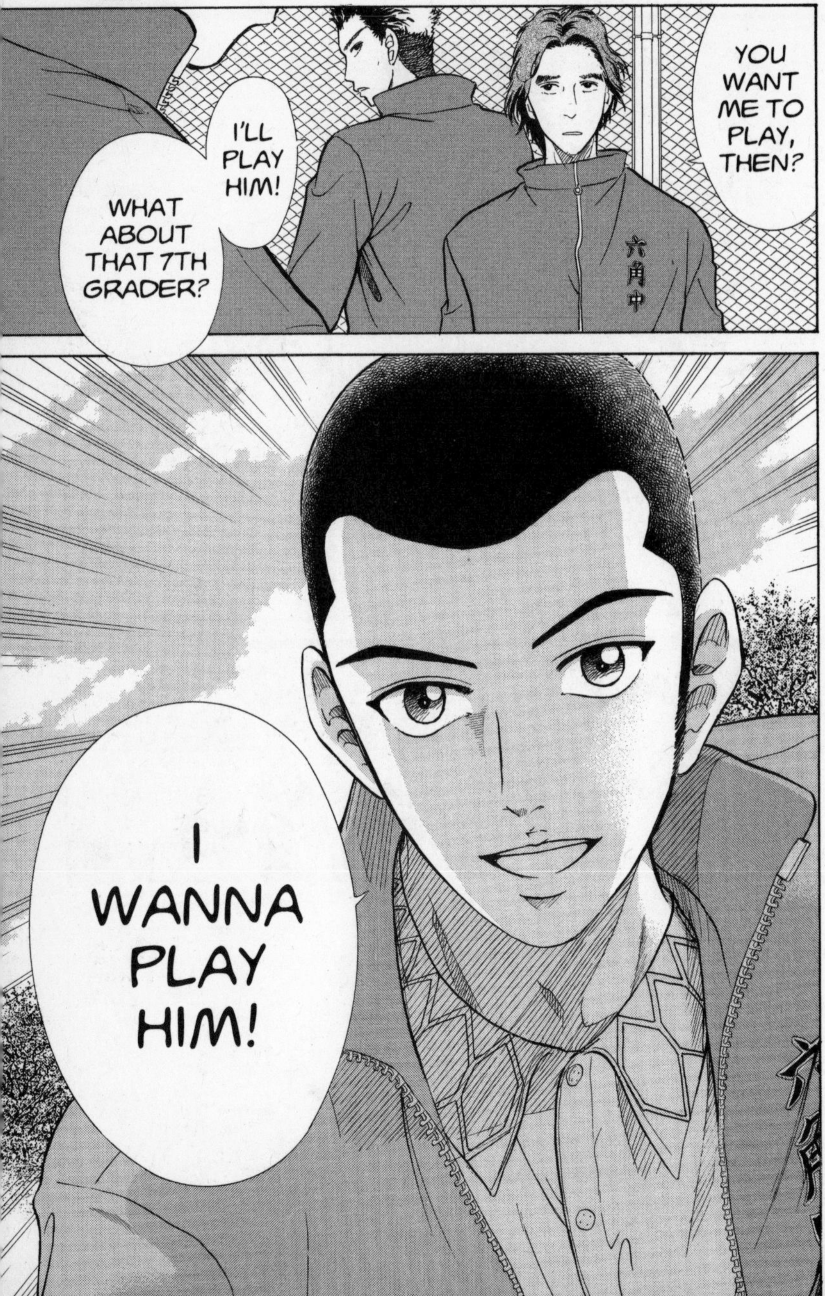
YOU WANT ME TO PLAY, THEN?
六角中
I'LL PLAY HIM!
WHAT ABOUT THAT 7TH GRADER?
I WANNA PLAY HIM!

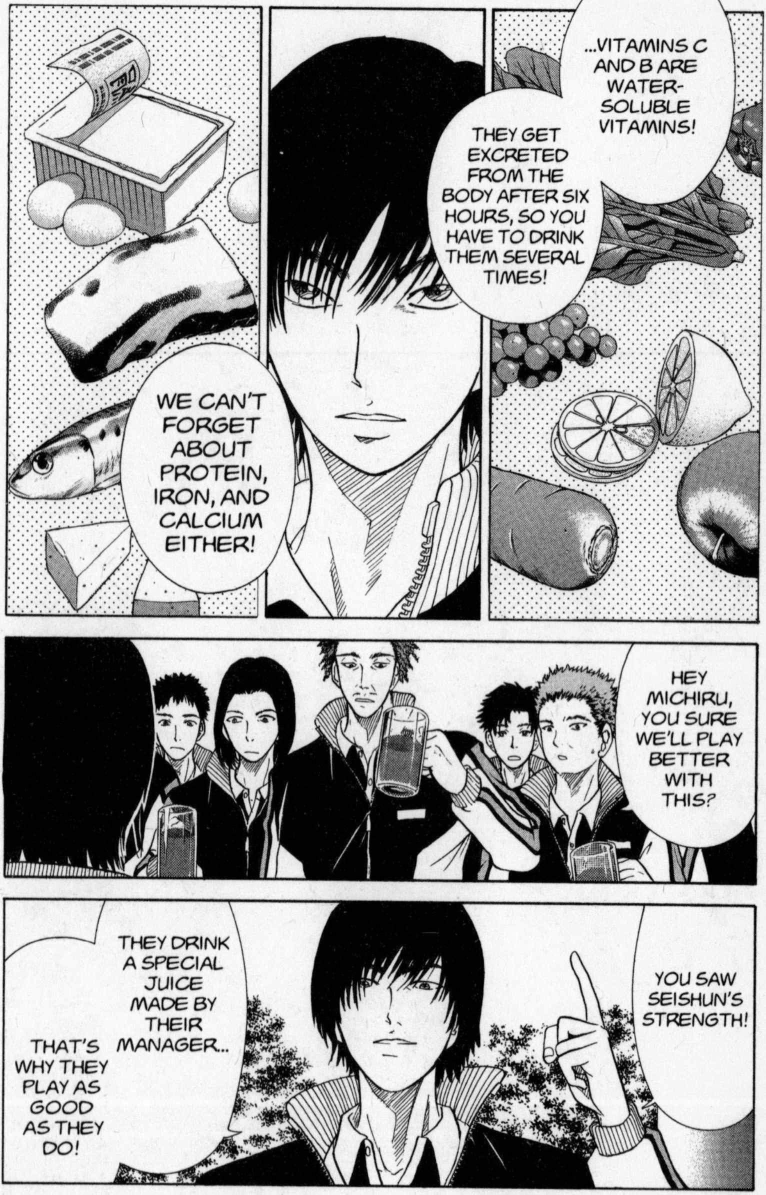
...VITAMINS C AND B ARE WATER-SOLUBLE VITAMINS!
THEY GET EXCRETED FROM THE BODY AFTER SIX HOURS, SO YOU HAVE TO DRINK THEM SEVERAL TIMES!
WE CAN'T FORGET ABOUT PROTEIN, IRON, AND CALCIUM EITHER!
HEY MICHIRU, YOU SURE WE'LL PLAY BETTER WITH THIS?
YOU SAW SEISHUN'S STRENGTH!
THEY DRINK A SPECIAL JUICE MADE BY THEIR MANAGER...
THAT'S WHY THEY PLAY AS GOOD AS THEY DO!

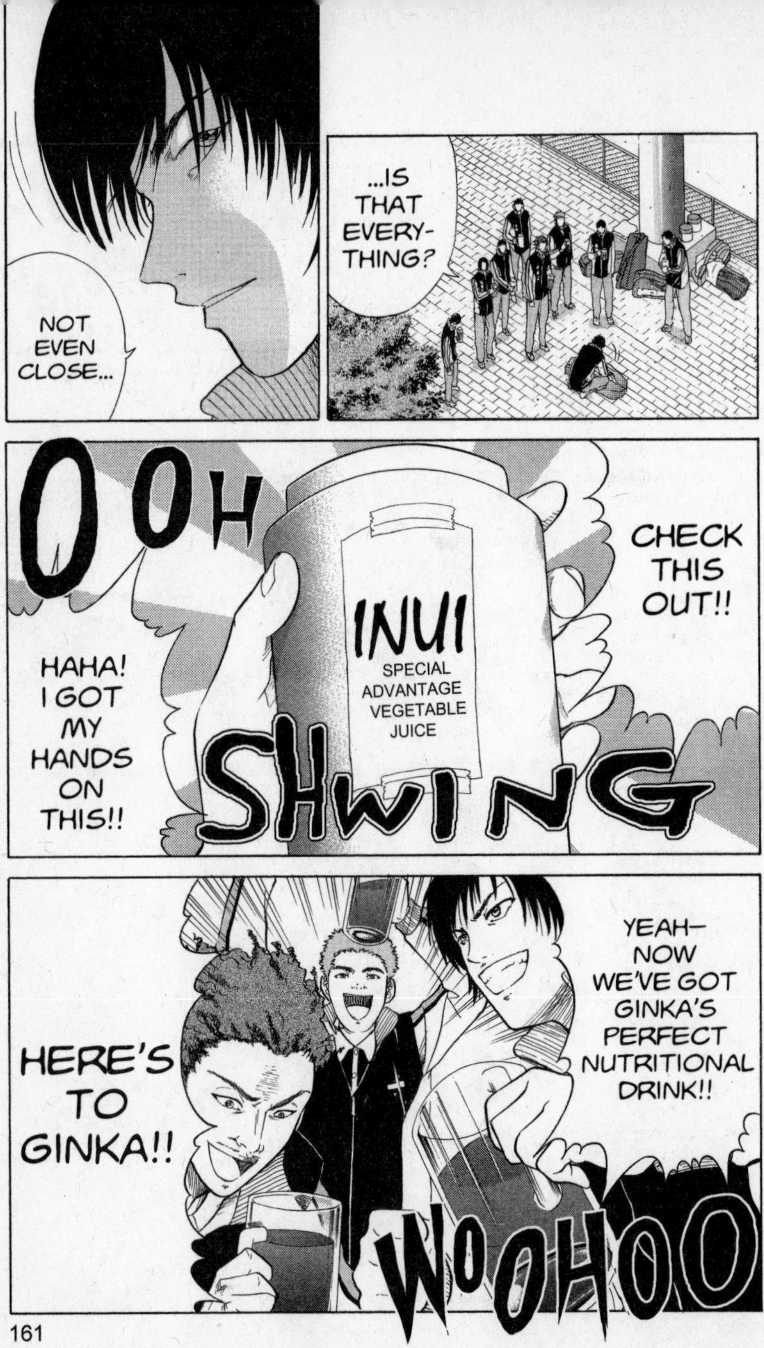
...IS THAT EVERY-THING?
NOT EVEN CLOSE...
CHECK THIS OUT!!
OOH
INUI
SPECIAL ADVANTAGE VEGETABLE JUICE
HAHA! I GOT MY HANDS ON THIS!!
SHWING
YEAH— NOW WE'VE GOT GINKA'S PERFECT NUTRITIONAL DRINK!!
HERE'S TO GINKA!!
WOOHOO

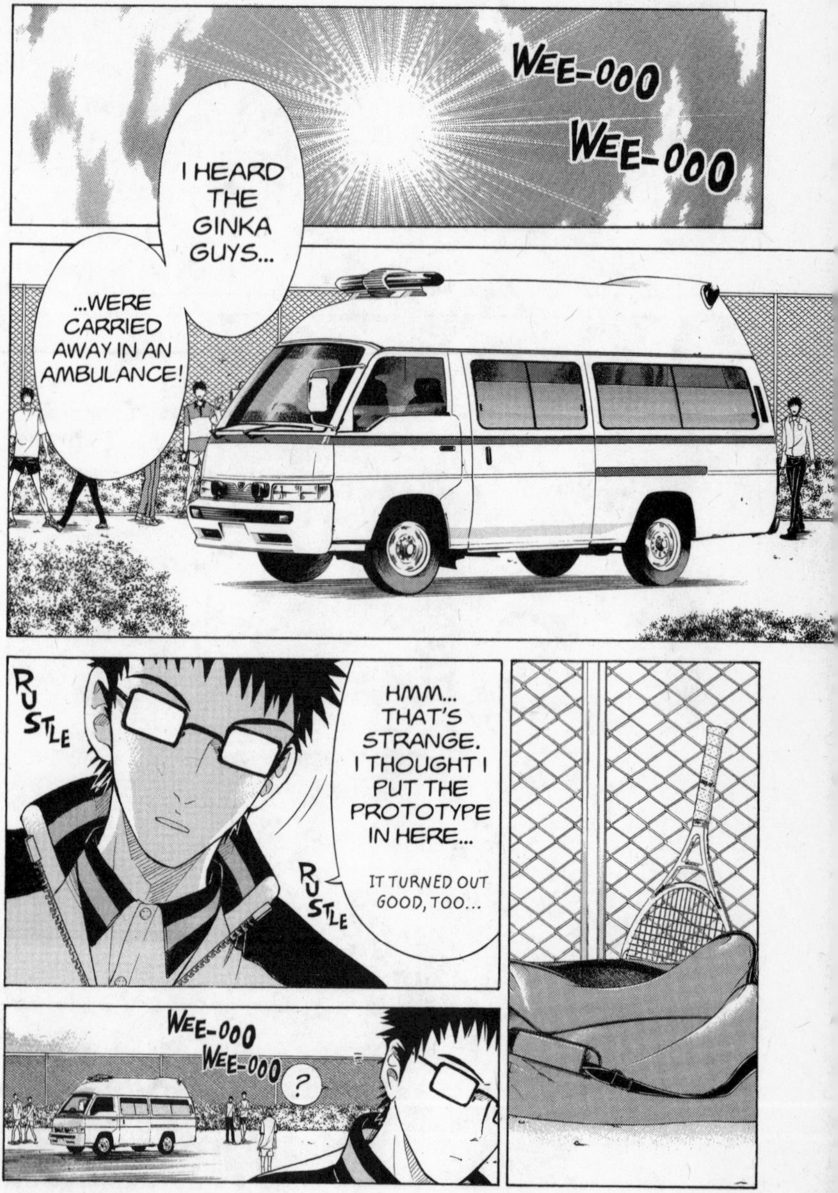
WEE-OOO
WEE-OOO
I HEARD THE GINKA GUYS...
...WERE CARRIED AWAY IN AN AMBULANCE!
HMM... THAT'S STRANGE. I THOUGHT I PUT THE PROTOTYPE IN HERE...
IT TURNED OUT GOOD, TOO...
RUSTLE
RUSTLE
WEE-OOO
WEE-OOO
?

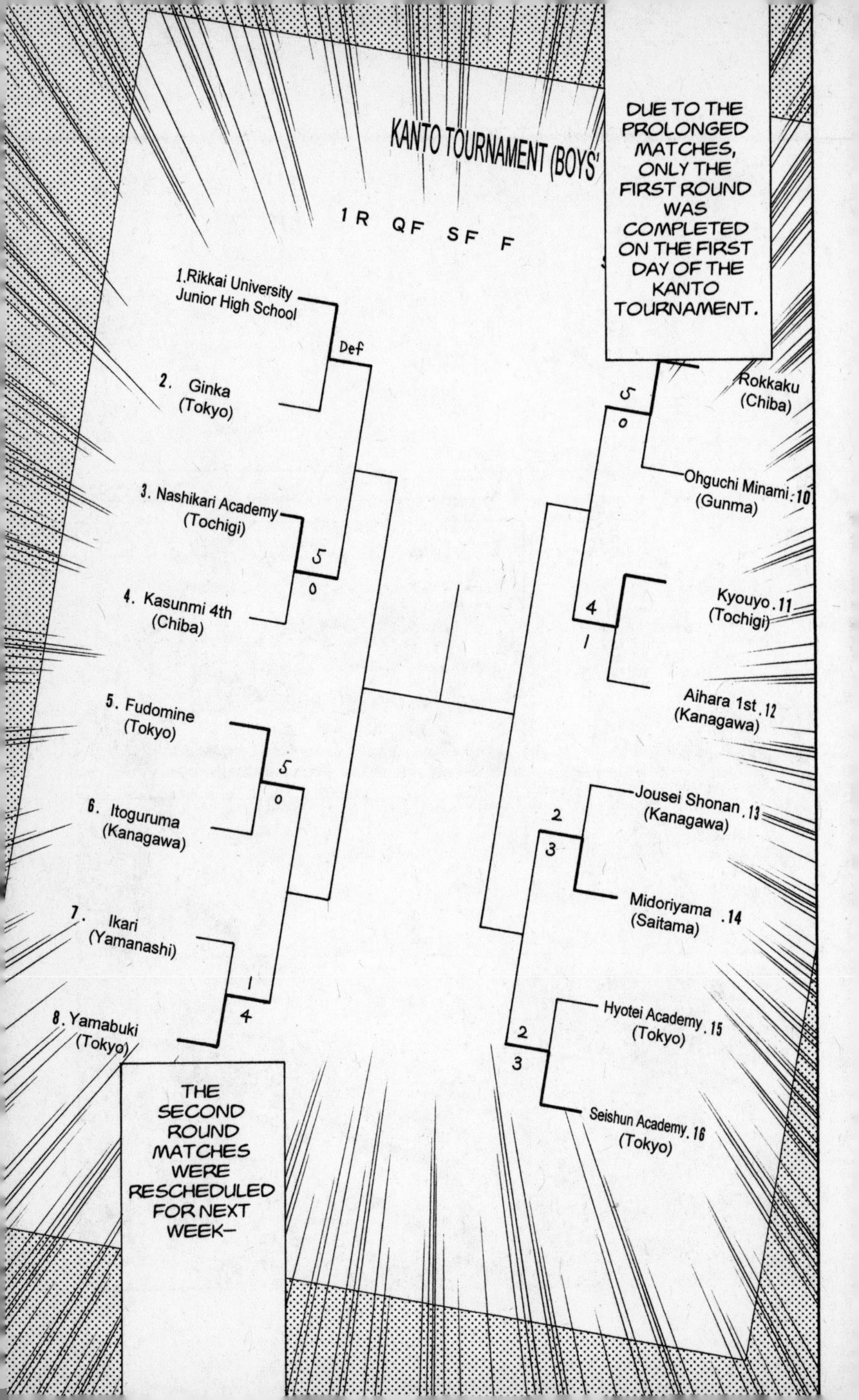
DUE TO THE PROLONGED MATCHES, ONLY THE FIRST ROUND WAS COMPLETED ON THE FIRST DAY OF THE KANTO TOURNAMENT.
KANTO TOURNAMENT (BOYS'
1R QF SF F
1.Rikkai University Junior High School
Def
2. Ginka (Tokyo)
3. Nashikari Academy (Tochigi)
5
0
4. Kasunmi 4th (Chiba)
5. Fudomine (Tokyo)
5
0
6. Itoguruma (Kanagawa)
7. Ikari (Yamanashi)
1
4
8. Yamabuki (Tokyo)
Rokkaku (Chiba)
5
0
Ohguchi Minami .10 (Gunma)
Kyouyo .11 (Tochigi)
4
1
Aihara 1st .12 (Kanagawa)
Jousei Shonan .13 (Kanagawa)
2
3
Midoriyama .14 (Saitama)
Hyotei Academy .15 (Tokyo)
2
3
Seishun Academy .16 (Tokyo)
THE SECOND ROUND MATCHES WERE RESCHEDULED FOR NEXT WEEK–

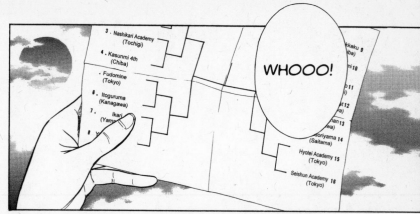

3 . Nashikari Academy
(Tochigi)

4 . Kasunmi 4th
(Chiba)

. Fudomine
(Tokyo)

6 . Itoguruma
(Kanagawa)

7 . Ikari
(Yama

8

kkaku 9
ba)

mi 10

)

st 12
a)

han 13
wa)

doriyama 14
(Saitama)

Hyotei Academy 15
(Tokyo)

Seishun Academy 16
(Tokyo)

WHOOO!

DESPITE EVERY THING HE SAID...

WH HNG

GNN NNG

WHOOO

GN NNG

READ THIS WAY

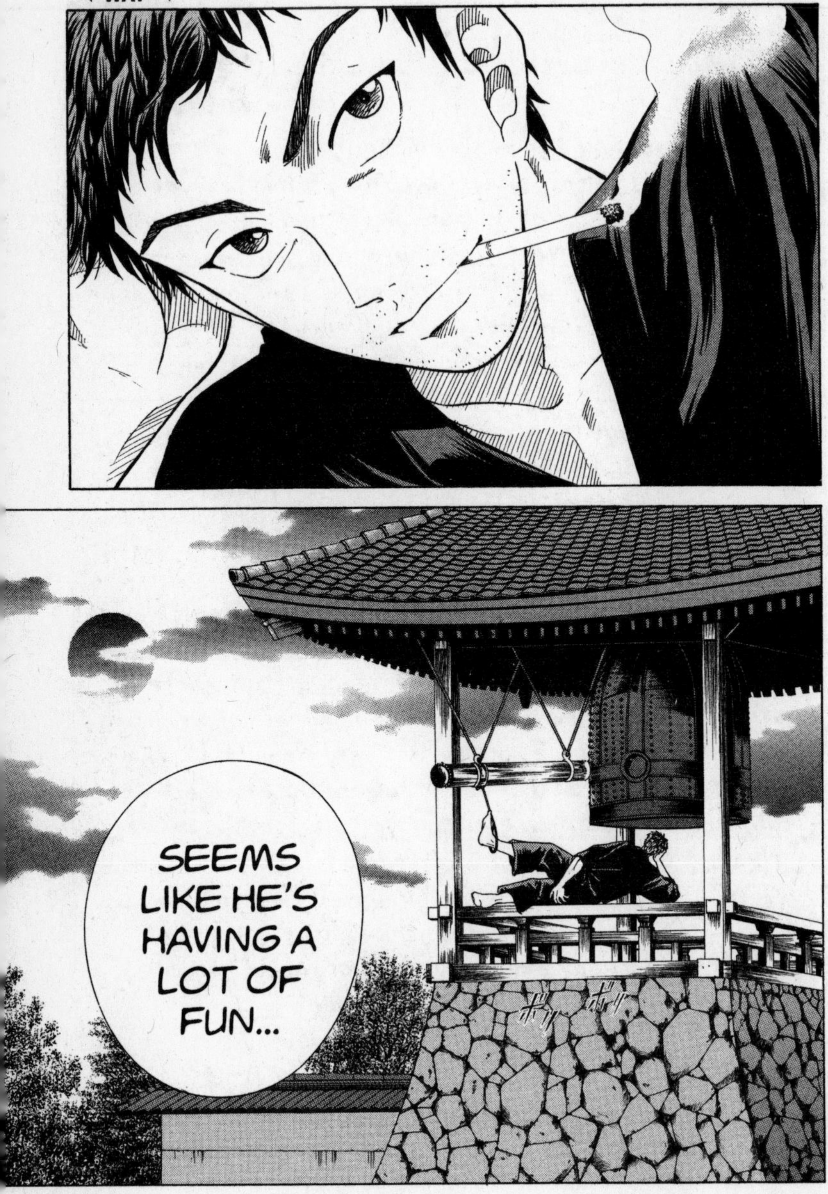
SEEMS LIKE HE'S HAVING A LOT OF FUN...

テニスの王子様
THE PRINCE OF TENNIS

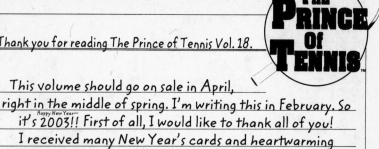

Thank you for reading The Prince of Tennis Vol. 18.

This volume should go on sale in April, right in the middle of spring. I'm writing this in February. So it's 2003!! (Happy New Year—) First of all, I would like to thank all of you! I received many New Year's cards and heartwarming messages this year! Thank you very much. I am so proud as an author to receive New Year's cards every year from readers from the beginning, new readers, families watching the animation, and many others! Every time I take one in my hand, it gives me the strength to keep going! If it weren't for these cards, I would've dropped dead from the intense schedule! Thank you so much!
I'm gonna keep doing my best in 2003!!

On a separate note, the long Seishun vs. Hyotei match has finally come to an end. Several of the matches' results changed from what I initially intended. (But whose matches those were is a secret!) I had a lot of fun writing it, and the match turned out to be a very memorable. The majority of you hated Hyotei, but toward the end there were many who claimed their eternal loyalty to Hyotei. I am very pleased. The very popular one-frame bits were a bit too difficult to include in the Kunimitsu-Keigo match, so they were excluded for this volume. I'm sorry.
A lot of new schools are being introduced in the magazine.
Let's keep charging ahead with Seishun!!

I'll see you in Vol. 19!!

テニスの王子様☆
T.KONOMI!
2003.2.28

GENIUS 158: BOWLING, GO!

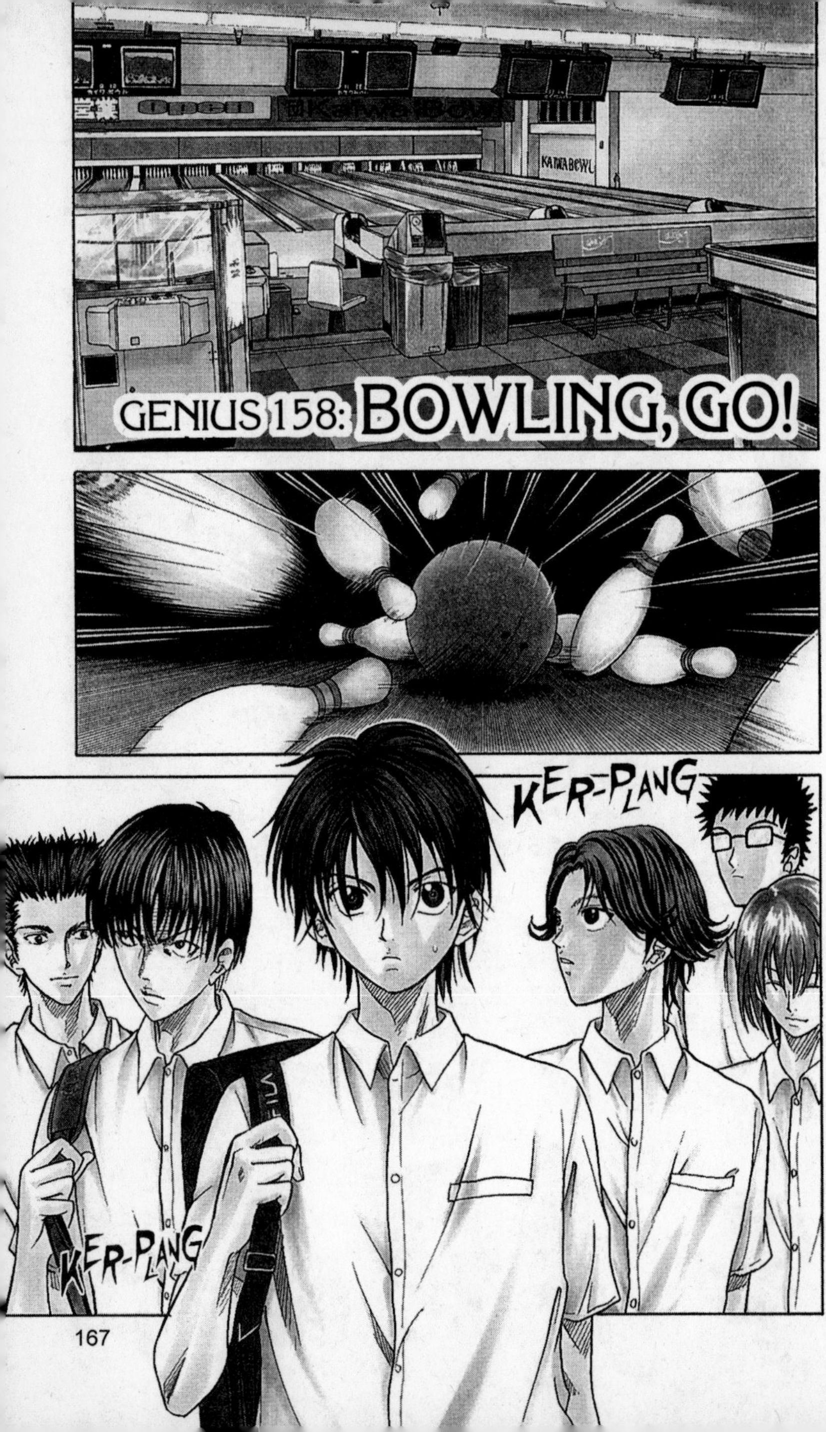
KER-PLANG
KER-PLANG

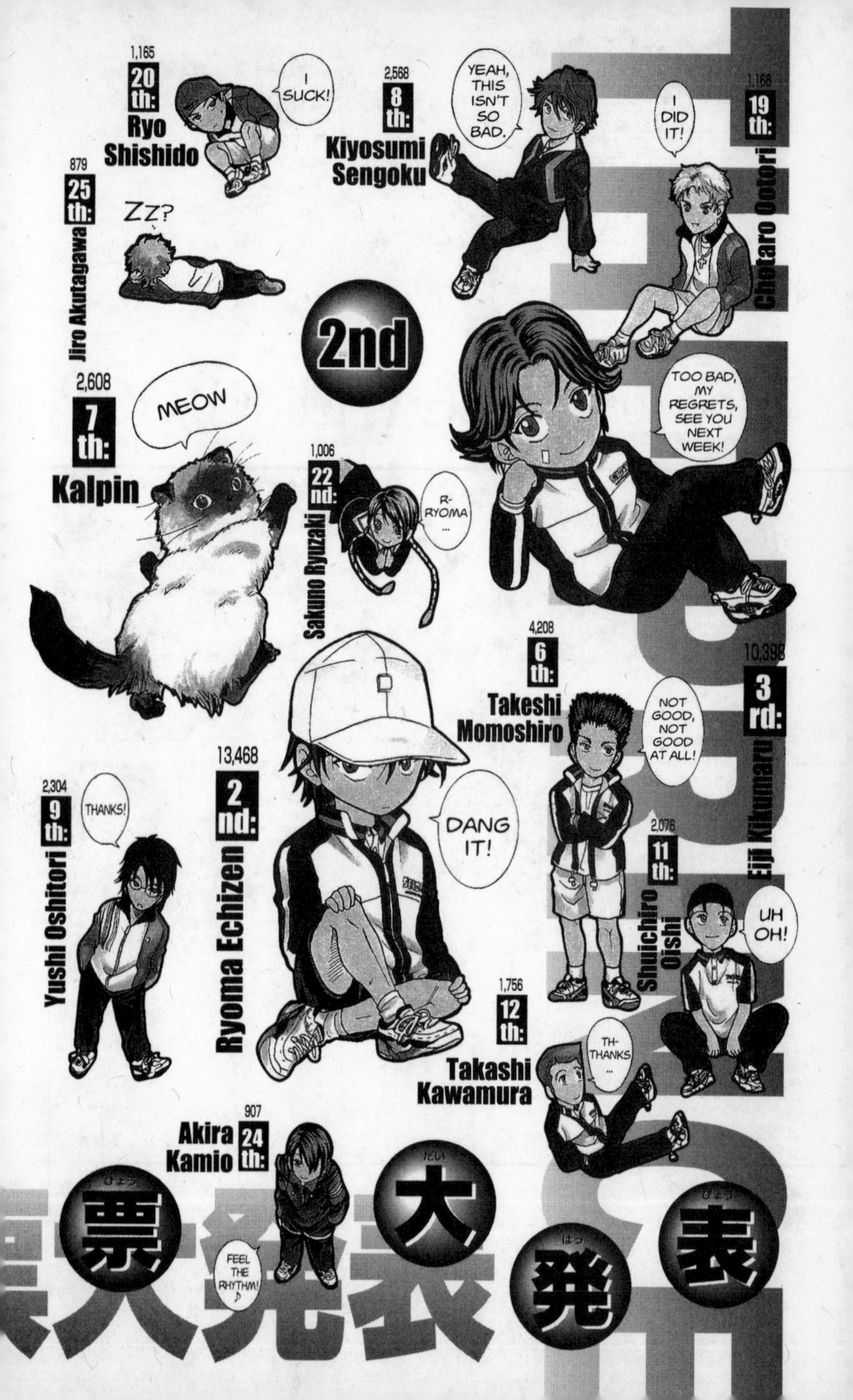
1,168
19th: Chotaro Ootori
I DID IT!
2,568
8th: Kiyosumi Sengoku
YEAH, THIS ISN'T SO BAD.
1,165
20th: Ryo Shishido
I SUCK!
879
25th: Jiro Akutagawa
ZZ?
2nd
TOO BAD, MY REGRETS, SEE YOU NEXT WEEK!
1,006
22nd: Sakuno Ryuzaki
R-RYOMA ...
2,608
7th: Kalpin
MEOW
10,398
3rd: Eiji Kikumaru
NOT GOOD, NOT GOOD AT ALL!
4,208
6th: Takeshi Momoshiro
2,076
11th: Shuichiro Oishi
UH OH!
13,468
2nd: Ryoma Echizen
DANG IT!
2,304
9th: Yushi Oshitori
THANKS!
1,756
12th: Takashi Kawamura
TH-THANKS ...
907
24th: Akira Kamio
FEEL THE RHYTHM! ♪
票大発表

Genius 158: Bowling, Go!

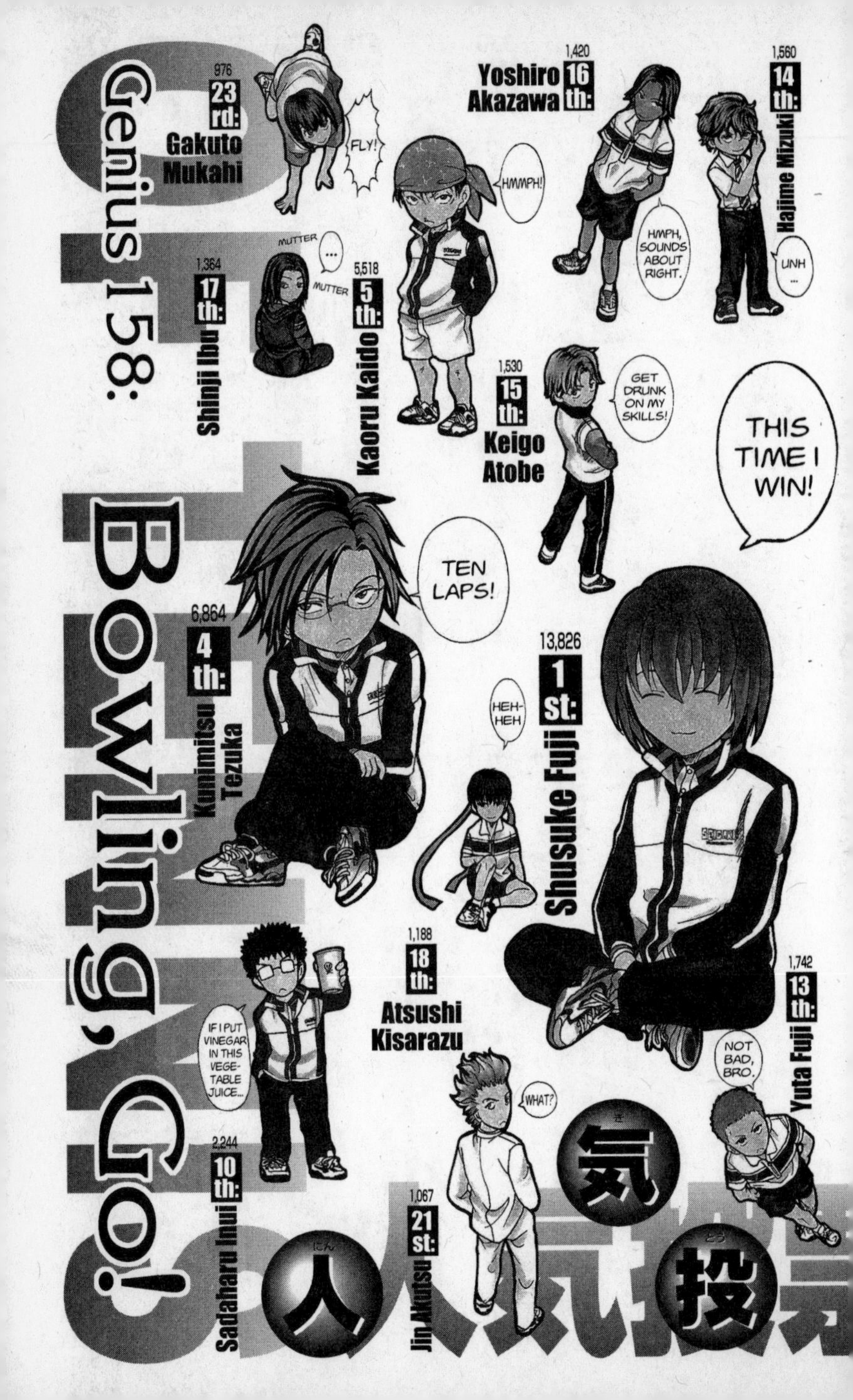
1,560
14th: Hajime Mizuki
UNH ...
1,420
16th: Yoshiro Akazawa
HMPH, SOUNDS ABOUT RIGHT.
1,530
15th: Keigo Atobe
GET DRUNK ON MY SKILLS!
THIS TIME I WIN!
5,518
5th: Kaoru Kaido
HMMPH!
976
23rd: Gakuto Mukahi
FLY!
1,364
17th: Shinji Ibu
MUTTER
...
MUTTER
13,826
1st: Shusuke Fuji
HEH-HEH
6,864
4th: Kunimitsu Tezuka
TEN LAPS!
1,742
13th: Yuta Fuji
NOT BAD, BRO.
1,188
18th: Atsushi Kisarazu
1,067
21st: Jin Akutsu
WHAT?
2,244
10th: Sadaharu Inui
IF I PUT VINEGAR IN THIS VEGE-TABLE JUICE...
人気投票

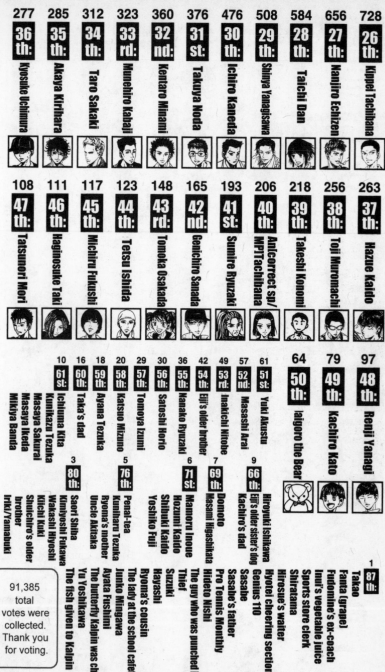

26th: Kippei Tachibana 728

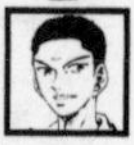

27th: Nanjiro Echizen 656

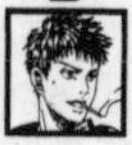

28th: Taichi Dan 584

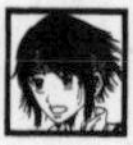

29th: Shinya Yanagisawa 508

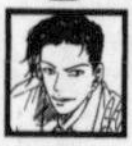

30th: Ichiro Kaneda 476

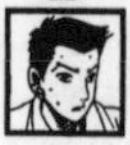

31st: Takuya Noda 376

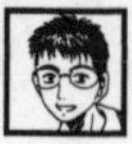

32nd: Kentaro Minami 360

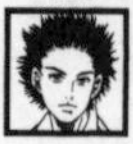

33rd: Munehiro Kabaji 323

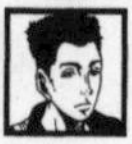

34th: Taro Sakaki 312

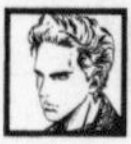

35th: Akaya Kirihara 285

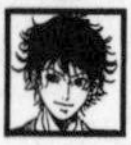

36th: Kyosuke Uchimura 277

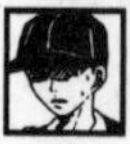

37th: Hazue Kaido 263

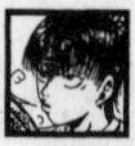

38th: Toji Muromachi 256

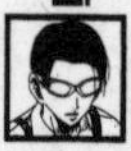

39th: Takeshi Konomi 218

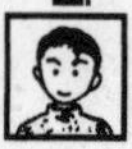

40th: Ani correct sp/ MP! Tachibana 206

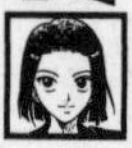

41st: Sumire Ryuzaki 193

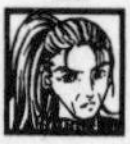

42nd: Genichiro Sanada 165

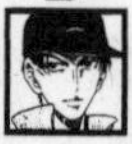

43rd: Tomoka Osakada 148

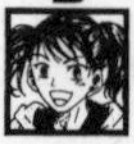

44th: Tetsu Ishida 123

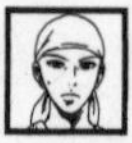

45th: Michiru Fukushi 117

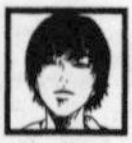

46th: Haginosuke Taki 111

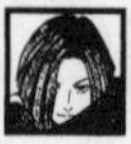

47th: Tatsunori Mori 108

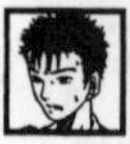

48th: Renji Yanagi 97

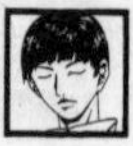

49th: Kachiro Kato 79

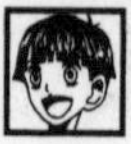

50th: Taigoro the Bear 64

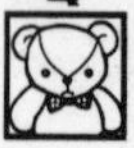

51st: Yuki Akustu 61

52nd: Masashi Arai 57

53rd: Inakichi Nitobe 49

54th: Eiji's older brother 42

55th: Nanako Ryuzaki 36

56th: Satoshi Horio 30

57th: Tomoya Izumi 29

58th: Katsuo Mizuno 20

59th: Ayana Tezuka 18

60th: Taka's dad 16

61st: 10
Ichiuma Kita
Kunikazu Tezuka
Masaya Sakurai
Masaya Ikeda
Mikiya Banda

66th: 9
Hiroyuki Ishikawa
Eiji's older sister's dog
Kachiro's dad

69th: 7
Domoto
Masami Higashikata

71st: 6
Mamoru Inoue
Hozumi Kaido
Shibuki Kaido
Yoshiko Fuji

76th: 5
Penal-tea
Kuniharu Tezuka
Ryoma's mother
Uncle Akitaka

80th: 3
Saori Shiba
Kimiyoshi Fukawa
Wakashi Hiyoshi
Kiichi Kuki
Shuichiro's older brother
Iriki/Yamabuki

87th: 1
Takao
Fanta (grape)
Fudomine's ex-coach
Inui's vegetable juice
Sports store clerk
Shiratama
Hirosue's waiter
Hyotei Cheering section
Genius 110
Sasabe
Sasabe's father
Pro Tennis Monthly
Hideto Nishi
The guy who was punched by Jin
Thief
Suzuki
Hayashi
Ryoma's cousin
The lady at the school cafeteria
Junko Mingawa
Ayata Fushimi
The butterfly Kalpin was chasing
Yu Yoshikawa
The fish given to Kalpin

91,385 total votes were collected. Thank you for voting.

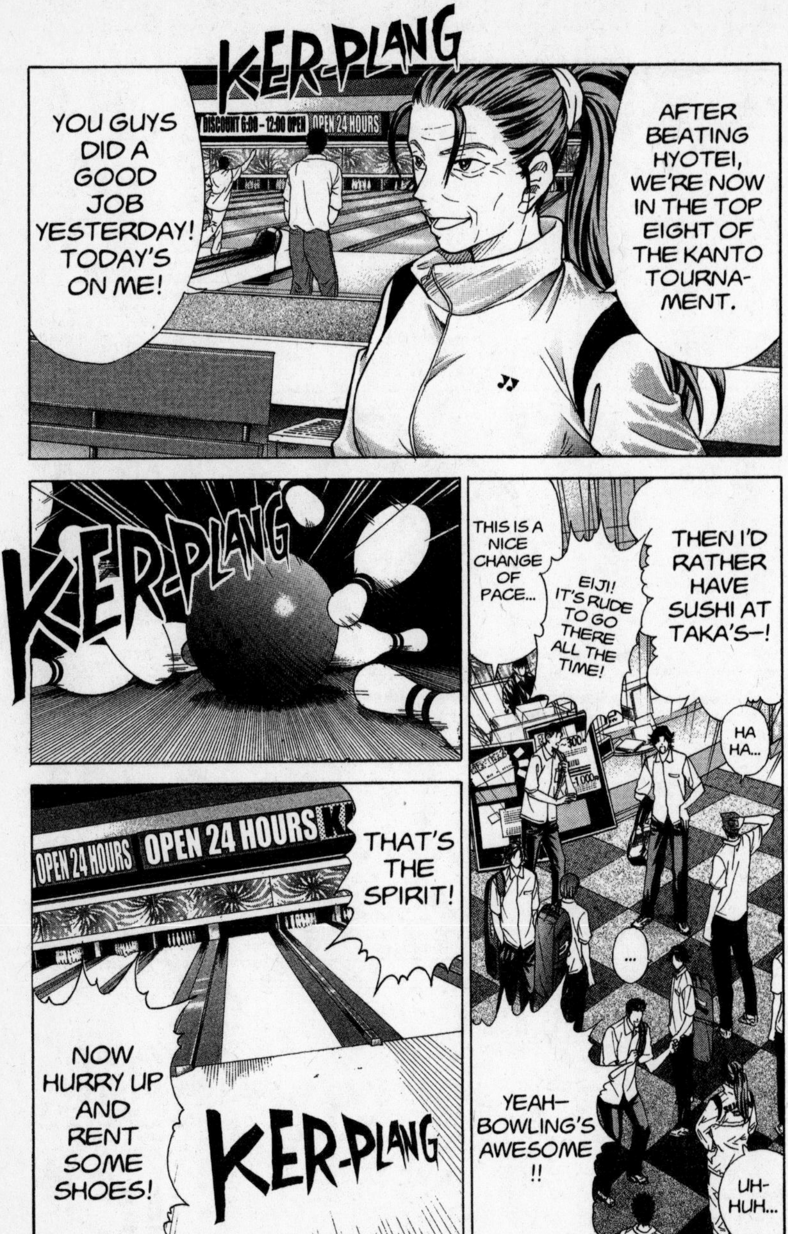
KER-PLANG
AFTER BEATING HYOTEI, WE'RE NOW IN THE TOP EIGHT OF THE KANTO TOURNAMENT.
DISCOUNT 6:00 - 12:00 OPEN
OPEN 24 HOURS
YOU GUYS DID A GOOD JOB YESTERDAY! TODAY'S ON ME!
THEN I'D RATHER HAVE SUSHI AT TAKA'S—!
EIJI! IT'S RUDE TO GO THERE ALL THE TIME!
THIS IS A NICE CHANGE OF PACE...
HA HA...
...
UH-HUH...
YEAH— BOWLING'S AWESOME !!
KER-PLANG
OPEN 24 HOURS
OPEN 24 HOURS
THAT'S THE SPIRIT!
NOW HURRY UP AND RENT SOME SHOES!
KER-PLANG

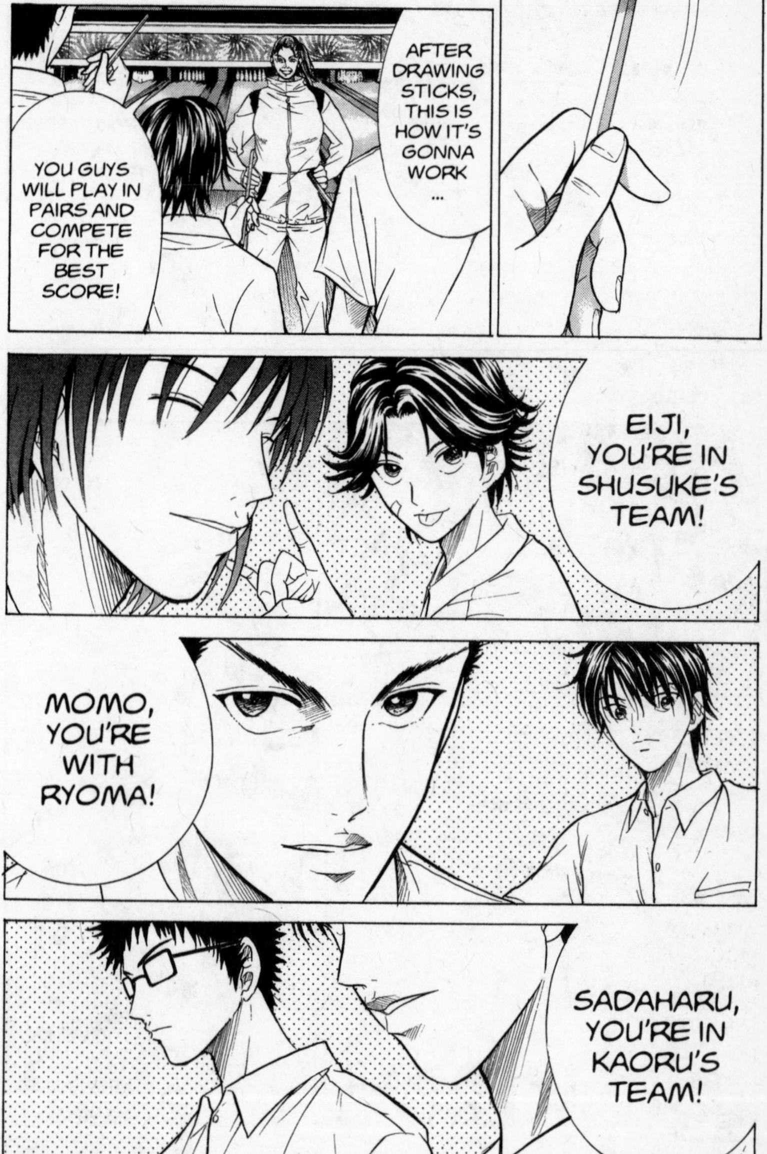
AFTER DRAWING STICKS, THIS IS HOW IT'S GONNA WORK ...
YOU GUYS WILL PLAY IN PAIRS AND COMPETE FOR THE BEST SCORE!
EIJI, YOU'RE IN SHUSUKE'S TEAM!
MOMO, YOU'RE WITH RYOMA!
SADAHARU, YOU'RE IN KAORU'S TEAM!

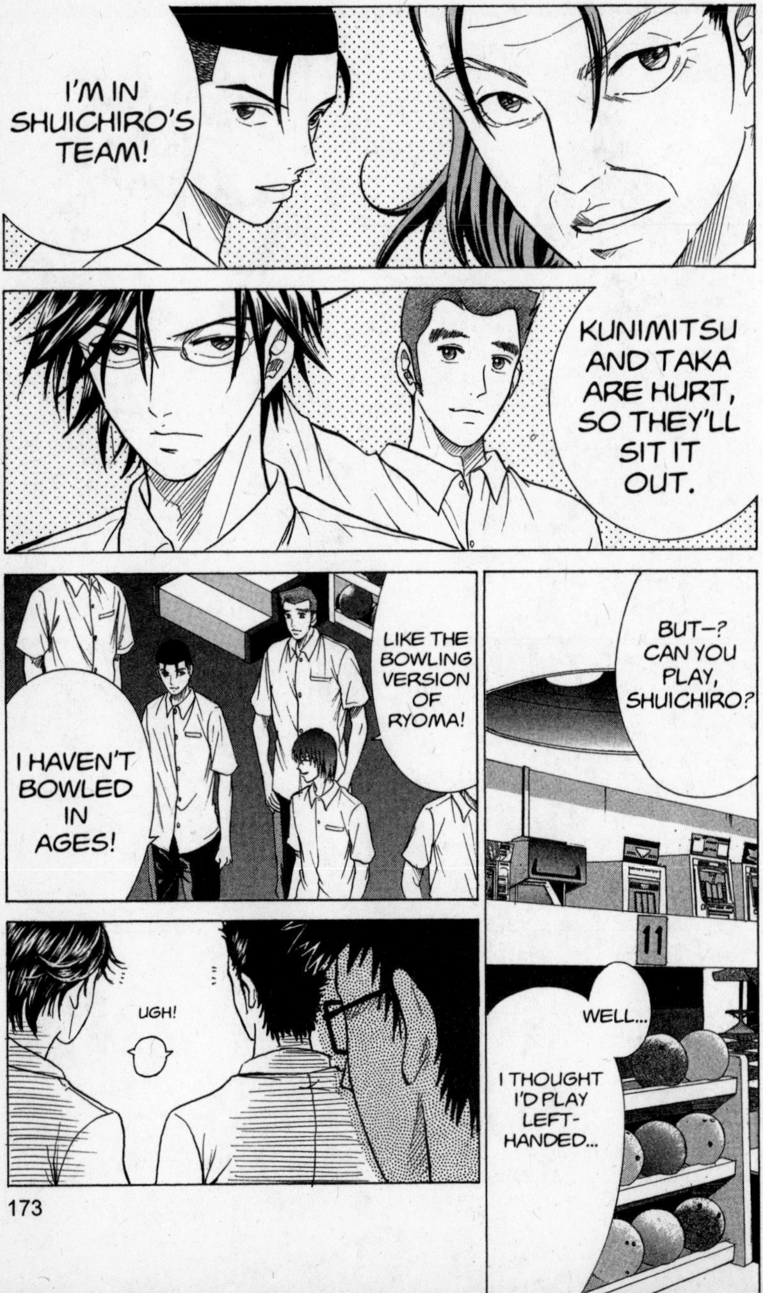
I'M IN SHUICHIRO'S TEAM!
KUNIMITSU AND TAKA ARE HURT, SO THEY'LL SIT IT OUT.
BUT–? CAN YOU PLAY, SHUICHIRO?
LIKE THE BOWLING VERSION OF RYOMA!
I HAVEN'T BOWLED IN AGES!
WELL...
I THOUGHT I'D PLAY LEFT-HANDED...
11
UGH!

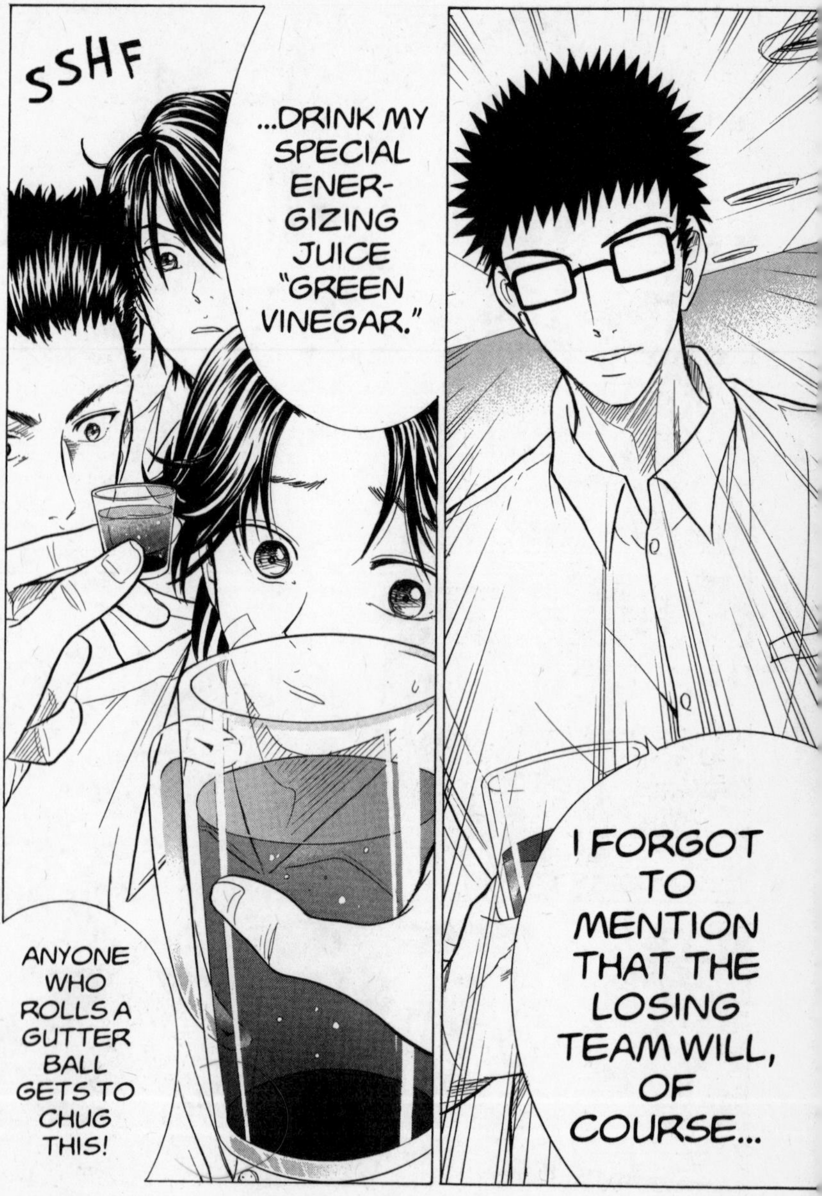
I FORGOT TO MENTION THAT THE LOSING TEAM WILL, OF COURSE...
SSHF
...DRINK MY SPECIAL ENER-GIZING JUICE "GREEN VINEGAR."
ANYONE WHO ROLLS A GUTTER BALL GETS TO CHUG THIS!

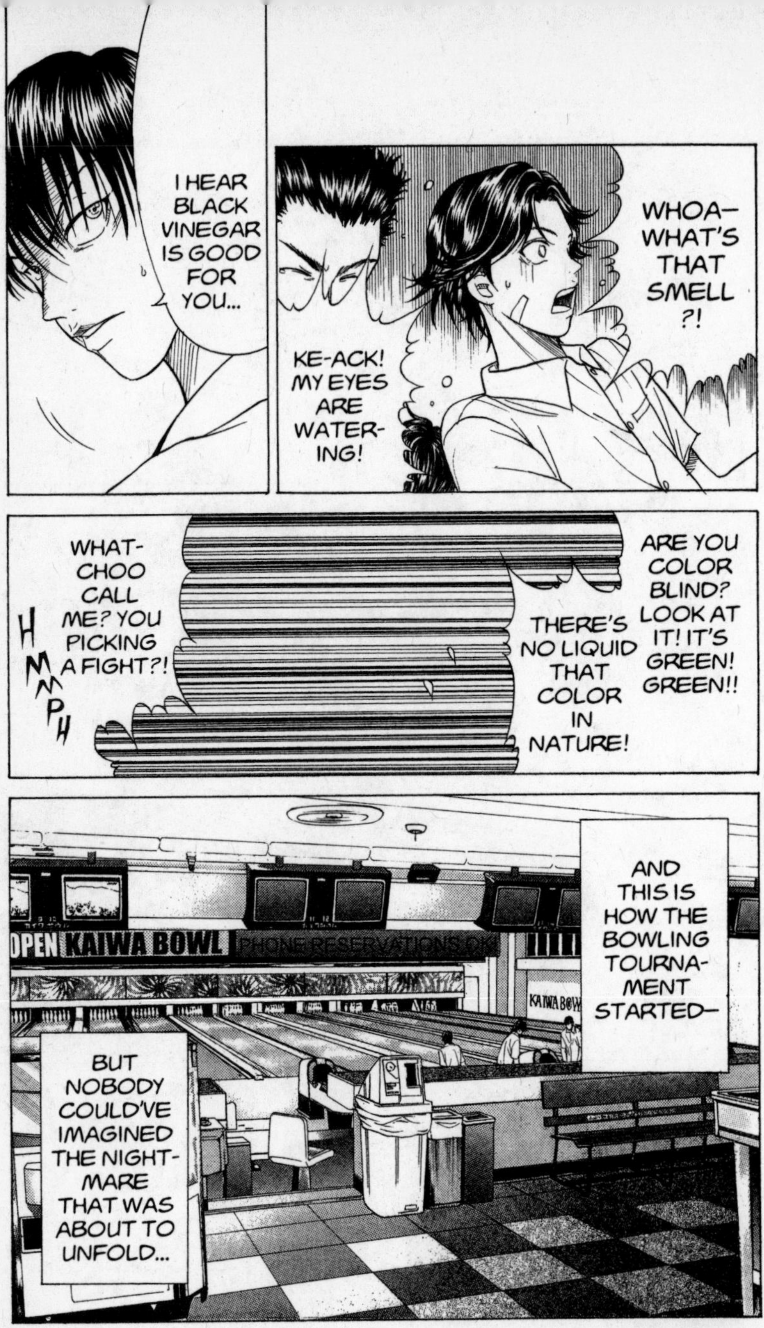
WHOA— WHAT'S THAT SMELL ?!
KE-ACK! MY EYES ARE WATERING!
I HEAR BLACK VINEGAR IS GOOD FOR YOU...
ARE YOU COLOR BLIND? LOOK AT IT! IT'S GREEN! GREEN!!
THERE'S NO LIQUID THAT COLOR IN NATURE!
WHATCHOO CALL ME? YOU PICKING A FIGHT?!
HMMPH
AND THIS IS HOW THE BOWLING TOURNAMENT STARTED—
OPEN KAIWA BOWL PHONE RESERVATIONS OK!
KAIWA BOW
BUT NOBODY COULD'VE IMAGINED THE NIGHTMARE THAT WAS ABOUT TO UNFOLD...

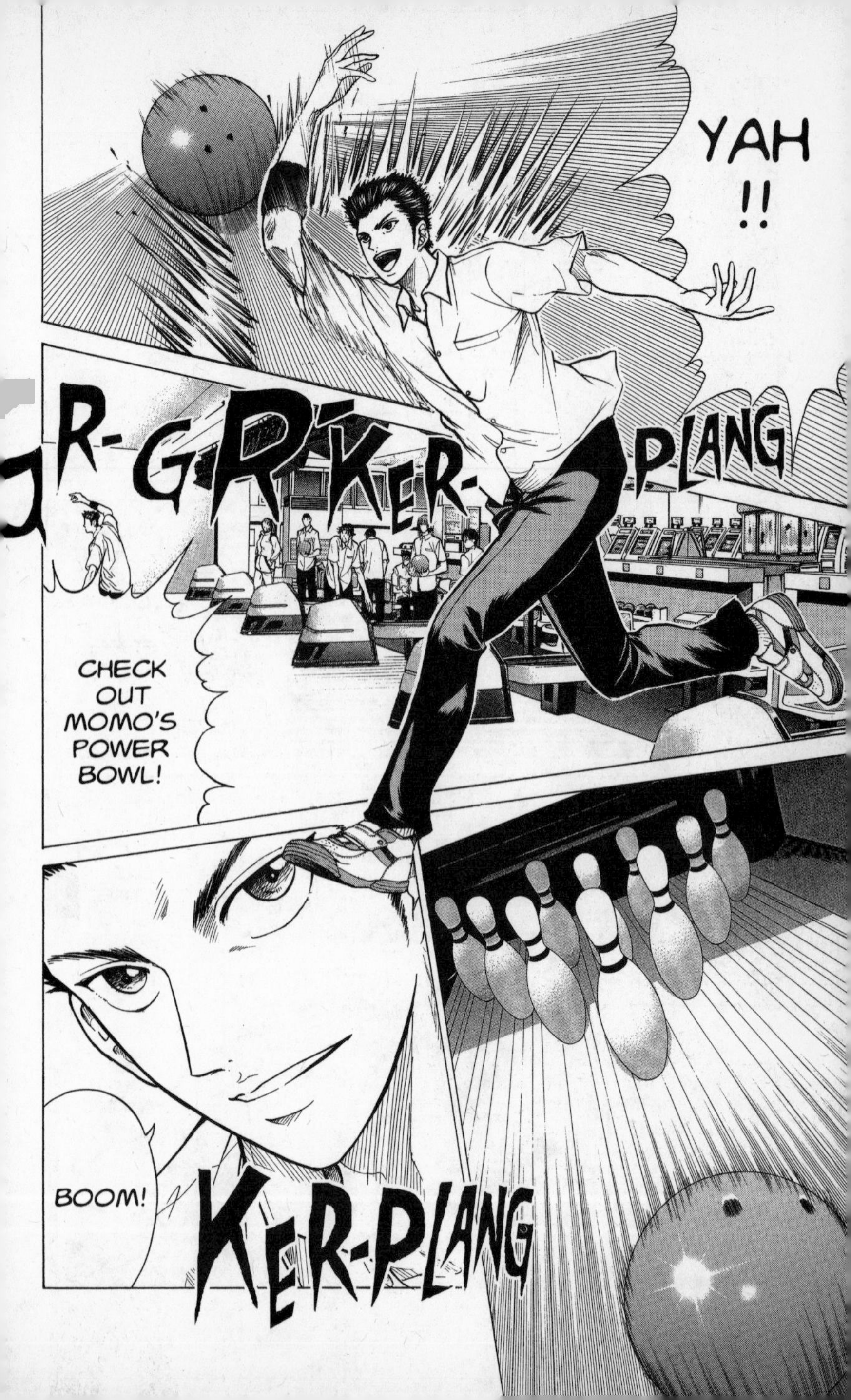
YAH !!
R-GR-KER-PLANG
CHECK OUT MOMO'S POWER BOWL!
BOOM!
KER-PLANG

READ THIS WAY

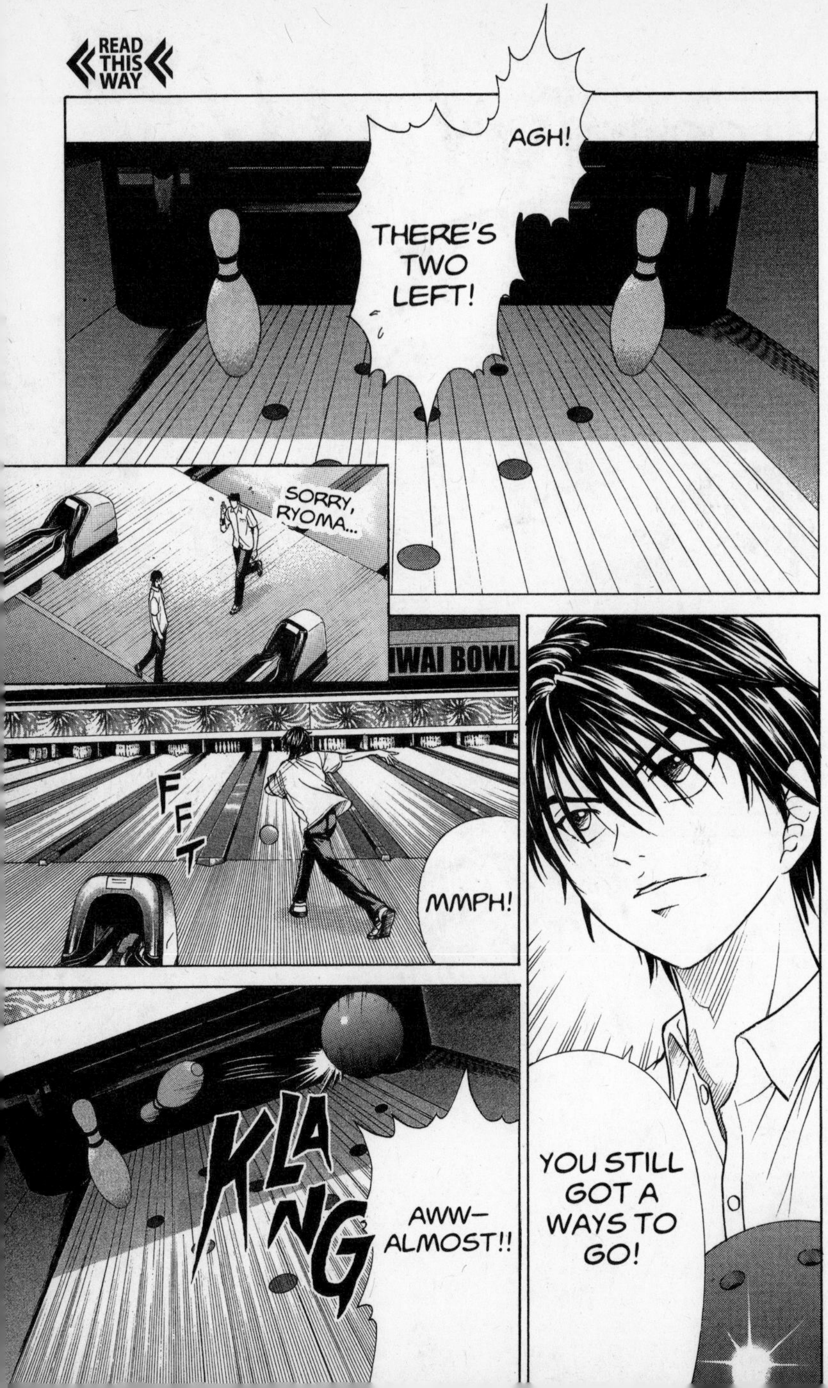
AGH!
THERE'S TWO LEFT!
SORRY, RYOMA...
YOU STILL GOT A WAYS TO GO!
IWAI BOWL
FFT
MMPH!
KLANG
AWW— ALMOST!!

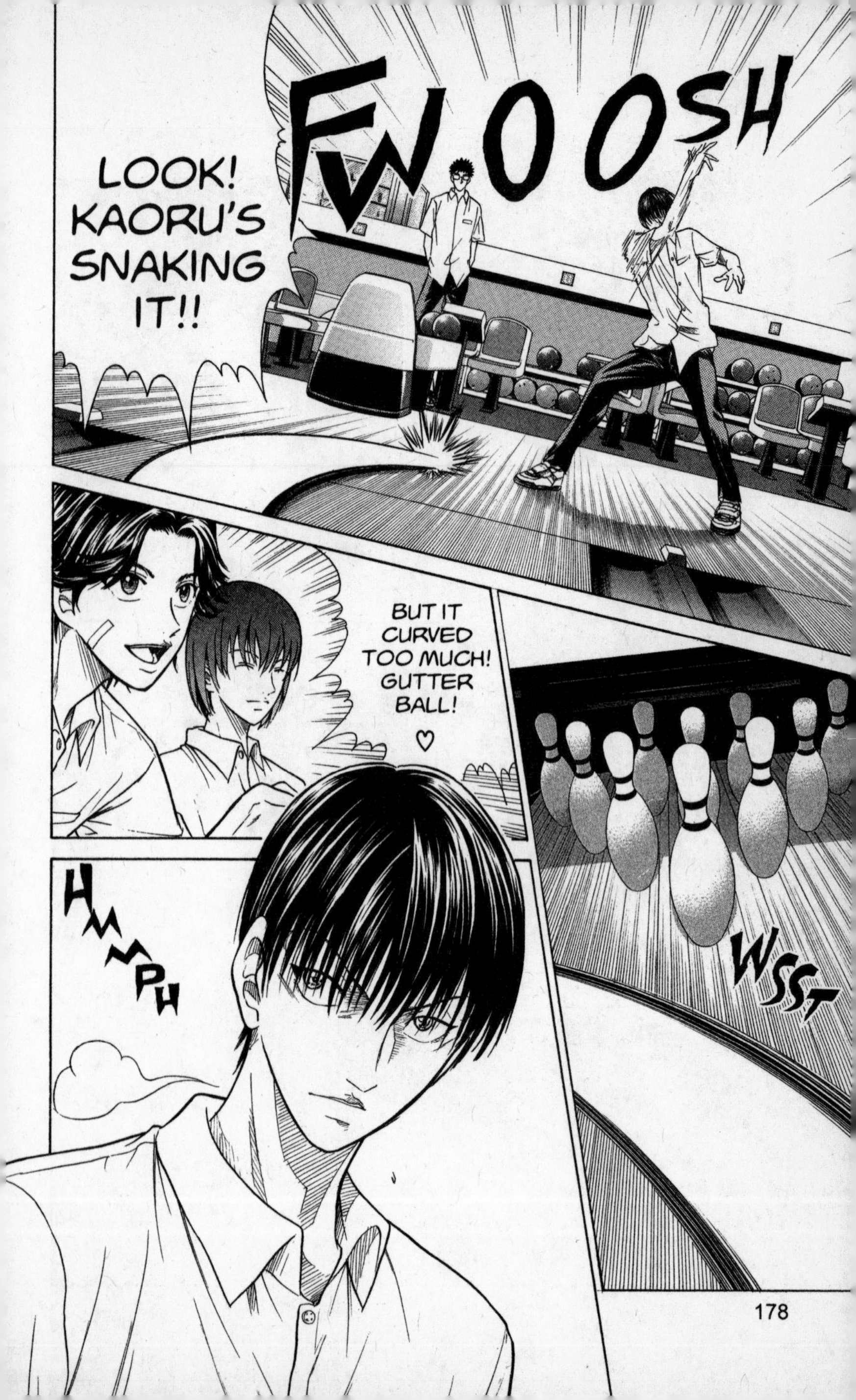
FWOOSH
LOOK! KAORU'S SNAKING IT!!
WSST
BUT IT CURVED TOO MUCH! GUTTER BALL! ♡
HMMPH

READ THIS WAY

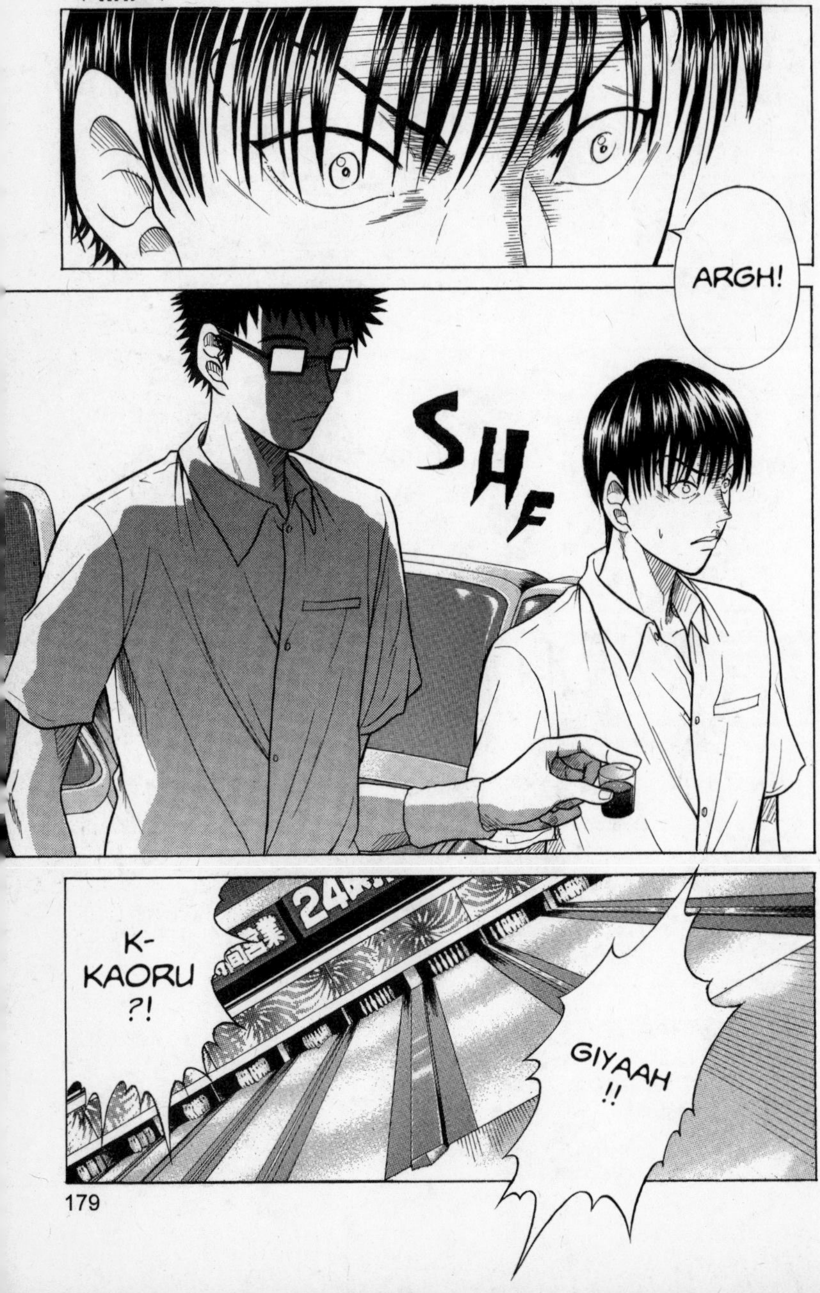

ARGH!
SHF
GIYAAH!!
K-KAORU?!

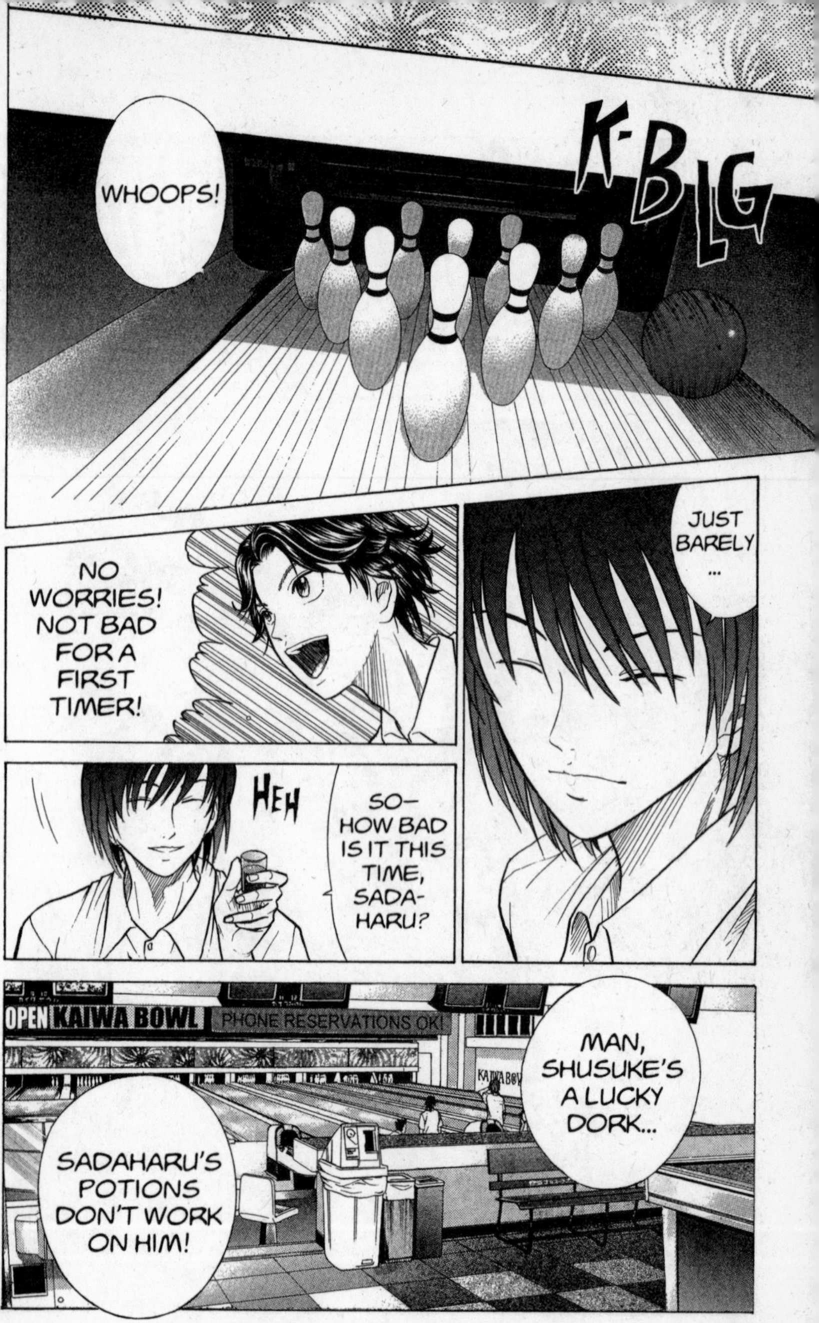
K-BLG
WHOOPS!
JUST BARELY ...
NO WORRIES! NOT BAD FOR A FIRST TIMER!
SO— HOW BAD IS IT THIS TIME, SADAHARU?
HEH
MAN, SHUSUKE'S A LUCKY DORK...
OPEN KAIWA BOWL
PHONE RESERVATIONS OK!
SADAHARU'S POTIONS DON'T WORK ON HIM!

READ THIS WAY

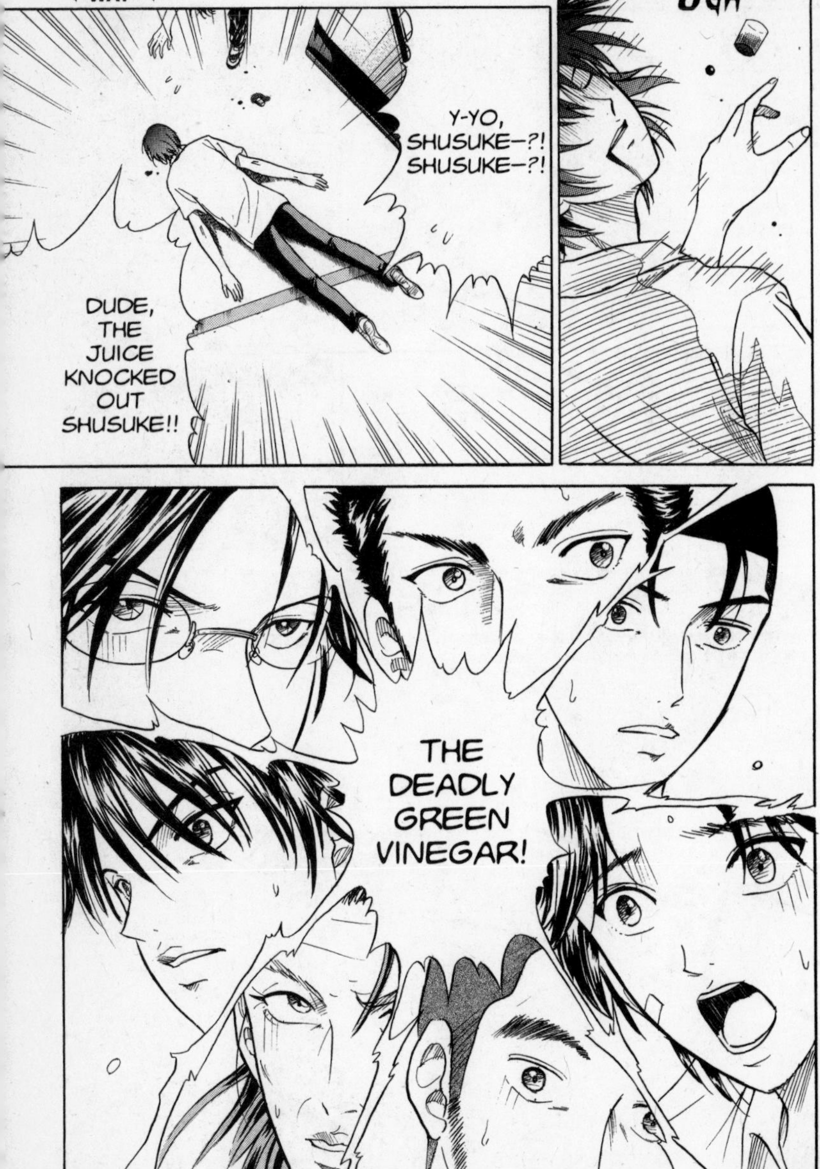
BLEOUGH
Y-YO, SHUSUKE-?! SHUSUKE-?!
DUDE, THE JUICE KNOCKED OUT SHUSUKE!!
THE DEADLY GREEN VINEGAR!

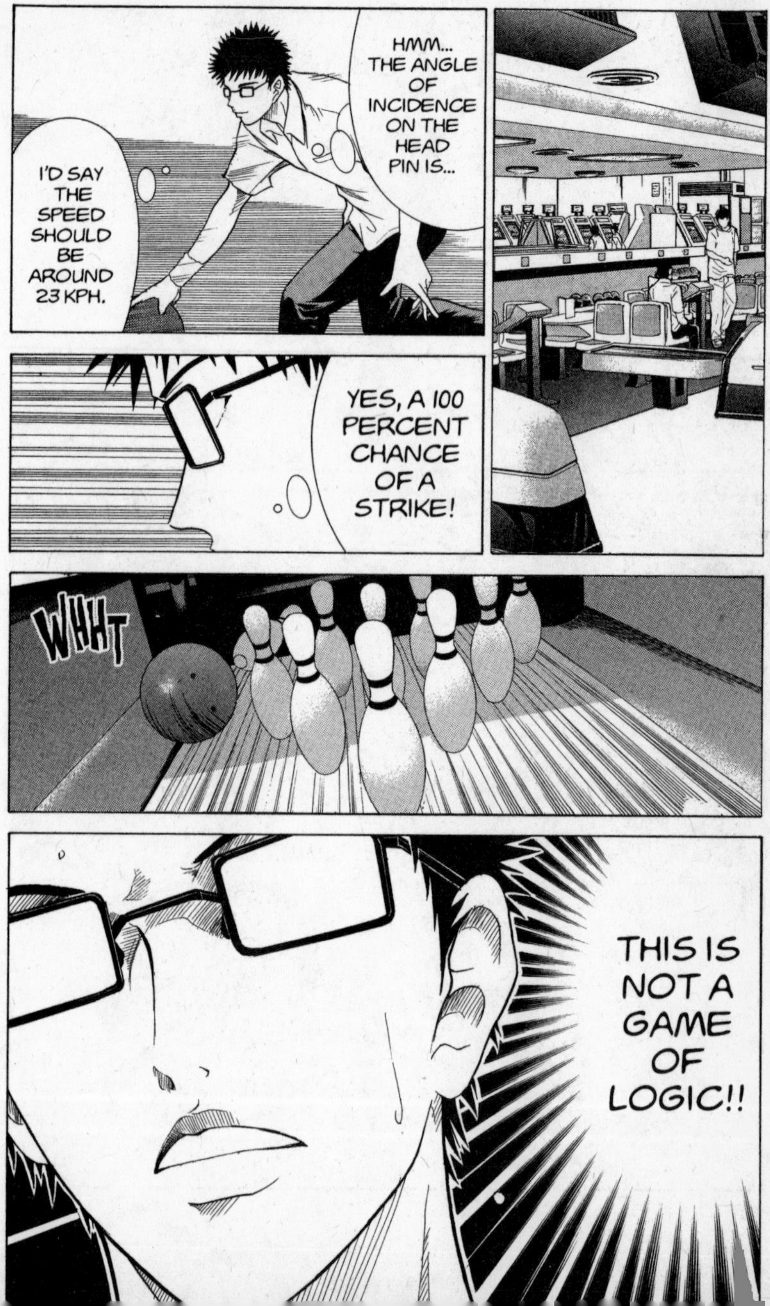
HMM... THE ANGLE OF INCIDENCE ON THE HEAD PIN IS...
I'D SAY THE SPEED SHOULD BE AROUND 23 KPH.
YES, A 100 PERCENT CHANCE OF A STRIKE!
WHHT
THIS IS NOT A GAME OF LOGIC!!

READ THIS WAY

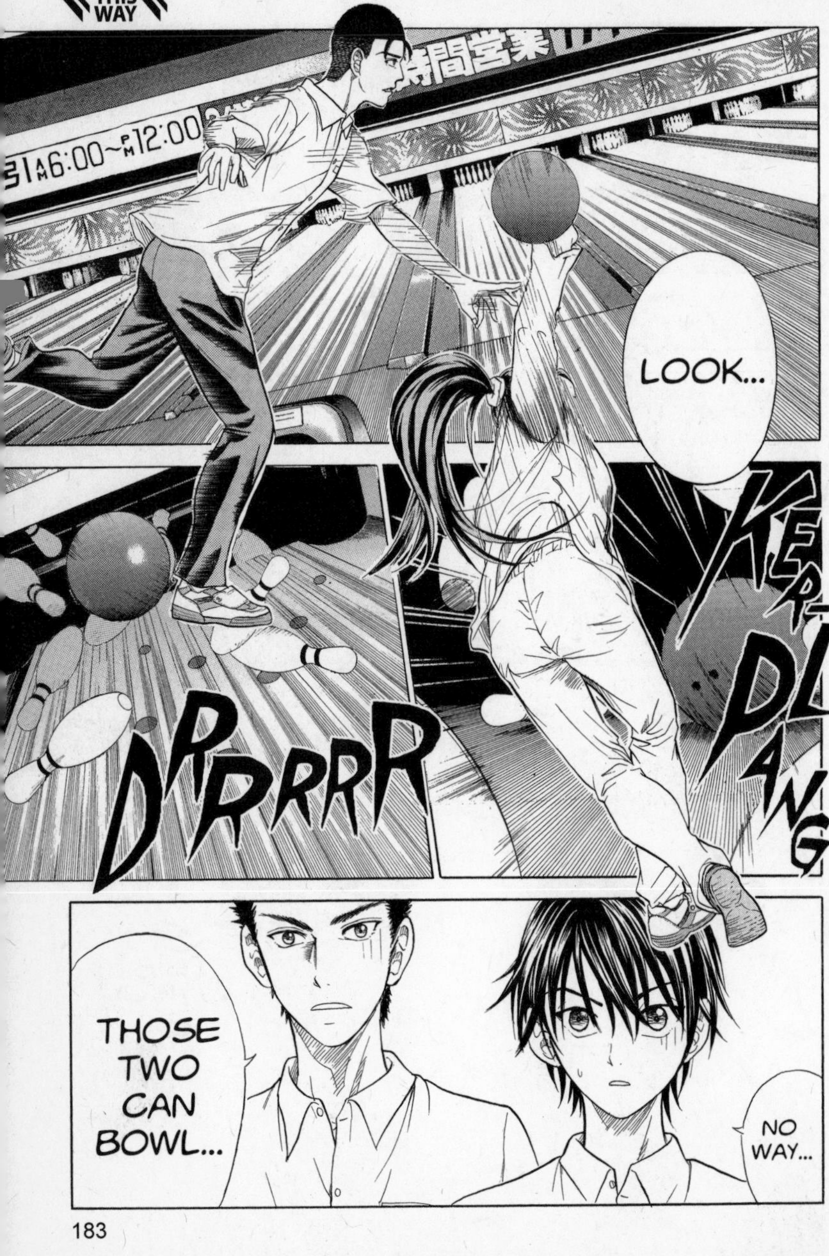

時間営業
AM6:00~PM12:00
LOOK...
KER-DLANG
DPRRRRR
NO WAY...
THOSE TWO CAN BOWL...

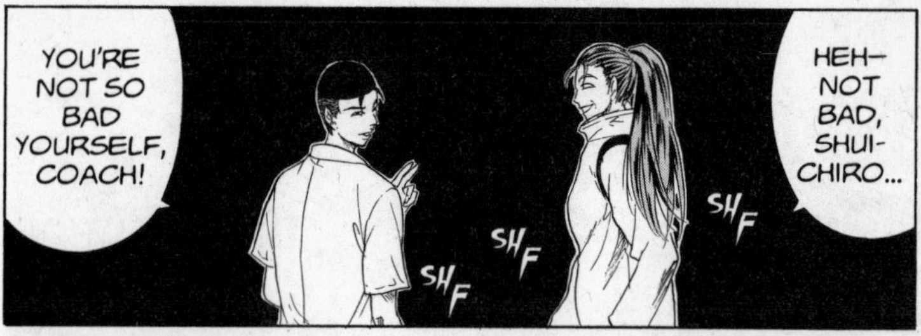
HEH— NOT BAD, SHUI-CHIRO...
SHF
SHF
SHF
YOU'RE NOT SO BAD YOURSELF, COACH!

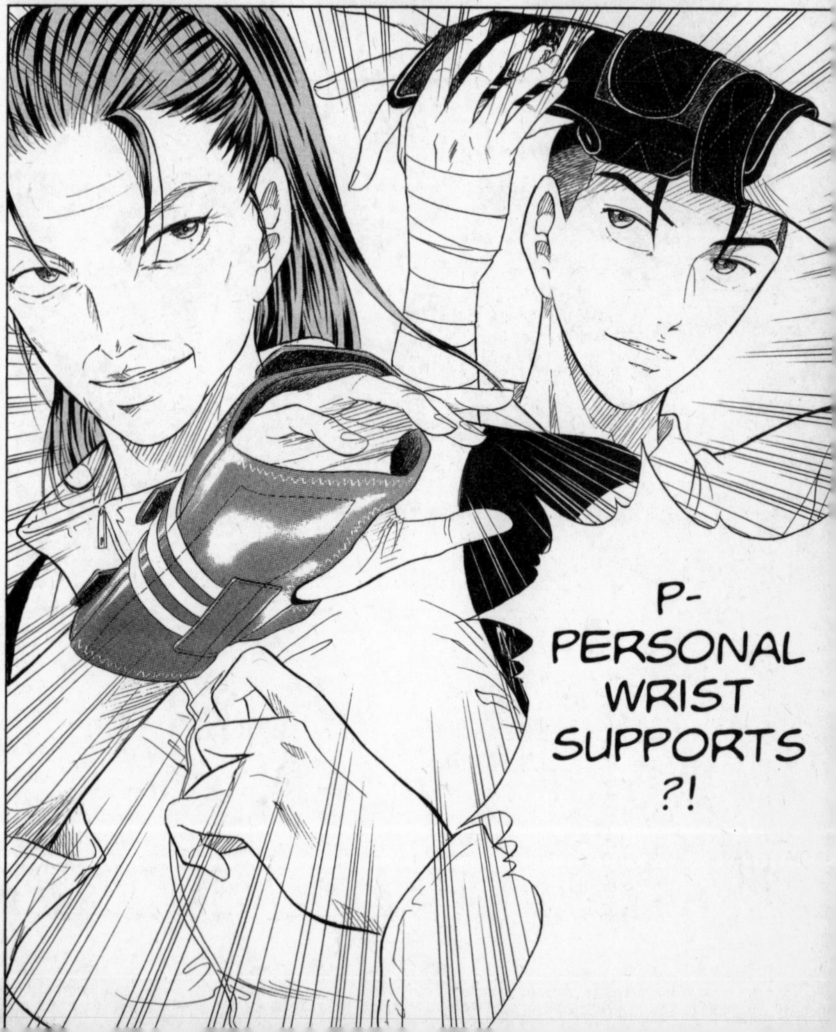
P-PERSONAL WRIST SUPPORTS ?!

READ THIS WAY

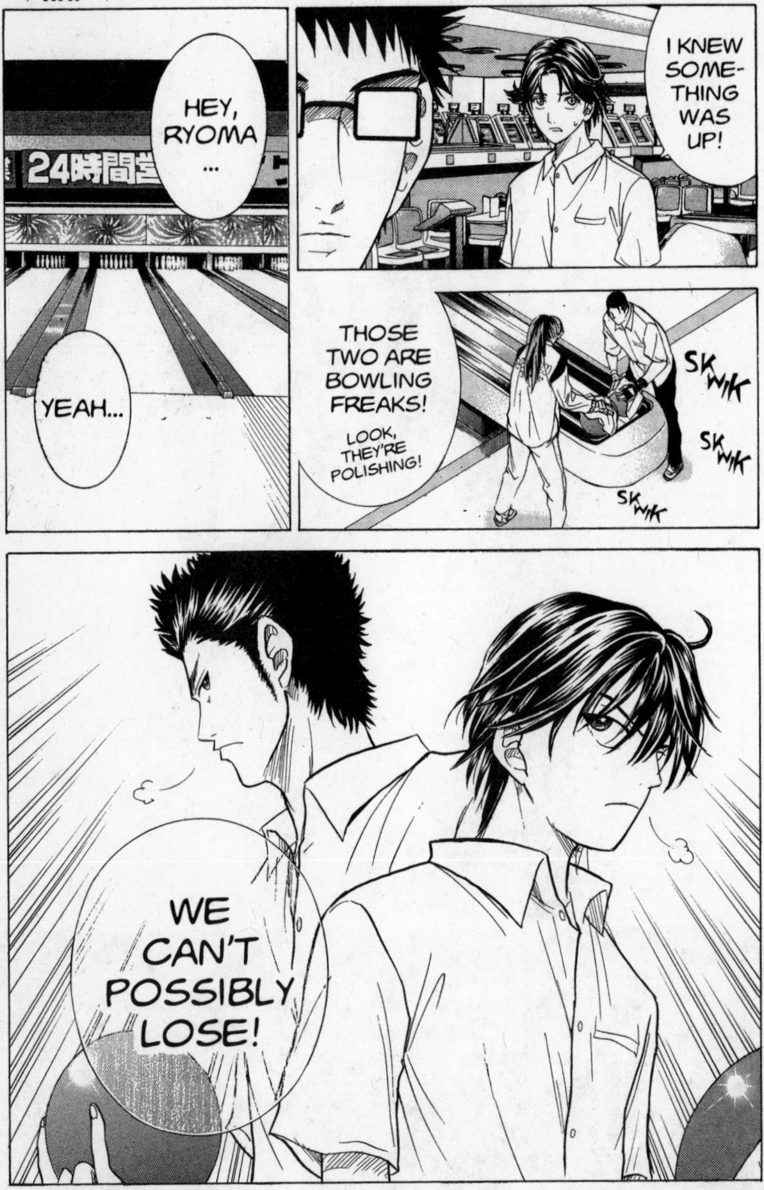
I KNEW SOME-THING WAS UP!
THOSE TWO ARE BOWLING FREAKS!
LOOK, THEY'RE POLISHING!
SKWIK
SKWIK
SKWIK
HEY, RYOMA ...
YEAH...
WE CAN'T POSSIBLY LOSE!

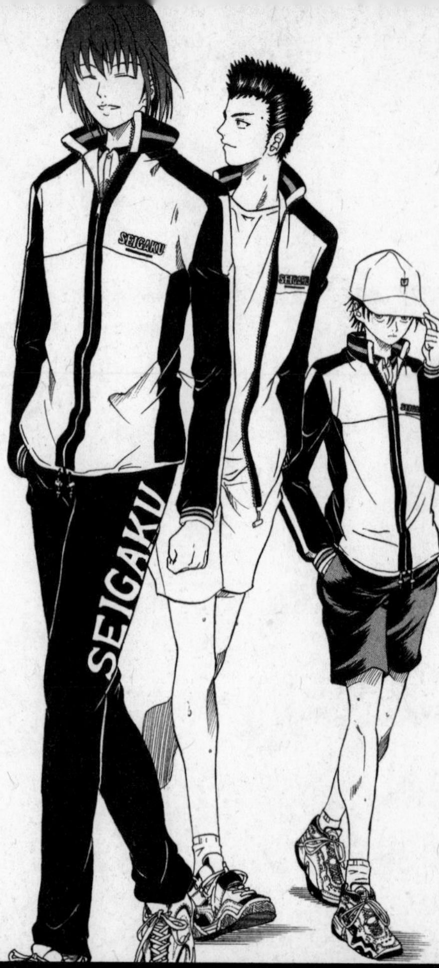
SEIGAKU
SEIGAKU

The pressure on the players mounts! Captain Kunimitsu is gone! Now, without him, Seishun's up against a team coached by a four-time Japan Open winner. It's time for serious stress

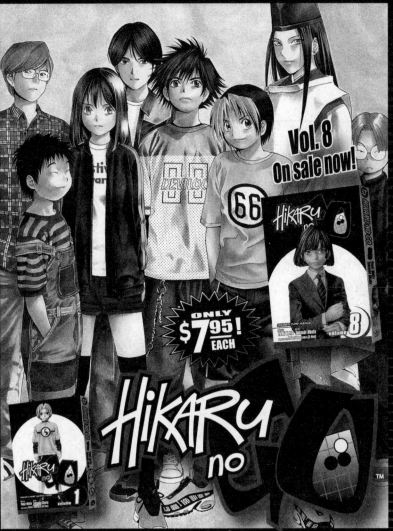